HOLMAN
New
Testament
Commentary

HOLMAN
New Testament
Commentary

Acts

GENERAL EDITOR
Max Anders

AUTHOR
Kenneth O. Gangel

HOLMAN
REFERENCE

Nashville, Tennessee

Holman New Testament Commentary
© 1998 Broadman & Holman Publishers
Nashville, Tennessee
All rights reserved

ISBN 10: 0-8054-0205-5
ISBN 13: 978-0-8054-0205-6

Dewey Decimal Classification 226.6
Subject Heading: BIBLE.NT. ACTS
Library of Congress Card Catalog Number: 98-39365

Gangel, Kenneth O.
        Acts of the Apostles / by Kenneth O. Gangel.
            p. cm. — (Holman New Testmanet commentary)
        Includes bibliographical references.
        ISBN 0-8054-0205-5
    BS2625.3G36 1998
    226.6'07—dc21   98-39365
                                                                                                     CIP

            7 8 9 10 11 12 • 10 09 08 07 06
                            D

*L*uke held a high view of women, and I share that position. Particularly, the three women who helped in the preparation of this manuscript. Dividing transcription and typing chores equally were my former administrative assistant, Virginia Murray, and my present administrative assistant, Karen Grassmick. Checking each text and reference for accuracy fell to my loving wife Betty. Readers who profit from this work will want to remember their efforts as well as my own.

• *Kenneth O. Gangel* •

October 1996

Contents

Editorial Preface ix

Holman Old Testament Commentary Contributors x

Holman New Testament Commentary Contributors xi

Introduction to Acts 1

Acts 1
We Are Witnesses 5

Acts 2
A Church Is Born 21

Acts 3
Surprised by Ministry 39

Acts 4
Christians with Courage 55

Acts 5
Honor and Dishonor in the Church 71

Acts 6
Who Serves the Church? 87

Acts 7
A Layman Makes His Mark 101

Acts 8
Catch That Chariot! 117

Acts 9
God's Chosen Instruments 135

Acts 10
No Favoritism Allowed! 155

Acts 11
Marks of a Biblical Church 173

Acts 12
Adventures of a Prison Escapee 189

Acts 13
How to Send Out Missionaries 205

Acts 14
Things Are Tough All Over 227

Acts 15
Church Business Meetings Can Work! 243

Acts 16
Singing in Our Struggles 263

Acts 17
The Gospel and the Greeks 281

Acts 18
Corinth! 299

Acts 19
Invading the Kingdom of Diana 317

Acts 20
How to Lead in the Church 335

Acts 21
Back to the Big Apple 351

Acts 22
Testimony of a Roman Citizen 367

Acts 23
Cavalry Escort 383

Acts 24
Politician on the Take 399

Acts 25
Festus—Foot Soldier for Rome 413

Acts 26
Apostle before a King 427

Acts 27
Mediterranean Cruise 443

Acts 28
God's Man in Rome 459

Glossary 475

Bibliography 483

Editorial Preface

Today's church hungers for Bible teaching and Bible teachers hunger for resources to guide them in teaching God's Word. The Holman New Testament Commentary provides the church with the food to feed the spiritually hungry in an easily digestible format. The result: new spiritual vitality that the church can readily use.

Bible teaching should result in new interest in the Scriptures, expanded Bible knowledge, discovery of specific Scriptural principles, relevant applications, and exciting living. The unique format of the Holman New Testament Commentary includes sections to achieve these results for every New Testament book.

Opening quotations from some of the church's best writers lead to an introductory illustration and discussion that draw individuals and study groups into the Word of God. "In a Nutshell" summarizes the content and teaching of the chapter. Verse-by-verse commentary answers the church's questions rather than raising issues scholars usually admit they cannot adequately solve. Bible principles and specific contemporary applications encourage students to move from Bible to contemporary times. A specific modern illustration then ties application vividly to present life. A brief prayer aids the student to commit his or her daily life to the principles and applications found in the Bible chapter being studied. For those still hungry for more, "Deeper Discoveries" take the student into a more personal, deeper study of the words, phrases, and themes of God's Word. Finally, a teaching outline provides transitional statements and conclusions along with an outline to assist the teacher in group Bible studies.

It is the editors' prayer that this new resource for local church Bible teaching will enrich the ministry of group, as well as, individual Bible study, and that it will lead God's people to truly be people of the Book, living out what God calls us to be.

Holman Old Testament Commentary Contributors

Vol. 1, Genesis
ISBN 0-8054-9461-8
Kenneth O. Gangel and
Stephen J. Bramer

Vol. 2, Exodus, Leviticus, Numbers
ISBN 0-8054-9462-6
Glen Martin

Vol. 3, Deuteronomy
ISBN 0-8054-9463-4
Doug McIntosh

Vol. 4, Joshua
ISBN 0-8054-9464-2
Kenneth O. Gangel

Vol. 5, Judges, Ruth
ISBN 0-8054-9465-0
W. Gary Phillips

Vol. 6, 1 & 2 Samuel
ISBN 0-8054-9466-9
Stephen Andrews

Vol. 7, 1 & 2 Kings
ISBN 0-8054-9467-7
Gary Inrig

Vol. 8, 1 & 2 Chronicles
ISBN 0-8054-9468-5
Winfried Corduan

Vol. 9, Ezra, Nehemiah, Esther
ISBN 0-8054-9469-3
Knute Larson and Kathy Dahlen

Vol. 10, Job
ISBN 0-8054-9470-7
Steven J. Lawson

Vol. 11, Psalms 1–75
ISBN 0-8054-9471-5
Steven J. Lawson

Vol. 12, Psalms 76–150
ISBN 0-8054-9481-2
Steven J. Lawson

Vol. 13, Proverbs
ISBN 0-8054-9472-3
Max Anders

Vol. 14, Ecclesiastes, Song of Songs
ISBN 0-8054-9482-0
David George Moore and Daniel L. Akin

Vol. 15, Isaiah
ISBN 0-8054-9473-1
Trent C. Butler

Vol. 16, Jeremiah, Lamentations
ISBN 0-8054-9474-X
Fred M. Wood and Ross McLaren

Vol. 17, Ezekiel
ISBN 0-8054-9475-8
Mark F. Rooker

Vol. 18, Daniel
ISBN 0-8054-9476-6
Kenneth O. Gangel

Vol. 19, Hosea, Joel, Amos, Obadiah, Jonah, Micah
ISBN 0-8054-9477-4
Trent C. Butler

Vol. 20, Nahum, Habakkuk, Zephaniah, Haggai, Zechariah, Malachi
ISBN 0-8054-9478-2
Stephen R. Miller

Holman New Testament Commentary Contributors

Vol. 1, Matthew
ISBN 0-8054-0201-2
Stuart K. Weber

Vol. 2, Mark
ISBN 0-8054-0202-0
Rodney L. Cooper

Vol. 3, Luke
ISBN 0-8054-0203-9
Trent C. Butler

Vol. 4, John
ISBN 0-8054-0204-7
Kenneth O. Gangel

Vol. 5, Acts
ISBN 0-8054-0205-5
Kenneth O. Gangel

Vol. 6, Romans
ISBN 0-8054-0206-3
Kenneth Boa and William Kruidenier

Vol. 7, 1 & 2 Corinthians
ISBN 0-8054-0207-1
Richard L. Pratt Jr.

Vol. 8, Galatians, Ephesians, Philippians, Colossians
ISBN 0-8054-0208-X
Max Anders

Vol. 9, 1 & 2 Thessalonians, 1 & 2 Timothy, Titus, Philemon
ISBN 0-8054-0209-8
Knute Larson

Vol. 10, Hebrews, James
ISBN 0-8054-0211-X
Thomas D. Lea

Vol. 11, 1 & 2 Peter, 1, 2, 3 John, Jude
ISBN 0-8054-0210-1
David Walls & Max Anders

Vol. 12, Revelation
ISBN 0-8054-0212-8
Kendell H. Easley

Holman New Testament Commentary

Twelve volumes designed for Bible study and teaching to enrich the local church and God's people.

Series Editor	Max Anders
Managing Editors	Trent C. Butler & Steve Bond
Project Editor	Lloyd W. Mullens
Marketing Manager	Greg Webster
Product Manager	David Shepherd
Page Composition	TF Designs, Mt. Juliet, TN

Introduction to

Acts

*F*rom Pentecostal fire in Jerusalem to unhindered gospel proclamation in a Roman prison, Acts unfolds the exciting story of God working to take the gospel message of salvation to the ends of the earth. A scholarly, exegetical commentary on Acts would spend thirty or forty pages introducing the book and the intricate scholarly theories about it and is beyond the scope and purpose of this work. The excellent commentary of Richard Longenecker deals sufficiently with all the intricacies of Acts introduction. We will spend a few paragraphs outlining the basics—authorship, date of writing, purpose, and style. This provides all you need for a user-friendly, teacher's companion commentary.

 A U T H O R S H I P

Luke seems almost unchallenged as the author of Acts. Common style and vocabulary unite Acts with Luke's Gospel. The Gospel's conclusion virtually forms an introduction to the Book of Acts. The connection of the ascension narratives and the internal evidence of the "we" sections (16:10–17; 20:5–21; 27:1–28:16) strongly suggest that one of Paul's traveling companions wrote much of the narrative. Luke was with Paul at Rome (Col. 4:14; 2 Tim. 4:11). Thus common style, common vocabulary, and common dedication to Theophilus give credence to the Lucan authorship of both books.

External evidence is strong as well. Putting it simply, Longenecker says,

> What we can say positively is that the tradition that Luke wrote the third Gospel and Acts goes back at least to the early second century, that it was unanimously accepted within the church, and that it would be very strange were it not true. . . . Consequently, there are no compelling reasons to reject the tradition that Luke, Paul's physician friend, who appears to have been a Gentile (Col. 4:10–15), was the writer of Acts (Longenecker, 240).

Who was Luke? His name appears only three times in the New Testament (Col. 4:14; Phlm. 24; 2 Tim. 4:10–11), but we know clearly he was a member of the missionary team who traveled extensively with the apostle and served as his companion during the Roman confinement. The conclusion he was a Gentile comes largely from his Greek style and cultural perspectives. His occupation is well attested in Colossians 4:14. The best conclusion is to place little weight on external tradition (though some have made elaborate arguments) and to base our knowledge of Luke solely upon the books of Luke and Acts.

DATE OF WRITING

Essentially, scholars offer three options for dating: before A.D. 64, explaining the abrupt ending; between 70 and 90, assuming Luke's Gospel knows the fall of Jerusalem in 70 as a past event; between 95 and 100, assuming Luke depends on Josephus. Most evangelical scholars support an early date. One can hardly imagine Luke not including the death of Paul (about A.D. 67) or the fall of Jerusalem (A.D. 70) in a book so committed to historical pattern. Polhill's willingness to accept a date sometime after 70 ("but no convincing reason for dating it later than sometime during that decade," Polhill, 31) seems an unnecessary yielding to critics of an early date. Dogmatism is hardly essential on this issue. A date not later than A.D. 64 seems most likely since Luke does not mention Paul's release (about A.D. 61), the Neronian fire in Rome with its ensuing persecution of Christians in A.D. 64, nor the fall of Jerusalem in A.D. 70. Such a view allows space for portions of Luke to be dependent on Mark but also views Luke's treatment of Jerusalem in his Gospel as prophetic rather than historic, a traditional evangelical position.

Who was Theophilus? A well-established Greek name, *Theophilus* literally means, "lover of God." Many have argued Luke used the name symbolically, thereby addressing his works to Gentile proselytes who had not yet grasped the full message of Jesus and the resurrection. Some suggest Theophilus was an influential Roman official; others equate him with Flavius Clemens, or even Agrippa II. Though Polhill finds the symbolic "God-fearer" theory attractive, I concur with Longenecker in the traditional view that Theophilus was a Greek gentleman, probably well educated, and probably very interested in the gospel—though unfamiliar with much of the story of Jesus and the work of the early church. This goes back at least to Ramsay in 1894 who identified Theophilus as a Roman officer who had become a Christian.

> We may safely say that in the first century a Roman official would hardly bear the name Theophilus; and therefore it must be a name given him at baptism, and used or known only among the Christians. The fact that his public name is avoided and only the baptismal name used, favours the supposition (though not absolutely demanding it) that it was dangerous for a Roman of rank to be recognized as a Christian (Ramsay, 388).

Roman official or not, the personal nature of the letters (when contrasted with the pastoral tone of New Testament epistles) certainly seemed to indicate that the author took aim at one person, a close and trusted friend.

P U R P O S E   O F   A C T S

Luke had multiple goals in putting together this complex work. One goal could be described as historical: to describe the establishment and growth of the early church from the ascension to the imprisonment of Paul. Another goal could be biographical: to set Paul within the larger framework of three decades of first-century Christianity. Some see Acts as a defense against Gnosticism. Others see a conciliatory account that attempts to reconcile conflict between Jewish and Gentile believers. Arrington writes:

> The broad scope of Luke-Acts strongly suggests that they were written for a wide audience. Luke's general aim was to relate how Jesus, enabled by the Holy Spirit, had accomplished his mission and how the gospel spread from Jerusalem to Rome though the power of the Spirit in apostolic preaching. . . . By addressing his two-volume work to an individual, Luke was in accordance with literary convention of his time. In Antiquity, authors frequently dedicated their works to an individual; this ensured that their works would gain a public hearing (Arrington, xxxvii).

Certainly we see throughout Acts a clearer historic record of the early church, a constant emphasis on the gospel to the Gentiles, and an apologetic of the resurrection of Jesus to Jews, Greeks, and Romans. Polhill finds eight different themes radiating through Acts: world mission, the providence of God, the power of the Spirit, a restored Israel, an inclusive gospel, faithful witnesses, the church's relationship with the world, and the triumph of the gospel (Polhill, 57–71).

S T Y L E   O F   A C T S

In simplest terms, Acts is historical and narrative theology. Using the form of the well-known Hellenistic monograph, Luke's Greek vocabulary is the largest of any New Testament writer (approximately 90 percent of his words are found in the Septuagint, the earliest Greek translation of the Old Testament). We have no evidence of an early title for the book we call "Acts." Shortly before A.D. 200, Irenaeus referred to it as "Luke's witness to the apostles." Tertullian shortly after A.D. 200 called it "Luke's commentary." Before

A.D. 300 the book seems to have received the lasting title, "The Acts of the Apostles."

As a physician, Luke had an eye for specifics and a heart for people. He was also an avocational historian who recorded numerous details other Bible writers seemed to overlook. He was interested in buildings, the role of women, speeches (which comprise 300 of 1,000 verses in Acts), and anecdotes about miracles, humorous events, and especially travel narratives. He enjoyed summaries, almost a hallmark of his writing style in the early chapters. Very much in the pattern of a contemporary cutting-edge theologian, he connected the story of Jesus with the wider history of the world, doubtless an idea he picked up from listening to the many speeches and sermons of Paul.

Foremost, his history is theological. His interest is not just in the events themselves but in the meaning of the events. Arrington puts it well:

> Luke utilizes historical data to stress the importance of salvation, to call people to confess Jesus as Lord, and to urge them to accept the charismatic work of the Holy Spirit. At the same time, he encourages those experiencing doubt, persecution, and disappointment to live out their faith under the Lordship of Christ. Both an evangelical and pastoral purpose can be discerned in Luke's writing of history and theology (Arrington, xxxvii).

Acts 1

We Are Witnesses

I. **Introduction**
The Power of a Witness

II. **Commentary**
A verse-by-verse explanation of the chapter.

III. **Conclusion**
Viewing Life from the End
An overview of the principles and applications from the chapter.

IV. **Life Application**
Tied to the Stake
Melding the chapter to life.

V. **Prayer**
Tying the chapter to life with God.

VI. **Deeper Discoveries**
Historical, geographical, and grammatical enrichment of the commentary.

VII. **Teaching Outline**
Suggested step-by-step group study of the chapter.

VIII. **Issues for Discussion**
Zeroing the chapter in on daily life.

"When we're trusting Jesus Christ as Lord as well as Saviour, He enables us to live and speak as faithful witnesses."

Paul E. Little

BOOK PROFILE: ACTS

- Third longest book in the New Testament (only Matthew and Luke are longer)
- Luke and Acts comprise 30 percent of the New Testament
- Probably written between A.D. 60 and 65
- Directed to Luke's personal friend Theophilus, a Greek believer, perhaps a sponsor of his ministry

AUTHOR PROFILE: LUKE

- A Christian physician
- Traveling companion of the apostle Paul
- Part-time historian
- An eyewitness of many of the accounts in this book
- A gifted storyteller with an eye for detail
- A good lay-theologian/historian

CITY PROFILE: JERUSALEM

- Ancient capital of Jewish religion and culture
- First mentioned in Joshua 10:5 (cf. Gen. 14:18)
- Birthplace of the church
- Destroyed by the Romans in A.D. 70

I N   A   N U T S H E L L

uke depicts the birth and growth of the early church through about thirty-three years, almost two generations. He begins with the ascension of Christ and ends with the imprisonment of Paul in Rome. Along the way he describes the earliest days of the church in Jerusalem, the church's beginning efforts to reach beyond the Jewish community, and three missionary journeys across Asia Minor and into Greece. He introduces ninety-five people, sixty-two of whom are not mentioned elsewhere in the New Testament.

The key verse of the book is probably 1:8: "But you will receive power when the Holy Spirit comes on you; and you will be my witnesses in Jerusalem, and in all Judea and Samaria, and to the ends of the earth."

We Are Witnesses

I. INTRODUCTION

The Power of a Witness

Chinese farmer, after having cataracts removed from his eyes, made his way from the Christian compound to the far interior of China. Only a few days elapsed, however, before the missionary doctor looked out his bamboo window and noticed the formerly blind man holding the front end of a long rope. In a single file and holding to the rope behind him came several blind Chinese whom the farmer had told about his operation. They all knew the farmer had been blind, but now he could see. He told them of the doctor who had cured him; naturally, all these other blind people wanted to meet the doctor who cured the blind man.

The cured man could not explain the physiology of the eye or the technique of the operation. He could tell others he had been blind, the doctor had operated on him, and now he could see. That was all the others needed to hear. They came to the doctor.

So it is in our Christian lives. We need not all be trained theologians. We need not understand all the intricacies of God's mysteries, nor be perfect examples of flawless Christian living. We can all tell everyone what Christ has done for us. We may not all be teachers. We may not all be like Mother Teresa. We can all be witnesses. That is the point of the Book of Acts, a written witness, a faithful telling of the work of God in the first days of Christianity and the church.

Acts is not a devotional book like the Psalms, nor a teaching letter like the epistles. It reads similiar to some of the historical books of the Old Testament, and even more like the four Gospels which precede it. We call this kind of Bible writing "narrative" and recognize that we can learn the truth of God's Word and principles of Christian living by seeing how God worked with people in the early church. These are our brothers and sisters who faced many of the same kind of issues and problems we have experienced or will yet experience.

Acts 1 delves immediately into the theme of the book. We enjoy the splendor of the Lord's ascension and immediately fall into the abyss of depression with this small and struggling group of believers who must deal with the "Judas issue" before they can get on with their work. Luke never avoids reality—he tells the story exactly as it happened.

When we grasp the significance of new life in Christ and the internal power of his resurrection through the Holy Spirit, we can live out the words of a modern chorus, "Get all excited and tell everybody" that Jesus Christ the Son of God lives today in the lives of his people even as he did back in the days of the New Testament.

II. COMMENTARY

We Are Witnesses

MAIN IDEA: *Because of Christ's ascension and the coming of the Holy Spirit, Christians can be effective witnesses in their communities, around their own states or provinces, throughout the country, and around the world.*

A Witnesses of the Lord's Life (vv. 1–5)

SUPPORTING IDEA: *From the time of the Lord's ascension until now, believers live their lives and do their work by the power of the Holy Spirit.*

1:1–3a. Book dedications were common among the Greeks. Luke had dedicated his Gospel to his Greek-speaking friend Theophilus (Luke 1:3). He continues his contact with Theophilus to complete the story from the birth of Christ to the establishment of the church all around the Mediterranean world. Immediately he emphasizes key ideas of his book: the command to witness; the role of the apostles; the significance of the Holy Spirit; and his literary launching pad, the ascension of the Lord. Luke connects Acts to his

Gospel with the simple words, **after his suffering.** He refused to point to the resurrected, glorious, ascended Lord without pointing to the suffering Servant.

During the forty days that separated the resurrection and the ascension Jesus further taught the disciples, preparing them to lead the early church. This is the only New Testament reference to these postresurrection days. You will probably find it helpful to read at least the last chapter of Luke to get a feel for how Luke makes the transition into this second letter to Theophilus. To lead, they first had to be convinced that death had turned to life. During this time he **gave many convincing proofs that he was alive . . . and spoke about the kingdom of God.**

1:3b. What did Jesus say during these question sessions? From everything we know, he used the Old Testament to emphasize that he was the Messiah Israel expected. Now he would turn the reins of responsibility over to the apostles and other believers. Jesus' life on earth was finished, but his work had only begun; the disciples now assumed the responsibility to carry on Jesus' work. We should never forget the full title of our book—"Acts of the Apostles"—though many have suggested it could more properly be titled "The Continuing Acts of Jesus Christ through the Apostles."

Luke uses the phrase "kingdom of God" throughout Acts as a summary for God's work in the world. We should not confuse it with references either in the Old Testament or in other New Testament books. Jesus' teaching did not center on prophecy alone but on the ongoing role of the King on earth through his people.

1:4–5. What would these disciples do after the Lord left them? The first command was to wait. They were not to engage in ministry until they had been empowered by **the gift my Father promised.** As we read words like this in the Bible, we're reminded of the great history of the church that has preceded us and the resources he has provided to continue that heritage.

Jesus taught the disciples, the disciples taught people of their generation, who taught others, until today you and I have both the opportunity and responsibility to enjoy the gift and to tell others about it. In this case the gift is not just the gospel in general, but the specific coming of the Holy Spirit. This was not a new theme. Jesus had talked about it in John 14:16–21; 15:26–27; 16:7–15.

Believers are somewhat divided on the terminology "baptism of the Holy Spirit." To argue that issue in detail here is beyond the scope of this work. Certainly Luke had in view that as the New Testament church got under way, Spirit baptism placed believers into that group of believers the New Testament calls the body of Christ.

Throughout the Book of Acts we will see different reactions when people receive the Holy Spirit so we should not conclude that any one particular pattern is the only way God deals with us. The coming of the Holy Spirit took place ten days after Jesus' ascension at which time the believers experienced the same power in which Jesus carried out his ministry.

What a lesson for us . . . wait. Don't rush off into ministry unprepared. Don't carry on the Lord's work in the strength of the flesh. The only way we can fulfill Christ's command to witness is to be under control of the Holy Spirit who energizes us for service.

Ⓑ Witnesses of the Lord's Message (vv. 6–8)

SUPPORTING IDEA: *Our call to witness rests on both Christ's command and his coming.*

1:6–7. The disciples' question revived their political goals, an ideal they could never quite stifle. Throughout the Gospels they wanted Jesus to throw off the iron hand of Rome, tell the nation he was their Messiah, and set up the kingdom. Surely now that he had risen from the dead and instructed his troops, it was time for the rebellion to begin. The Lord's answer offers a warning Christians have not heeded very well for almost two thousand years: **It is not for you to know the times or dates the Father has set by his own authority** (v. 7).

How many Christian leaders have embarrassed themselves by announcing to the world when the Lord would return! The *fact* of that return is absolute as we shall see in a moment. The *time* was not revealed to Jesus' own disciples at the time of the ascension, and it will never be known by any human until the Lord comes again, regardless of what someone may claim.

We can't criticize the disciples too much, however, because the Old Testament links Spirit baptism with the coming kingdom (Isa. 32:15–20; Ezek. 39:28–29; Joel 2:28–3:1). The Lord did not deny the kingdom is coming but only warned the disciples that God's schedule is none of their business.

1:8. Some have suggested that this key verse of our book may contain a three fold table of contents: Jerusalem, Acts 2:42–8:3; Judea and Samaria, Acts 8:4–12:24; ends of the earth, Acts 12:25–28:31. We cannot know if Luke had that kind of division in mind, but the book unfolds in a fascinating manner somewhat along that pattern.

Notice that the call to witness is not limited to any select group of people since it spreads from the apostles to the 120 believers and on throughout the pages of Acts. Nor can we restrict it only to service in our own churches or to some kind of "professional ministry." Every believer should be a "world Christian," able to function for the Savior from the other side of the street to the other side of the world.

C Witnesses of the Lord's Ascension (vv. 9–11)

SUPPORTING IDEA: *Jesus now reigns in heaven with the Father—but he is coming again.*

1:9–10. We hear a great deal around Easter about the "seven last words of Christ." This phrase commonly refers to sayings on the cross such as "I thirst" and "Father forgive them." Here in the NIV translation of Acts 1 we find the seven last words of Christ on earth: **and to the ends of the earth.** Immediately after uttering those words he ascended and was hidden by a cloud, even as they watched. The concept of a cloud linked with God is a common Old Testament theme (Exod. 13:21; Ps. 68:4; Isa. 19:1; Dan. 7:13). We refer to it as the *Shekinah* glory explained in Ezekiel 11:14–25.

This account elaborates on Luke's earlier report to Theophilus. No serious Bible scholar doubts that the **two men** were angels who announced this great event in history. Angels taking the form of men was hardly unknown, even in New Testament times (Matt. 28:2–3; John 20:12; Luke 24:4). Picture the disciples standing in fear and awe **looking intently,** a phrase which appears fourteen times in the New Testament, twelve of them in Luke-Acts. We know this was the eleventh appearance of the Lord after his resurrection and that the ascension took place on the Mount of Olives in the vicinity of Bethany (Luke 24:45–53).

1:11. These disciples were literally **men of Galilee,** citizens of the northern portion of Israel. The angelic question took on special poignancy in the light of the Lord's command; but rather than scolding, the angel assured the disciples that Jesus would return. Let's not miss the emphasis of Luke's specific words: **This same Jesus . . . will come back in the same way you have seen him go into heaven.** Not some different Jesus but a literal, physical, resurrected Savior. The Jesus they knew and loved would come again *to* earth just as he ascended *from* earth. Other New Testament passages such as 1 Thessalonians 4–5 explain the details more fully.

Why would the Lord return to heaven? Why did he continuously say to the disciples that his exit was essential to the Holy Spirit's entrance? Certainly it fits God's plan and purpose, and that reason alone would be enough. We can also see some practical things. The second coming has no appeal for unbelievers, only for us as believers. With Jesus in heaven we must live our lives by faith and turn our hearts and vision upward and forward. During the time he is there and we are here, he serves as our heavenly intercessor and advocate. That ought to encourage us in our efforts to live and witness for him.

Ⓓ Witnesses of the Lord's People (vv. 12–14)

SUPPORTING IDEA: *The foundation of unity in ministry can only be found in believers praying together.*

1:12–13a. The apostles returned the half-mile to the city and went to a specific room. Normally second-story rooms were large in first-century Jerusalem, so they offered a likely meeting place. We must avoid making a holy shrine of this or any place. It could have been the same room in which they met for the Last Supper, or the one in which the events of John 20 occurred; the specific location is of no concern. Mystical fantasies arise when we designate special locations as unusually touched by God. Remember the Samaritan woman's argument about worshiping in Samaria or Jerusalem? Jesus regarded place unimportant; only heart attitude mattered.

1:13b. This is the same list of disciples we find in Luke 6, but not in the same order. We see no superstars here, only ordinary people. How crucial in our day to resist a celebrity Christianity. All believers form the church and must function in response to the Lord's command. The outstanding thing about these men is that they were not outstanding. God chose ordinary men to do an extraordinary task.

1:14. They not only prayed, but they prayed *together* and they prayed *constantly*. Luke characteristically reminds us that women were included along with the disciples and Jesus' physical brothers. This is the last New Testament mention of Mary the mother of Jesus. His half brothers, born after the virgin birth of Jesus, have already appeared in Luke's Gospel (8:19–21). Did the group pray for the Holy Spirit to come? Probably not, since Jesus had already said that would happen. Perhaps the important thing here is not the content of their prayers but the fact and nature of their praying. A crucial moment filled with expectation and wonder was also a moment of prayer.

Ⓔ Witnesses of the Lord's Word (vv. 15–22)

SUPPORTING IDEA: *When you have a difficult task to do, base it on Scripture.*

1:15–17. One hundred twenty people in Jerusalem do not account for all the believers in Palestine. Many more lived in Samaria and Galilee. Peter, however, assumed the leadership here and (we can imagine somewhat grudgingly) moved the group from the mountain to the muck. He called them "brothers" after the words of Jesus in John 20:17. Then he explained that a replacement for Judas was necessary, not because of his death, but because of his defection. Judas was an active member of the group. We should not miss Peter's reverence for Scripture throughout this section. He quotes Psalms

69:25 and 109:8 and certifies their inspiration as coming directly from the Holy Spirit.

1:18–20. As much as modern Christians love to talk about successes, sometimes the failures of the church need airing. Peter's explanation of Judas' failure offers us a look at the difference between *apostasy* and *backsliding*. Peter was a temporary backslider when he denied the Savior at the time of the crucifixion. Judas was an apostate; he revealed his true nature—an unbeliever—by his behavior in betraying Jesus (1 John 2:18–19). He did not have faith to ask for forgiveness and restoration. He yielded to despair and suicide, actions Peter recognized as fulfillment of Scripture. Why use these particular Psalms in this context? Because they were written about David's companions who became his enemies.

The differences between Luke's and Matthew's account of how Judas died should not worry us. Matthew tells us Judas hanged himself, but it is certainly possible that after the hanging, the body fell to the ground and burst open.

Our fascination with drama gives birth to so many more questions about Judas than this passage answers. Luke wants our attention turned to the positive advance of the church, not their agony over Judas' failure.

1:21–22. Peter spelled out the qualifications of the new leader: part of the believers from the beginning; witness of the resurrection; handpicked by the Lord. The apostles' important task was to tell others of Jesus' resurrection, the central distinguishing mark of Christian faith. Why twelve apostles? Why not just go on with the eleven? Apparently the New Testament carries forward a Jewish symbolism such as we find in Matthew 19:28 (twelve thrones) and Revelation 21:14 (twelve foundations).

F Witnesses of the Lord's Sovereignty (vv. 23–26)

SUPPORTING IDEA: Sovereignty simply means that the Lord knows what he is doing and he is doing it.

1:23–26. Note the participatory meeting; the whole group became part of the process as the believers nominated the candidates. The name Barsabbas means "son of the Sabbath." He also used the Greek name Justus. This was not an election for church management but a completion of the group who would lead the witness ministry. Again the believers prayed, and we are warmed and convicted by what they said: **Lord, you know everyone's heart.** Indeed, this is no election at all. These Christians have reverted to a time-honored Old Testament pattern for ascertaining God's will, the use of two stones in a container, not unlike the way we use dice in table games today. This was the Lord's choice, not theirs. They were perfectly happy to respond to whatever he directed.

In sovereign selection, God chose Matthias to become the twelfth apostle. Some commentators criticize these believers for rushing too quickly to fill the vacancy Judas left. Paul, not Matthias, they argue was the choice for that important role. We can't ignore the simplicity of the text. They prayed directly for God's will, and he gave it. At no point in Luke's narrative does he suggest even the slightest hint of wrongdoing in this process. Furthermore, as Acts unfolds, we discover that the number of apostles was hardly confined to twelve since it will include both Paul and Barnabas as well as others.

MAIN IDEA REVIEW: *Because of Christ's ascension and the coming of the Holy Spirit, Christians can be effective witnesses in their communities, around their own states or provinces, throughout the country, and around the world.*

III. CONCLUSION

Viewing Life from the End

What a powerful chapter! We can certainly imagine Theophilus already well into the flow of Luke's narrative, for he has captured our interest as well. After commissioning the disciples, the Lord made a spectacular departure from this earth in full view of the eleven apostles. We hear the promise of his return. We see the early church in sincere prayer. We read Peter's affirmation of Old Testament texts as Scripture. We watch a young and small group of Christians struggle with a very difficult problem, totally dependent upon the Lord. We know in the second chapter we will see the coming of the Holy Spirit and the power of the gospel explode in the city of Jerusalem.

Samuel Coleridge, a few days before his death on July 13, 1834, wrote a letter to his grandson which included this paragraph:

> I have known what the enjoyments and advantages of this life are, and the refined pleasures which learning and intellectual power can bestow upon us; and with all the experience that more than three score years can give, I, now, on the eve of my departure, declare to you that health is a great blessing; competence a great blessing; and a great blessing it is to have kind, loving, and faithful friends and relatives; but that the greatest of all blessings is to be indeed a Christian. . . . And I, on the very brink of the grave, solemnly bear witness to you that the Almighty Redeemer, most gracious in his promises to them who truly seek him, is faithful to perform what he has promised.

PRINCIPLES

- Jesus' resurrection was affirmed by many convincing proofs.
- All Christians are to be God's witnesses.
- Jesus is coming again.
- New Testament believers considered the Old Testament to be inspired Scripture.
- God leads his church as they make decisions.

APPLICATIONS

- Avoid any teacher or writer who sets dates for the coming of the Lord.
- Begin to look for witnessing opportunities in your life and family.
- Live in the expectation of Christ's return.
- Pray often with other believers.
- Trust God's sovereignty for all issues and problems in your life.

IV. LIFE APPLICATION

Tied to the Stake

Throughout the Book of Acts we see how Christians should function in the world. Paul's epistles explain doctrine and introduce deep and important truths which govern that life; Acts describes how we live it out day by day. Revelation gives us a glimpse into the end of that life and what lies beyond the grave; Acts forces a present view of our responsibilities.

In this book we must learn from history. Unlike Romans or Galatians, this book will not explain specific behavior patterns God wants from his children. We will look at the lives of people God used and allow the Holy Spirit to transfer the meaning of their experience into our modern-day world. By seeing how God worked with other people, we can understand what he can do in and through us.

As we have already seen, this first chapter starts with a bang. Central to everything we have studied stands that key verse: **But you will receive power when the Holy Spirit comes on you; and you will be my witnesses in Jerusalem, in all Judea and Samaria, and to the ends of the earth** (1:8). *How Christians and congregations interpret that commission (and others like it in the Gospels) will determine how they see their roles in the world and how their church programs unfold.* Obviously, telling others what we know about Jesus forms a basic responsibility in Christian living.

Our key verse lies between two other passages which emphasize the importance of the Lord's return. In verse 7 Jesus explains to the disciples that they cannot know times and dates of his return and the beginning of the kingdom. In verse 11 angels announce, **This same Jesus, who has been taken from you into heaven, will come back in the same way you have seen him go into heaven.** So the *command* is inseparably linked with the *coming*; we serve the Savior not only because of what he did for us in the past, but because we know he could come again any day.

Dr. W. A. Criswell, former pastor of First Baptist Church of Dallas, tells a story about a Louisiana farmer who caught a wild duck and tied it to a stake by his pond. Throughout the summer the duck seemed content. With plenty to eat he showed no desire to wander beyond the boundaries of his newly confined territory.

Then fall came, and wild ducks began migrating to the marshes. As they flew over the farmer's pond and called, the domestic ducks paid no attention whatsoever. They had no interest in flying off to the marshes; the pond was their home. Not so with the wild mallard. Every time the ducks flew over the pond, he would strain at the cord which tied him to his alien home. Finally, he broke the cord and rose upward to join his own kind and fly off to the marshes.

This story reminds us that the second coming holds no appeal for unbelievers. For Christians, however, the awareness of Christ's soon return enhances enthusiasm for the mission, the witness. Not only that, but it should increase our efforts and discipline at godly living. Look at what John has to say: "Dear friends, now we are children of God, and what we will be has not yet been made known. But we know that when he appears, we shall be like him, for we shall see him as he is. Everyone who has this hope in him purifies himself, just as he is pure" (1 John 3:2–3).

These Christians understood the huge difference between *going* to church and *being* the church. They understood the essential biblical qualifications of church leaders. They understood the absolute necessity of praying and serving together. They understood how important it was (and is) to obey the Lord even if it meant waiting at a time when they thought they should rush out and do something. They understood how the sovereignty of God transcends all human efforts, and they trusted him completely.

God makes this kind of maturity available to us through the Holy Spirit. Yes, now we are like wild ducks tied to the stake of an alien society. We look in horror at some of the things Hollywood and television feed our culture. We recoil in fear at the cruelty and violence which dominate our streets. Jesus told us this world is no friend to him nor to his people. So as we live our lives around the pond, we keep one eye on heaven. Soon that same Jesus, perhaps in the same cloud, will come just as the apostles saw him go. By his power we can break the cord and fly off with him to our eternal home.

V. PRAYER

Sovereign Lord, please give us a fresh awareness of the reality of your return. Meanwhile, let us serve with power as your witnesses in a desperately needy world.

VI. DEEPER DISCOVERIES

A. Jerusalem (v. 4)

Two different versions of this word appear in the New Testament. *Ierousalem* appears seventy-six times and offers an almost sacred connotation. *Hiersoluma* is used sixty-three times, in the secular or earthly sense. Interestingly, Luke uses the first (sacred) exclusively in chapters 1–7 and after that seems to use the terms interchangeably.

We should not draw any significant theological conclusion from this (remember, we are reading a history book); but Luke leaves no doubt that the action in the early church passes from Jerusalem to Antioch after the death of Stephen. Despite its importance, Jerusalem does not remain the "mother church" of the New Testament very long. All the churches we read about in Acts, those to whom Paul wrote the letters of the New Testament, resulted from the missionary effort launched at Antioch.

B. Witnesses (v. 8)

As we have already noticed, this word appears thirty-nine times in our book and links all portions of Luke's history. Here the eleven apostles are called "witnesses." The term also applied to Stephen (22:20), Paul (10:39–41; 13:31; 22:15; 26:16), and others.

The word comes from the Greek *martys* which is the root for our term *martyr.* Not all witnesses were martyrs, but in the New Testament sense, all martyrs were witnesses. Stephen, Peter, and Paul illustrated for us the reality of witnessing all the way to martyrdom.

C. Ascension (vv. 9–11)

In the entire New Testament, only Luke records this event in both his Gospel and his history. Although brief, this account reminds us of the Old Testament departures of Enoch and Elijah and particularly the transfiguration of Christ (Luke 9:28–36).

Let's not wander from Luke's emphasis. The ascension is historical, important, and very real—but Luke immediately moves on to a reminder of the apostle's task in the light of the Lord's return. In other words, we don't dwell on Jesus' departure; we emphasize what he does for us now in heaven and the fact that he will soon come again.

D. Sovereignty (vv. 25–26)

We wonder at the method these believers used to determine God's will (lots), but they were acting within their traditional patterns. Obviously, passages like this provide no basis for us to throw dice or draw straws to determine God's will. We have his Word, the Holy Spirit, and the godly advice of friends and church leaders to help us with life's tough decisions. The issue in our text was the determination of God's sovereign will.

Though the word *sovereignty* does not appear, the behavior of the early Christians shows us how important that doctrine was to them. Numerous passages in the New Testament emphasize the sovereignty of God; these are only a few:

Ephesians 1:4–5 — He chose us in him . . . he predestined us to be adopted.

Romans 8:29–30 — Those God foreknew, he also predestined to be conformed to the likeness of his Son. . . . And those he predestined, he also called; and those he called, he also justified; those he justified, he also glorified.

John 6:44 — No one can come to me unless the Father who sent me draws him.

Matthew 11:28 — Come to me, all you who are weary and burdened, and I will give you rest.

John 3:16 — For God so loved the world that he gave his one and only Son, that whoever believes in him shall not perish but have eternal life.

1 Timothy 2:1,3–4 — I urge, then first of all, that requests, prayers, intercession and thanksgiving be made for everyone. . . . This is good and pleases God our Savior, who wants all men to be saved and to come to a knowledge of the truth.

2 Peter 3:9 — The Lord . . . is not wanting anyone to perish, but everyone to come to repentance.

VII. TEACHING OUTLINE

A. INTRODUCTION

1. Lead Story: The Power of a Witness
2. Context: Merging the Gospels and epistles, Acts shows us how Jesus' disciples understood and put into action what he taught them for three and one-half years. Written in the early 60s, possibly from Caesarea or Rome, the book shows us a growing group of people genuinely excited about the resurrection, the power of the Holy Spirit, and the coming of the Lord.
3. Transition: This chapter launches our adventure with the early Christians as they take the gospel from Jerusalem and Antioch around the Mediterranean world. Luke makes six points about the early church.

B. COMMENTARY

1. Witnesses of the Lord's Life (vv. 1–5)
   a. Convincing proofs (vv. 1–3)
   b. Command for power (vv. 4–5)
2. Witnesses of the Lord's Message (vv. 6–8)
   a. Message of the kingdom (vv. 6–7)
   b. Message for the world (v. 8)
3. Witnesses of the Lord's Ascension (vv. 9–11)
   a. "He was taken up" (vv. 9–10)
   b. "He will come back" (v. 11)
4. Witnesses of the Lord's People (vv. 12–14)
   a. Together in an upper room (vv. 12–13)
   b. Praying together (v. 14)
5. Witnesses of the Lord's Word (vv. 15–22)
   a. Prophetic fulfillment (vv. 15–17)
   b. Honest explanation (vv. 18–20)
   c. Clear qualifications (vv. 21–22)
6. Witnesses of the Lord's Sovereignty (vv. 23–26)
   a. Candidates nominated (v. 23)
   b. Commitment affirmed (vv. 24–25)
   c. Choice concluded (v. 26)

C. CONCLUSION

VIII. ISSUES FOR DISCUSSION

1. What evidence shows that your church has received the Holy Spirit's power?
2. Describe the prayer ministry of your study group and of your church.
3. How does the way your church selects leaders compare with that of the first Jerusalem church?

Acts 2

A Church Is Born

I. Introduction
Symphony of the Spirit

II. Commentary
A verse-by-verse explanation of the chapter.

III. Conclusion
A Model Church
An overview of the principles and applications from the chapter.

IV. Life Application
The Clever Monk
Melding the chapter to life.

V. Prayer
Tying the chapter to life with God.

VI. Deeper Discoveries
Historical, geographical, and grammatical enrichment of the commentary.

VII. Teaching Outline
Suggested step-by-step group study of the chapter.

VIII. Issues for Discussion
Zeroing the chapter in on daily life.

"*T*he Holy Spirit longs to reveal to you
the deeper things of God.
He longs to love through you.
He longs to work through you.
Through the blessed Holy Spirit you may have:
strength for every duty,
wisdom for every problem,
comfort in every sorrow,
joy in His overflowing service."

T .   J .   B a c h

GEOGRAPHICAL PROFILE: PARTHIA

- Ancient empire to the east, south of the Caspian Sea
- Approximately the site of modern Iran
- As many as a million Jews may have lived in the East
- Peacefully coexisted with Rome through the first century A.D.
- A warrior society which never developed education and literature

GEOGRAPHICAL PROFILE: MEDIA

- A territory of 150,000 square miles
- A polytheistic society which later practiced Zoroastrianism
- Mentioned more than 20 times in Scripture, often in connection with Persia

GEOGRAPHICAL PROFILE: ELAM

- A country located on the east side of the Tigris River
- One of the earliest known civilizations
- Mentioned in Gen. 14:1; Isa. 21:2; 22:6; Jer. 25:25; 49:34–39
- Named for and founded by Elam a son of Shem (Gen. 10:22)

GEOGRAPHICAL PROFILE: MESOPOTAMIA

- The area between the Tigris and Euphrates Rivers
- Territory roughly equivalent to modern Iraq

- Abraham's original home (Acts 7:2)
- Babylon arose out of the central section of Mesopotamia

CITY PROFILE: CYRENE

- A Libyan city in North Africa, founded in 60 B.C
- Given to Rome by the last Ptolemy of Egypt
- Simon of Cyrene carried Jesus' cross (Luke 23:26)
- Cyrenians helped establish the church at Antioch

I N   A   N U T S H E L L

In summary, Luke writes to Theophilus in chapter 2: "You won't believe what happened next. On the Day of Pentecost God sent the Holy Spirit upon these 120 believers in Jerusalem, and they began to proclaim the gospel in different languages. Peter preached a powerful sermon after which 3,000 people trusted Christ and the first New Testament church was born."

A Church Is Born

I. INTRODUCTION

Symphony of the Spirit

*D*onald Barnhouse tells the story of driving in a car with a friend and being asked, "What's your favorite symphony?" Barnhouse began whistling Brahms' First Symphony. Then he thought, "How silly of me to try to convey the impact and splendor of Brahms through a whistle while driving." He thought also of the magnificence of the human mind and how it somehow translated that meager whistle into brass, strings, and timpani in the mind of his friend who was also familiar with Brahms.

That is precisely how these early Christians felt as they waited and waited. They knew the facts about Jesus but lacked the power to deliver these facts to the city and the world. The Holy Spirit translates our meager whistling melodies into heavenly music others can grasp and understand. Then and now he makes witness possible by creating in us not just a strange sounding note or two but the symphony of the Spirit.

At the end of chapter 1 the believers gathered in silence and prayer. Obediently, they awaited the promise of the Holy Spirit's coming and the Lord's command for them to do nothing until that event occurred. Apart from the business of selecting Matthias to replace Judas, the believers engaged in no ministry activity, at least none that Luke reports. Now the second chapter bursts upon the scene with both audio and visual effects choreographed by God. Now the believers began to speak, and their message was clear from the beginning. What is found in these forty-seven verses represents one of the great miracles of the New Testament. It follows right on the heels of the resurrection. The chronological and theological linking of the resurrection and Pentecost keep these two events in the minds of believers throughout Acts. There seems to be an unwritten preaching code, sort of a first-century homiletical rule: "When in doubt, proclaim the resurrection, and let the Holy Spirit do the rest."

This is not the first time we've seen the Holy Spirit in the New Testament. Luke introduced him in his Gospel (1:15) as a witness to the coming of Christ at the incarnation. Luke also recorded the role of the Holy Spirit in the virgin birth (1:35) and the descending of the Spirit upon Jesus at the time of his baptism (3:22).

The major teaching about the Holy Spirit thus far has come from John's inkwell. In chapter 14 John recorded Jesus' promise of the Spirit's coming and emphasized that he will be in you (14:17). Then in chapter 16 John explained the link between the ascension and the coming of the Holy Spirit: "Unless I go away, the Counselor will not come to you; but if I go, I will send him to you" (16:7b). Later in the same chapter, "But when he, the Spirit of truth, comes, he will guide you into all truth. He will not speak on his own; he will speak only what he hears, and he will tell what is yet to come. He will bring glory to me by taking from what is mine and making it known to you" (16:13–14).

Just as the disciples had never understood the reality of the resurrection until they experienced it, they could never have grasped what the Lord intended for this miraculous day at Pentecost. Hesitant, confused, perhaps frightened, they burst forth as a group with the wonderful message of life. Across Jerusalem that day in multiple languages and with spiritual fervor, thousands heard the symphony of the Spirit.

Pentecost, commonly known as the Feast of Weeks, was established fifteen centuries before the birth of Christ and became one of the three great pilgrim festivals of the Jews. The name derived from the fact that the Jews celebrated it the fiftieth day after Passover. In the Old Testament it was viewed as the anniversary of the law given at Sinai. Now under the new covenant, it became the birthday of the church.

II. COMMENTARY
A Church Is Born

MAIN IDEA: *Through the power of the Holy Spirit, Christians can proclaim the gospel of Jesus Christ, and people will believe and become a part of his body, the church.*

A Symbols of the Spirit's Coming (vv. 1–4)

SUPPORTING IDEA: *God empowers his church for ministry through the coming of the Holy Spirit.*

2:1–2. Throughout this book Luke records the togetherness the early Christians enjoyed. Here, at the beginning of everything, we find them **all together.** They heard a sound **like the blowing of a violent wind,** certainly an experience with which all of us can identify. The word for *wind* is *pneuma,* the same word Jesus used in talking about the Spirit and the wind with Nicodemus (John 3:7–8).

Wind filling the whole house reminds us of God's presence filling the temple in the Old Testament. If you live in the south, the midwest, or parts of Canada, you might imagine a tornado *inside the house.* East coast and Gulf state people might recognize the experience of a hurricane, but again, *inside the house.* Luke was probably not present for this event, but we can imagine that he heard his colleagues describe it scores of times, for it was a day they could never forget.

2:3. We need to be careful with the language of the text. The sound was not a wind but **like** a wind. They saw **what seemed to be tongues of fire.** Apparently, the fire started as one and then separated and came upon them. Like wind, the Bible commonly associates fire with the presence of God, as Moses found out one day in the desert (Exod. 3:2). Since this entire experience was highly symbolical, it may not be inappropriate for us to see in the single then multiple fire the unity and diversity in the body of Christ.

2:4. A third physical phenomenon experienced on the Day of Pentecost was the use of different languages. Throughout Acts, Luke uses different verbs to describe the coming of the Spirit upon new believers. This first time was a unique event, never again repeated in exactly the same way. When we look at the entire New Testament teaching on the Holy Spirit, we see the word *baptism* associated with initial conversion and the word *filling* with ministry. The first seems to happen once without repetition; the second occurs with frequency as believers allow God's Spirit to produce powerful work through them.

Most evangelical scholars believe the **tongues** of Pentecost were genuine languages, not the ecstatic sounds Paul dealt with at Corinth (1 Cor. 14:1–12). Two arguments rise strongly to emphasize that these tongues represented languages not previously learned. First, the use of the word *dialektos* in verses 6 and 8 can only refer to a language or dialect. Second, the paragraph that follows (vv. 5–12) specifically emphasizes the fact that people of different languages understood the message of the Christians in their own language.

Some argue for a miracle of hearing as well as speaking in this chapter. The text does not really justify that. On the other hand, when people filled with the Holy Spirit proclaim the gospel, a supernatural ministry always takes place. When the hearers respond, a miracle of understanding certainly follows.

ⓑ Results of the Spirit's Coming (vv. 5–13)

SUPPORTING IDEA: *Sometimes unbelievers make fun of Christians who act in ways God empowers them.*

2:5–6. Like Paul, Luke occasionally engages in deliberate exaggeration such as his suggestion that there were pious Jews residing in Jerusalem **from every nation under heaven**. Probably we should understand him to mean that people speaking many other languages were present on the Day of Pentecost and each heard the message in his or her own language or dialect. We might ask, if they resided in Jerusalem, wouldn't they have understood Aramaic, or at least Greek? Doubtless many of them did; but part of the miracle was God's ability to proclaim his message in multiple languages through uneducated people who spoke almost exclusively Aramaic and Greek.

Some have suggested that the Feast of Pentecost might very well have attracted over two hundred thousand Jews from all over Palestine and the Mediterranean world. Nothing indicates that they heard the wind or saw the flames; but the sound of languages—perhaps dozens of them—captured their attention immediately.

2:7–11. The speakers amazed Jerusalem's visitors as much as did the language: **are not all these men who are speaking Galileans?** After the introductory question raised by the bewildered guests, they identified fifteen language groups, roughly scattered from east to west, who heard the believers declaring the wonders of God in their own languages. Luke tells us they were bewildered and perplexed. Twice he used the word **amazed**. Many of the disciples (all of the eleven) came from Galilee, but that label for the group does not necessarily mean that all 120 came from that province. Jesus was a Galilean, and his followers were therefore known by that group name.

Luke's list of fifteen geographical locations was a group of nations or areas in which known Jewish populations existed and would likely have sent representative groups to the Feast of Pentecost. Everyone there who spoke a language other than Greek or Aramaic heard the message of the Christians in that language—maybe fifteen languages, maybe fifty, maybe more. The languages differed; the message remained the same: **the wonders of God.**

2:12–13. What a wonderful question to hear after one has proclaimed **the wonders of God.** Surely every pastor would like to have a congregation ask about every sermon, What does this mean? Like most congregations, not everyone agreed that this event had significant meaning. Some simply mocked, **they have had too much wine** (v. 13). This word for wine (*gleukos*), used only here in the Bible, leaves no doubt of the mockers meaning. Peter's explanation in the following verses says pointedly, **These men are not drunk, as you suppose** (v. 15). People shocked by a supernatural phenomenon may choose to accept God's hand at work in his world, or they may turn away and chalk it up to something else. When they make the latter choice, drunkenness offers as good an explanation as any.

 Prophecy of the Spirit's Coming (vv. 14–21)

SUPPORTING IDEA: *When God makes a promise, he keeps it, and we had better pay attention to how it applies to us.*

2:14–16. Now filled with the Holy Spirit and fresh from the Pentecost experience, Peter found new courage. He commanded immediate attention and addressed his remarks **to fellow Jews and all of you who live in Jerusalem.** Drunkenness? Not a chance. Not at nine in the morning. On feast days a Jew would not break fast until ten.

Most scholars believe Peter spoke in Aramaic, the common dialect of Jerusalem which all there would have understood. It was the third hour of the day, a customary hour of prayer. Peter's interesting argument may contain a bit of humor. He sounds rather like a pastor saying to a crowd gathered outside the church, "Our deacons aren't drunk yet—it's too early for that." Obviously, there is no intent to indicate that the believers ever became drunk, but to provide a clear-cut, nonchallengeable argument against the charge of drunkenness.

2:17–21. Peter launched into a recitation of Joel 2:28–32 reproduced by Luke from the Greek Old Testament, the Septuagint. No doubt Peter saw this passage fulfilled at Pentecost, at least in part. Men and women, young and old who gathered in Jerusalem after the ascension had experienced the pouring out of the Holy Spirit and subsequently proclaimed God's wonders. Are we to understand that Peter thought the wonders in the heavens of verses 19 and 20 had also been fulfilled at Pentecost? The context implies that the remainder of Joel's prophecy, the full experience of cosmic wonders, would await the full repentance of God's chosen nation. Nevertheless, it is part of the passage in Joel, so he thunders on to get to his major theme, **And everyone who calls on the name of the Lord will be saved.**

In terms of the earthly life and ministry of Jesus, this was the end of the beginning. The Christians will now carry on what he began to do (1:1–2). In terms of the unfolding of the church era however, the New Covenant age, this was the beginning of the end. Prophecy had been renewed in fulfillment after four hundred years. God was at work again among his people—the resurrection and Pentecost had proven that.

What does it mean to be saved? Certainly for Peter the "Lord" in the Joel passage is Jesus Christ. The spokesman for the twelve and all the other believers called all who would listen to turn to the Savior, God's Messiah, and in doing so, find life through his name. We will see this message and challenge many times in Acts.

🄳 Explanation of the Spirit's Coming (vv. 22–36)

SUPPORTING IDEA: *The message of the gospel rests on historical facts coupled with prophetic foundations intended to lead believers to a repentant faith.*

2:22–28. The Book of Acts contains twenty-three sermons or speeches, including seven by Peter and eleven by Paul. Verse 22 stands in the middle of Peter's first public sermon. Verses 14–16 constitute the introduction; verses 17–21 make up the text; verses 22–36 form the body; and verses 38–41 offer the conclusion/application.

2:22. During Jesus' time on earth his ministry was guaranteed by three-fold evidence—miracles, wonders, and signs—precisely the marks of an apostle which Paul identified in 2 Corinthians 12:12. Interestingly, first-century Jews didn't deny Jesus' miracles; that seems to be a theological characteristic of more modern times. The key term of the verse is surely the word **accredited,** used often in first-century Greek for people holding some official office. Jesus' mighty acts pointed to divine power behind his life and ministry, thereby certifying that he was the Messiah.

2:23. Frequently the New Testament links predestination and free will, the two elements of a divine paradox. God **handed over** Jesus for crucifixion, but wicked men **put him to death.** So often people ask, "Does God choose us for salvation, or do we choose to believe the gospel?" Human reason searches for philosophical solutions, but the only biblical answer is a simple *yes.* Somehow in God's eternal plan these two seemingly parallel roads come together.

2:24–28. Peter's sermon progresses well; in typical New Testament form, he comes right to the point: *resurrection.* Verses 25–35 in this chapter contain four evidences of the resurrection: David's tomb, the witnesses, that very Day of Pentecost, and the ascension witnessed by the eleven disciples. God may have handed Jesus over for crucifixion, but he also raised him from the dead. As strange as it might seem to the human mind, Messiah's death was God's will.

Thus Peter turns to Psalm 16:8–11. Surely readers of the Old Testament up to this point had applied Psalm 16 only to David. Peter, speaking through the Holy Spirit, now certified it as a messianic prophecy. He did not use the psalm to prove the resurrection, but to affirm the messiahship of Jesus. Peter didn't bother to prove the resurrection at all—he just proclaimed it. God raised Jesus to experience **joy in your presence.**

2:29–30. Something new has been added. Not only was David's psalm a messianic prophecy, but the application of the psalm to Jesus is also linked with the fact that the Messiah came in David's line. David may have considered himself a shepherd and a king, but Peter tells us he was also a prophet, whether aware of it or not. We see here a major key to understanding Scripture, namely—*Christ is the unifying link between Old and New Testaments.* Luke had already concluded his first report to Theophilus on precisely this point: "Then he opened their minds so they could understand the Scriptures. He told them 'This is what is written: The Christ will suffer and rise from the dead on the third day, and repentance and forgiveness of sins will be preached in his name to all nations, beginning at Jerusalem. You are witnesses of these things'" (Luke 24:45–48).

2:31–32. Not only did David understand Jesus' coming, he also foretold his resurrection. Standing in the crowd that day were many local residents who were familiar with the events that had transpired in Jerusalem less than two months earlier. Just in case their memories had lapsed, Peter raised again the broad banner of those courageous early Christians: **we are all witnesses of the fact.**

2:33–36. Peter wanted to proclaim the whole gospel, so he could not stop at the crucifixion and resurrection. In these verses he moves on to the exaltation and the coming of the Holy Spirit, bringing his listeners right up to the moment. Another quote from the Psalms (110:1) surely must have stabbed their collective attention. The humble carpenter of Nazareth was not only the Messiah, but now he lives in heaven and has caused all the Pentecostal commotion which evoked this sermon in the first place. Showing an enormous confidence in his God and his message, Peter used a phrase appearing only here in the New Testament (**all Israel**) and hammered home his final point: **God has made this Jesus, whom you crucified, both Lord and Christ.** In fine homiletical style he returned to his original text (v. 21) and, along with the prophet Joel, extolled the messiahship of his Lord. The one you think dead is your living Lord, Master, and Messiah!

E Response to the Spirit's Coming (vv. 37–41)

SUPPORTING IDEA: *Jesus Christ the Son of God died and rose again to provide forgiveness of sins to all who believe.*

2:37. The combination of God's Scripture and God's Spirit working through God's servant had the intended effect. From their initial question **What does this mean?** (2:12), the people now progressed to specific response—**Brothers, what shall we do?** The phrase **cut to the heart** translates *katenugesan* meaning "stung" or "stunned." Had some people listening to Peter that day also screamed for blood in Pilate's hall? While the word *conviction* does not appear in our verse, this clearly reflects that heart attitude. The New Testament uses this word to describe the work of the Holy Spirit by which we see ourselves as we are in God's sight.

2:38–39. Peter hesitated not a moment for the answer to their question, calling for repentance and baptism and offering forgiveness and the gift of the Holy Spirit. Repentance is not a new theme in the New Testament, having appeared in the ministry of John the Baptist (Mark 1:4; Luke 3:3) and in the preaching of Jesus (Mark 1:15; Luke 13:3). The context shows baptism here refers to water, not the Holy Spirit. In the New Testament, water baptism became the uniform of the Lord's people. Today we call it "believers' baptism," the conscious identification with Jesus on the part of those who have trusted him for salvation. The gift of the Holy Spirit then became the seal of salvation. To whom is this available? For all whom the Lord our God will call.

2:40–41. Luke hastens to tell us we do not have the entire sermon recorded in his book. Peter spoke many other words and pleaded with his hearers who responded. That day God added three thousand people to the small number of believers already serving as Christ's witnesses. But wait. Don't miss the importance of what Luke does not say. This time there was no sound, no flame, and no foreign language. These people received the Holy Spirit because that's what Peter promised in Jesus' name. Pentecost was a one-time event, with only a mild echo or two appearing elsewhere during the first century.

Are we to believe that Peter baptized three thousand people on that one day? Of course not. The Bible knows no hierarchical system whereby people must be baptized at the hand of some official or titled clergy. We should probably assume all 120 believers assisted in this magnificent demonstration.

In the space of just a few verses, we see what happens when people trust Christ for salvation. First, they must recognize their need; then, they must receive God's gift; and finally, they must obey the message.

⬛ Purpose of the Spirit's Coming (vv. 42–47)

SUPPORTING IDEA: *Unity affords the greatest identifying mark of the people of God. That's why Luke emphasizes, **all the believers were together and had everything in common.***

2:42. At various times in Acts, especially in the early chapters, Luke gives summary reports of how the church is doing. Here we have the first. In it our author describes what a biblical church really looks like, not only in the first century, but in every century from the Lord's ascension until his second coming.

A biblical church is marked by teaching. Thousands of new converts needed to understand precisely how Peter linked Old Testament text with the ministry of Jesus. Theologians call it "Messianic Christology". It became the core of New Testament doctrine.

Furthermore, the new Christians engaged in fellowship. Someone called the church "the colony of heaven." Here the believers fulfilled the words the Lord gave his disciples just before the crucifixion: "A new command I give you: Love one another. As I have loved you, so you must love one another. By this all men will know that you are my disciples, if you love one another" (John 13:34–35).

Then the believers joined in breaking bread—Luke's term for what Paul calls "the Lord's Supper." Quite possibly they practiced it differently than many churches do now, likely with a full meal. Still, the memorial to the Lord's death until he comes again remains the central theme of believers breaking bread together. Quite likely, the phrase also describes Christians fellowshipping together at meal time.

Their worship also included prayer, in our text literally, "the prayers." New prayers and old. Probably public and private.

2:43–45. In addition to their worship, these believers became actively involved in the work of the Lord. Luke uses the same language to describe the apostles that he used of Jesus in 2:22. The miracles showed evidence of a new era. God gave miracles when Moses brought down the law and when Elijah and other prophets thundered a new message across Israel. "Miracles" does not appear in Acts after chapter 15, even though God continued to do miracles beyond that point.

Their work also included learning how to live and love together. They sold their possessions and made sure everybody had plenty. Communism? Absolutely not—this was voluntary, contemporary, and discretionary.

2:46–47. The early church was marked by faithful attendance—meeting together daily in the temple courts. They prayed, gave, ate, and rejoiced together. They practiced the presence of Jesus—still a good idea for his people. Luke makes good use of the Greek word *homothumadon*, translated **together**, applying it in 1:14; 2:46; 4:24; and 5:12.

Their witness included a demonstration of hospitality. No home would be large enough to house even a small group of believers for a short time, so they literally went house to house. Luke wants us to see how good it was—they enjoyed favor with the people. Not the Sanhedrin, but common folks all around the city. *Witnessing* may be the main theme in Acts, but *praising* certainly represents a secondary strain common in Luke's writings (the word *ainountes* is used nine times in the New Testament, seven by Luke). What happens to believers who worship, work, and witness for their Lord? The Lord grows the church. Let's not miss the order—first godly relationships with each other, then growth.

MAIN IDEA REVIEW: *Through the power of the Holy Spirit, Christians can proclaim the gospel of Jesus Christ and people will be saved and become a part of his body, the church.*

III. CONCLUSION

A Model Church

What a magnificent chapter! Instead of a humble and subdued group of Christians praying quietly in an upper room, we now have over three thousand people all over the city praising, praying, and witnessing for Jesus. The early church was a healthy church, a veritable model of what congregations can be in our day when they take seriously the biblical qualifications of what it means to be the church.

Irenaeus served as bishop of Lyons from approximately A.D. 175–195. In his book *Against Heresies* he wrote

This preaching, as cited, and this Faith, as aforementioned, the Church although scattered in the whole world, diligently guards as if it lived in one house, and believes, like the above, as if it had one mind and the same heart, and preaches and teaches and hands on these things harmoniously, as if it had but one mouth. And although there are different languages in the world, the force of the tradition is one and the same.

PRINCIPLES

- The controlling power of God's Holy Spirit is available to all believers.
- The gospel calls for repentance and faith.
- Both historical facts and Bible prophecy affirm that Jesus is God's Messiah.
- Every believer has the Holy Spirit within them.
- Healthy churches pay careful attention to teaching, fellowship, prayer, and witness.

APPLICATIONS

- Trust God's Spirit for the power to serve him.
- Proclaim Jesus' resurrection at every opportunity.
- Understand how the Old Testament and New Testament fit together.
- Participate with other believers in biblical behavior.
- Enjoy your Christian faith.

IV. LIFE APPLICATION

The Clever Monk

I once heard a wonderful story about a young monk who was called on to preach his first sermon at the monastery. Frightened and intimidated, he opened with a question: "How many of you know what I am about to say?" When no one raised a hand, he timidly admitted, "Well I don't either" and dismissed the assembly with the traditional *Dominus vobiscum*, "the Lord be with you."

Of course, his superiors would not let him off the hook with that kind of behavior, so a week later he was back on the same platform. To everyone's surprise, he asked the same question: "How many of you know what I am about to say?" This time the brothers determined to teach him a lesson, so everyone present raised a hand. Courageously, the young monk smiled and said, "Well, since you already know, you don't need to hear the sermon. *Dominus vobiscum.*"

After a severe reprimand he slowly ascended the stairs of the platform yet a third time. Slowly, but deliberately, he astonished the audience with his now traditional question: "How many of you know what I am about to say?" To completely unbalance this clever amateur, half the brothers raised a hand, the other half did not. "Well," said the young monk, "those of you who know tell those who don't know. *Dominus vobiscum.*" And he dismissed the group.

We may feel like that young monk. We may think we don't know enough to preach to others or that we are not mature enough to present ourselves as prime examples of the Christian faith. We can all share with others the experiences we have had in our lives up to this point. If we are new Christians, we can at least tell others that we know Jesus and can help others know him. We don't need to be trained theologians. We can simply tell others what our own experience has been.

"**We are witnesses**," said Peter. Luke makes that theme the banner of his book. Like the early Christians, witnesses are simply people who know, telling people who don't know, what God has made possible through the death, resurrection, and exaltation of his Son, Jesus Christ. We do not need to be brilliant theologians to fulfill that mission, but we do need to be biblical Christians.

The last part of our chapter forces us to examine our own congregations and our individual roles in those congregations. Do our contemporary churches feature these biblical characteristics? If so, special programs and growth formulas are probably unnecessary.

God understands all our shortcomings, our failures, and our problems. Yet he has no other plan for sharing the good news with the world than the proclamation of his people. When we truly believe the power of Peter's message and truly behave like these early believers, some day a future historian may write of our churches, **And the Lord added to their number daily those who were being saved**.

V. PRAYER

Father, thank you for the wonderful gift of the Holy Spirit. May we allow him total control of our lives so that our behavior as individuals, family members, and participants in the body of Christ may be everything God wants to show a needy world. Amen.

VI. DEEPER DISCOVERIES

A. Filled With the Spirit (v. 4)

This special filling at Pentecost was unlike other fillings described both in the Book of Acts and in Paul's epistles. Luke used an adjective and two verbs for *filling*. The adjective was also used of Stephen (7:55), and one of the verbs (*pleroó*) appears in Acts only once in reference to the Holy Spirit (13:52). The form of the verb indicates that the believers *were being filled*, suggesting a continuous process, not only throughout the Day of Pentecost, but repeatedly. For the Christian there is one baptism and many fillings. *Baptism* places believers in the body of Christ, and *filling* enables them to minister in the power of the Holy Spirit. Not all Christians would make this distinction, however; some believe that baptism and filling form exactly the same event or process.

Notice that Luke emphasizes the outward demonstration. Since the concepts of Spirit and wind are linked together, perhaps we can use yet another illustration—steam. Steam is not visible and, technically, not wet. What comes out of a boiling tea kettle forms a visible mist as steam condenses into water droplets. We know what happens as heat creates steam in the kettle, but we don't see it. We do, however, observe what steam does: it burns a hand passed through it; it coats windows in a bathroom during a hot shower or bath; and it serves a multitude of uses from clearing sinuses to softening a piece of frozen food.

In reading Acts 2 we must at the same time recognize the enormous miracle Luke describes and acknowledge it as a historical, never-repeated event. That balance does not minimize the work of the Holy Spirit in contemporary believers, but brings us into an awareness of how God's Spirit is so essential in everything we do. So essential in fact, that Peter makes it a part of the promise of salvation in verse 38.

Paul picked up precisely the same analogy Peter used of drunkenness and Spirit-control when he wrote the Ephesians, "Do not get drunk on wine, which leads to debauchery. Instead, be filled with the Spirit. Speak to one another with psalms, hymns and spiritual songs. Sing and make music in your heart to the Lord, always giving thanks to God the Father for everything, in the name of our Lord Jesus Christ" (Eph. 5:18–20). Obviously, the Spirit empowers for worship, service, and testimony. Just as too much alcohol controls a person's behavior in the wrong way, so the Holy Spirit intends to control the Christian's behavior in God's way. Believers are to submit themselves voluntarily to the control of the Holy Spirit who lives in them, resulting in peace, joy, and harmony with other believers.

B. Foreknowledge (v. 23)

The death of Jesus was not accidental, nor was it under the control of Jewish religious leaders or Roman politicians. His death fulfilled prophecy, and all the human instruments involved served God's eternal plan. Without realizing it, they carried out the will of God (Acts 13:27). This is the eternal paradox of divine sovereignty and human freedom. God works in human events to bring about his will, even events tainted by human sin.

Many times, perhaps most times, we do not understand how or why he is working. Who can explain God's plan through Adolf Hitler? What did God have in mind in the genocide of Bosnia? What are we to make of the brain cancer death of a young wife who leaves behind a grieving husband and three small children? Certainly, we shall never understand any of it this side of heaven. We know that God sovereignly carries out precisely what he intends in the world and the ultimate eternal result is good, because God is good.

Perhaps the key here again is balance—not to allow one truth to throw another into lesser importance. Our verse is most helpful. Peter clearly says that God's foreknowledge and purpose brought about the cross. In the same breath he tells the men of Israel that they put him to death by nailing him to the cross. Human responsibility cannot be absolved because they became instruments in carrying out God's greater plan.

How does all this relate to the issue of personal salvation? Do we "find God"? Or does God elect us to salvation? The Scriptures affirm both truths. There is no possibility, nor any need, for us to understand everything that goes on in the mind of God. That is why the Bible so often refers to the Christian life as faith.

C. Repentance (v. 38)

The word *repentance* (*metanoia*) derives from two other words, *meta* meaning "after" and *nous*, the word for "mind." Repentance means "to change one's mind" or even more precisely, "to turn and go in the opposite direction." The dominant idea of this verse clearly centers in repentance with the other aspects following logically in order. Repentance moves a person to baptism, forgiveness, and the gift of the Holy Spirit, not necessarily in that specific order.

Verses like Acts 2:38 remind us of that wonderful and deeply theological hymn, "Once For All."

> Free from the law, O happy condition,
> Jesus hath bled, and there is remission;
> Cursed by the law and bruised by the fall,
> Grace hath redeemed us once for all.
> Now we are free—there's no condemnation,
> Jesus provides a perfect salvation;
> "Come unto me," O hear His sweet call,
> Come, and He saves us once for all.
> Children of God, O glorious calling,
> Surely His grace will keep us from falling;
> Passing from death to life at His call,
> Blessed salvation once for all.
> Once for all—O sinner, receive it;
> Once for all—O brother, believe it;
> Cling to the cross, the burden will fall,
> Christ hath redeemed us once for all.

D. Church (vv. 42–47)

How interesting that the actual word *church* does not appear in these six verses, though Luke describes it precisely. We use the word in at least four different ways, to identify a *building*, a *denomination*, a local *congregation*, and *the body of Christ*.

We may say of the building in which we meet on Sunday mornings, "I'm going down to the church to pick up some materials for my Sunday school class next week." It may be Tuesday morning, and we understand that the body of Christ is not there, just the building in which they meet. This usage works in casual conversation as long as we understand the Bible never applies the word to describe a building or a specific place of worship. The New Testament claims that God's people do *not* have to be in a specific place to worship.

Nor does the word *church* appear in the Bible to describe a denomination. Today we talk about the Methodist Church, the Baptist Church, or the Church of God. We do no harm with such terminology as long as we understand that this human construct does not constitute theological truth. What we mean is that groups of congregations have come together to form a larger representation of the body of Christ, and so we use the word *church*.

The New Testament regularly uses the word *church* in reference to local congregations. We read about the Church of Ephesus and the Church at Philippi. The Book of Revelation opens with letters to seven churches. In every case, these are gatherings of believers who likely did not meet in specific buildings and had no affiliation with any larger group other than geographical connections. This is the most common New Testament use and the one we find in our passage at the end of Acts 2.

Finally, all believers of all places and ages are placed by the Holy Spirit into the body of Christ and, therefore, become a part of the universal church. The universal church finds embodiment in local churches (congregations) like the one developed at Jerusalem after Peter's sermon. Ephesians tells us much about the universal church.

VII. TEACHING OUTLINE

A. INTRODUCTION

1. Lead Story: Symphony of the Spirit
2. Context: We dare never forget that the Book of Acts is history, and chapter 2 describes a pivotal point in that history. It is inseparable from chapter 1, for we have read of the believers gathered in Jerusalem waiting for the coming of the Spirit. Now in chapter 2, the Holy Spirit comes, and thousands more believe to form the church. We have become part of them. The same resurrected and ascended Lord gives the same Holy Spirit to believers in our day. We are

baptized into the body and filled with his Spirit to carry out appropriate works of service for Jesus. The more we behave like the believers described in verses 42–47, the more the Lord can add to our numbers those who are being saved.

3. Transition: Acts 2 introduces the dispensation of the New Covenant church. The word *dispensation* obviously is built on *dispense*, meaning "to give." The Father gave the Son; the Son gave the Spirit; the Spirit gives us life, that we may give the gift of love—and the gift goes on. Luke mentions six things related to the birth of the church in chapter 2:

B. COMMENTARY

1. Symbols of the Spirit's Coming (vv. 1–4)
    a. Sound of wind (vv. 1–2)
    b. Appearance of flame (v. 3)
    c. Use of languages (v. 4)
2. Results of the Spirit's Coming (vv. 5–13)
    a. Popularity (vv. 5–6)
    b. Proclamation (vv. 7–11)
    c. Perplexity (vv. 12–13)
3. Prophecy of the Spirit's Coming (vv. 14–21)
    a. Drunkenness denied (vv. 14–16)
    b. Prophecy affirmed (vv. 17–21)
4. Explanation of the Spirit's Coming (vv. 22–36)
    a. Historical facts (vv. 22–28)
    b. Prophetic foundation (vv. 29–36)
5. Response to the Spirit's Coming (vv. 37–41)
    a. People must see their need (v. 37)
    b. People must receive God's gift (vv. 38–39)
    c. People must obey the message (vv. 40–41)
6. Purpose of the Spirit's Coming (vv. 42–47)
    a. Worship (v. 42)
    b. Work (vv. 43–45)
    c. Witness (vv. 46–47)

C. CONCLUSION: THE CLEVER MONK

VIII. ISSUES FOR DISCUSSION

1. Should your church be praying for a Pentecost experience in your midst? Why?
2. What message does verse 21 have for you and your church?
3. How would you explain who Jesus is to an unbeliever?
4. Who needs to repent and be baptized? Why?

Acts 3

Surprised by Ministry

I. **Introduction**
When Darkness Hides in Light

II. **Commentary**
A verse-by-verse explanation of the chapter.

III. **Conclusion**
The Hearer's Choice
An overview of the principles and applications from the chapter.

IV. **Life Application**
Taking Off the Dunce Cap
Melding the chapter to life.

V. **Prayer**
Tying the chapter to life with God.

VI. **Deeper Discoveries**
Historical, geographical, and grammatical enrichment of the commentary.

VII. **Teaching Outline**
Suggested step-by-step group study of the chapter.

VIII. **Issues for Discussion**
Zeroing the chapter in on daily life.

Q u o t e

"*H*is name above all names shall stand, exalted more and more; At God the Father's own right hand, where angel hosts adore."

W . H . C l a r k

BUILDING PROFILE: HEROD'S TEMPLE

- Begun by Herod the Great in 20–19 B.C.
- Completed in a.d. 64 and destroyed in A.D. 70
- Built on twenty-six acres surrounded by a high wall
- Constructed of white marble with gold plates facing the rising sun

I N   A   N U T S H E L L

*F*ervent Jews in Jesus' time met at the temple three times daily for prayer—during morning sacrifice, during the afternoon sacrifice, and at sunset. In this chapter Peter and John attended the temple. Although not looking for ministry opportunities, they were met with a challenge from God to take their faith seriously. What follows is the first public healing miracle described in our book, and one of the most eloquent sermons concerning the name and power of Jesus found anywhere in the Bible—delivered spontaneously. Luke wants his readers to see that everything the early Christians accomplished was because of the power of Jesus Christ in their lives and the guidance of the Spirit.

Surprised by Ministry

I. INTRODUCTION

When Darkness Hides in Light

*H*ave you ever flown at night into Miami? The same can be said for other cities as well, but this city in particular offers the passenger in a window seat a lighting spectacular which gives every promise of splendor and beauty awaiting on the ground. Many times passengers flying into Miami International Airport comment about the enchanting rows of orange lights in the streets just north and east of the airport. Sometimes they'll even connect them with the Orange Bowl and other "orange" metaphors of the Sunshine State.

Living in that city, however, gives a person a different perspective. Those are crime lights! Heavy orange lights are used in parts of the city particularly known for crime and trouble. Darkness hides in that light.

Such was the case as Peter and John went to afternoon worship at the temple. They entered by the Eastern Gate and took the fifteen steps that led down to the Court of the Gentiles and Solomon's Colonnade (which contained four rows of white marble columns). Behind ran the Kidron Valley and, rising just above it, the Mount of Olives. In front of them was the beautiful temple of Herod. Josephus tells us the temple had ten gates into the sanctuary, nine overlaid with silver and gold, and the tenth formed of Corinthian bronze, so massive it took twenty men to close it.

Apparently this gate's adornments included the symbol of a vine reflecting the Old Testament picture of Israel as part of God's vineyard (Isa. 5). With beauty surrounding them, perhaps on a bright and cheery day, surely still riding the spiritual cloud of Pentecost, Peter and John came face-to-face with sickness and pain—darkness hiding in the light.

How often our lives are like that. A lonely woman returns to a magnificent apartment which has become hers through a bitter divorce settlement and sees only the pain and suffering of that experience. Tourists wander from monument to monument in Washington, D.C., scarcely aware they are surrounded by some of the worst street crime and drug trafficking in America. Boaters, seemingly pushed by the gentle rays of the setting sun, float into San Francisco harbor under the Golden Gate Bridge perhaps not thinking for a moment they will soon dock at a city which houses the largest homosexual community in the world.

Even day-to-day life demonstrates this stark contrast. A new car, so joyously purchased last month, turns out to be a lemon. A vacation trip to

Orlando in February finds us in a week of fifty degree weather and shivering rain.

One lesson Peter and John learned that day, we must also learn if we want to become mature Christians. God's grace and power are neither governed by, nor limited to, any set of circumstances. The beggar formed a pitiful sight and, at first glance, reflected only the common curse of sin in the world, about which Peter and John could do nothing. They were wrong. Sometimes when darkness hides in the light, the light, because of Jesus, overpowers the darkness. How did John put it? "In him was life, and that life was the light of men. The light shines in the darkness, but the darkness has not understood it" (John 1:4–5).

II. COMMENTARY

Surprised by Ministry

MAIN IDEA: *God provides for his glory spontaneous opportunities for ministry and will also grant us the power to seize those opportunities.*

A Opportunity for Ministry (vv. 1–5)

SUPPORTING IDEA: *Some opportunities for ministry call on us to determine the real needs of the ones to whom we minister and the resources we have that will help them.*

3:1. The early Christians were still faithful Jews. At three in the afternoon, the hour of prayer, they were headed to church as we might do on a Sunday morning. We see no special connection between Peter and John except that they were part of the inner circle present at the transfiguration (Luke 9:28–36). Everything about the Christian faith still revolved around Jerusalem. The believers saw no reason to separate themselves from the city and the religion that had openly rejected and even crucified their Lord. Their goal was not to turn away, but rather to proclaim the name of Jesus to the very ones who had shouted "Crucify him!"

3:2. Luke has already told us in his Gospel that the healing of lame people would be a sign of the Lord's return (Luke 7:22). These apostles believed they lived in the end times and, in the broad sweep of human history, they did, just as we do. The man had chosen an excellent place for begging, since alms giving was a virtuous act for the Jews. Luke tells us the man was **crippled from birth**, using a Greek term which commonly described paralysis in the ankles or heels, making walking impossible. This had been his plight for more than forty years. Each day someone brought him to the temple along with dozens of other beggars. Each sought to catch the attention of the good worshipers passing their way.

Ogilvie observes, "I have watched beggars in cities all over the world. They have a highly developed sense of who will respond. While walking down a street one day, I spied a beggar at the end of the block. I noticed his eyes darted from person to person as they passed by him, and he called out for a gift from only certain people. He could tell which ones were likely to stop" (Ogilvie, 81).

Traditional translations such as King James give the literal phrase "the ninth hour" instead of translating into modern idiom, **three in the afternoon,** as does NIV. Since a Jewish day began at 6:00 A.M., those two time references coincide.

3:3. The man sat outside the temple. A person with a **defect** was not allowed to enter temple worship (Lev. 21:16–18). Luke wants us to notice that the beggar picked Peter and John out of the crowd, perhaps for the same reason Olgivie mentions above. Then, he did exactly what beggars do—he asked them for money. The Greek verb here is interesting. The word *erota* appears in the inchoative imperfect, suggesting an oft-repeated appeal he had made for years.

Remember our theme for this first section—opportunity for ministry. Because they faithfully attended worship, because believers maintained contact with the real world, and because Peter and John understood that the *size of ministry was not an issue,* God gave them opportunity for a miracle.

These men had recently been involved in an evangelistic effort which brought thousands to Christ. Now God tells them, this one lost sheep is just as important to him as the thousands to whom they preached at Pentecost. This lesson should sound a clarion note in a society obsessed with numbers and size. A pastor or congregation serving Jesus Christ in a rural church of fifty renders just as important service for the kingdom of God as the pastoral staff and sprawling congregation in an urban megachurch of five thousand. God is not interested in the number of people you and I teach or disciple or influence; he watches how faithfully we seize opportunities for ministry.

3:4–5. Peter had never been famous for indecisiveness (except at the time of the crucifixion), although he often chose the wrong direction. Here he was right on target. We can almost sense the drama as Peter's eyes locked on those of the beggar. Rather than reaching in their money pouches as he expected, these two unusual men stared straight at him. Not only that, but Peter commanded, **Look at us!** The Greek form tells us the man gave the apostles his total attention, possibly expecting some unusual generosity.

Why call for his attention when he had already addressed them? Because a veteran beggar would be looking well beyond his immediate clientele to whomever might be next in line. Beg to everyone, and hope a few will respond. Peter, filled with the Spirit of God, had more in mind. God forced them into a ministry opportunity they had not anticipated, but they were ready. In the seconds that passed during this brief encounter, this man could not have known what his Creator was about to do through these two potential donors.

🅱 Power for Ministry (vv. 6–10)

SUPPORTING IDEA: *Service for the Savior cannot be carried out in our own strength. Only divinely-empowered responses to ministry can count in any way.*

3:6. What a stunning and eloquent statement from this former fisherman. In seconds the beggar must have gone from disappointment at hearing about Peter's financial condition to disbelief when told to walk. In his many years at that spot he had heard countless people claim their own poverty as an excuse for passing his bowl. No one had ever said anything like this. What a dramatic call to action this verse gives us—**what I have I give you.**

A missionary asks for support during the annual missionary conference, but our budgets simply cannot tolerate another five or ten dollars a month. What can we give? Can we pray? Can we write? Can we encourage and affirm, even during that week? Can we invite this missionary or someone during next year's conference into our homes? God never asks us to give what we don't have; he expects us to give to those in need from what he has given us, and always to do it **in the name of Jesus Christ of Nazareth.**

Within moments Peter will preach about this **name,** but here it becomes the power, the leverage for the first of three healings of cripples in Acts (9:32; 14:8). Longenecker reminds us:

> In Semitic thought, a name does not just identify or distinguish a person; it expresses the very nature of his being. Hence the power of the person is present and available in the name of the person. Peter, therefore, does not just ask the risen Jesus to heal but pronounces over the crippled beggar the name of Jesus, thereby releasing the power of Jesus, compare 3:16; 4:10 (Longenecker, 294).

3:7–8. The text is unclear whether the beggar was unable to walk just from hearing the words or whether he did not even have time to try. Peter grasped his hand, helped him up, and in that process **the man's feet and ankles became strong.** This was a clear miracle of rehabilitation. Luke chose the word **instantly** which he also used on several other occasions in his two books. Other than Luke and Acts, the Greek word (*paraxrema*) only occurs in Matthew 21:19–20. Those heels and ankles which had been out of socket rejoined and immediately became strong.

To this point in the text we find no reference to the man's faith. Throughout Scripture both salvation and healing come through faith (though not always the faith of the sick, compare James 5:14–15). As we glance ahead in our chapter, we see in verse 16 that somehow the man responded spiritually as well as physically. Even as strength entered his ankles, faith entered his heart.

What does one suddenly able to walk for the first time in forty years do? Dr. Luke leaves us no doubt as he unleashes a handful of bouncing verbs— **walking, jumping, praising**. He uses an interesting word for *jumping*. In the Greek text of Isaiah 35:6 the word refers to a deer. In the midst of all that walking, jumping, and praising, this former cripple, this outcast, entered the temple courts.

3:9–10. Miracles should cause amazement and usually do (Luke 4:36; 5:9,26; 7:16). Surely only the people immediately in the area heard Peter attribute the miracle to Jesus, but **all the people** saw this well-known beggar walking, jumping, and praising. No one doubted what had happened.

Think with me for a moment about the contrasts in these five verses. First is *the contrast between what the disciples were and what they are at the temple*. Larry Burkett tells the story of trying to determine whether God could use him in some way in Christian service. As part of his decision process he listed the disciples' traits as if he were a businessman hiring employees. In the group he was able to find three or four positive traits, but at least three times that many were negative. Yet here two of them are about to turn a city upside down for God. What made the difference? The resurrection of Jesus Christ and the power of the Holy Spirit in their lives—both ministry dynamics within our grasp today.

Then *consider the contrast between what the beggar expected and what he got*. A heresy rampages through our churches today. This heresy identifies God's blessing with money, possessions, fame, and other such worldly measures. Often called the "prosperity gospel," it completely denies the message of the New Testament, for the Bible identifies Christians as pilgrims and strangers on earth. The Bible never denotes money or celebrity status as a sign of God's blessing (2 Cor. 6:3–10). Trouble or struggle in our lives does not evidence the lack of God's blessing upon us or our families. Peter was on a high right here, but deep lows lay ahead.

Finally, consider *the contrast between the physical miracle and the spiritual miracle*. Both occurred in the same man at the same time. Which was greater? To the immediate crowd, surely the jumping and walking. To the angels that day, the recognition that another person would spend eternity in heaven. We will address the question of healing a bit later in our study of this chapter, but let's remember here that spiritual miracles are no less miraculous and certainly no less important than physical miracles.

ⓒ Source of Ministry (vv. 11–16)

SUPPORTING IDEA: *Our service for Jesus begins with self-denial, centers on him, and proclaims faith in his name.*

3:11. Solomon's Colonnade was a covered portico running the entire eastern portion of the temple's outer court. On that porch, a large crowd gathered as a result of the miracle. Peter's third of seven addresses in Acts was about to commence. The pattern of this chapter seems not at all unlike our Lord's ministry, particularly as John recorded it. I like to call it the "miracle-message method." Jesus would perform a miracle (like the feeding of the five thousand) and follow with a message related to the same theme (the bread of life in John 6). Whether Peter intended it or not, that is precisely what he did.

3:12. All effective ministry begins with self-denial. John the Baptizer once said, "He must become greater; I must become less" (John 3:30).

Peter challenged their astonishment at a miracle, aware of course that apart from what Jesus had done, miracles had been nonexistent in Israel for years. His listeners must understand that the source of the miracle and the source of the ministry could not be found in the two men now clutched by the healed cripple. They had neither power of the spirit nor power of moral example to be able to claim to do miracles.

3:13–15. All Christian ministries center on Jesus. God's work did not begin with Jesus' earthly life. The gospel rests in history so Peter began there. As a Jew speaking to Jews, he invoked the revered names of Abraham, Isaac, and Jacob. He had no interest in abstract theology, nor did he bother (with this audience) to develop an elaborate introduction, as we shall see later with both Stephen and Paul.

Interestingly, Peter's recollection of the crucifixion seems to exonerate, or at least ignore, Pilate. The good people of Jerusalem, those who worshiped regularly at Herod's temple, disowned **the Holy and Righteous One** and chose rather a murderer. Don't miss the direct accusations: you handed him over; you disowned him; you asked that a murderer be released; you killed the author of life.

Peter left no doubt about the blame for the death of Jesus, God's messianic servant (Isa. 52:13–53:12). All this was certainly stunning revelation to people who had **acted in ignorance** (v. 17). Their ignorance did not diminish their guilt. Verse 15 is particularly stunning: **You killed the author of life, but God raised him from the dead.** The very architect of breathing had his breath taken away by these people. The Creator of the universe gave that breath back.

We dare not miss the last five words of the verse—**we are witnesses of this.** In the first chapter we noted how the word *witness* stands so strategic in Luke's history of the early church in Acts. As we study through the sermons in Acts, we will find these early preachers moving as rapidly as they can to the fact and meaning of the resurrection. They saw him. They touched him. They watched him ascend into heaven. Nothing could daunt their faith nor diminish their resolve to be his witnesses.

3:16. Effective Christian ministry proclaims faith **in the name of Jesus.** Luke uses this phrase thirty-three times in the Book of Acts. Here we have the key verse of the chapter, the answer to the questions raised in verse 12. How was this man healed? How is all this possible? Because of Jesus' name **and the faith that comes through him.** The beggar need not understand resurrection, the ascension, or any other Christian theology. His response to Peter's command and outstretched right hand demonstrated faith which God had placed in his heart.

We must remember that Jesus had probably entered this very gate of the temple many times and would have been well-known to a man who sat there every day. When Romans talked about the name of Caesar, they implied all the authority and power of the emperor. So here Peter referred to Jesus and everything about him as he delivered what we might call the first pure gospel in Acts.

Message of Ministry (vv. 17–26)

SUPPORTING IDEA: *By God's grace, repentance brings forgiveness through Christ, and that forgiveness is available to all who call upon his name.*

3:17–18. What a magnanimous gesture in this spontaneous sermon. Without backing away from his condemnation of their guilt, Peter acknowledged they had no idea what they were doing, nor did their leaders. Furthermore, crucifixion fulfilled prophecy because God had said the Messiah would suffer. Peter continued to jolt his audience with word after word. The God of Abraham, Isaac, and Jacob actually prophesied and then fulfilled the death of his own Son, the Messiah! This gracious appeal to Israel to accept the gospel reminds us of Jesus' words on the cross, "Father, forgive them, for they do not know what they are doing" (Luke 23:34).

3:19–20. Don't touch that dial; there's more. The Messiah is alive, he has ascended, and he will return. If the nation would only turn to God for the washing of sins, **times of refreshing may come from the Lord,** and Jesus would come again. Peter used two unprecedented expressions in these verses. His references to **times of refreshing** in verse 19 and **the time . . . for God to restore everything** (v. 21) have had commentators scratching their theological heads for years. One truth emerges with clarity: prophecy which determined Christ's death also will determine a time of restoration. It seems that Israel will repent before Jesus comes again, though we probably cannot conclude from the passage that Christ's return depends upon Israel's repentance.

Meanwhile, Jesus will remain in heaven until the promised restoration (Ps. 110:1). We need not conclude that Peter had specific prophetic passages in mind, though that certainly might have been the case. In general, he intended to remind his fellow Jews that the hope of Israel's restoration should not be forgotten and, indeed, could only be fulfilled in Jesus.

3:22–23. Faith in Christ, coupled with repentance, is required for salvation, so Peter used a messianic proof text from Deuteronomy 18:15,18–19. Any group wanting a hearing in Israel had to link itself with the heroes of the past, and it surely didn't hurt to drop Moses' name in the process. As well-taught Jews, Peter's hearers would have immediately understood the identification and continuity—belief in Moses should produce belief in Jesus.

Belief in Jesus in no way destroys belief in Moses. When John the Baptist began preaching, the priests and Levites asked him: **Are you the Prophet?** (John 1:21). Of course not! Now Peter picked up the same theme to say that the prophet of whom Moses spoke was the very one through whose power the lame beggar had just been healed.

3:24–26. Peter's Jewish audience represented the natural heirs to promises dating all the way back to Genesis (22:18; 26:4). The earliest Christian preaching rested on Old Testament theology which emphasized the importance of a faithful remnant waiting for the Messiah. This spontaneous proclamation on a temple porch provided a brilliant example. Every genuine prophet looked forward to the coming of Messiah, and those prophets lived from Samuel right up to John the Baptist, or better yet, to Jesus who was raised up as God's servant.

MAIN IDEA REVIEW: *God provides for his glory spontaneous opportunities for ministry and will also grant us the power to seize those opportunities.*

III. CONCLUSION

The Hearer's Choice

The church age, the days in which you and I now live, were foretold by the prophets of old. First the gospel came to the Jews as a blessing, for God had chosen that nation to give the world his Messiah and his message of salvation. True, this sermon represented the gospel for Jews at a particular point in history, but it was the gospel no less. Everything good in this world comes because of the life, death, and resurrection of Jesus Christ. God's sovereign grace makes possible anything of worth or pleasure in our lives. We corrupt his gifts; we scorn his grace; we reject his goodness; but still he sent Jesus who blesses us continually.

The gospel requires response. In both Acts 2 and 3 Peter intended his listeners to do something about what he said. It was, as we might say, the hearer's choice.

In September of 1900, a killer hurricane bore down on Galveston Island. One old bridge connected the island to the mainland, serving as the only evacuation route for thousands. Even without modern-day detection systems, the coming hurricane was spotted, and ample warnings given. There were no visible signs; people living on the island couldn't actually see the hurricane nor hear its fury—so they chose to do nothing. When that terrible storm struck, six thousand people were killed, and the city of Galveston destroyed. Today a strong concrete sea wall stands as a barrier against such disaster, but also as a reminder that a century ago, thousands of people heard a message of warning and chose not to respond.

PRINCIPLES

- God works through his people to accomplish miraculous results, both physically and spiritually.
- People are amazed when they see God's power in action.
- God's work in the world gives his people opportunity to minister and proclaim his message.
- The Christian message begins and ends in the name and person of Jesus Christ, God's righteous Servant.
- Some ministry opportunities come when we least expect them and have not programmed them into our lives.

APPLICATIONS

- Be ready for any opportunity for ministry God may put in your path.
- Don't be afraid to speak boldly in the name of Jesus.
- Never draw attention or acclaim to yourself as a Christian.
- Thank God daily for all the great blessings you have in Christ.
- Look for the return of the One who waits in heaven until God will restore everything.

IV. LIFE APPLICATION

Taking Off the Dunce Cap

Have you ever wondered where that expression came from? Actually, right out of church history. John Duns Scotus was a theologian who entered the Franciscan order at the age of fifteen and was ordained a priest in 1291. His intricate theology prompted Roman Catholics to give him the title "Subtle Doctor." Protestant reformers picked up on the idea, calling anyone whose ideas seemed obscure a "duns" from which, of course, the word "dunce" arose.

On one occasion, Scotus and the Pope walked through the Vatican Gold Chambers. As the story goes, the Pope turned to the theologian and said, "Dr. Scotus, no longer can the church say 'silver and gold have I none.'" To which Scotus reportedly replied, "And no longer can it say, 'in the name of Jesus Christ of Nazareth, rise up and walk.'"

Whether true or not, the incident certainly applies to our day as well as the thirteenth century. We build gigantic buildings worth millions of dollars and put on lavish programs to call attention to ourselves, hoping people will come to a certain place, at a certain time, to hear a certain person proclaim a message of importance. Capturing God in a building with some kind of special group often seems like wearing the dunce cap, proclaiming a message nobody wants and nobody heeds. This chapter calls us to be ready for spontaneous ministry, to look for blind beggars in our path, and to trust God to give us the wisdom and the power to do something about every ministry opportunity he affords.

Peter's example also reminds us to avoid intricate meanderings of theological knowledge so typical of John Duns Scotus. Rather he shows us how to drive home the point of salvation through the name of Jesus, and forgiveness through repentance because of his resurrection.

Yet we feel so inadequate, so ill-prepared to respond like Peter and John. Let's not forget their struggles in the first four books of the New Testament. Let's not forget how ordinary they were, how incompetent, how ill-fitted for tasks Jesus sent them to do.

Then they got a glimpse of resurrection power and God filled them, as he does all Christians, with his Holy Spirit. Completely dependent upon him, they encountered situation after situation with total trust that God's sovereign grace would produce whatever he wished in their lives.

Is it possible that we try too hard? Of course, careful preparation for preaching and teaching is important, but it can never replace complete dependence upon God for every word we speak. Let's know the Scriptures so well and trust our heavenly Father so completely that we need never be "surprised by ministry."

V. PRAYER

God, please help us be ready to serve you at any time, always dependent upon the Holy Spirit's power and not upon ourselves. Amen.

VI. DEEPER DISCOVERIES

A. Beautiful Gate (v. 2)

The gate in question may well have been the huge Corinthian or Nicanor Gate and briefly described that entrance to the temple area. However, it is important to observe that not everyone agrees with that choice. Our problem comes because there was no gate formally called **Beautiful** even though Luke seems to use this as a proper name in the text. For hundreds of years scholars identified **Beautiful** gate as the Shushan Gate located on the eastern wall and providing access to the temple for those coming from the east. Yet few worshipers would have chosen that difficult entrance with its high cliffs, making it a less than enviable location for a veteran beggar.

Items like this in our study of the Bible should not throw us off balance. Luke says the gate was **called Beautiful**, and names stick in the same way today. Perhaps people spoke of the Corinthian Gate so often as "that beautiful gate" it no longer became fashionable to use the formal names Corinthian or Nicanor. We say, "I'm going down to that big store" or "Let's eat at the restaurant with the green awning." Whether or not we can pinpoint the gate with accuracy is not important; Luke's reader(s) would have understood it immediately.

B. Healing (vv. 7–8)

No serious Christian doubts God can heal whomever he chooses in a miraculous way, whether the crippled beggar in our chapter or a loved one with cancer today. Yet the gift of healing we find in Acts seems somewhat different from most claims around us today. In the early church God healed people through Peter, Paul, and others. As in this record, the immediate response often included no apparent faith or knowledge on the part of the person healed.

Today "faith healers" seem to select certain people; they go through very public and sometimes bizarre behaviors; and they blame any failure on a lack of faith in the sick person.

Perhaps the biggest difference is one we have already noted. After the healing, Peter and John completely disavowed any power of their own and immediately directed all healing power to God. They took no money; used no mailing list; built no multimillion dollar homes or churches; and calmed down a crowd rather than driving it into a frenzy.

C. The Name of Jesus (vv. 13–16)

This amazing sermon by Peter uses five different names or titles for the Lord: **his servant Jesus** (v. 13); **the Holy and Righteous One** (v. 14); the **author of life** (v. 15); **the Christ** (v. 20); and **a prophet like me** (v. 22). Remember that **the name** would trigger in all pious Jews a connection with the sacred, never pronounced personal name of God and his divine presence and power. Now Peter applies that most sacred name to Jesus of Nazareth.

Imagine that your pastor has announced on a certain Sunday that next week he will preach on "the name of Jesus." The congregation arrives, the title is printed in the bulletin, but the pastor became seriously ill and cannot come to church. After the worship, singing, giving, and Scripture reading, an official of the congregation comes to you and says, "The board has decided you should speak in the pastor's absence. We want you to deal with the same theme he announced"; then he personally conducts you to the pulpit microphone.

What would you say? Most of us would mumble some apologetic line about being unprepared and surprised. In a similar situation Peter spontaneously offered this magnificent portrayal of the power and person of Christ residing in his name. It's tempting to focus on this passage only for the theology Peter preached that day. Without denying the importance of that theme, let us not for one moment lose sight of the practical application of Scripture truth in the lives of his listeners. Every time we have an opportunity to preach or teach God's Word, we should try to relate it to the lives of our listeners.

D. Repentance (v. 19)

How often we have heard that repentance means being sorry for our sin, and often that posture appropriately accompanies genuine repentance. But the word *metanoia* really refers to a change of mind. Sometimes it describes turning around and walking in a different direction. The Jews in Peter's audience had rejected and crucified the Messiah; now they needed to accept him as the Savior of Israel.

The Bible often links repentance with faith because saving faith includes genuine repentance. The unbeliever changes to a believer, a complete difference of direction and thought (Acts 11:17–18; Acts 20:21).

Let's not worry about the order. Somehow, as part of the salvation process, we turn from our sins, reject and repudiate our former behavior, and cast ourselves in total faith upon the finished work of Jesus Christ.

E. Interpreting Scripture (vv. 24–26)

Although this is not a book on interpretation, we should always remember hermeneutical principles when dealing with the text of Acts. Perhaps the most important one is style or what some scholars call *genre*. This historical book, quite unlike Paul's theological epistles, David's psalms, or Solomon's list of proverbs, is subject to different understanding.

Furthermore, in the early chapters of Acts, Luke describes everything within the framework of a Jewish culture in which almost everybody who appears in his narrative has strong familiarity with the Old Testament. In the last paragraph of our chapter, for example, Peter uses the principle of *verbal analogy*. This argues that when the same *words* are applied to two separate cases, it follows that the same *considerations* apply to both. In these verses it works like this: since the ancient prophets made promises to Israel and God now fulfilled them in Christ, those promises and this new prophet obviously apply to first-century Jews.

Another aspect of interpretation is what Hebrew scholars call a *pesher* from the Hebrew term meaning "interpret." We find this type of interpretation in the Dead Sea Scrolls which quote an Old Testament text and then insert the word *pesher*. They used an ancient Scripture passage to interpret a present situation. This is the second pesher in Acts, the first one appearing in 2:14–21. Without explanation Peter applies the prophecy of Joel to first-century Christians, basically implying, "What Joel said then, God says now."

Again, the idea here is not to delve deeply into Hebrew hermeneutics, but to recognize that these apostles, filled with the Spirit, confidently proclaimed Scripture and applied it to the needs and struggles of people around them. That offers an outstanding model for us today.

VII. TEACHING OUTLINE

A. INTRODUCTION

1. Lead story: When Darkness Hides in Light
2. Context: After Luke's exciting description of the coming of the Holy Spirit at Pentecost, Peter's sermon, and the founding of the church, Luke ended the second chapter by telling us what the church looked like and how it behaved. Verse 46 said, **Every day they continued to meet together in the temple courts,** so we should hardly be surprised when chapter 3 opens with Peter and John doing precisely that.
3. Transition: In Acts 3 we see how alert Christians respond to ministry opportunities. We learn also how important it is to know Scripture and be able to proclaim it, even publicly if necessary, with solid

application to real life and an unmistakable emphasis on Jesus Christ and the resurrection. In chapter 3 Luke mentions four aspects of ministry.

B. COMMENTARY
1. Opportunity for Ministry (vv. 1–5)
    a. Because Christians were in the right place at the right time (v. 1)
    b. Because God placed opportunity in their path (vv. 2–3)
    c. Because Peter and John were ready to serve (vv. 4–5)
2. Power for Ministry (vv. 6–10)
    a. Ministry power resides in the name of Jesus (v. 6)
    b. Ministry power brings results (vv. 7–8)
    c. Ministry power attracts attention (vv. 9–10)
3. Source of Ministry (vv. 11–16)
    a. It begins with self-denial (vv. 11–12)
    b. It centers on Jesus (vv. 13–15)
    c. It proclaims faith in his name (v. 16)
4. Message of Ministry (vv. 17–23)
    a. God prophesied and fulfilled Christ's death (vv. 17–18).
    b. Christ is alive, ascended, and coming again (vv. 19–21).
    c. Repentant faith is required for salvation (vv. 22–23).
    d. All the prophets from Samuel to Jesus have proclaimed his coming (vv. 24–26).

C. CONCLUSION: TAKING OFF THE DUNCE CAP

VIII. ISSUES FOR DISCUSSION

1. How would you and your church respond to a beggar on the steps of your church?
2. What do you have besides financial resources that you could give to God's work?
3. What is repentance?

Acts 4

Christians with Courage

I. Introduction
    The College Fleet

II. Commentary
    A verse-by-verse explanation of the chapter.

III. Conclusion
    Termite Teachings
    An overview of the principles and applications from the chapter.

IV. Life Application
    Bloom Where You Are Planted
    Melding the chapter to life.

V. Prayer
    Tying the chapter to life with God.

VI. Deeper Discoveries
    Historical, geographical, and grammatical enrichment of the commentary.

VII. Teaching Outline
    Suggested step-by-step group study of the chapter.

VIII. Issues for Discussion
    Zeroing the chapter in on daily life.

Quote

"*Courage is a special kind of knowledge: the knowledge of how to fear what ought to be feared and how not to fear what ought not to be feared.*"

Ben Gurion

BIOGRAPHICAL PROFILE: ANNAS

- Name means "merciful" or "gracious"
- Appointed High Priest about A.D. 6 by Quirinius
- Father-in-law of Caiaphas
- Most influential member of the high priestly family

BIOGRAPHICAL PROFILE: HEROD ANTIPAS

- Tetrarch of Galilee and Perea (Luke 23:1–24)
- Son of Herod the Great
- Murderer of John the Baptist
- Involved in the trial and crucifixion of Jesus

GEOGRAPHICAL PROFILE: CYPRUS

- An island in the northeast Mediterranean Sea
- 148 miles long and 40 miles north to south
- In Greek mythology, the birthplace of Zeus
- Mentioned in Ezekiel 27:6

 I N A N U T S H E L L

In chapter 4 Luke continues the story of public reaction to the healing of the crippled beggar. Now, rather than crowd response, we see the official follow-up by the infamous Sanhedrin. Through the entire chapter the early Christians show courage because of their complete faith in God's sovereignty and in the resurrection of the Lord Jesus.

Christians with Courage

I. INTRODUCTION

The College Fleet

*W*hile still vice president, former President Bush told an interesting story of an event which occurred during the Spanish-American War. Apparently the Congress of the United States came up with the idea of renaming captured Spanish vessels after American universities, thereby creating "The College Fleet."

Admiral Dewey, already a seasoned officer in charge of American Naval Forces, heard that two ships already captured were to be rechristened the *Harvard* and the *Yale*. He received orders to follow that pattern as the war progressed. The Admiral understood education and naval warfare, but failed to see why the two should be mixed. Nevertheless, obedient to his superiors, he named the next captured Spanish vessel *The Massachusetts Institute of Technology* and yet a fourth, *The Vermont Normal College for Women*. As Bush tells the story, Congress promptly abandoned the idea for a college fleet.

Two things surface in Dewey's response. The first shows his clever courage in defying Congress while achieving an end he felt important for the navy, namely, giving warships appropriate names. We also see an interesting relationship between act and attitude in the process of obedience. Dewey obeyed in act but demonstrated that his heart was not in it.

In our chapter, the early Christians demonstrated precisely the reverse. Here we see act and attitude going hand in hand. The courage was there. Holy boldness permeates all the verses as believers put into practice what they claimed they knew and understood about the Savior.

We need chapters like this for spiritual growth. We focus on Peter and John courageously proclaiming God's message **in the name**. We observe the church confidently at prayer for God's work through them. We see them sharing what they had so all the needy could be cared for. This kind of behavior, this kind of courage, could transform a modern congregation in just a few weeks.

II. COMMENTARY

Christians with Courage

MAIN IDEA: *Christians with holy courage know how to handle opposition, how to pray, and how to take care of each other.*

🅰 Courage and Proclamation (vv. 1–7)

SUPPORTING IDEA: *Religious leaders often provide the believer's strongest opposition.*

4:1. Notice how chapter 4 really continues the story of chapter 3. The religious officials approached Peter and John **while they were speaking to the people.** Early Jewish opposition came mainly from the Sadducees, priests from the tribe of Levi who saw themselves the protectors of tradition. They believed the Messiah was an ideal not a person, so all this talk of fulfilled prophecy in Jesus would have been offensive to their theology. Furthermore, they cooperated with Rome and would hardly want this kind of apocalyptic talk reaching Pilate or any other Roman official.

4:2. At the heart of Sadducean theology lay the denial of the resurrection (Luke 20:27–40). Surely this aspect of Peter's sermon **greatly disturbed** them more than any other. These strong words indicate annoyance and indignation. Luke uses the term to describe Paul's reaction to the possessed girl in Acts 16. Keep in mind that one official function of the Sadducees was to teach and interpret the Scriptures. Now these two unschooled former fishermen taught great crowds who seemed eager to hear what Peter and John had to say.

4:3–4. Luke introduces the first act of open opposition against the Christians by telling us Peter and John were held in custody overnight. The **captain** was the commanding officer of the temple police who certainly had the authority to do this, especially backed by the Sadducean priests described in verse 1. **But,** says Luke. We might say, "meanwhile." Even though Peter and John might have been the first Christians to spend the night in jail for their faith, the message still spread, and more people trusted Christ. Now the total number of Jewish Christians had reached five thousand. One would not want to make any dogmatic points about the number, but five thousand may well be the complete total, despite the use of the word **men.** This term, because of the way Luke uses it in Acts, does not necessarily exclude women.

4:5–7. Three groups formed the Sanhedrin, the supreme court and senate of the nation: rulers, elders, and scribes (teachers of the law). Annas was high priest from A.D. 6–15, and Caiaphas from 18–36. Annas had arranged for five sons and one son-in-law to become high priest after him. Obviously, he still functioned in something of a "godfather" role. Both Annas and Caiaphas took part in the crucifixion of Jesus, and we could probably conclude they were prepared to take such action again among Christ's followers if they deemed it necessary. The names John and Alexander are not known to New Testament scholars, nor do they seem particularly important to

Luke's narrative except to emphasize the dominance of the family (perhaps both were related to Caiaphas).

Their opening question reminds us again of Peter's emphasis in chapter 3 on the name of Jesus: **By what power or what name did you do this?** How often do we look for openings to witness for the Savior! How difficult it seems at times to find appropriate places in a conversation to raise the issue of the gospel. No problem here. The gathered religious leaders could not have asked a question which more easily led into precisely what Peter and John had been saying out in the temple courts.

The last word of verse 7 (**this**) likely refers to the apostles' teaching rather than the healing of the crippled beggar—both the miracle and the message might be in view. As they sat in jail overnight, or perhaps as they faced the stern, demanding faces of the Sanhedrin, Peter and John might well have remembered Jesus' words on the night before his death:

> If the world hates you, keep in mind that it hated me first. If you belonged to the world, it would love you as its own. As it is, you do not belong to the world, but I have chosen you out of the world. That is why the world hates you. Remember the words I spoke to you: "No servant is greater than his master." If they persecuted me, they will persecute you also. If they obeyed my teaching, they will obey yours also. They will treat you this way because of my name, for they do not know the One who sent me. If I had not come and spoken to them, they would not be guilty of sin. Now, however, they have no excuse for their sin. He who hates me hates my Father as well. If I had not done among them what no one else did, they would not be guilty of sin. But now they have seen these miracles, and yet they have hated both me and my Father. But this is to fulfill what is written in their Law: "They hated me without reason" (John 15:18–25).

B Courage and Public Witness (vv. 8–12)

SUPPORTING IDEA: *Since salvation comes through the name of Jesus, Christians must courageously proclaim that name even in the most difficult of situations.*

4:8–9. Peter was delighted to reply. Partly because he knew the answer, and partly because he was **filled with the Holy Spirit**. We dare not minimize that brief reference by Luke, appearing as it does, at the beginning of Peter's defense. How easy it seems to depend upon our own resources in the service of the Lord; but how futile. Here a humble fisherman, quite unaccustomed to public speaking until just a few days earlier, courageously addressed the highest authorities in the land. Jesus had promised such power and boldness for occasions just like this (Luke 21:14–15). Christians with courage never have to stand alone when they stand for the Lord. The words **called to account** translate *anakrinomai*, suggesting a preliminary inquiry rather than a full trial. Peter's immediate reference to the cripple suggests that perhaps the inquiry dealt with the miracle more than the following sermon.

4:10–12. Here it is again—just one more of the thirty-three times Luke uses the phrase **the name of Jesus** in his book. Peter didn't read a new text or refer to a new set of notes; he simply reiterated what he had said to the temple crowds the previous day (3:13–16).

Notice how much Peter packed into one Greek sentence (vv. 8–10). Everyone should know that only by the name of Jesus Christ of Nazareth, crucified and risen from the dead, do his disciples have the power to heal and teach. To seal his argument, Peter used a *pesher* (see "Deeper Discoveries," chap. 3) to apply Psalm 118:22 to Jesus. Today we sing "Jesus is the cornerstone," a theme developed to a greater extent in Peter's epistles. Rejected at the beginning, he becomes the capstone at the end—the alpha and omega (1 Pet. 2:7).

How easy it would have been for Peter and John to answer the high priest's question by simply saying, "God did it." That would have been a religiously and politically correct response, and the apostles could have been dismissed immediately. When they brought Jesus, his crucifixion, and his resurrection into the argument, the whole complexion of the Council changed. The issue now revolved not around a healed cripple, but around the authority of Jesus of Nazareth.

ⓒ Courage in Position (vv. 13–22)

SUPPORTING IDEA: *Christians with courage should be law-abiding citizens until that law exceeds the clearly written law of God, at which point a higher authority takes over.*

4:13–14. The courage of these men couldn't be doubted, but they were certainly vulnerable on other accounts. They **were unschooled** which means they had no formal rabbinical training. They were **ordinary** which means they had no religious credentials. They were courageous, clearly evident by Peter's powerful response to the opening question. And, they were Christ taught: they **had been with Jesus.**

Hymn writers and preachers often spiritualize this passage indicating that the Sanhedrin may have seen some deep spiritual qualities in Peter and John. No doubt those qualities were evident, but that's not what the text says. Actually, the Sanhedrin likely had negative feelings about the connection between the hated Galilean they had killed and these two men who now proclaimed his resurrection. Nevertheless, they could not deny the miracle because the healed man stood right there; so they retreated in silence.

4:15–17. The Sanhedrin had few options in this case. They finally concluded that punishment was unnecessary and denial, impossible. Now they had to practice damage control by keeping these two from using that **name** any further.

Notice how central Jesus has already become in the Book of Acts. Notice how Luke wants to emphasize repeatedly the significance of the Savior by appealing to his name, thereby emphasizing all that he stood for. The gospel was about to become "illegal" in Jerusalem all because of the **name**.

Let's not miss the impact of this chapter. Religion doesn't save. Philosophy doesn't save. Eternal relationship with God does not rest in the Sanhedrin, nor Buddhism, nor Hinduism, nor Islam. Salvation does not come in the Ayatollah or in the name of Mohammed (even though the latter is the world's most common name). The exclusivity of verse 12 prevails: **There is no other name under heaven given to men by which we must be saved.**

4:18–20. Socrates once said to the Greek authorities, "I shall obey God rather than you." The Sanhedrin could have brought back several judgments with which Peter and John would likely have complied as solid Jewish citizens, but they were told to do the one thing they could not—stop speaking in Jesus' name (Acts 1:8; Matt. 28:19–20). A clear choice: obey civil authority or God. For Peter and John this was no choice. They knew what they had **seen and heard**.

4:21–22. We know from history that religious and political leaders will always try intimidation, because often it works. But not here. The warning was publicly discounted, the threats seemed to do no good, and they had no basis for punishment. Politicians (civil or religious) also have to play to the crowds, and in this case, **all the people were praising God for what happened,** so any further action would have been a lost cause.

Nevertheless, the Council faced not just a passing conversation but a legal precedent. We shall see as we make our way through this book that the illegality of the gospel surfaces repeatedly, especially in connection with Jerusalem. The Greek text of verse 22 uses the word *semeion* meaning "sign." Throughout the Gospels and Acts miracles are "God's signs," quite obvious in the visual presence of the healed beggar.

Two themes have dominated our chapter thus far: exclusive one-way salvation through Jesus with no room for compromise, and the courage of the early Christians to proclaim that message.

Courage in Prayer (vv. 23–31)

SUPPORTING IDEA: *Christian courage depends upon biblical praying grounded in the sovereignty of God.*

4:23–24. As Peter and John went back to the believers praying for them, they reported what must have been viewed by all as a victory. What follows is one of the most dramatic prayers of the New Testament because it reflects the way the early Christians prayed.

They began with creation—**you made . . . everything.** The word for **sovereign Lord** is *despotes*, literally "lord of the house," used ten times in the New Testament, three to address God in prayers (Luke 2:29; Rev. 6:10; and here) and three referring to Christ (2 Tim. 2:21; 2 Pet. 2:1; Jude 4). As its English cognate *despot*, the term can imply harshness of rule and caprice, but the Greek Old Testament uses it for God twenty-five times, emphasizing God's unlimited power.

Notice also that they prayed **together.** Peter and John came back **to their own people,** and now they prayed together. Luke repeatedly emphasizes unity throughout the Book of Acts, a theme which might well be more highly developed in contemporary churches.

Why begin with creation? Why remind God of what he had done? Because creation remains foundational to every other doctrine, and it certainly demonstrates the sovereignty of God, the very foundation for this prayer (cf. Acts 14:15; 2 Pet. 3:1–14).

4:25–26. The second theme of the prayer is revelation—**you spoke . . . through . . David.** Here Luke delivers another pesher to describe the praying of the early Christians as they found their present dilemma well outlined in Psalm 2:1–2. They just assumed the **nations** were Gentile authorities; the **peoples,** the religious leaders of Israel; the **kings of the earth,** a reference to Herod; and the **rulers,** likely pointing to Pilate. All that seems confirmed by the flow of the prayer beyond these two verses.

Let's back up. This Creator whom the believers addressed in verse 24 is self-revealed. Since we cannot test creation by scientific methods which deal only with repeatable events, it must be understood by faith (Heb. 11:3). Furthermore, faith in a Creator demands a recognition of his involvement in his world (Rom. 1:18–20).

Most people have little difficulty dealing with a Creator, a vague concept accepted by many who have no faith in Jesus. It takes quite another step to recognize that the Creator has personally revealed himself and therefore made his creation responsible for what he has said.

4:27–28. Creation and revelation are followed by a discussion of the *incarnation.* Not only did the Sovereign Lord create the world, but he controls suffering—both of Jesus and now of his people. Human leaders may deliberate, but God ultimately determines destiny. An ancient king by the name of Nebuchadnezzar learned that the hard way (Dan. 4). Now incarnation becomes a highlight of revelation. All these people clearly understood that God had spoken through prophets for hundreds of years. The praying church emphasized that now he has spoken through Jesus Christ his Son (cf. Heb. 1:1–3).

A little boy finished his bedtime prayers with mommy. Holding her tight, he said, "Momma, I like you better than God." In shock the Christian mother pointed out how important it is for even little boys to love God more than they love their parents. She inquired why the youngster would say that he loved his mommy more than God. After only a brief pause the boy responded, "Because I can hug you."

The incarnation made God "huggable." All that had been heard in the thunderous words of Elijah and Elisha or read in the tomes of Isaiah and Jeremiah had now been seen on earth in the person of Jesus Christ.

4:29–31. At this point the prayer turned to the practical outworking of their dilemma. Creation, revelation, and incarnation are doctrines and important ones. Life and its daily problems are also important to you and to God, so now the prayer turns to *motivation.* "Sovereign Lord: you made everything; you spoke through David; you anointed Jesus; and now you enable your servants." They reached out for even more courage, even greater boldness. They continued their witness as God confirmed it through miraculous signs in the name of Jesus.

This was not a prayer for relief, but a prayer for courage, an excellent pattern for the modern church. The prayer assumes dependence and faith. These believers expected to do nothing by themselves; everything rested in the sovereign power of God and the name of Jesus.

How did God respond? The room shook, and he filled them anew with the Holy Spirit and sent them out to speak **the word of God boldly.** Here they received no baptism, nor did they speak in foreign languages (see chap. 2); it was not necessary. These born-again, functioning believers only needed a fresh filling to continue their effective service.

The model of this prayer is still very applicable for us today. Like these early believers, we need to understand that the self-revealed Creator who sent his Son to earth to die and rise again for our salvation will give us the courage we need to carry out whatever ministry he places before us.

E Courage in Provision (vv. 32–37)

SUPPORTING IDEA: *Courageous Christians demonstrate the kind of generosity which makes possible the care of people more needy than ourselves.*

4:32–33. In a paragraph reminiscent of Acts 2:43–47, Luke again emphasizes the unity of the church and, this time, adds a note about its generosity. What were these early Christians like? They were clearly united. They not only prayed together but **were one in heart and mind**—perhaps because of the way they prayed together! The witness to the resurrection continued. The Christians were neither a monastic order nor a closed society like some cults. Christianity contains clear-cut social implications, and sharing with others is one of them (John 13:35).

4:34–35. Not only were they united; they were unselfish. This passage shows us a distinctly Christian view of possessions which centers not in ownership, but stewardship; not in creed, but need; not in fad, but family. We have no other New Testament record of communal sharing, and we should not apply this passage universally to other groups of believers. God deemed it necessary at this time and place and laid down a general principle of sharing with others. Notice the result: **There were no needy persons among them.**

United, unselfish, and unafraid. Looking back at the prayer, we see its fulfillment in their power for witness and their clear focus of that witness—the resurrection of Jesus Christ.

Unlike so many congregations today, these early Christians knew their identity and precisely what God expected of them. They moved forward with courage to achieve their goals.

4:36–37. We can almost feel Luke searching for an example to demonstrate the generosity and unity of the believers. He came up with exhibit A, **Joseph a Levite from Cyprus**. We call him Barnabas, a nickname he earned because of his encouraging spirit in the church at Jerusalem. He appears in Acts 4; 9; 11; 13; 14; and 15. Luke's clear-cut wording about the meaning of the name Barnabas has troubled scholars since the Bible was written. *Bar* clearly means "son" in Aramaic, but *nabas* has escaped scholarly explanation as an Aramaic or Semitic root related to *paraklesis*, the Greek word for encouragement. Such things are not our concern nor Luke's. We need to see Barnabas as Luke saw him, a positive demonstration of how courageous Christianity operated in the first century, giving of their resources and making other people feel better.

MAIN IDEA REVIEW: *Christians with holy courage know how to handle opposition, how to pray, and how to take care of each other.*

III. CONCLUSION

Termite Teachings

How the sovereign power of God rings through the verses of this chapter! From the second the eyes of Peter and John met those of the beggar to the selfless behavior of Barnabas, we are captivated by how God controls his word and his people. These early Christians understood that although we may have a creed, Christianity stands for more than that. Christianity centers on the person of Jesus Christ around whom everything else gathers like metal fragments to a magnet. As believers draw closer to their Lord, they become a powerful force, proclaiming his message with boldness.

We don't dote on insects in our society and certainly not on termites. They probably top the most hated list, but a community of termites is a rather remarkable group. One or two operating alone can do virtually nothing. When they reach a critical mass, they organize platoons and create a cathedral in which the colony will live out its entire life. That termite cathedral, constructed of small pellets of wood, is air-conditioned, humidity controlled, and quite comfortable. Remarkably, the builders are stone blind. They simply follow a chemical blueprint the divine Creator coded in their genes.

A direct comparison of Christians with termites would be counterproductive, but certainly the group cooperation metaphor helps us to think about coming together as believers—just like these early Christians with courage.

PRINCIPLES

- God always blesses the proclamation of his word.
- God gives courage to his people every time they need it.
- Civil disobedience is only biblically permissible when human law defies divine law.
- Christians find both power and joy in prayer.
- Believers should be marked by unity and generosity.

APPLICATIONS

- Speak out for the Lord with courage whenever you have an opportunity.
- Demonstrate that being a citizen of heaven makes you an even better citizen on earth.
- Learn to pray like the early believers, and do it often with groups of other Christians.
- Share generously what God has given you, especially to those who really need help.

IV. LIFE APPLICATION

Bloom Where You Are Planted

You can still remember our study of chapter 1, where the disciples anticipated kingdom restoration, each doubtless wanting to claim the important roles Jesus had promised them (see Luke 22:28–30). Now they have had their first touch of opposition and can sense the potential persecution against their church and their message. It was not supposed to be like this. They intended the Lord to throw out the Romans and let the good guys take over Israel again.

Through the Holy Spirit's wisdom and power they adapted to the changing surroundings and learned to serve the Lord in whatever situation they found themselves. Peter could have no idea at this point (chap. 4) that he would someday be proclaiming the gospel in the house of a Gentile (Acts 10). John could have never guessed that his life of ministry would extend beyond age ninety, and that he would write four books of the New Testament.

Regardless of our ages, we cannot anticipate what God has ahead. We simply learn to bloom where we are planted.

Some years ago I was on the roster of speakers at the annual Moody Founder's Week. The music program was led by Pastor Jim Reece from Canada. Just before that conference, Pastor Reece's retarded son celebrated his tenth birthday for which his father had written a song. He sang it for us during the week.

> Bloom where you are planted, God's sun still shines above.
> Bloom where you are planted, he showers you with love.
> Weeds may grow, and winds may blow,
> But keep your head up high.
> And bloom where you are planted;
> Keep growing toward the sky.

That's what you and I must do if we are to be courageous Christians. We cannot prescribe an ideal situation and then ask God to place us in it. Christian witness is not designing some program for the holodeck on the *Enterprise*. In two chapters Peter and John, along with the other believers, learn to fit in where and when God needs them, and to be faithful to their message. In short, they learn to bloom where they are planted.

V. PRAYER

God, please increase our faith and courage so that, like these early believers, we may learn to pray and witness in the name and power of Jesus. Amen.

VI. DEEPER DISCOVERIES

A. Sadducees (v. 1)

The Sadducees and Pharisees were two religious parties who held the balance of power in the Sanhedrin. The Pharisees had adopted a strong nationalistic posture committed to the defense of the law and, as we know from their conflict with Jesus in the Gospels, a minute and detailed observation of religious ritual. They hated the Romans, believed in the resurrection, and anticipated the coming of a personal Messiah albeit one that fit their particular definition.

The Sadducees controlled the wealth and much of the land. They coexisted with the Romans, a practice that afforded them material advantage. Theology was less important to them than peace, a position which often brought them into conflict with the Pharisees. They denied the resurrection or life beyond the grave and, as we noted earlier, viewed the concept of Messiah as an ideal rather than a person.

The Sanhedrin appears to have consisted of seventy-one members (Num. 11:16), including the high priest at its head. The Pharisees had been admitted to the Sanhedrin only in the last century B.C. and probably still represented the minority, though popular with the people. The Sanhedrin was also known as the "Council," and met in a hall adjoining the southwest part of the temple near a meeting place called the *Xystos*.

Jesus encountered problems with the Sadducees in the gospels, but the Pharisees provided a much more prominent nemesis. In Acts, however, and especially in Jerusalem, the Sadducees ran the show. They brought Peter and John up on charges before the Sanhedrin.

B. Universalism (v. 12)

From the time of Origen—a prominent figure in the early church about A.D. 185 to 253—some Christians have believed that God will eventually restore everything and everyone to its created order. Indeed, some have preached this doctrine of universal salvation from the text of Acts 3:21. Others have argued from 1 Corinthians 15:27–28 that God will devise some way to save everyone, even if it means a second chance or some different way to heaven.

Acts 4:12 chops that tree at its very base. God does *not* plan several ways up the mountain of conversion or multiple tracks on the railway to heaven. Agreement that God exists is not enough to eventually meet him face-to-face. These pious Jews needed repentance, for they had rejected the only way to heaven: **Salvation is found in no one else, for there is no other name under heaven given to men by which we must be saved** (4:12).

C. Luke's Insider Information (vv. 15–17)

Luke's careful description of the conversation between the Sanhedrin and the apostles has fascinated scholars. How did he know what went on and what was said in council meetings? Very likely he heard the story from Peter and John themselves and recorded it. Certainly their lifetimes overlapped sufficiently, and we have no reason to think that Luke would not have had ample opportunity to research such details for his manuscripts. Some have suggested that Paul was already present in the Sanhedrin and he could have served as Luke's information source. Others argue that Paul heard the story from his mentor Gamaliel and then passed it on to Luke.

Such mental meanderings are interesting, but not crucial to how we interpret the text. Clearly, the Council would have denied the miracle if that had been possible. Failing that, they took the one avenue they felt open to them to stop this heresy before it got out of hand.

D. Civil Disobedience (vv. 19–20)

Under normal conditions, Peter and John would not hesitate to obey the word of the Sanhedrin. Adherence to civil authority, taught by Jesus, became a major theme in the New Testament in the writing of both Peter (1 Pet. 2:13–17) and Paul (Rom. 13:1–7). Civil disobedience and anarchy defy established law, and the passages cited above clearly require subservience to government.

Yet there are exceptions! Two of them occur in back-to-back chapters in Acts 4 and 5. When a duly appointed civil authority requires a Christian to do something explicitly forbidden in God's word, civil disobedience is not only permissible, but the appropriate choice. In chapter 5 the Sanhedrin reminds the apostles of the earlier warning and hears from them once again; **We must obey God rather than men!** (Acts 5:29).

Let's be careful here. God does not give us the right to judge whether laws are "good or bad." Our own interpretation of how we should respond to civil government does not enter into the issue. Biblical responses of civil disobedience must be supportable by appeal to God's revelation—the Bible.

VII. TEACHING OUTLINE

A. INTRODUCTION

1. Lead story: The College Fleet
2. Context: Chapter 4 begins with a public hearing and ends with a summary of the events that formed the early church. Apart from the Council's warning, all has been well now for four chapters, undisturbed by internal sin or external strife. That will soon change as we give our attention to chapter 5, but for the moment Luke wants us to focus on the unity, unselfishness, and courage of these early believers.
3. Transition: Acts 4 continues Acts 3. With the exception of the concluding summary (vv. 32–37), the entire narrative deals with fallout from the healing of the crippled beggar at the temple gate. We should come away from this chapter with a stronger faith in the power of the Lord, in the church, and in God's Word. Luke mentions five examples of courage by the apostles and the Christians in Jerusalem.

B. COMMENTARY

1. Courage in Proclamation (vv. 1–7)
   a. Reaction to the proclamation (vv. 1–3)
   b. Blessing from the proclamation (vv. 4)
   c. Questions about the proclamation (vv. 5–7)
2. Courage in Public Witness (vv. 8–12)
   a. Courage to speak (v. 8)
   b. Courage to heal (vv. 9–11)
   c. Courage to tell the truth (v. 12)
3. Courage in Position (vv. 13–22)
   a. Ordinary people (vv. 13–14)
   b. Logical conclusion (vv. 15–17)
   c. Civil disobedience (vv. 18–19)
   d. Public praise (vv. 20–22)
4. Courage in Prayer (vv. 23–31)
   a. Creation by the Sovereign Lord (vv. 23–24)
   b. Revelation through David (vv. 25–26)
   c. Incarnation of Jesus (vv. 27–28)
   d. Motivation for service (vv. 29–31)
5. Courage in Provision (vv. 32–37)
   a. Explanation of the believers (vv. 32–35)
   b. Example of the believers (vv. 36–37)

C. CONCLUSION: BLOOM WHERE YOU ARE PLANTED

VIII. ISSUES FOR DISCUSSION

1. Why did the Sadducees oppose Jesus and the church?
2. What part did the resurrection have in the apostles' preaching? Why?
3. How did the apostles have courage to face the powerful enemies of the gospel?

Acts 5

Honor and Dishonor in the Church

I. Introduction
The Embarrassing Accordion

II. Commentary
A verse-by-verse explanation of the chapter.

III. Conclusion
Honoring or Dishonoring Jesus
An overview of the principles and applications from the chapter.

IV. Life Application
Witness in New Guinea
Melding the chapter to life.

V. Prayer
Tying the chapter to life with God.

VI. Deeper Discoveries
Historical, geographical, and grammatical enrichment of the commentary.

VII. Teaching Outline
Suggested step-by-step group study of the chapter.

VIII. Issues for Discussion
Zeroing the chapter in on daily life.

"*O*nly he who believes is obedient; only he who is obedient believes."

D i e t r i c h   B o n h o e f f e r

PERSONAL PROFILE: GAMALIEL

- Possibly the grandson of the great Rabbi Hillel
- The most highly respected Pharisee of his day
- Mentor to Saul of Tarsus (Acts 22:3)

I N   A   N U T S H E L L

*T*his chapter falls into two distinct parts—the sin and judgment of Ananias and Sapphira and the second appearance of the apostles before the Sanhedrin. Luke continues his witnessing theme and ends the chapter on a mountain top: **They never stopped teaching and proclaiming the good news that Jesus is the Christ.**

Honor and Dishonor in the Church

I. INTRODUCTION

The Embarrassing Accordion

*T*he time was World War II. As a child in a family with only one believing parent, I had not yet learned how the dynamic of Christianity both enriched and antagonized real life. We had no car, so it required a train ride and two bus trips just to get to church on Sunday. The church was located in a large eastern city with one of the bus stops right in front of city hall. There, sometime between noon and 1 P.M., we would come upon a Christian man playing an accordion and singing gospel songs. He may have done it every day, but I saw him only on Sundays. Though I had just come from church, my childish embarrassment at being identified with someone who would do church-like things in a public street caused inward turmoil week after week.

I remember his name, though I choose not to state it here, and I remember discussions with my mother. With six- and seven-year-old logic I tried to explain why he should be playing somewhere in church, not out here in public. Patiently, my mother would explain the importance of courageous public witness and faithfulness to God which proclaimed his message among those who would never visit a church.

I never conquered that childhood embarrassment, but now I look back and see that man as a hero of the faith. In reality he practiced in a more modern-day sense precisely what the early Christians did in this chapter. Having been told they could speak no longer in the name of Jesus, they marched right back to Solomon's Colonnade—and from there to jail.

As a little boy I wanted my religion neatly packaged, surrounded by hymnbooks, a robed choir, and dignified men in dark suits and white shirts who passed the plates each Sunday. It seemed incongruous to hear those same hymns on the concrete by a bus stop. Now I face embarrassment of a different sort. Recognizing in adulthood the boldness of his witness, I cringe for the ineffectiveness of my own, so often limited by the same childhood boundaries of how and where God's message should be delivered.

To grasp Acts, we must recognize the difference between God's ministry strategy in the Old Testament and the New. In the era before Christ, God's people had to go to a certain place with specifically arranged religious ornamentation, be taught by a certain class of people (the priests), and carry out fastidious rituals to be acceptable to God. Sadly, some churches still practice Old Testament witness: "If you will come where we meet at the time we gather, we will tell you something that could change your life."

New Testament believers turned the formula upside down and literally took to the streets with the gospel. Like Luke, we will first have to deal with the Ananias and Sapphira disaster; but once we get beyond that event, we will see again in this chapter the magnificent blessing of God upon people willing to be his witnesses in the public arena. First we see dishonor in the church; then Luke shows us great honor.

II. COMMENTARY
Honor and Dishonor in the Church

MAIN IDEA: *God will allow nothing to stand in the way of the proclamation of his gospel and the expansion of his church.*

A Rebellion in the Church (vv. 1–4)

SUPPORTING IDEA: *God knows when you are lying to him and will not let you stand in the way of the proclamation of his gospel.*

5:1–2. Like Paul, Luke is ever the master of contrast. Immediately following the brief testimony of Barnabas, he tells us about two other Christians who sold property so they could participate in the church's communal care program. The name Ananias means "God is gracious," and Sapphira means "beautiful." This was a joint effort even if the cultural patterns of the time put Ananias first. Luke tells us **he kept back part of the money**, using the verb *nospizo* which means "to put aside for oneself." Already this narrative reminds us of Achan in Joshua 7:1–26.

This couple wanted acclaim without sacrifice and comfort without commitment. They caused the first demonstration of defeat within the ranks since the betrayal of Judas and denial by Peter. The outward act seemed so appropriate. Notice the identical wording in 4:37 and 5:2: **Put it at the apostles' feet**. What appeared to be public generosity was actually family conspiracy, but God was looking.

5:3–4. Apparently, the Holy Spirit revealed this deception to Peter. The Spirit had created unity in the church and was now offended at its rupture. We are amazed to discover that Satan can fill the heart of a Christian, especially since Luke uses a verb for *fill* which also appears in Ephesians 5:18.

Peter faced up to the responsibility much in the way he did in chapter 1 when explaining the Judas suicide. We see immediately that the sin lay not in failing to give all the money, but rather in pretending to do so. The basic issue here was lying, not only to the church but to the Spirit. Above all, the church had to maintain integrity in its alien surroundings, and this behavior could quickly erode the shields of that credibility. Integrity describes those standards of moral and intellectual honesty on which we base our conduct and from which we cannot swerve without cheapening ourselves.

This passage also offers an important New Testament text on the deity of the Holy Spirit. Peter tells Ananias that he lied to the Holy Spirit and follows by saying, **You have not lied to men but to God**. Notice the emphasis on the voluntary nature of participation in communal property. Some see Communism at the end of chapter 4, but Peter makes it clear that Ananias was under no obligation to participate. Once he did, however, he betrayed the unity and community of the congregation. Tom Constable writes,

> Lying to the Holy Spirit is a sin that Christians commit frequently today. When Christians act hypocritically by pretending a devotion that is not there or a surrender of life that they have not really made, they lie to the Holy Spirit. If God worked today as he did in the early Jerusalem church, undertakers would have much work (Constable, 39).

B Reaction to the Crime (vv. 5–11)

SUPPORTING IDEA: *Sickness and death do not always result from sin, but God reserves the right to deal with sin in his church, even to the strongest possible penalty.*

5:5–6. We are stunned to read the results of Ananias' lie—God killed him. The word for died is *ekpsycho*, "to breathe one's last," used of General Sisera in the Septuagint of Judges 4:21 (cf. Acts 5:10; 12:23). We will deal with this judgment at greater length in "Deeper Discoveries." Here we should not obscure the clarity of the text. We can explain what happened. We must still remember God is the ultimate cause. One psychological explanation of what happened suggests that Ananias died from the shock of discovery. As one commentator puts it, "The fear of exposure was so drastic, their nervous systems could not take it" (Ogilvie, 120). To be sure, death from seemingly natural causes could have its origin in a supernatural act (as in the case of Herod at the end of Acts 12), but it is no less God ordained. Here we have the ultimate discipline in the church. God can remove a spiritual cancer by surgery and may very well choose to do so on some occasions (1 Cor. 11:30–32).

In this case the death resulted from sin, but the Bible reminds us that immediate death does not always occur. In the early verses of John 9, the disciples concluded that the blind man must be suffering because of his sin or that of his parents. Jesus reminds them that neither is the case, "But this happened so that the work of God might be displayed in his life" (John 9:3). God sees what happens in our hearts; and when hidden sin threatens to thwart the church's ministry, he may choose to deal with it severely.

5:7–10. The young attendants had buried Ananias and returned in three hours, quite possibly a record for first-century Jewish funerals. Amazingly, Sapphira came in with the same story, and it was deja vu all over again. Sapphira's narrative offers nothing new. In neither case did Peter pronounce a curse of any kind. Peter explained the sin, but God took care of the judgment.

5:11. The death of Ananias and Sapphira brought two results: fear in the church and fear in the city. This is the first appearance in Acts of the Greek word for church (*ekklesia*). Perhaps Peter remembered this incident when he wrote: "It is time for judgment to begin with the family of God" (1 Pet. 4:17). Fear in the city centered on the power of God and perhaps the ugliness of sin.

As tempted as we might be to push this story into some dark corner of early church history, that would be a tragic mistake. It deals with money, greed, and deceit—all very popular problems in today's church. Deceit, disunity, and duplicity always undermine the Holy Spirit's work and always erode the effectiveness of the Christian community.

Ⓒ Reputation in the City (vv. 12–16)

SUPPORTING IDEA: *Christians are responsible to proclaim the gospel and leave the results to God.*

5:12. This opening paragraph of the second part of our chapter shows the reason for the Sadducees' jealousy—the apostles broke the "no witnessing law." Furthermore, rather than just Peter and John healing one lame man, all the apostles performed miracles. They continued to meet in the very place where that first miracle had happened. Three groups of people come into view as Luke introduces this section: the church (believers); the unbelieving Jews (the people); and those who believed and **were added to their number** (v. 14). God has answered the prayer recorded in chapter 4.

5:13–14. What exactly does Luke mean when he tells us that **No one else dared join them**? He does not mean that new believers did not become part of the church, for verse 14 declares they did. He might mean that no one dared join them on his or her own authority or perhaps that no one dared antagonize them or prevent their meetings. Most likely this is a geographical reference. Many new believers became part of the congregation, but they did not meet in Solomon's Colonnade since that seemed to be the center of Sadducean attack. As Polhill notes:

> It is the same two-sidedness of the Spirit's power that had just been demonstrated in Ananias and Sapphira. The power of the miracles attracts. The awesome power of the Spirit that judges also demands commitment and responsibility. Before that power the crowd kept its distance with healthy respect, unless they were willing to fully submit to that power and make a commitment (Pohill, 163).

5:15–16. Instead of going to the Colonnade, people brought sick loved ones into the streets so that Peter's shadow might fall on them as he walked by. Once again, the wording of the New Testament seems so foreign to our experience. Or does it? Even today people search for some kind of physical demonstration of God's presence in their lives. From Gideon's fleece (Judg. 6:36–40) to the touching of a television set, humanity seems to crave some physical contact with a spiritual God.

In the ancient world, a person's shadow was believed to represent that person. Superstitious to be sure, but these people behaved in line with everything we know about their culture. Notice that the text does not say people were healed by the shadow, though God may very well have chosen to do that. Nevertheless, Luke tells us: **Crowds gathered . . . and all of them were healed** (v. 16).

Notice the geographical spread of the gospel; all these people have come from the towns around Jerusalem. Despite the awful episode recorded in verses 1–11, the church continued to grow and to spread its vital life-giving message throughout the city and even beyond its urban boundaries.

Release of the Captives (vv. 17–26)

SUPPORTING IDEA: *Overt efforts to proclaim the gospel in an alien environment will often result in persecution, but God takes care of his people.*

5:17–20. Enter the bad guys in the black hats, the same crowd we met in chapter 4. As they had done earlier, they arrested the apostles and put them in the public jail. At that point the story changes. These verses record the first of three "jail door miracles" in Acts (12:6–10; 16:16–28). In chapter 4 God's grace intervened in the minds of the Sanhedrin, and the apostles were released. Here we have a physical deliverance and a divine revelation directing them precisely back to what they were doing, preaching the gospel in the temple courts.

A new word enters the narrative at the end of verse 20—life (*zoe*). It appears thirty-six times in the New Testament, often as a synonym for the Lord himself (John 1:4; 1 John 1:1–2). Since the Sadducees did not believe in angels, we might find it a bit amusing to see God's choice for the instrument of delivery.

5:21–26. These verses expand the explanation of how the apostles experienced divine deliverance from prison. Luke carefully reminds us how miraculous the escape was, since the guards still stood at their posts, apparently undisturbed by the previous night's events. The captain of the temple guard, second in command to the high priest, decided to handle this matter himself and gingerly marched to the temple courts to bring back the apostles yet again. Of course, he found them at their posts in God's service **teaching the people.**

Notice the increasing popularity of Christianity. Rather than forcefully chaining these fugitives and returning them to their cells, the captain and his cohorts feared for their own lives. Certainly, Luke intends to show us that God completely controlled all these events. The apostles were pliable servants who moved at his bidding; and the members of the Sanhedrin, pawns in his hand to accomplish his purpose.

E Responses in the Council (vv. 27–40)

SUPPORTING IDEA: *Witnessing Christians work with the Holy Spirit to proclaim the message of crucifixion and resurrection. Those who oppose that message find themselves fighting against God.*

5:27–28. Undoubtedly, the Sanhedrin was exactly correct in their assessment of the situation and well within their rights to enforce the "no witnessing law." Observe how they describe the faithful public proclamation of the Christians—**you have filled Jerusalem with your teaching.** Not only that, in the eyes of the Sanhedrin this new gospel made them directly responsible for Christ's death. That should not surprise us, since Peter told them earlier, **It is by the name of Jesus Christ of Nazareth, whom you crucified but whom God raised from the dead, that this man stands before you completely healed** (4:10). Just a few weeks earlier these very religious leaders had told Pilate, "Let his blood be on us and on our children!" (Matt. 27:25).

We find the absence of some statements interesting here. The high priest makes no mention of the escape (the last thing he wants here is to concede another miracle). Nor does he mention Jesus by name. The opposition was now in full swing, for these apostles no longer merely represented an annoyance; as lawbreakers they must be dealt with.

5:29–32. Here again we find the one exception to the Bible's rule against civil disobedience as Peter explains why they had been foolish enough to go out and do precisely what they had been ordered not to do. They were simply obeying **the God of our fathers**, not some new God. The message sounds like what we heard by the temple gate and in the earlier meeting with the Sanhedrin. Polhill points out that the dramatic statement of Peter, **We must obey God rather than men!** must be viewed in the context of overall biblical commands lest it be abused by power-hungry religious leaders.

> His saying has continued to be used by Christians throughout the centuries, by Christian martyrs making the ultimate sacrifice in obedience to their Lord, and by power-hungry medieval popes exerting their influence over the secular rulers. It is a dangerous saying, subject to abuse and misappropriation; and one should be as clear as Peter was about what God's purposes really are before ever using it (Pohill, 169).

Christians do not respond with violence or resistance (Luke 22:49–51). Peter offers no defense, only a witness, an offer of salvation to Jesus' murderers. Verses 30–32 are pure gospel. **Repentance and forgiveness of sins** offered to Israel. There is no anti-Semitism here, but a frank explanation of historical events and a free offer of salvation to those who believe. How can they know this is true? Eyewitnesses! Apostles and the Holy Spirit. Notice the Spirit comes as God's gift to **those who obey him.**

5:33–34. All of a sudden help arises from an unlikely source—a Pharisee. The Sadducees screamed for a Roman-type execution, but God put it in the heart of a respected rabbi to call for reason. Remember, the Pharisees were the minority party; it probably required someone of Gamaliel's stature to carry the day on an issue like this. We should not think him concerned for the welfare of the church or the truth of the gospel. He was apparently a good man, wise enough to know that nothing could be accomplished by killing members of this new Jewish cult whose popularity had already spread beyond the city of Jerusalem.

5:35–39. Gamaliel's argument seems very simple. The Sanhedrin should remember that twice before religious leaders appeared making claims contrary to the views of the Council. In both cases the zealots came to an untimely death, and their views dissipated when their followers scattered. Why might that not happen again? Furthermore, if what these men said comes from God, any kind of severe punishment would bring his wrath upon the Council.

The Jewish historian Josephus, who lived and wrote just after Jesus' crucifixion, refers to Judas the Galilean as a rebel who refused to give tribute to Caesar. Theudas cannot be as easily identified, but some scholars suggest he may date back to the insurgencies which arose in Palestine after the death of Herod the Great in 4 B.C.

This passage holds two great lessons for us. First, the calm, quiet logic of Gamaliel should appeal to Christians repeatedly told in Scripture to be sober and controlled. Second, though committed believers must speak out against heresy and cultic error, attacks against fellow Christians on minor matters are out of place and out of character. People whose views do not agree with ours should be left to God, lest we discover they were right and we were wrong and find ourselves fighting against God. Such was the case of the apostle Paul who all his life could never forget he had once been God's vigorous enemy.

5:40. No release with a warning this time, and certainly no angelic deliverance. It's time to suffer for the faith—thirty-nine lashes used as a warning to lawbreakers in that day (2 Cor. 11:24). Let us not think this a slap on the wrist; more than one man had died from such punishment. While blood still ran down their backs, the apostles heard again the prohibition against speaking **in the name of Jesus,** and then they were released.

⊞ Rejoicing in the Congregation (vv. 41–42)

SUPPORTING IDEA: *Somehow God's grace can produce joy even in the midst of suffering and public disgrace.*

5:41. Small wonder Peter picked up a "suffering for Jesus" theme in his epistles (1 Pet. 4:13; 2:18–21; 3:8–17). They had beaten Jesus, and now they had beaten his disciples who praised God that they could suffer **for the Name**. How great the name of Jesus had already become!

5:42. We don't expect the apostles to obey the Sanhedrin even after the beating, and they did not disappoint us. Luke seems to emphasize that their witnessing activity moved to a higher level—**day after day**, and **from house to house, they never stopped**. The unstoppable Christians. The irresistible forward advance of the gospel. The obvious blessing of God upon his people.

MAIN IDEA REVIEW: *God will allow nothing to stand in the way of the proclamation of his gospel and the expansion of his church.*

III. CONCLUSION

Honoring or Dishonoring Jesus?

How often we hear the name of Jesus today, and how rarely in connection with praise. The most crude and ignorant people somehow learn to curse by using the name of God's Son. Because we live in a society like that, and because as Christians we must uphold and honor that name, we should ask God daily to give us courage and power to *honor* rather than *dishonor* Jesus' name and his church. We should affirm with John Newton,

> How sweet the name of Jesus sounds in a believer's ear.
> It soothes his sorrows, heals his wounds, and drives away his
>   fears.
> Dear Name—the Rock on which I build, my shield, and Hiding
>   Place,
> My never-failing treasury with boundless stores of grace.

PRINCIPLES

- God reserves the right to use whatever punishment he wishes when sin occurs in the church.
- Sinning Christians do not always get the opportunity to repent and change their ways.

- Sometimes God gives his word great credibility and reception among alien crowds.
- Christians can be called upon to suffer painful physical abuse in the name of Jesus.
- No suffering should deter or defeat us in our efforts to live out the gospel and proclaim its saving truth.

APPLICATIONS

- Be open and honest with God and fellow believers at all times.
- Fear the great power of God which he can unleash against sin.
- Learn to proclaim the gospel message with simplicity and clarity.
- Never let civil authorities intimidate you with regard to your Christian faith.
- Trust God to deliver you from or in suffering.

IV. LIFE APPLICATION

Witness in New Guinea

Born at Ardrishaig, Scotland, James Chalmers heard God's call at the age of fifteen and committed his life to take the gospel to cannibals. Actually, he didn't come to Christ until three years later in 1859. Eight years later in 1877, he sailed for the Cook Islands of Polynesia to join a pioneer work in New Guinea where he served for twenty-four years.

At the end of twenty-one years of missionary service, Chalmers reportedly prayed, "Recall the twenty-one years. Give me back all its experiences. Give me its shipwrecks, its standing in the face of death, surrounded by savages with spears and clubs . . . give it back and I will still be your missionary." He continued to press on with the gospel, and his success is attributed by reliable sources to the fact that he never doubted he had a gospel for the people of New Guinea. In 1901 he was murdered by cannibals at the age of sixty.

The story doesn't end there. During World War II, some American fighter pilots shot down over New Guinea were led to Christ by former cannibals impacted by the witness of James Chalmers, pioneer missionary.

The apostles and early Christians in our chapter can be called pioneer missionaries. They pressed the gospel in places where it was not wanted. Though they did not have to learn new languages or enter new cultures, they suffered and, as we shall see in the case of Stephen, died for their faith. Yet the effect of their witness spread to us today; and we, as someone has said, go forward on the backs on those who have gone before.

Chalmers, Peter, John, the other apostles, and all the early believers have shown us how to be faithful Christians with honor. Since God usually does not discipline today with the severity he used on Ananias and Sapphira, we have deceit and hypocrisy in the church. How desperately that needs to be offset by new generations of people (like Barnabas and Chalmers) whose witness may not be in New Guinea or even on the temple colonnade, but across the back fence or during the morning commute. May others say of us and of our congregations, **they never stopped teaching and proclaiming the good news that Jesus is the Christ.**

V. PRAYER

God, we thank you for this wonderful record of the courage and honor of the early Christians. May we also proclaim the gospel in clarity without concern for the inconvenience or even suffering our witness might bring. Amen.

VI. DEEPER DISCOVERIES

A. Christian Sinning (vv. 1–2)

Were Ananias and Sapphira really believers? Scholars answer in at least two ways: 1) they were members of the church (so-called nominal Christians) who never entered in faith into a personal saving relationship with Jesus; 2) they were Christians whose sin (possibly the sin unto death of 1 John 5:16–17; cf. 1 Cor. 11:27–30) God punished as an example to the church but who gained eternal salvation. The entire narrative seems to indicate that these people were born-again Christians and very much a part of the Jerusalem congregation. It is not unusual in the Scripture to find death coming to believers at the hand of God. Admittedly these are difficult verses, and it is not in our best interest to take on additional explanations beyond Acts. It seems the best approach to the passage is to consider that Ananias and Sapphira had committed a sin that leads to death and God proceeded with the ultimate punishment.

B. Divine Punishment (vv. 5, 10)

We are stunned in this passage by the suddenness of God's judgment and the seeming lack of pity or remorse on the part of Peter and the others. Furthermore, there seems to be no opportunity for repentance apart from Peter's question to Sapphira in verse 8. Stories like this were quite common in the Old Testament, such as Nadab and Abihu consumed by the illegitimate fire they used (Lev. 10). Repeatedly in Deuteronomy, God told his people to root out evil from among them (Deut. 13:5; 17:7,12; 19:19). Let's not confuse lying to the Holy Spirit with blaspheming the Spirit (Mark 3:29). There seems to be no parallel here between death as physical punishment and what has often been called the unpardonable sin. Nowhere in Luke's record does he condemn Ananias and Sapphira to eternal punishment. Most scholars take the opinion that these believers retained their salvation and will experience eternal life. Surely, we must learn here the necessity for purity and unity in the body of Christ.

C. Church (v. 11)

The New Testament Greek word for church (*ekklesia*) is used commonly in Acts (7:38; 8:1; 9:31; 11:22; 13:1; 14:23; 15:22,41; 16:5; 19:32,41; 20:28). Throughout this book and elsewhere in the New Testament the term can refer to the universal church (all believers of all times and places) or a local congregation such as here in Jerusalem. We do not find, however, the common and popular uses of today such as reference to a building or a denomination appearing anywhere in the New Testament text. That does not mean such usages are wrong, simply that they reflect popular conversation and not theological truth. The word comes from two Greek words meaning "called" and "out." Literally, the church of Jesus Christ is called out from among unbelievers to be the family of God, the body of Christ, and his eternal bride.

D. Signs and Wonders (v. 12)

No serious Christian doubts that real events stand behind this text and behind the many references to **signs and wonders**, both in the Gospels and in the remainder of Acts. The problem comes when we apply passages like this to the modern-day church. Some claim the church is insipid and ineffective today because it does not experience signs and wonders. Others argue that signs and wonders have passed from the scene since they were only necessary to authenticate the apostles as genuine messengers of the heavenly Father and his Messiah, Jesus. Still others claim that God is giving signs and wonders to churches today.

Whatever position we take, we must see in our text the power for **signs and wonders** emanating directly from God and not dependent on any person(s). We should contrast the superstitious behavior of placing sick people in Peter's shadow with his own words from chapter 3: **Why do you stare at us as if by our own power or godliness we had made this man walk?** God can choose to extend or withhold signs and wonders as he wishes, hardly dependent on any special person or movement.

E. Gamaliel (v. 34)

Gamaliel appears not only in Scripture, but various places in rabbinical literature. The time of the events in Acts coincided with the prime of his influence in the Sanhedrin (A.D. 25–50). He so endeared himself to the entire Jewish community that they called him "Rabban" (our teacher) rather than

Rabbi (my teacher). The *Mishna* records, "When Rabban Gamaliel the Elder died, the glory of the Law ceased and purity and abstinence died" (Polhill, 171).

VII. TEACHING OUTLINE

A. INTRODUCTION

1. Lead story: The Embarrassing Accordion
2. Context: Not only does Acts 5 flow immediately from Acts 4 virtually without any break in Luke's narrative, but it actually represents a conclusion to the first segment of his history of the early church. Immediately, he will introduce Greek-speaking Christians and move on to the tumultuous times of Stephen and Saul. At the conclusion of chapter 5, we find another reminder that all was well in Jerusalem (despite the Sanhedrin), since the early Christians, pure and unified, **never stopped teaching and proclaiming the good news that Jesus is the Christ**.
3. Transition: As we reflect on this chapter we should ask the Holy Spirit to empty us of petty and phony excuses we use to miss church shirk our responsibilities in the congregation. We should ask him to straighten our reversed and confused priorities in life, to subject our personal pride and feelings before the Lord, and to use us to do what is best for his church and his kingdom in the world. We will learn a lesson of dishonor contrasted with honor, yet always focused on the name of Jesus. This chapter contains an explanation of six events in the early days of the church:

B. COMMENTARY

1. Rebellion in the Church (vv. 1–4)
   a. Family conspiracy (v. 1)
   b. Public generosity (v. 2)
   c. Congregational responsibility (vv. 3–4)
2. Reaction to the Crime (vv. 5–11)
   a. The ultimate discipline (vv. 5–6)
   b. The necessary corollary (vv. 7–10)
   c. The resulting attitude (v. 11)
3. Reputation in the City (vv. 12–16)
   a. Continuing meetings (v. 12)
   b. Public popularity (vv. 13–14)
   c. Regular healings (vv. 15–16)
4. Release of the Captives (vv. 17–26)
   a. Angelic intervention (vv. 17–20)

    b.   Confused politicians (vv. 21–24)

    c.   Liberated apostles (vv. 25–26)

5. Response in the Council (vv. 27–40)

    a.   Peter's response: "We must obey God" (vv. 27–32)

    b.   Gamaliel's response: "Leave these men alone!" (vv. 33–39)

    c.   Sanhedrin response (v. 40)

6. Rejoicing in the Congregation (vv. 41–42)

    a.   Worthy to suffer (v. 41)

    b.   Called to proclaim (v. 42)

C. CONCLUSION: WITNESS IN NEW GUINEA

VIII. ISSUES FOR DISCUSSION

1. Why would anyone lie to God? Could anything make you lie to God?

2. How can you worship a God who would cause people to die?

3. What situations can you see rising in our culture where you would have to obey God rather than government?

Acts 6

Who Serves the Church?

I. **Introduction**
Cross-Cultural Worship

II. **Commentary**
A verse-by-verse explanation of the chapter.

III. **Conclusion**
Counting for Eternity
An overview of the principles and applications
from the chapter.

IV. **Life Application**
Animal Football
Melding the chapter to life.

V. **Prayer**
Tying the chapter to life with God.

VI. **Deeper Discoveries**
Historical, geographical, and grammatical enrichment
of the commentary.

VII. **Teaching Outline**
Suggested step-by-step group study of the chapter.

VIII. **Issues for Discussion**
Zeroing the chapter in on daily life.

Quote

"*It* is strange that sometimes the church is written off by those who know little or nothing about it. They are not involved in its process or mission. In no other field would we take the word of a bystander as a word of authority and appraisal."

C .   N e i l   S t r a i t

GEOGRAPHICAL PROFILE: ALEXANDRIA

- Founded by Alexander the Great in 332 B.C.
- Chief grain port for Rome in Egypt
- Educational center known for studies in mathematics, astronomy, medicine, and poetry
- Library was the largest and best known in the ancient world
- Home of the Septuagint, the Greek translation of the Old Testament

GEOGRAPHICAL PROFILE: CILICIA

- Province in southeastern Asia Minor
- Tarsus was the main city of its eastern section
- Governed by the Roman orator Cicero from 51–50 B.C.
- Location of several Christian churches by the time of Paul's second journey

IN A NUTSHELL

Every church needs leaders selected by the congregation to serve the congregation. Those leaders must be qualified and committed to biblical ministry. In this chapter we see the first example of that as Luke tells us about the first group of elected leaders in the church.

Who Serves the Church?

I. INTRODUCTION

Cross-Cultural Worship

*S*ome years ago my wife and I ministered to a Chinese congregation in the city of Seattle. After various seminars Friday evening and Saturday, we concluded the weekend of ministry with the regular Sunday worship. We discovered two different groups meeting in two separate services that day, but they were really only one congregation.

In the first service I preached to young, American-born Chinese, who spoke primarily English and whose culture was clearly North American. They knew virtually nothing about the old country other than what they had been told by parents and grandparents. They sang praise choruses, wore sweaters and slacks, and conducted the entire service in English. Scarcely thirty minutes later I found myself facing people in dark suits and white shirts who sang and studied Scripture in Chinese, who had been born in China or Hong Kong (or perhaps Taiwan), and for whom the sermon had to be translated into Chinese.

News magazines and books often describe cross-culturalism as a late twentieth-century phenomenon. In fact, it existed in the first-century church, and Luke describes it in the early verses of this chapter. The Jerusalem congregation consisted of those who spoke primarily Greek, read the Scriptures in the Greek version of the Old Testament (the Septuagint), and belonged to families of the dispersion, (Jews born and raised outside of Palestine). These people worshiped side-by-side with those whose conversational language was Aramaic, who read the Scriptures in Hebrew and were probably born in Palestine.

Luke honestly shows us the realities of the first-century church and some of the problems it encountered. It was a good congregation, unified, generous, and zealous about proclaiming the gospel; but it was not perfect because, like us, it functioned in an imperfect world.

In this chapter we will find a way to deal biblically with church issues and problems, as well as how to elect qualified leaders for the local church.

II. COMMENTARY

Who Serves the Church?

> **MAIN IDEA:** *God calls certain people to lead in his church and insists that we require of them faithfulness and commitment in the execution of their duties.*

A Need for Servants (vv. 1–2)

> **SUPPORTING IDEA:** *God calls different people to accomplish different tasks in his church.*

6:1. If we applied modern terms to the two groups of people we find in our verse, we might call the Grecian Jews the "liberals" and the Aramaic-speaking Jews the "conservatives." That would not describe their theology, but rather their cultural practices and the attitudes of most of them toward the law as it pertained to New Covenant Christians. Since the Jerusalem church was located in the heart of Palestine where Aramaic-speaking Jews would have been the majority population, the question of discrimination arose (Eph. 4:31; Heb. 12:15). The particular issue was the distribution of food to widows, but the real problem was much wider.

The word **disciples** appears twice in the early verses in our chapter, used first here in Acts and, interestingly, never in Paul's epistles. We should view it as synonymous with *believers* or later, *Christians,* for Luke distinguishes disciples from the Twelve to which he refers in verse 2. Chapters 1–5 have dealt solely with Jews and Jerusalem. Now chapters 6–9 will focus on Greek ("Hellenistic") Christians and those connected with them. The stories of Stephen, Philip, and Saul in the following chapters are all linked to this opening verse about Grecian Jews.

Luke gives us an honest look at the age-old problem of prejudice. This was not essentially a racial division, since these people were all Jews; but we do see a definite cultural problem. The "outsiders" didn't act, talk, or live like the pure-blooded Palestinian Jews, so they were treated like second-class citizens.

Some commentators suggest that widows came immediately into focus because many older Jews who lived outside of Palestine returned to that country to live out their final years and die on holy soil. As in our society, widows often struggled more than others to provide for themselves. Unlike our society, no Medicare or Medicaid programs, no pensions or insurance policies could take care of older people. God gave the church that responsibility.

The Bible has a great deal to say about widows, both in the Old Testament as well as in the New (1 Tim. 5:9–16; Jas. 1:27). The word **overlooked** indicates that this neglect was neither direct nor intentional. The busy apostles had not appointed anyone to handle these matters, so they simply slipped through the cracks.

The translation of **daily distribution of food** seems somewhat unfortunate. Luke uses the common New Testament word for ministry (*diakonia*) which appears four times in the first four verses of Acts 6.

6:2. The Twelve (a term which appears only here in Acts) gathered all the believers together. They noted that though the problem was real, they themselves could not and should not handle it. Here again in verse 2 the word *diakonia* appears twice—once translated **ministry**, but the second time it takes the English words **wait on**. Literally, the passage could be translated "to minister at table."

The key idea seems to be that *ministry is ministry whether it consists of teaching God's Word or taking care of widows*. We tend to look at a passage like this and make distinctions of importance between taking care of widows and teaching God's truth. Luke does not seem to make such distinction, nor does it appear that was what the Twelve intended. Yes, teaching and prayer claimed priority, but not all disciples were involved in that. God calls different people to different kinds of ministries, and the key lies not in spelling out some level of importance, but being faithful to the call.

The word for **table** (*trapezai*) appears in the Gospels to describe the money tables Jesus overturned in the temple. Quite possibly, Luke is not talking about a soup kitchen here, but the administrative procedure of gathering and dispensing funds for the care of Christian widows in the Jerusalem church and making sure that the handling of those funds and their distribution was done fairly.

The Twelve refused to get involved in matters of church finance because they considered themselves already busy enough with the proclamation of the Word. This might be a helpful suggestion in some modern churches where senior pastors control checking accounts and other church-related business enterprises, sometimes to public ruin and disgrace.

The Twelve gathered **all the disciples together**, not just a select group. From the earliest days of the New Testament the church practiced strong congregational involvement in church decisions. We see it here, and we'll also see it in chapters 11; 13; and 15. This was not a problem for the apostles; it belonged to the congregation, and they had to deal with it.

B Qualifications of Servants (vv. 3–4)

SUPPORTING IDEA: *Ministry is everyone's responsibility, but different ministry tasks require different ministry qualifications.*

6:3–4. The Twelve challenged the entire congregation to elect seven leaders who would undertake this ministry. Why seven? No mystical or theological reason. Jewish courts commonly consisted of seven members, and that would have been the logical choice for Jerusalemite Christians. They were men, though one would hardly make a universal declaration of this applicable to the modern church. In the culture of first-century Judaism that would have been the only possible selection.

This point however, raises the wider issue of whether these seven men became the first deacons, a view commonly espoused from this passage. It seems unlikely that the church had any concept of "officers" at this point, though certainly Paul clearly treats the office of deacon in 1 Timothy 3. The issue here was taking care of widows, not electing officers. The word *diakonia*, though it certainly gave birth to the word *deacon*, hardly seems related to any kind of title in this passage.

The words **from among you** draw interest. Do they imply that the leaders selected should come from the group complaining about the injustice? Though we might not conclude that from verse 3, a quick glance at the Greek names in verse 5 suggests that the people selected seven Hellenists.

What about reputation? These were not just people who looked as though they might be effective or who signed up as volunteers. The first essential qualification required that they be **known to be full of the Spirit and wisdom**. How often we reverse that in our day. We select officers or teachers for various aspects of church ministry and hope they will grow into the task. Not so here. The candidates not only possessed the qualities desired; those qualities had to be obvious to the total congregation!

So Luke has already mentioned three kinds of ministries in four verses: the ministry of food distribution, the ministry of serving tables (money or otherwise), and the ministry of the Word.

Selection of Servants (vv. 5–7)

SUPPORTING IDEA: *Church leaders can only be effectively chosen when a congregation submits to the leading of the Holy Spirit and to the qualifications the Bible requires.*

6:5. Notice that the Twelve offered a suggestion, not a dictatorial decision. The apostles put forth the idea, but the church elected the leaders (just as they chose Matthias in chapter 1). Look at the names of the seven men. As I suggested earlier, most commentators believe they were all Hellenists, though that cannot be proven since Palestinian Jews also had Greek names. One stands out as a Gentile convert (proselyte).

6:6. The selection was followed by a commissioning service in which the apostles dedicated the candidates (cf. Exod. 18:13–27; Num. 27:16–23).

Though many churches still practice physical laying on of hands at ordination services, we should probably not read that back into this text. This Jewish ritual practiced by Jewish Christians gave no hint that God intended to create a new church office. In fact, Luke uses laying on of hands several ways in Acts, including healing (9:17); the giving of the Spirit (8:18); and as here, commissioning to a task (13:3).

As a longtime teacher of leadership courses, I cannot leave this passage without pointing out several fascinating patterns we find in this model:

1. The early church took seriously the combination of spiritual and material concerns. This was not just a soul-saving center, but a congregation which recognized the genuine needs of its widows and designed a practical, biblical plan to take care of them.
2. The early church always seemed ready to adjust its organization to meet needs. We tend to get so locked into structure that we bypass needs if we have no pattern to handle them. *In the New Testament church, structure only developed to meet needs.*
3. The early church practiced positive attitudes of restraint. In this particular case they fixed no blame, showed no paternalism toward the Hellenistic widows, and certainly gave no hint of autocratic leadership on the part of the Twelve.

Can we find a key word in all this? Certainly it has to be the word *ministry* or *service* (*diakonia*). The one who rows a boat seldom has time to rock it, and here were seven new rowers about to take on significant congregational responsibilities.

6:7. Luke updates us, and the news is still good. Not only does he tell us that the number of disciples in the city increased rapidly, but **a large number of priests became obedient to the faith.** Priests served in twenty-four weekly courses at the temple each year, in addition to the function of the high priestly family. At this particular time we would expect as many as eight thousand priests and ten thousand Levites to be involved in temple functions.

Most Bible scholars agree we should not equate the *priests* of this passage with the Sanhedrin henchmen of 4:1. Considerably poorer, these priests quite likely practiced sincere piety and devotion to God. Consequently, the message of a risen Messiah alive in the hearts of his people would have attracted them.

🄳 Opposition to Servants (vv. 8–11)

SUPPORTING IDEA: *When one is selected for church leadership, the type of ministry experiences may be very different than what one expects.*

6:8. Luke placed Stephen first on the list in verse 5 because he doubtless already knew he would later develop the story of this Christian hero. We know from verse 3 that he was **full of the Spirit and wisdom** and from verse 5 that he was **full of faith and the Holy Spirit**. Now Luke describes him as **full of God's grace and power**. Those qualifications led to far more than widow supervision; Stephen did signs and wonders, words we have encountered before in the text of this book. He was the first New Testament character (apart from Jesus and the apostles) described as a miracle worker. Nothing in the text implies that Stephen's ministry in signs and wonders only began after the church selected him as one of the seven servants. That is a possible conclusion, but it cannot be grammatically proven.

6:9. External opposition arose again, this time from Hellenistic Jews, particularly those from Cyrene, Alexandria, Cilicia, and Asia. For whatever reason, Stephen's teaching (Luke does not tell us the exact content) was not well received by his cultural peers, and he found himself in a theological quarrel.

6:10. Luke intends us to understand that Stephen was no second-rate debater. Through wisdom and the power of the Holy Spirit, he argued effectively against his detractors. As we shall see more than once in the pages of this book, criticism for Christian leaders often arises when least expected, undeserved, and often comes from those who ought to know better. Stephen would soon fall prey to vindictive false charges by his fellow Hellenists.

6:11. The charge? Blasphemy. Not only against Moses but also against God himself. The Greek word translated **secretly persuaded** is *hypoballo*, indicating someone put up to this by others, perhaps even given the words to say.

▣ Persecution of Servants (vv. 12–15)

SUPPORTING IDEA: *In the most difficult of situations, God can provide comfort and peace—even at the time of death.*

6:12. Luke tells us the rumors affected almost everybody as these false witnesses stirred up the people, the elders, and the teachers of the law—three groups you would not want chasing you through the streets of Jerusalem in the first century. Here we see the first time the general population (**people**) turned against the Christians. The elders (representing the Sadducees) and the Scribes (representing the Pharisees) were also involved. So a third arrest of Christians took place, and a third "trial" before the Sanhedrin begins to unfold.

6:13–14. The Synagogue of the Freedmen vigilante group fell on Stephen's trail, as false witnesses (perhaps even new ones) charged that he attacked the temple and the law. More precisely they claimed they heard him say that Jesus would destroy the temple and change the traditions of Moses.

This whole scenario reminds us of the way Jesus himself was treated, and of the charges against him (Matt. 26:61; Mark 14:58). Yes, Jesus intended to bring change in Jewish society, but he never threatened to destroy the temple, and he certainly affirmed the law. In the next chapter we shall see precisely what Stephen said, but the charge stands—nothing less than heresy and sedition.

6:15. Stephen came before the Sanhedrin like Peter and John before him. The Council sitting, he standing, they stared at each other for just a moment. The word for **looked intently** (*atenizo*) is a Lucan favorite. We can almost see Stephen making eye contact with the high priest and other members of the Council. What they saw must have startled them. No anger. No fear. No bitterness. Instead, a quiet confidence, peace, security, and courage obviously brought about by the presence of the Holy Spirit and God's grace in his life. Even at that, Luke's choice of words seems remarkable—**his face was like the face of an angel.**

MAIN IDEA REVIEW: *God calls certain people to lead in his church and insists that we require of them faithfulness and commitment in the execution of their duties.*

III. CONCLUSION

Counting for Eternity

How magnificent to serve God when called upon by others to do so! How rewarding and fulfilling to be chosen for a need-meeting ministry such as the one described in this chapter. Dostoevski once wrote,

> If it were desired to reduce a man to nothing—to punish him atrociously, to crush him in such a manner that the most hardened murderer would tremble before such punishment—it would be necessary only to give his work a character of complete uselessness . . . let him be constrained to pour water from one vessel to another and back again. Then I am persuaded that at the end of a few days the prisoner would strangle himself or commit a thousand crimes punishable with death, rather than live in such an abject condition and endure such torments (*The House of the Dead*).

Christian ministry is hardly meaningless time-wasting. It counts for eternity even though others might not see and applaud it here on earth.

PRINCIPLES

- The genius of the New Testament church centers in lay leadership, not dominant pastors.
- Christians need to balance their concern between spiritual and physical ministries, to serve people as well as souls.
- Leadership often brings with it a magnet for the criticism of others, even making some of us targets for false charges.
- Ministry is ministry, whether preaching the Word or taking care of widows.
- The doctrine of the universal priesthood of believers requires that all Christians have a strong voice in the operations of their congregations.

APPLICATIONS

- Develop your devotional life and your spiritual gifts so you can be ready when God calls.
- Be available for various kinds of ministry, not just those which others see and applaud.
- Sense a need and fill it.
- Don't attempt to serve God without the proper qualifications.
- If you are involved in any kind of public ministry, expect opposition.

IV. LIFE APPLICATION

Animal Football

An interesting fable concerns a football game between the little animals and the big animals. The score was 84 to 0 at halftime. In hopelessness, the little animals kicked off to begin the second half.

Somehow, the chimp who handled the kickoff was tackled on the 10 yard line, the worst field position of the day for the big animals. On first down they ran the elephant through the middle—no gain. On second down they threw a zebra screen pass—no gain. On third down, a deep pass to the tight giraffe, and again, no gain.

As the defensive unit of the little animals came screaming off the field, the coach (a gopher) shouted over their excited roar: "Who made the tackle on the kickoff?" The centipede responded, "I did, Coach." "Who stopped the elephant down the middle?" Again, the centipede, "I did, Coach." "Who knocked down those two passes?" To the gopher's amazement the centipede again acknowledged his surprising feat on defense.

Having heard the report, the coach screamed at the centipede, "Where were you the first half?" To which the centipede replied, "In the locker room taping my ankles."

This ridiculous story has only one basic point—*too many of us stay in the locker room taping our ankles when our teams desperately need us on the field.* This passage of Scripture tells about men not only willing, but ready to serve when a ministry need surfaced. The church is a group of people who serve God together, not a group of people who pay others to do so, praise them when they succeed, and fire them when they don't.

Stephen offers us an example of one who knew the Word of God well enough to proclaim it publicly and eloquently. We shall see more of this in chapter 7, but already Luke has spoken of **his wisdom**.

What is your ministry? How do you involve yourself in your local congregation? Might they have selected you that day in Jerusalem to take care of the widows? *The only important ministry is the one to which God has called you and expects you to be faithful.*

V. PRAYER

God, please help us understand how important we are to the function of our congregations. Fill us with the Holy Spirit, wisdom, faith, God's grace, and power so we may serve you effectively whenever and wherever you call us. Amen.

VI. DEEPER DISCOVERIES

A. Hellenism (v. 1)

For a full discussion of this term readers may want to consult a Bible dictionary, encyclopedia, or *The Expositor's Bible Commentary, Volume 9* in which Longenecker devotes several pages to the subject. He discusses an identification of "Hellenists" exclusively by language and geographical origin, as a reference to Jewish proselytes, as a term which means only to live as a Greek, and in connection with the Essene movement or even the Samaritans.

All of these views he finds somewhat limiting and prefers to side with Bishop Moule by suggesting, "that the Hellenists were 'simply Jews (whether by birth or as proselytes) who spoke only Greek and no Semitic language, in contrast to *Hebraioi* which would then mean the Jews who spoke a Semitic language in addition, of course, to Greek'" (Moule, 328–329).

These people were commonly considered second-class Israelites, especially by the Pharisees. Such a definition emphasizes intellectual orientation rather than just geography or language. These Jews resided in Jerusalem, but had come there from other countries and, therefore, lived under some kind of suspicion because of their speech, their behavior, or their culture.

B. Widows (v. 1)

Luke includes more references to widows and women than any other Gospel writer. The word for widow (*chera*) is used once by Mark, not at all by Matthew and John, and six times by Luke in his Gospel. He speaks of widows three more times in Acts which means out of its twenty-two appearances in the New Testament, the word *widow* was penned nine times by Luke. Luke refers to women sixty times in his two books, quite possibly reflecting his care for them in his vocation as a physician. Whatever the reason for his concern, he stands directly in line with the Old Testament on the theme of caring for widows (Deut. 10:18; 16:11,14; 24:17,19–21; 26:12–13). In fact, the Old Testament offers a curse for failing to take care of widows (Mal. 3:5; cf. Isa. 1:17–23).

During their days of wilderness wandering, God reminded his people that when they finally came into their own land they must not forget "widows, strangers, and orphans." That admonition apparently carried over into the early church, and certainly offers a relevant challenge for us today.

C. Believing Priest (v. 7)

Every homegrown Jew clearly knew the difference between priestly families, ordinary priests, and priests who represented minor cultic groups. Luke would not necessarily have been familiar with those distinctions. He certainly learned from his sources that a great number of people, somehow associated with priestly status, believed in Jesus and became Christians. He tags it on to the end of a section without much explanation to demonstrate that it happened as fact, but perhaps lay beyond his ability or interest to interpret.

D. Synagogue of the Freedmen (v. 9)

Sixty million slaves inhabited the Roman Empire during the days of the New Testament, and thousands of them became Christians. **The Synagogue of the Freedmen** implies that the membership of a synagogue in Jerusalem quite possibly consisted of former slaves or the descendants of slaves. Certainly it included dispersed Jews from North Africa and Asia. Remember the apostle Paul was a Cilician Jew who ran into trouble with Asian Jews accusing him of violating the temple (Acts 21:27–29).

In addition to slaves in general, the population of the synagogue might very well have included Jews taken prisoner by Roman armies and later released. As we read Acts, we should not forget that Israel had been under the domination of other powerful nations (Syria, Babylonia, Persia, Greece, Rome) for most of the last seven hundred years.

VII. TEACHING OUTLINE

A. INTRODUCTION

1. Lead Story: Cross-Cultural Worship
2. Context: Acts 5:42 brought down the curtain on Act I in this book. Our present chapter opens a new thought from Luke's pen. He moves on to show how the gospel will spread first to Greek-speaking Jews and then eventually to pagan Gentiles. Stephen becomes Luke's point man, his transition from Jerusalem to Caesarea, on a spiritual, missionary journey that would eventually reach around the Mediterranean world.
3. Transition: As we look at this chapter, we will see a congregation at work trying to solve a simple problem. Their reaction offers a model for us in dealing with church issues and appointing church leaders. One of their number, Stephen, also demonstrates how God can take us beyond our immediate spheres of ministry and use us for his glory in a wider arena. In this chapter Luke makes five observations about servants.

B. COMMENTARY

1. Need for Servants (vv. 1–2)
   a. The problem identified (v. 1)
   b. The responsibility delegated (v. 2)
2. Recruitment of Servants (vv. 3–4)
   a. Qualification (v. 3a)
   b. Delegation (v. 3b)
   c. Specialization (v. 4)
3. Selection of Servants (vv. 5–7)
   a. The line up (v. 5)
   b. The dedication (v. 6)
   c. The result (v. 7)
4. Opposition to Servants (vv. 8–11)
   a. Expanded ministry (v. 8)
   b. Surprising enemies (vv. 9–10)
   c. Illicit testimony (v. 11)
5. Persecution of Servants (vv. 12–15)
   a. The arrest (v. 12)
   b. The charge (vv. 13–14)
   c. The defendant (v. 15)

C. CONCLUSION: ANIMAL FOOTBALL

VIII. ISSUES FOR DISCUSSION

1. How is the organization of your church related to the ministry opportunities your church faces?
2. How do you determine job assignments for the ministerial staff of your church? for the lay workers in your church?
3. Do some people feel like second-class citizens in your church? How can you change the situation?

Acts 7

A Layman Makes His Mark

I.   Introduction
     Humility at Thirty Thousand Feet

II. Commentary
     A verse-by-verse explanation of the chapter.

III. Conclusion
     The Martyr's Crown
     An overview of the principles and applications from the
     chapter.

IV. Life Application
     The Day the Gospel Reached Korea
     Melding the chapter to life.

V.   Prayer
     Tying the chapter to life with God.

VI. Deeper Discoveries
     Historical, geographical, and grammatical enrichment
     of the commentary.

VII. Teaching Outline
     Suggested step-by-step group study of the chapter.

VIII. Issues for Discussion
      Zeroing the chapter in on daily life.

Quote

"*Cowards die many times before their deaths; the valiant never taste of death but once.*"

William Shakespeare

IN A NUTSHELL

Standing before the Sanhedrin with his life hanging in the balance, Stephen offered a brilliant proclamation of the Christian message in terms of popular, first-century Judaism. Rather than a historical survey of the Jews, Stephen delivered a theological explanation of how God has dealt with his people. He showed that God's blessing is not inseparably linked with the land or with any particular geographical location.

A Layman Makes His Mark

I. INTRODUCTION

Humility at Thirty Thousand Feet

Perhaps you remember Ray Donovan, the first Secretary of Labor in the Reagan administration. A business leader from New York, he did not even last out the president's first term. He liked to tell the story of his first ride aboard *Air Force One*. As Donovan recalls, he sat in the cabin immediately behind the president, the only other Cabinet officer on board. As lunchtime approached, a presidential aide came into the cabin to say, "Mr. Secretary, the President would like you to join him in his cabin for lunch in approximately fifteen minutes." Donovan straightened his tie and puffed out his chest a bit, enormously proud to be such an important man, dining with the president at thirty thousand feet on *Air Force One*.

In exactly fifteen minutes he opened the door to enter the president's cabin. At precisely that moment, the red phone next to the president rang. Donovan says, "I couldn't take another step; I felt part of history in the making. Which head of state would be calling? What global question might we discuss over lunch?" His self-importance, already inflated, grew yet another pound-per-square-inch.

The president picked up the phone and Donovan heard him say, "Yes . . . Yes . . . Yes . . . I understand. What are my options?" A long pause until he spoke again: "All right then, I'll have the iced tea." Donovan says he walked into the president's cabin with a considerably different viewpoint of his own importance and prepared for some leisurely banter over that day's luncheon menu.

When the Lord taught his disciples leadership, he emphasized that they should watch him and learn from him for he was "gentle and humble in heart" (Matt. 11:29). We already know Stephen was full of the Spirit, wisdom, God's grace, and power; in this chapter of brilliantly-developed theology, we learn that the speaker has been a humble servant of God, quite willing to die if it would advance the cause of his Savior.

Attitudinal inflation relentlessly claws at the face of modern Christianity. Though Paul warns us not to think more highly of ourselves than we ought (Rom. 12:3), we boast about our attendance, our buildings, and our television and radio ratings. In addition, we have developed the false notion that God wants ministry carried out by trained professionals who have degrees and stand on platforms. Stephen (and in the next chapter Philip) demonstrates once again the significance of lay leadership and every member ministry in the church.

Acts begins and ends that way. We must remember through every word of this chapter that the speaker is a layman who took the time to learn the theological history of his own nation and could articulate it in relation to the coming of the Messiah, his death and resurrection, and what that meant for the future of the nation.

II. COMMENTARY

A Layman Makes His Mark

MAIN IDEA: *In this longest speech recorded in Acts, Stephen intended to show that the Christian gospel squared with Old Testament revelation. In view of that, he returned to the beginning of the nation, even back beyond Moses, back to Abraham to tell the story of God's work with Israel up to his day.*

Abraham and the Land (vv. 1–8)

SUPPORTING IDEA: *God's history with his people began with God's call to Abraham to leave his country for an unknown destination.*

7:1–3. Throughout the days of the Old Testament the Jews could never disassociate God's blessing from his gift of and call to a specific parcel of land. Stephen challenged that idea, showing that God's blessing often occurred outside the land and demonstrating that wherever God meets his people should be viewed as holy ground. Stephen never directly answered the high priest's question, but launched directly into his speech.

To those who emphasized the land, Stephen said that Abraham had wandered far from Palestine when God first met him. So the very formation of the nation dated back to Abraham's initial call (Gen. 12), showing that God can be anywhere at any time he chooses. God is far too big to be tied to a specific geographical area; and Abraham, the first Israelite, provided a good example of the pilgrim nature of God's people right from the beginning. Stephen's address picked up on the common Old Testament themes of rest and remnant (Deut. 12:9–10; Josh. 1:13; Joel 2:32; Mic. 4:6–7).

7:4–5. Not only did God appear to Abraham *before* he ever saw the holy land, but Abraham never had an inheritance there. Palestine was never *his* land in any way.

The key theme here is *promise*. Jews and Christians have always understood God as the God of promise who never fails to deliver. When Christian music talks about the "Promised Land," it almost always refers to heaven. For Abraham, promise could have only meant some geographical area where God would allow his descendants to live. Notice Stephen's emphasis as he attempts to make his case against the land as the ultimate evidence of God's blessing—**not even a foot of ground**.

7:6–8. The four hundred years ran from about 1845 to 1445 B.C., from the original enslavement in Egypt to the year of Exodus. Stephen may have generalized, but Exodus 12:40 puts that time at 430 years. Just like Peter in the temple courts, Stephen offered a spontaneous declaration, not a scholarly paper. Stephen's quote comes from Genesis 15:13–14, and he added the note of circumcision as God's sign of his promise, taken from Genesis 17.

Although **this place** sounds very much in context as though Stephen had in mind the land of Palestine, the phrase is often taken by scholars to refer specifically to the temple. If we do understand it that way, it emphasizes again the breadth of God's grace to his people, not only unlimited in geography and time, but also unrestricted by any particular house or form of worship.

Verse 8 forms a bridge from Abraham to the Patriarchs, about whom Stephen will speak in the next section.

Ⓑ Joseph and Egypt (vv. 9–16)

SUPPORTING IDEA: *Though Stephen never mentioned the Lord's name, the parallel between Joseph and Jesus would likely surface in the minds of his listeners. Both were loved by their fathers; both were sent to a foreign land; both brought blessing to people in those lands; and both were restored to positions of glory at the end of their ordeals.*

7:9–10. No fewer than six times in verses 9–16 do we find the name "Egypt." Reminders of the horrors of history stand in contrast to a gracious God working through and in that history to provide for his people. Notice **God was with him**, and God **rescued him.** God **gave Joseph wisdom** and **enabled him to gain the goodwill of Pharaoh.** Stephen gives us more than history; he gives us theology. Above all futile actions of pagan rulers in all times from Egypt to the modern world, the Sovereign God controls all of his world, not just those who trust in him.

7:11–16. Here Stephen lapsed for just a moment back to the "land argument" to show that even after God fulfilled his promise by providing the land, his great deliverance and blessing to Jacob's family occurred in Egypt through the hands of Joseph whom God had sent there to deliver and protect two nations. Not only that, Jacob's entire family died in Egypt (as did Joseph), and only later were their bodies brought back to Shechem in the land God promised to Abraham.

Let's not lose practical reality in this theological history. Our unlimited, omnipotent God accepts no humanly-designed prohibitions on the way he carries out his work. He is not bound to temples, churches, families, nations, geographical districts, or time. The New Testament continues the Old Testament's emphasis on the sovereignty of the Creator. The men judging Stephen had put God in their little box, and Stephen's speech vividly and quickly untied the wrappings to let God out. If Stephen had met J. B. Phillips before this day, he might have said to the Sanhedrin, "Your God is too small."

Ⓒ Moses and Deliverance (vv. 17–38)

SUPPORTING IDEA: *God will take care of his people wherever they are and provide for their deliverance from trouble and suffering.*

7:17–22. Abraham's son and grandson had lived in the land. Abraham's great-grandchildren had been buried there. Still, the promise was not fulfilled. God did another great thing after the four hundred years (v. 6). He sent another leader to inaugurate this next step. Most of this section of Stephen's speech dealt with Moses, each segment covering forty years of his life (Deut. 34:7 tells us Moses lived to be 120). The phrase **no ordinary child** might be more accurately translated "beautiful to God." Obviously Stephen's audience knew all this very well, so it was only necessary to touch on high points as he made his way to the conclusion.

How interesting that Stephen should call Moses **powerful in speech** when Moses himself doubted his eloquence (Exod. 4:10). Two things may be in view here. First, Stephen described Moses after forty years of leadership during which time he made many eloquent pronouncements in delivering God's messages to the people. Second, Stephen might have had in mind the writing of the Pentateuch in which Moses certainly displayed great power in oral tradition until he wrote it as Scripture.

7:23–29. Picking up on the record of Exodus 2, Stephen reviewed how Moses' first attempts at godly leadership failed miserably and sent him, this specially born and highly educated choice of God, out to the wilderness for forty years. We cannot bypass the comparison between Moses and Jesus in this segment, both rejected by their own people. The incarnation and life of Jesus cannot be compared with Moses' bumbling attempts to start a slave deliverance campaign, but the reaction was essentially the same. In both cases we see a God-appointed leader driven away from the people he came to help.

7:30–38. Now begin the final forty years of Moses' life, the period of actual ministry. Once again God appeared outside the land to deliver a message to his chosen servant. In verse 35 Stephen describes an angel, though that is not the precise record of Exodus 3. Nevertheless, the current view in Stephen's time insisted that God never appears directly to humanity (John 1:14–18), and the angelic connection to the bush is mentioned in Galatians 3:19 along with the Septuagint text of Deuteronomy 33:2.

The empowerment not available to Moses forty years earlier was now his. No longer would he undertake things in his own strength. Notice the emphasis of this historic event does not rest on Moses; it directs our attention immediately to God. Where God dwells and where God speaks is holy ground though it be miles from the "holy land" and completely unrelated to special buildings. Stephen made his first reference to Jesus (again, without the name) in verse 37 as **a prophet like me from your own people.** The text of Deuteronomy 18:5 was commonly referred to Jesus by first-century disciples and Bible writers. Peter had already directly applied this verse to Jesus in 3:22, and doubtless the Sanhedrin would have remembered that, especially with Stephen's special emphasis again here.

The phrase **assembly in the desert** (v. 38) translates the Greek *ekklesia*, the common word for *church* in the New Testament. Here it simply means a group of people called to a specific purpose and should not lead us to find the church in the Book of Genesis.

The style of Stephen's speech changes in this section at about verse 35. The word *deliverer* (redeemer) is *lytrotes* and appears only here in Luke's writings. In Luke 24:21 he applies the verb form to Christ. Stephen clearly says that Moses typified Christ because they were both prophets and deliverers of Israel. Furthermore, both had been denied; both performed miraculous signs; both were prophets raised up by God. As Polhill suggests, "It is hard to resist the comparison between Moses standing in the assembly of Israel mediating between the Israelites and the angel of God and the presence of Christ and his church fulfilling the same role" (Pohill, 199).

Moses associated with angels, and angels were heavily involved in the birth and life of Jesus. Moses gave living words of the law, and Jesus became the living word of grace. Everything Stephen said about Moses and the law is entirely positive. He made no attempt to place the gospel above the law or to criticize anything about that Old Testament system. So far in the speech, the charges have been proved false that **this fellow never stops speaking against this holy place and against the law** (6:13).

 ## Israel and the Temple (vv. 39–50)

SUPPORTING IDEA: *Stephen brings his speech to a close with a demonstration of what we call today "preevangelism," intended to give people who do not understand the gospel enough background to make sense of what they hear.*

7:39–40. Moses' promise of a new prophet (v. 37) means that Israel could not limit its veneration to him and the law. Peter used essentially the same argument in 3:22–23. After rejecting Moses' leadership, the Israelites **in their hearts turned back to Egypt.** How interesting to notice what we have already seen, that basic sin occurs in the heart not in the act. They never returned, of course, but in their hearts they wanted to go back to the pagan surroundings where at least they had the bare essentials of life.

At this point Stephen stopped sounding like Peter who had spoken quite gently to the Sanhedrin **heirs of the prophets** (3:25). For Stephen these rejecters were cut in the same pattern as the aliens in the desert who told Aaron to make new gods (Exod. 32:1). The Talmud records the golden calf incident as Israel's worst sin, but does not interpret it as a rejection of Moses; that special twist belongs to Stephen. The clear emphasis of this entire section argues that the rejection of Christ parallels the rejection of Moses, and the guilt that wilderness Israelites bore for the golden calf incident is not at all unlike the guilt Stephen's contemporaries held for crucifying Christ.

7:41–43. The result of the rejection? **God turned away** and, says Stephen, **gave them over to the worship of the heavenly bodies**. To support this assertion he quotes Amos 5:25–27. The phrase **the book of prophets** was a common first-century way of referring to the minor prophets collected together in a single book of the Hebrew Bible. These verses focus not on astrology but apostasy. All this happened at the time of rejection—God "gave them over," used in Romans 1:24 to refer to the move from idolatry to immorality.

So, Stephen said, forget the sacrifices and the temple to which people bring them. The rejection has turned God away. In denying Jesus, the Jews were heading for another wilderness experience. They considered the land and the temple more important than the God who gave them. At the end of the quote from Amos, Stephen lays to rest his defense against the charge of blaspheming Moses and turns to the charge of blasphemy against the temple.

7:44–47. The tabernacle represented a glorious history for the Jews. In this brief summary, Stephen dwells exclusively on the tabernacle with only the slightest mention of the temple in verse 47. Once again the geography question arises. The temple was stationary, a fixed building in a fixed city to which everyone had to come. Even the tabernacle, though it represented a specific place for God's dwelling, moved around Canaan from place to place right up to the time of David. It offered a flexible form of worship.

In verse 47 Stephen may well have had in mind a text in 2 Samuel 7:5–7 where God spoke through the prophet Nathan to affirm his satisfaction with the tabernacle and declined David's offer for a special house. True, the Lord later indicated Solomon could carry out the task, but apparently Stephen did not consider that a final fulfillment of God's words to David in 2 Samuel 7.

The main point seems to be that God never really needed a place in which to live. He can hardly be confined to **temples built by hands** (Acts 17:24). What a refreshing view of God Stephen offers! Nothing can confine him. Nothing can explain him. Nothing can define him in terms of limited human experience. Stephen seems to emphasize how far the ritualistic traditionalism of first-century Israel had strayed from the simple basics of Old Testament revelation—**In the beginning, God** (Gen. 1:1).

7:48–50. In view of the quotation above from Acts 17:24, we must remind ourselves that Saul attended Stephen's defense and heard these words even as Stephen spoke them. Here Stephen appealed to Isaiah 66:1–2 to demonstrate the foolishness of trying to capture the God of the universe in some spatial setting with a label. The answer to the rhetorical question appears in the second half of Isaiah 66:2: **This is the one I esteem: he who is humble and contrite in spirit, and trembles at my word**. Actually, Judaism never taught that God lived in the temple, but Stephen makes the point that their behavior seemed to support that notion.

Keep in mind that Stephen was a Hellenistic Jew, a Greek speaking outsider who had probably spent most of his life worshiping God in some place other than Palestine, and especially not in the temple. He could not stomach the rigid institutionalism he encountered as a liberated Jewish Christian living in Jerusalem.

Remember, another false accusation brought against Stephen was that he spoke out against the holy place (6:13). Consequently he felt it necessary in this defense to raise the issue of the temple along with Moses and the land. Certainly the basic theme of early Christian theology centered on Jesus as the mediation of God's saving presence among his people, replacing tabernacle, temple, or anything else. Stephen moved headlong toward the important New Testament doctrine we call "the universal priesthood of believers," though that will only be fully developed later by Paul.

ᴇ Sanhedrin and Indictment (vv. 51–53)

SUPPORTING IDEA: *Stephen sets an entirely new tone in Christian preaching which became quite popular during historic revivals: direct and pointed accusation at those who offended God.*

7:51–52a. The **our** now switches to **you** as Stephen drives home his indictment of prophet killing, not a new theme in Scripture (2 Chron. 36:15–16; Neh. 9:26; Jer. 2:30). The accusation of stubborn people (Exod. 33:5) he couples with a stirring theological metaphor **uncircumcised hearts** (Lev. 26:41; Deut. 10:16). In short, they behaved like pagans, precisely the way their fathers behaved when they killed the prophets. Their ancestors had persecuted and murdered those who predicted Jesus' coming. Now that he had come, the present generation treated him exactly the same way. Stephen grasped the temporary nature of all physical aspects of God's work in the world. The land, though it will someday be restored again, was not the issue of God's blessing. Tabernacles, temples, rituals, traditions come and go, but God lives above them all.

7:52b–53. Theoretically, Israel had learned great lessons down through the years through the struggles Stephen described. He intended precisely the reverse—no lesson had been learned, a fact apparent from the behavior of the Sanhedrin toward Jesus. This was flagrant apostasy, especially from a Hellenist. He had begun with **men, brothers and fathers**. He had affirmed his deep love and commitment for Abraham, the patriarchs, circumcision, the tabernacle, and the law. Now he wanted out. He did not wish to be linked with a nation that murdered the righteous one, a nation that received the law through angels but didn't obey it. All of a sudden Stephen became a thundering Elijah, declaring that no forgiveness was possible without acknowledgment of sin, sin which rested right on the robed shoulders of the Sanhedrin.

Stephen never finished his address. He might very well have gone on to offer repentance as did Peter (3:19–21). He was at the accusation point when attacked, so any further words he may have intended to say were stifled under the flurry of stones.

Some have suggested, and perhaps correctly, that this constituted no defense at all. They indicate that Stephen considered his situation so hopeless that he took this opportunity to give direct witness as a Christian. Perhaps. One wonders, however, why he would not have spoken more precisely of Jesus (as Peter did earlier) rather than dwelling so long on historic events well-known to his audience. At any rate, by the time we reach the end of verse 53, the case was closed. We will never know until heaven what else Stephen might have wanted to say before his death.

F Stephen and Heaven (vv. 54–60)

SUPPORTING IDEA: *"Precious in the sight of the Lord is the death of his saints" (Ps. 116:15). Stephen now becomes the first to die for Jesus.*

7:54–56. The mob had no time for the mediating voice of Gamaliel in this situation. Such heresy deserved a death penalty—and not tomorrow. In their vicious anger they could not wait to get their hands on him. The text implies wild, jeering shouts of hatred and hostility. They ground their teeth at Stephen, making a hissing sound. This scholarly assembly of religious leaders had become a murderous lynch mob. Stephen's response hardly served his cause. He saw a vision and boldly described it—Jesus, standing at the right hand of God (Mark 14:62). We might say he added insult to injury. In the New Testament the phrase **the Son of man** appears outside the gospels only here and in Revelation 1:13; 14:14. The mob never questioned nor doubted what Stephen described.

Even more striking than Stephen using the phrase "the Son of man" (the only time in the New Testament it was spoken by anyone other than Jesus), was this vision of the Savior standing next to God, when even Christians acknowledged he was seated at God's right hand (Luke 22:69). Did he stand to welcome the first martyr in honor? Did he stand, as Bruce suggests, to assume the posture of a witness in a heavenly court pleading Stephen's case there? (Bruce, 210). Or was he standing as Daniel saw him (7:13–14), the Ancient of Days ready to step into a judgmental rule against all nations who rejected him?

We can only conclude it may have been all of these or none of them. Certainly the last fits in well with the judgmental message Stephen had just concluded. If it had been his intent to evoke the Danielic image, his hearers would have had no difficulty grasping the connection.

7:57–58. This identification of God, heaven, and Jesus affirmed the deity of Christ and so, though it would seem difficult, they added to their screaming and hissing the covering of their ears lest they hear any additional heresy. Even though this heretical apostasy called for the death penalty, the law of the land was clear: they had to wait at least one more day, and they needed approval from Roman authorities. Obviously, this crowd no longer thought about law and order. Assuming the Pharisees were as offended as the Sadducees (an assumption quite easy to make in light of Stephen's remarks), no one lifted a restraining hand at the moment of their charge. The actual stoning resembled a formal execution rather than the result of mob action. We know that because Luke tells us **the witnesses laid their clothes at the feet of a young man named Saul**. These **witnesses** knocked the victim down and were privileged to throw the first stones.

Most scholars believe Saul did not just stand by to serve as a coatrack. He apparently had some official role in the execution. We cannot determine whether he was actually a member of the Sanhedrin, but he definitely exercised some kind of delegated authority in the death of Stephen. Stephen became the first Christian the Rabbi from Tarsus would kill. At that time Saul was a young man *(neanias),* generally considered to be between the ages of twenty-four and forty.

So far we have seen three trials in the Book of Acts. The first ended in threats (chap. 4); the second, in beatings (chap. 5); and the third, in death (chap. 7).

7:59–60. We began this section by talking about humility. That is precisely where the chapter ends. We dare not take Stephen's harsh condemnation as anything less than the cry of his heart at the rejection of his Savior. We have already been told of his qualities, and now we see them in practice as he literally prayed his way into heaven. Did he recall in that moment the words of his Lord on the cross (Luke 23:34–36)? Imagine Saul's emotions as he heard this dying martyr call upon the name he so despised!

Normally victims of stoning would lie on their backs, but Stephen fell to his knees when the witnesses pushed him over. The words of forgiveness uttered by both Jesus and Stephen are based on an old Jewish prayer. Jewish families taught their children to pray this prayer at bedtime, and it certainly would serve the modern church well to use it more frequently. What a wonderful way to end each day—by forgiving all who have offended us during its hours.

Sleep is a common New Testament euphemism for death. It translates the Greek word *(ekoimethe)* from which we construct the English noun *cemetery*. A cemetery—supposedly fearsome and spooky—affords a Christian word of faith. Christians who die are not gone; they sleep temporarily until Jesus wakes them up. That sleep, of course, does not mean cessation of existence or awareness, because we learn later in Paul's writings that to be absent from the body is to be present with the Lord (2 Cor. 5:1–10).

MAIN IDEA REVIEW: *In this longest speech recorded in Acts, Stephen intended to show that the Christian gospel was consistent with Old Testament revelation. In view of that, he returned to the beginning of the nation, even back beyond Moses, to Abraham and told the story of God's work with Israel to his day.*

III. CONCLUSION

The Martyr's Crown

We have seen repeatedly throughout history that the blood of the martyrs is indeed the seed of the church. God planted it here and countless times on all the continents of the world. In the late 1970s missiologists estimated a population of one million Christians inside China. Fifteen years later, after severe persecution by the Communists, experts reported thirty to fifty million believers. It also seems important that the first martyr was a layman, not a professional minister of some type. People willing to lay their lives on the line for the Lord hardly need any special training or certification for such ultimate sacrifice.

Amazingly, there have been more martyrs in the twentieth century than all previous nineteen centuries. This kind of statistic boggles our minds since we think of martyrdom as arising from medieval practices or the struggles of the Reformation. Countless Stephens have met their Lord during the last hundred years and are still doing so in countries around the world. *Stephanos* is the word for *crown*, and Stephen will wear one someday. Of this man Alfred Lord Tennison once wrote,

> He heeded not reviling tones,
> Nor sold his heart to idle moans,
> Though cursed and scorned and bruised with stones.
> But looking upward, full of grace;
> He prayed—and from a happy place
> God's glory smote him on the face.

PRINCIPLES

- We can worship God anywhere at anytime.
- God cannot be confined by any human endeavors or patterns.
- Those who reject Jesus reject God, and only punishment can follow.
- God's people, filled by the Holy Spirit, are able to die in joy even when that death is hideous and cruel.

APPLICATIONS

- Learn to worship God in places other than the traditional church or meeting place.
- Develop a full grasp of Scripture so that you can talk freely about God's plan on earth as Stephen did.
- Allow God to give you freedom to talk openly about Jesus and your own witness of faith.
- Trust God to provide whatever courage and peace you need in times of struggle, and ultimately, at the time of death.

IV. LIFE APPLICATION

The Day the Gospel Reached Korea

At this point in history, Korea is the only Asian country where the Christian population exceeds 20 percent of the total. Yet the gospel has only been in that land for a little over one hundred years. Robert J. Thomas, a Welsh missionary, served in China with the Scottish Bible Society. Upon learning that the Korean language was related to Chinese, and at least some in Korea could read it, he decided to take his literature there. He sailed aboard an American ship called the *General Sherman* headed for Pyong Yang.

As the ship drew near shore, a fight broke out between the American officers and the Korean "Coast Guard." The ship was burned, and all the passengers killed. Yet somehow, while all this was happening, Thomas struggled to reach shore and staggered out of the water, with his arms filled with Bibles. As he thrust these into Korean hands, they clubbed him to death. The gospel was now on Korean shore—literally.

Enormous lessons arise from stories like those of Stephen and Robert J. Thomas. One lesson emphasizes the importance of prayer for the safety of missionaries, especially in high risk areas of service. We should know their names if possible, but when we don't, we can pray for those who proclaim the gospel to remote tribes in South America or among Islamic peoples in Africa and the Near East.

Second, we ought to learn from this chapter how fleeting life is. Doubtless when the church appointed Stephen to leadership (chap. 6), he anticipated many fruitful years, perhaps even decades, to serve the Lord. Somehow in the providence of God, his life ended a short time later. Every day is a gift from God, and we should use it as such.

Finally, this passage calls us to be ready for death at any time. How we fear, not only death, but the ravaging diseases which line the highway to that dreaded point: cancer, heart attacks, strokes, Alzheimer's disease, AIDS—all horrible paths. There are few good ways to die. Yet here we see a man in one of the worst possible situations—stoning—who serenely looked to Jesus and forgave his tormentors. What a challenge for us to walk more closely with the Lord, to be more highly disciplined and governed by his Spirit.

V. PRAYER

God, please give us the grace to be like Stephen. May our hearts depend completely on you for serenity and calm when difficult struggles attack our lives. Amen.

VI. DEEPER DISCOVERIES

A. God's Call (v. 34)

In the modern church we seem to have lost some sense of call. Yet throughout Acts and, indeed, throughout the entire Scripture, God called men and women to various positions and places of service. When we compare this brief verse with the account in Exodus 3, we recognize again how important it is never to attempt to do God's work in our own strength or our own timing. The key word in Acts 7:34 consists of just one letter—I.

Earlier Moses tried to break up fights to rally the slaves; now God brought the power of heaven, using a dispensable tool to carry out his work in the world. That precisely describes Moses, and it describes us as well. We are dispensable tools whom God chooses to use for his purposes, and our pliability holds the key to our effectiveness.

B. Heaven (vv. 49,56)

This familiar word, so prominent at the time of Stephen's death, has already taken on significant meaning in Acts. In chapter 1, Jesus was taken up into heaven (1:2,11). In chapter 2, the sound of the wind comes from heaven (2:2). Also in Peter's Pentecost sermon he referred to wonders in heaven (2:19) and the fact that David did not ascend to heaven (2:34). In chapter 3, Jesus will remain in heaven until he comes again (3:21). Chapter 4 tells us there is no other name under heaven given to men (4:12), and the believers also prayed to the one who made heaven and earth (4:24). Now this dwelling place of God opens its portals to receive the first Christian martyr. Who follows in his train?

C. Son of Man (v. 56)

Here we have the only time in the New Testament where this phrase was spoken by anyone other than Jesus. This title of the Messiah implied the universal aspect of his rule described by Daniel (Dan. 7:13–14) and later Jesus himself (Mark 14:62). **Son of man** was Jesus' most common reference to himself, used eighty-one times in the Gospels. He clearly intended it as a messianic claim, and it appears with striking contrast in Mark 8 where, after Peter says, "You are the Christ" (v. 29), Mark says: "He then began to teach them that the Son of Man must suffer many things and be rejected by the elders, chief priests and teachers of the law, and that he must be killed and after three days rise again" (v. 31).

The **Son of man** title directs our attention to God incarnate, the eternal Spirit God having taken human flesh and become the child of a virgin. Fully aware of the many Old Testament references to this phrase (particularly the one in Daniel), Stephen chose the title for Jesus when he saw him in heaven. The eternal Lord of glory who existed forever in the past in heaven came down to offer himself as a redemptive sacrifice; and after his rejection and death, he once again returned to heaven—but he is still the **Son of man**.

VII. TEACHING OUTLINE

A. INTRODUCTION

1. Lead story: Humility at Thirty Thousand Feet
2. Context: Acts 7 is a continuation of Acts 6. The Sanhedrin has already convened in 6:15, and our present chapter opens with the high priest's question to Stephen, serving as an invitation for him to answer the charges brought against him. Furthermore, the first verse of chapter 8 is, in reality, the last verse of chapter 7. Luke's historical narrative will expand immediately, as did the church from the moment of Stephen's death. As difficult as it may seem at times to plow through the historical theology of Acts 7, the chapter forms a pivotal point in the book as the gospel, because of Saul's vigorous persecution of Christians, spreads well outside Jerusalem and Palestine.
3. Transition: The spiritual reality of this passage helps us see ourselves in Stephen's shoes. Most of us cannot relate directly to standing before an official council explaining our faith and then being stoned for what we say. We can, however, quickly grasp the idea of witnessing for Jesus in an alien environment like an office or school and receiving scorn and perhaps even ill treatment because of our witness. Chapter 7 tells the story of God's work with Israel, with a focus on six key people.

B. COMMENTARY

1. Abraham and the Land (vv. 1–8)
   a. Introduction of Abraham (vv. 1–3)
   b. Call of Abraham (vv. 4–5)
   c. Promise to Abraham (vv. 6–8)

2. Joseph and Egypt (vv. 9–16)
   a. God rescues Joseph in Egypt (vv. 9–10)
   b. God rescues Jacob in Egypt (vv. 11–16)
3. Moses and Deliverance (vv. 17–38)
   a. Moses in Pharaoh's house (vv. 17–22)
   b. Moses in Midian (vv. 23–29)
   c. Moses in Sinai (vv. 30–38)
4. Israel and the Temple (vv. 39–50)
   a. Rebellion in the desert (vv. 39–40)
   b. Idolatry in the desert (vv. 41–43)
   c. Tabernacle in the desert (vv. 44–47)
   d. The temporary temple (vv. 48–50)
5. The Sanhedrin and Indictment (vv. 51–53)
   a. Ancient Israel killed its prophets (vv. 51–52a)
   b. Current Israel killed the Christ (vv. 52b–53)
6. Stephen and Heaven (vv. 54–60)
   a. Heavenly revelation (vv. 54–56)
   b. Horrible persecution (vv. 57–58)
   c. Holy death (vv. 59–60)

C. CONCLUSION: THE DAY THE GOSPEL REACHED KOREA

VIII. ISSUES FOR DISCUSSION

1. How would you answer someone with the power to sentence you to death if you professed to be a Christian?
2. Are you able to use the narratives in the Bible to show someone why you believe in Christ?
3. How is the story of your church like the story of Israel? How is it different?

Acts 8

Catch That Chariot!

I. Introduction
Take My Factories

II. Commentary
A verse-by-verse explanation of the chapter.

III. Conclusion
Prototype of Lay Evangelism
An overview of the principles and applications from the chapter.

IV. Life Application
A Gravestone in Olney
Melding the chapter to life.

V. Prayer
Tying the chapter to life with God.

VI. Deeper Discoveries
Historical, geographical, and grammatical enrichment of the commentary.

VII. Teaching Outline
Suggested step-by-step group study of the chapter.

VIII. Issues for Discussion
Zeroing the chapter in on daily life.

"*T*he way from God to a human heart
is through a human heart."

Samuel Gordon

GEOGRAPHICAL PROFILE: SAMARITANS

- Descended from the northern tribes of Israel
- Intermarried with Canaanites and other peoples whom the Assyrians resettled in their territory
- Worshiped at a temple on Mt. Gerizim
- Continued to look for a Messiah
- Constantly in conflict with the Jews over ethnic and theological differences

IN A NUTSHELL

*L*uke interrupts his narrative of the church a second time to introduce another one of God's chosen servants. Whereas Stephen showed us a layman skilled in preaching, Philip demonstrates effective evangelism.

Catch That Chariot!

I. INTRODUCTION

Take My Factories

*A*ndrew Carnegie, who made a fortune around 1900 manufacturing steel ,was famous for his deep commitment to the quality of people who worked for him. "Take away my people but leave my factories," he said, "and soon grass will grow up through the floors of the factories. But leave my people and take my factories, and those people will soon build new and better factories." The dedication and competence of his employees accounted for Carnegie's remarkable success.

The key ministry ingredient is always dedication. Luke has already shown us one "home video" of the death of Stephen. We have been mesmerized by his understanding of the Old Testament, his ability to explain messianic history, and his courage in the face of death. Now it's time to open another box with a very different label. In this chapter we encounter Philip, also selected as one of the servants in chapter 6. Luke seems to contrast Stephen and Philip in their personalities, their types of ministries, and the way God chose to take one home to heaven immediately and leave the other on earth for many more years.

Luke introduces the chapter with a brief record of the persecution which broke out after the death of Stephen (a bridge in the text which also gives him opportunity to introduce Saul). At first, this persecution must have seemed like some horror story to those young believers, especially the Hellenistic Christians who appeared to bear the brunt of the attack. Then—as Luke reminds us—we see God's plan realized as the gospel spreads from Jerusalem to Judea and Samaria bringing to reality the ascension commission of the Lord (1:8).

All of us who are a part of Christ's body, the church, should be greatly interested in the vast differences among Christians. The original twelve disciples did not have much in common except for certain occupational and personality traits. In Acts 8 we find the final reference to Stephen, a brief introduction of Saul, and the story of Philip—three people who came from considerably different backgrounds. God's grace brings together vastly different people into one body. We see, both in the New Testament and in our churches today, the genius of Christian unity. Paul praised it in the early verses of Ephesians 4: "Make every effort to keep the unity of the Spirit through the bond of peace. There is one body and one Spirit—just as you were called to one hope when you were called—one Lord, one faith, one baptism; one God and Father of all, who is over all and through all and in all" (Eph. 4:3–6).

We find the same theme in a dramatic passage in Romans 12, where Paul pointed to unity and diversity, something we shall see repeatedly lived out through Acts: "Just as each of us has one body with many members, and these members do not all have the same function, so in Christ we who are many form one body, and each member belongs to all the others" (Rom. 12:4–5).

According to the *Chronicle of Church Fund Raising* released by Resource Services, Inc. in Dallas, modern churches invest in enormously expensive property. This organization has assisted local congregations in stewardship funding for the construction of church buildings, raising over thirty million dollars. Andrew Carnegie was right. How important for us to recognize that we should be able to say, without hesitation, "Take away my factories." The church consists of people, not buildings. The ongoing ministry of the gospel until Jesus comes again, rests squarely with committed Christians such as Philip who make themselves available for the service of Jesus Christ whenever and wherever the Holy Spirit wills.

II. COMMENTARY

Catch That Chariot!

MAIN IDEA: *Leading other people to Christ requires that we be ready, unafraid, able to use God's Word, and filled with the Holy Spirit.*

A Context of Philip's Ministry (vv. 1–8)

SUPPORTING IDEA: *Christian witness brings great joy.*

8:1. New Testament scholars do not agree on what role Saul actually played in the death of Stephen. Luke did not feel it important at this point to explain in detail. He simply reported that Saul was there and approved of the stoning. Luke in his wonderful writing style carries us through the narrative of Acts with an amazing smoothness when we consider that journalism represented a second avocation (after historian) for this medical doctor. Here he created a bridge from martyrdom to persecution and from martyrdom to evangelism.

In this verse we encounter the first use in Acts of the word *persecution*. It is likely that the persecution was aimed primarily at Hellenistic Christians in Jerusalem. They already suffered from cultural discrimination in the local Jewish community. Now with Stephen's blatant "heresy" and the public act of killing him, opponents of the gospel may have felt they found a vulnerable point in the church—Greek–speaking Jewish Christians.

This would explain two important aspects of Luke's message in Acts. First, the apostles are able to remain at Jerusalem, a point he makes briefly but which serves us immeasurably in understanding this persecution. Second, in chapter 11 we shall discover a continuation of the narrative from 8:4 and see that these scattered Christians felt comfortable in proclaiming the gospel to Gentiles, a characteristic more likely of Hellenists than Hebraic Christians. This scattering shows God's hand working through evil persecutors to disperse his people into places he wanted the gospel to reach.

8:2–3. Note another Lucan contrast—**Godly men . . . but Saul.** Luke clearly wants us to understand that Stephen was deeply loved by his brothers and sisters in the Jerusalem congregation. In contrast to this wild zealot of a Pharisee named Saul, they mourned with broken hearts for their fallen comrade. The word translated "godly" is *eulabes*, used of Simeon in Luke

2:25 and also to describe devout Jews open to the gospel at Pentecost in Acts 2:5.

Does this persecution find single focus in one destructive personality? Yes, Saul of Tarsus. Saul did not just persecute the church: he **began to destroy** it. The word for *destroy* is used of wild boars in the Greek text of Psalm 80:13. The picture here does not describe some religious administrator seated at a desk and sending others to do his dirty work. Saul led the charge in the streets, house to house, men and women. He did not just arrest Christians; he dragged them off. The Bible fleshes out this portrait of Saul in other New Testament passages (Acts 22:4–5; 26:10–11; 1 Cor. 15:9; Gal. 1:13–14,22–23; Phil. 3:5–6; 1 Tim. 1:13).

8:4–5. Any congregation needing a verse for every-member evangelism can find it right here. Remember, the apostles stayed at Jerusalem, so the scattered Hellenists were essentially lay leaders; yet wherever they went, they proclaimed the Word of God. What a magnificent picture of dedicated believers. Picture them as they run for their lives, grasping what few possessions they could take with them when the persecution broke out. See them praying for deliverance but also for courage to be faithful to their Savior and to proclaim his message effectively wherever they went.

Luke introduces Philip for the second time in his narrative. Previously (6:5) he was just one of seven leaders appointed to handle ministry to the widows. Now, as Saul embodied the persecution, Philip embodies the behavior of the scattered Christians. He went down (from a higher area to the plains) and proclaimed the message of Messiah. An outcast Hellenist in the land of the outcasts—no wonder the Samaritans responded so well.

The gospel moved out into Samaria. Luke must not have considered it important for us to know which city became the point of first contact. Before this event concludes, the Lord's people are **preaching the gospel in many Samaritan villages** (v. 25).

8:6–8. As a historian, Luke enjoyed recording great speeches, but he says nothing about Philip's preaching, again a possible contrast with the eloquent Stephen. This does not in any way demean Philip's ministry, since communicating the message of the gospel in a less-than-polished form is considerably better than not communicating it at all. In Stephen we saw courageous eloquence; in Philip we see aggressive and effective evangelism.

Luke emphasizes the miracles this lay leader performed in Samaria—exorcism (casting out demons) and healings. Such powerful signs made the people interested in what he had to say.

Verses like this lead some to wonder whether response to the gospel today might not be much more widespread if the same kind of miracles were regularly done by God's people. Several things must draw our attention here. First, the accompaniment of the gospel by miracles—though not limited to the early chapters of Acts, certainly represents the transitional time in which God did a new work with a new message. Second, we must see the miracles as secondary—as in the ministry of Christ. The purpose of the miracle is to attract attention to the gospel. Verse 12 clearly indicates that the message of Christ, not the experience of signs and wonders, was the issue. Nevertheless, a combination of miracle and message brought great joy to the city. The gospel had reached "foreign soil" for the first time. In the text of Acts, Philip was the first missionary, even though Samaria lay just a few miles away and did not require the learning of a different language.

Ⓑ Con Man in Samaria (vv. 9–19)

SUPPORTING IDEA: *Whenever God accompanies the gospel with physical miracles, the potential for perversion exists. Christians willing to proclaim God's truth must expect trouble from those who want to distort it.*

8:9–11. Philip had come to Samaria to proclaim the gospel, not to sell it. In bringing the name of Jesus and the liberating power of his message to Samaria, Philip had invaded the stronghold of the occult. Had Philip known what lay ahead, he might have said to his comrades, "I'm off to see the wizard," for that is precisely what Simon the sorcerer proclaimed and precisely what people around him believed.

We will explore the identification of Simon and the phrase **the Great Power** a bit later in "Deeper Discoveries." Here let's just recognize that Luke wants us to know what Philip was up against. A lay preacher, in a strange land, face-to-face with a magician who had amazed people **for a long time with his magic.** Whether Simon's dabblings in the occult centered in astrology or some other form of sorcery, whatever power people saw in him probably came from demonic sources (cf. Acts 16:16–20). Now those sources are about to be challenged by the God of the universe and the message of the gospel.

8:12. When the power of Jesus Christ encounters the power of Satan, there is no contest. Philip's message is clear. It reminds us of the basic gospel in Acts 4:12. Again, this Bible writer so concerned about the role of women in God's plan, emphasizes that they, too, heard Philip's message, trusted Christ, and were saved. Furthermore, they were baptized. Luke has not made much of this yet in his account, but we shall see it again in a strategic way before this chapter finishes.

8:13. We are almost as astonished as the Samaritans must have been when we read that Simon also **believed and was baptized.** Was this magician, whether charlatan or sorcerer, genuinely converted? The following paragraph will show us enough information to demonstrate that he was not. Remember that the word *believe* does not always mean saving faith in the

New Testament (John 2:23–25; Jas. 2:19). Apparently Simon was caught up in the excitement of the moment. Having recognized that Philip's miracles were considerably greater than his own, he followed the evangelist around to learn some new tricks. Any earning of God's gift denies God's grace. Somehow Simon never quite caught that basic message of the gospel.

Arrington puts it this way: "His only hope was genuine evangelical repentance which he had not experienced. He had no real spiritual understanding of the faith that he claimed. His faith was imperfect; it was centered in man, not in Christ" (Arrington, 88–89).

8:14–17. Time to bring in the first team. When Jerusalem heard what was happening up north, they not only sent apostles, they dispatched Peter and John, the earliest heroes of Luke's narrative (chap. 3). The Holy Spirit had not yet been given in Samaria, indicating that the baptism of verse 12 was water baptism for repentance in the name of Jesus.

A host of questions thrust themselves at us from these few verses. Why did the Jerusalem apostles come to Samaria? Certainly not because of "apostolic succession," since this was an event and not a practice. In chapter 11 when the gospel spreads to Antioch, another lay leader (Barnabas) is sent to assist the church there.

We also do not find some kind of "second blessing" here in which the Holy Spirit comes to believers sometime subsequent to their salvation. Yes, that happens here, but Acts is a transitional book. The entire New Testament makes it plain that people who do not have the Spirit of God are not born again. The very act of the Spirit in our hearts brings about salvation. Having taken up residence for that act, he never leaves.

Luke seems to emphasize the importance of church unity here. This was not some new movement, some cultic subset of mainline Christianity. Believers in Samaria linked immediately with believers in Jerusalem to protect the unity of the church, an issue especially crucial when Jerusalem and Samaria were involved. We find no lessening of Philip's ministry here, but rather an affirmation by Jerusalem. Philip, a layman on the run, had no experience in dealing with new converts. His submission to the authority of Peter and John offers a model for believers today. Not a model of subservience of laypeople to clergy, but a model of inexperienced, younger Christians to more experienced, older Christians. Let us apply to the interpretation of any passage everything we know about New Testament theology. The Holy Spirit unifies the body of Christ, and surely no two segments of that body needed unifying more than traditional Christians in Jerusalem and newborn Christians in Samaria.

Luke does not tell us what actually happened when the Samaritans received the Holy Spirit, but we may assume that similar visible signs, possibly speaking in other languages, attended this event as they did previous events in Acts.

8:18–19. Simony. That's what we call it, and here's how the word came into the language. Simony describes the buying or selling of religious office, precisely what the Samaritan sorcerer wanted to do. Whatever Simon saw fascinated him. Watching Philip do miracles had been exciting and attractive, but now the unleashing of some new power in the lives of people by an unseen presence of the living God was downright irresistible. This man was a professional who immediately saw the profit potential in this kind of power. How much would it cost for Peter and John to pass this on to him? After all, they would soon return to Jerusalem, and someone in Samaria needed to carry on this amazing gift.

Sadly, people who name the name of Jesus have not abandoned simony down through the centuries. Luther was enraged by the activity of John Tetzel selling "indulgences" right across the river from Luther's parish. Tetzel even had a catch phrase which surely attracted the attention of German listeners: *So bald der Pfennig in Kasten klingt, die Seele aus des Fegefeuer springt.* Translation: "As soon as you drop your money in the pot, the soul [of the person you pay for] jumps right out of the fire of purgatory."

Today misguided "evangelists" use radio, television, mailing campaigns, and even the Internet to garner money for religious favors of one kind or another. In many cases, they are no better than Simon the sorcerer, exchanging funds for God's grace. *We talk often about blasphemy of belief, but there is also a blasphemy of behavior.*

Ⓒ Conflict Between Truth and Error (vv. 20–25)

SUPPORTING IDEA: *Only a heart attitude of repentance can bring genuine salvation.*

8:20. Leave it to J. B. Phillips to lay it on the line. He translates the first part of Peter's response, "To hell with you and your money." Where truth exists, so does error. Where reality exists, we find sham. The true heart of Simon begins to emerge. Whatever he believed back in verse 13, it was certainly not faith for salvation, else Peter could never have said he would perish.

Quite obviously the statement of belief, water baptism, and perhaps even the laying on of hands conveyed no genuine indication of heart condition. That has hardly changed in today's church. Baptism, communion, membership, office holding, and any other kind of external recognition mean nothing to God who looks directly at the heart condition.

8:21–23. Simon's wicked heart had no part in the evangelical ministry of Samaria. Peter's earlier statement was not a prophecy of ultimate condemnation.

Simon still had opportunity to repent. Peter, interestingly, did not guarantee forgiveness. If we had any question about Simon's spiritual condition earlier in the chapter, it is surely erased by verse 23. Apparently one can create a counterfeit response to the work of the Spirit, and for a professional like Simon, no problem at all. Whatever Simon understood of the gospel, he certainly didn't understand the grace of God. Furthermore, Luke speaks so clearly about the significance of the coming of the Spirit at Pentecost! Throughout Acts he wants to emphasize that God energizes the gospel exclusively by the power of the Holy Spirit in the lives of believers.

8:24. Understandably, Simon had no interest in perishing, especially when a new business of such promising lucrative dimensions lay before him. Let's not confuse his request for prayer with repentance. He fears the consequence, but we see no indication that he practices *metanoia* (repentance) which, as we have noted previously, means to turn around and go the other way.

8:25. Caught up in the excitement of the gospel in Samaria, Peter and John taught for a while in that city and then returned home, but not without stopping at **many Samaritan villages** on the way to proclaim the gospel. Something new has been added. This evangelistic mission, begun by a Hellenistic lay evangelist, was continued in Samaria by Hebraic Jews. Philip broke the ice, but Peter and John enjoyed the fishing.

Ⓓ Contrast in Evangelism (vv. 26-29)

SUPPORTING IDEA: *In God's value system, it matters not whether one's preaches to hundreds in a city or one in the desert. Faithfulness to call is the only issue.*

8:26. The southernmost of the five chief Philistine cities, Gaza lay about fifty miles southwest of Jerusalem. It was destroyed about 98 B.C. and then later rebuilt by Pompey. Philip, sent by an angel, would soon enter a new phase of ministry.

Surely the place and timing seemed inappropriate. Why would God move him from an area-wide evangelistic campaign just getting underway in Samaria, down to this lonely desert road? Luke wants us to see what the early Christians were really like. Contrast Philip with Jonah. Empowered by the Holy Spirit, this lay evangelist went wherever God sent. Philip was on his way to the end of the Palestinian world of that time. South and west of Gaza the desert trailed off across Sinai into Egypt. There was nothing.

8:27-28. Philip was in God's plan again and functioning through the Spirit. Gaza was not the target at all, but rather an Ethiopian eunuch, treasurer to the queen, on his way home from temple worship, presumably in an ox-drawn chariot. Both *eunuch* and *Candace* are probably government titles.

In that case the man probably was, like Nicolas in 6:5, a proselyte or full convert to Judaism. This would mean he was a Gentile who had embraced the Jewish religion and Scriptures which he now read. Some commentators believe that because Luke uses both *eunuch* and the title of *treasurer*, that the two terms mean different things: physical castration and political office. If that is the case, the Ethiopian could not have been a full participant in temple worship (Deut. 23:1) though he was certainly a full participant in God's promise (Luke 14:12–14).

8:29. How easy we find it to picture Philip plodding southward on that desert road, casually observing the common sight of a foreign visitor returning from Jerusalem and, in the custom of the day, reading aloud, this time from Isaiah 53. What might the evangelist have been thinking? Perhaps mixed emotions—the loneliness of the place, possibly regret at leaving the thriving effort in Samaria, and even a wish that this stranger could really understand the Messiah of whom the prophet had written.

Silent musings appealed neither to Philip nor Luke. This is an action story, and since an ox-drawn vehicle hardly moved at blazing speed, the Spirit can easily say to Philip, "Catch that chariot!"

Contact with the Target (vv. 30–35)

SUPPORTING IDEA: *When a willing Christian communicates the gospel to a prepared listener, spiritual miracles take place.*

8:30–31. Philip's question, doubtless placed in his mind by the Holy Spirit, illustrates a basic theme in Luke and Acts—how to find Jesus in the Old Testament. Luke had already written to Theophilus that Jesus is the key to understanding that ancient Scripture (Luke 24:45).

This problem has never disappeared. People caught up in religion of various kinds not only fail to understand the intricacies of their chosen religion, but make no connection between that dogma and God's genuine revelation through the Bible. Has there ever been a better invitation to proclaim the gospel than this? **He invited Philip to come up and sit with him**.

8:32–33. Imagine the exhilaration in Philip's heart as he realized why the Spirit had sent him to the desert. Here is a good man in need of grace, a serious searcher whose religion had not satisfied his quest for reality. God had prepared not only his heart but his mind. What better Old Testament text from which to preach Jesus than Isaiah 53:7–8. Indeed, it is so dramatic, Luke spells out the verses. This common messianic text in Judaism was hardly interpreted by the rabbis in light of God's suffering servant, an unthinkable concept in first-century Jewish theology.

Jesus had said repeatedly he had not come to wrest power from the Romans and build an earthly kingdom. "The Son of Man had not come to be served but to serve" (Mark 10:45) and even to die. This Christian interpretation of Isaiah Philip knew well. He was quite prepared to explain Jesus from this venerable text.

8:34–35. Not only did the eunuch invite Philip to sit with him and explain the text, but he asked the very questions that lead to an introduction of the Savior. Could Philip have begun somewhere in Deuteronomy or Job and explained the new covenant gospel to this man? Quite probably. God made it much easier. Jesus had repeatedly quoted portions of Isaiah 53 as being fulfilled in his death (Matt. 8:17; John 12:38; Luke 22:37), and the disciples certainly passed that information on to the Christians in the early church. With joy Philip explained, and with joy Luke recorded this good man hearing for the first time the **good news about Jesus**.

Can we conceive of a modern parallel to this incident? Picture yourself waiting in the departure lounge of an airport. A stranger sitting next to you has an open Bible on his lap. He may not be reading aloud, but his finger moves along the lines as he ponders the words. You glance over and discover he's in John 3 rapidly approaching verse 16. God prompts you to speak, and you say something like, "How unusual to find someone reading a Bible in an airport; isn't that third chapter wonderful?" The stranger turns to you and replies, "It is interesting; but I'm stumped on this sixteenth verse. What exactly does it mean to believe in Jesus and have eternal life?" Could you handle that situation without a seminary degree? Any serious Christian would offer a prayer of thanks and plunge in with a simple explanation of the gospel.

Convert in the Desert (vv. 36–40)

SUPPORTING IDEA: *God has ordained believer's baptism as a way of demonstrating that we have come to faith in his Son.*

8:36–37. We cannot know whether Philip closed his explanation of the gospel with a mention of baptism as he had heard Peter do earlier (2:38). Verse 12 indicates Philip clearly understood that baptism follows faith so he may have done that. Or, as a Jewish proselyte, the eunuch may have understood that when one places faith in God, water baptism symbolizes that internal act.

8:38. Luke seems to take pains to talk about going **down into the water** and coming **up out of the water**. Since the word *baptizo* always carries the idea of total immersion, we must assume that is what happened here. The focus of this passage is not baptism but the conversion of a black, non-Jewish official to Christ.

8:39–40. Even as they emerged from the water, a miracle occurred as the Spirit **took** Philip away. He disappeared immediately from the eunuch's vision. The word here is *herpasen*, a forceful and sudden action with no resistance. In this chapter only the Holy Spirit is more active than Philip. Leaving a rejoicing new Christian behind, Philip showed up at Azotus and continued evangelizing **in all the towns** as he made his way northward to Caesarea, where he apparently put down roots (Acts 21:8–9).

Luke's Gospel speaks often of joy (twenty-two times compared to thirteen in Matthew and three in Mark). We should not be surprised therefore that he emphasized a rejoicing treasurer on his way back to Ethiopia. Luke is carefully detailing the spread of the gospel. This double-barreled record of Philip's ministry is a potent part of Luke's gospel story. First, the gospel to the hated Samaritans, a half-breed race with distorted theology in the eyes of all good Palestinian Jews. Now, a Gentile secular official from a foreign land will take Jesus home with him. The church of Jesus Christ began sending missionaries to Africa almost two thousand years ago. The first was an African, a high government official, possibly a man with physical limitations.

MAIN IDEA REVIEW: *Leading other people to Christ requires that we be ready, unafraid, able to use God's Word, and filled with the Holy Spirit.*

III. CONCLUSION

Prototype of Lay Evangelism

Visionary evangelism has always been on the front lines of the progress of the church. Many other activities make up the full ministry and are no less important. In Philip we see a forerunner, someone who goes where others have never been and makes contact with people beyond the normal reach of the gospel. He was a true pioneer, a genuine missionary evangelist, though he never left his own country. Surely Luke wants us to see in this passage the significant contribution of a dynamic lay leader. Hovering over the entire text of Acts 8 is the role of the Holy Spirit. Philip's miraculous ministry and mobility depended on the Spirit's power at every point. Luke makes sure we understand that. If Stephen shows us a prototype of lay theology, Philip offers a prototype of lay evangelism.

Another theme runs through this fascinating chapter. People need not become Jews to become Christians. Just because the first Christians were Jews, that ethnic or religious connection did not carry over. True, the eunuch was probably a proselyte, but Luke emphasizes his Ethiopian connections much more strongly.

The major controversy of the first-century church centered around this basic question: "What do Gentiles need to do to become Christians?" If we do not feel fully satisfied in the answer from this chapter, Luke will come back to it in chapter 10 and especially in chapter 15 to make sure. Gentiles do not need to become Jews first; they move directly from whatever spiritual condition the gospel finds them to full status in the family of God through faith in Jesus Christ. Paul will tell us that more than once before we finish our study of this book.

PRINCIPLES

- God can do amazing things through an available layperson.
- Every believer should be ready to explain the gospel.
- The good news about Jesus is not limited to any ethnic or cultural group.
- All service for the Lord must be engendered and empowered by his Spirit.

APPLICATIONS

- Be ready to go any place for God at any time.
- Know your Bible well, and grow in your ability to use it.
- Don't minimize the importance of the Old Testament. Instead, know how to find Christ there as often as possible.
- Be ready to catch *your* chariot whenever and wherever it comes along.

IV. LIFE APPLICATION

A Gravestone in Olney

Born in 1725, John Newton was the son of a merchant sea captain. Enduring a difficult childhood and turbulent youth, he ran away from a forced tour of duty in the Royal Navy and became the slave of a white slave trader's black wife. During a storm at sea in 1747, he turned to God but continued in the slave trading business. Finally, in 1764 he became curate of the Olney Parish in Buckinghamshire and served there for fifteen years as an Anglican clergyman and hymn writer. We remember Newton well for songs like "Glorious Things of Thee Are Spoken," "How Sweet the Name of Jesus Sounds," and especially, "Amazing Grace."

When God took his servant home in 1807, friends wrote an epitaph for the gravestone in Olney. It reads, "John Newton; once an infidel and libertine, a servant of slaves in Africa, was by the rich mercy of our Lord and Savior Jesus Christ preserved, restored, pardoned, and appointed to preach the faith he had long labored to destroy."

Few modern Christians will have a testimony anything like that of John Newton, but the African connection between the eunuch of our text and this historic version of a slave trader reminds us again of the magnificent grace of God in their lives—and in ours.

What did these early believers do? They testified and proclaimed the gospel of Jesus wherever they went. Like Newton they had been touched "by the rich mercy of our Lord and Savior Jesus Christ," and like Newton they determined to share it with others.

Unlike Newton, however, and unlike the Ethiopian eunuch as well, it is hardly necessary to have some dramatic conversion story to serve Christ effectively. We can imagine the eunuch returning to Ethiopia enthralling his family and friends at court with the story of this amazing man he met in the desert whose message had changed his life. We know Newton repeatedly drew on illustrations of his past to demonstrate God's "Amazing Grace" in bringing people to himself.

Those of us who heard the gospel as children or committed our lives to Christ in Sunday school or perhaps at summer camp have no less right, no less authority, to proclaim God's message than did Philip, the eunuch, or John Newton. So many things in this chapter clamor for our attention today. Repeatedly I have emphasized *Philip's readiness and availability to God*. Yet that precise beginning of ministry so often eludes us in the busyness of modern life.

We surely see as well *Philip's acute understanding of the basics of Christianity*, his grasp of the centrality of Jesus Christ in the only Scripture he had, the Old Testament. Philip began at Isaiah 53, for the eunuch was reading there; but verse 35 seems to imply that he also introduced other texts to explain fully the message of Jesus. So many modern Christians own Bibles and carry them to church, but struggle to use them effectively in family worship, personal spiritual growth, and certainly in evangelism.

Finally, we can be as repetitious as Luke in emphasizing *the role of the Holy Spirit* in all this. What a combination—a willing servant, available Scripture, and the empowering Spirit. That combination is no less available today! There is no earthly or heavenly reason why Christians at the beginning of the twenty-first century cannot function in the same kind of vital witness we encounter in this magnificent record of Philip here in Acts 8.

V. PRAYER

God, wake up your church. Instill in us again the kind of zeal and vitality we see in these early Christians here in Acts. Give us both the burden for evangelism and the blessing of seeing others come to Christ through our efforts. Amen.

VI. DEEPER DISCOVERIES

A. The Samaritans (v. 5)

This interesting race of people lived on the northern border of Judea. The break between Jews and Samaritans dated back to 1000 B.C. when the ten tribes separated from Judea and Benjamin after Solomon's death. Their capital, Samaria, was destroyed by Sargon of the Assyrians in 722 B.C. At that time the mixed-blood population began because of the Assyrian practice of populating conquered areas with people of other conquered areas so that no unified racial group could rise up against them.

The final blow apparently occurred in 127 B.C. when John Hyrcanus led Jews in the destruction of the Gerizim temple and again, the city of Samaria. Herod offered to rebuild the temple in 25 B.C., but the Samaritans turned him down since he also intended to rebuild the temple at Jerusalem (which, of course, he did). Since the Samaritans never gave up their commitment to the Pentateuch and also their hope for Messiah, Philip had a connecting point to proclaim his message of a new covenant.

B. Simon (vv. 9–13)

What might Simon have meant by calling himself **the Great Power?** Possibly he claimed to be God himself, but more likely some great emissary from God who served as his primary spokesman and miracle worker in Samaria. Luke depicts him as a tinhorn charlatan with a bag of tricks, but extrabiblical sources suggest that his influence extended far further than that of a local magician. In the second century, Justin Martyr, himself a Samaritan, claimed that his countrymen revered Simon as a high god. Other second-century sources describe a Simon Magus whose heresy reached as far as Rome and whose teachings Peter was often required to refute. In the late second century, Tertullian talked about Simon, honored with a statue in Rome carrying the inscription "To Simon the holy god," though some scholars believe that was merely the misreading of another well-known statue to an ancient Sabine deity.

All of this is speculation of course, though the parallel between Luke's account in Acts 8 and traditional stories gathered one or two hundred years later cannot be ignored. Certainly we dare not conclude that because Simon refused grace and repentance in this chapter, he no longer posed any kind of threat or obstacle for the gospel in the years beyond.

C. Holy Spirit (vv. 15–17)

Christians have struggled with this time separation between accepting Christ and receiving the Spirit. Earlier we talked about this as an event, something not representative of common practice in the New Testament. Yet some Catholics argue this text is a basis for the separation between baptism and confirmation. Some modern charismatics see the baptism of the Holy Spirit as a second work of grace subsequent to salvation emanating from this passage.

Longenecker suggests that God may have designed this unique arrangement precisely because of the Samaritan context. He asks,

> What if the Spirit had come upon them at their baptism when administrated by Philip? Undoubtedly what feelings there were against Philip and the Hellenists would have carried over to them, and they would have been doubly under suspicion. But God in his providence withheld the gift of the Holy Spirit until Peter and John laid their hands on the Samaritans—Peter and John, two leading apostles who were highly thought of in the mother church at Jerusalem and who would have been accepted at that time as brothers in Christ by the new converts in Samaria. In effect, therefore, in this first advance of the gospel outside the confines of Jerusalem, God worked in ways that were conducive not only to the reception of the good news in Samaria but also to the acceptance of these new converts by believers at Jerusalem (Longenecker, 359).

D. Baptism (v. 37)

Bible students familiar with the King James text will pause at the NIV marginal reading for verse 36: "Some MSS add verse 37: Philip said, 'If you believe with all your heart, you may.' The eunuch answered, 'I believe that Jesus Christ is the Son of God.'" Scholars generally argue that it appears in the King James Version because Erasmus, a sixteenth-century scholar who produced his own translation of the Bible, included it. Generally speaking, however, the better manuscripts omit the verse, and consequently the NIV does not include it.

Polhill offers this suggestion as to why it appears in some manuscripts.

> Evidently a scribe felt this was lacking and so provided the missing confession of faith. He did not need to do so. Luke had summarized Philip's sharing the gospel with the eunuch in v. 35 and one can assume it included an appeal for the eunuch to respond. The eunuch's desire for baptism would indicate a favorable response to Philip's appeal. The added verse, however, has considerable value. It seems to embody a very early Christian baptismal confession where the one baptizing asked the candidate if he believed in Christ with all his heart, to which the candidate would respond by confessing Jesus Christ as the Son of God. This old confession has a real significance

to the history of early Christian confessions and would be appropriate to the baptismal ceremony today. To that extent we can be grateful to the pious scribe who ascribed to the eunuch the baptismal confession of his own day (Polhill, 226).

VII. TEACHING OUTLINE

A. INTRODUCTION
1. Lead story: Take My Factories
2. Context: In Acts 8 Luke has begun his transition from the containment of the gospel at Jerusalem to the spread of the gospel all over the Mediterranean world. He uses the stoning of Stephen as the springboard event but will now take us on to Saul and Cornelius before we actually find a church established in the Gentile city of Antioch (Acts 11).
3. Transition: We have already seen that God can use anyone available to him. That basic New Testament concept appeared in the slow-learning disciples who became apostles and then in the brilliance of the first martyr, Stephen. Now we see another ordinary man, selected to serve the Hellenistic widows, launched by God into citywide and then individual evangelism. As we enter the second quarter of our book, already the relevance of Acts for the church in our day jumps at us from every page.

B. COMMENTARY
1. Context of Philip's Ministry (vv. 1–8)
   a. Local persecution (vv. 1–3)
   b. Lay preaching (vv. 4–8)
2. Con Man in Samaria (vv. 9–19)
   a. Simon's profession of faith (vv. 9–13)
   b. Visit of Peter and John (vv. 14–17)
   c. Curse of simony (vv. 18–19)
3. Conflict between Truth and Error (vv. 20–25)
   a. Fitting rebuke (vv. 20–23)
   b. Faulty response (v. 24)
   c. Faithful representative (v. 25)
4. Contrast in Evangelism (vv. 26–29)
   a. On the road again (v. 26)
   b. In God's plan again (vv. 27–28)
   c. Through the Spirit again (v. 29)

5. Contact with the Target (vv. 30–35)
   a. Making the connection (vv. 30–31)
   b. Using the Bible (vv. 32–33)
   c. Explaining the gospel (vv. 34–35)
6. Convert in the Desert (vv. 36–40)
   a. Baptism follows faith (vv. 36–38)
   b. Rejoicing follows regeneration (v. 39)
   c. Philip follows the Spirit (v. 40)

C. CONCLUSION: A GRAVESTONE IN OLNEY

VIII. ISSUES FOR DISCUSSION

1. Is your church prone to concentrate on what is happening in the church rather than finding ways to scatter its members into God's harvest field? What can you do to encourage your church to be more evangelistic?
2. Does your church bring joy to your city? Why? Why not? What can you and your church do to help your city know the joy of the gospel?
3. How is money a source of temptation for you and your church? What do you and your church do to make sure that money is a holy resource and not a temptation?

Acts 9

God's Chosen Instruments

I. **Introduction**
Testimony of God's Call

II. **Commentary**
A verse-by-verse explanation of the chapter.

III. **Conclusion**
God's Little People
An overview of the principles and applications from the chapter.

IV. **Life Application**
Satan's Strategy Session
Melding the chapter to life.

V. **Prayer**
Tying the chapter to life with God.

VI. **Deeper Discoveries**
Historical, geographical, and grammatical enrichment of the commentary.

VII. **Teaching Outline**
Suggested step-by-step group study of the chapter.

VIII. **Issues for Discussion**
Zeroing the chapter in on daily life.

Q u o t e

"*S*alvation is moving from living death
to deathless life."

J a c k   O d e l l

GEOGRAPHICAL PROFILE: DAMASCUS

- Large commercial center of Syria
- One of the ten cities in region called "Decapolis" (Mark 5:20; 7:31)
- Contained a large Jewish population
- Located 150 miles northeast of Jerusalem

GEOGRAPHICAL PROFILE: TARSUS

- Capital of the province of Cilicia
- Center of a lumbering and linen industry
- University town steeped in Greek thought
- Located in southeastern portion of modern Turkey, about ten miles north of Mediterranean Sea

GEOGRAPHICAL PROFILE: JOPPA

- Ancient seaport for Jerusalem located thirty-five miles northwest of Jerusalem
- Known in Old Testament as Japho (Josh. 19:46) and today as Jappa or Haifa
- Only natural harbor between Egypt and Ptolemais
- Jonah's departing seaport (Jonah 1:3)

I N   A   N U T S H E L L

*T*his chapter contains the first of three accounts in Acts of Saul's conversion. That very repetition shows how important Luke considered this historical record. The chapter also includes the story of the raising of Dorcas through which Luke establishes Peter's ongoing importance in the church.

God's Chosen Instruments

I. INTRODUCTION

Testimony of God's Call

*C*hristians today appear to me to have a less-developed sense of God's call. My experience as a college student may have made me overly sensitive to this, and I certainly have no intention of reading my encounter with God into the lives of my students.

I had been a believer for most of my life, having placed faith in Christ at the age of six. That conversion, though quite real and definitive, had very little impact on day-by-day living through childhood, high school, and even the first two years at an outstanding Christian college. God often uses some kind of vehicle in a divine call; but, unlike Moses, mine was no burning bush event. Because of my interest and involvement in music, I was privileged after my sophomore year in college to travel in Europe with a male quartet from the college. Participating in three services a day in evangelistic tent campaigns around southern Germany, I became aware of a growing sense of confidence and joy in serving the Lord.

Only after I returned for my junior year at college did I experience a genuine *call*. Sitting in a Sunday morning worship service at a small church in central Indiana that September, I felt in my heart that God wanted me on church platforms instead of in church pews, proclaiming his Word in some way rather than following along while listening to someone else. No bells and whistles rang forth, no voices in the night, no chills or thrills while praying. Just an inner confidence that God had laid his hand on me for some kind of "ministry." Not until six years later did God thrust me into what has become my life work in theological education.

Not a dramatic story, hardly paralleling the experience of Saul on the Damascus Road. For one thing, he was called to salvation, then almost immediately to definitive service. Furthermore, here we see a fully-trained adult already practicing a religious vocation. The point of these paragraphs is not a favorable comparison between my meager experience and the drama of Acts 9, but an emphasis on the genuine biblical fact that God calls people *both* to salvation and to service.

We can go back as far as Genesis 12 to find God's specific call to Abraham, focusing on both geography and a covenantal promise. Then the Old Testament characters line up so fast we can hardly count them—Joseph, Moses, Joshua, Samuel, David, Elisha, and most of the prophets. In the New Testament God called Mary to bear Jesus. Jesus handpicked his disciples.

Now, in this chapter, we come to one of the most dramatic calls in the biblical record. Romans 11:29 tells us that God's gifts and his call are irrevocable. Paul opens his first letter to the Corinthians by telling them that he was **called to be an apostle of Christ Jesus** (1:1), a phrase he repeats various times in his letters.

A biblical sense of vocation cannot be limited to a formal public ministry. God calls some Christian teachers to serve in public education, others in Christian schools. Businessmen like R. G. LeTourneau have testified repeatedly that God called them to be effective in business and use their money and influence to advance the cause of Christ in the world. High school graduates sensitive to God's leading may be called to college "A" instead of college "B" and a few years later into a certain profession. Young mothers may sense God's call to quit a job and stay home to raise a new baby.

The form of the call is unimportant; a sovereign God surely reserves to himself the right to contact any of us as he chooses. An awareness of call, however, a sense of Christian vocation, must be present for effective godly living. In this chapter we encounter one of the most dramatic examples in history of what happens when God invades a person's life.

II. COMMENTARY

God's Chosen Instruments

MAIN IDEA: *God is now ready to appoint a highly trained, full-time missionary to the Gentiles. He selects Saul of Tarsus and changes his life to fit this role. Even the shorter narrative of Peter at the end of the chapter shows that very Jewish apostle taking the first step at the house of Simon, the tanner, from which God will also send him to a Gentile, Cornelius of Caesarea.*

Ⓐ Confrontation (vv. 1–9)

SUPPORTING IDEA: *God can call anyone he chooses to open new work for his kingdom.*

9:1–2. Tough and crafty, this young rabbi from Tarsus zealously wanted to exterminate Christians. He had no intention of letting the persecution of the church end with the death of Stephen and the expulsion of believers from Jerusalem. He obtained permission from the high priest and headed northeast to Damascus in Syria, intending to bring back as prisoners any Christians he might find. He had scheduled no random burning and looting but rather a sophisticated, officially authorized persecution.

Damascus was an important city, about six days journey on foot, and apparently a place to which many Christians had fled following the death of

Stephen. Furthermore, it appears that "extradition papers" from Jerusalem could be conveniently served in Damascus so Saul made this his first target, doubtless intending to follow up this campaign in many more cities.

The disciples were not called Christians until Antioch (Acts 11:26). The terminology here refers to them as followers of the Way, possibly taken from passages like John 14:6. This title occurs elsewhere in Acts (16:17; 18:25,26; 19:9,23; 22:4; 24:14,22).

Luke wants us to know this is not a roundup of men but a gender-inclusive persecution. Saul intended to arrest **any there who belonged to the Way** and bring them back to Jerusalem for imprisonment. The intensive ferocity of this young rabbi reminds us of the relentless Javier tracking down Jean Val Jean in the brilliant musical play *Les Miserables*. Both Javier and Saul considered themselves righteous representatives of the righteous. In reality, both intended to imprison those more righteous than they.

9:3–4. Saul had nearly completed the six-day journey as he approached Damascus, 175 miles northeast of Jerusalem, the second oldest city in the world still in existence (Tarsus is the oldest). Now God turned a mission of hate into a message from heaven. Saul saw a light and heard a voice from heaven; for a devout Jew, this would always mean a word from God.

This was no ordinary light. Remember it shone at midday (22:6). Saul describes it as **a light from heaven, brighter than the sun** (26:13). The various accounts of this event suggest that only Saul understood the message from heaven although those with him heard the sound. The Greek word for "voice" (*phone*) supports that idea since it means both sound and specific articulated speech. The question from heaven must have stunned Saul into disbelief. Persecuting God? He was doing exactly the reverse—persecuting those who blasphemed God.

9:5–6. The Greek *kyrios* could mean "sir." Some have suggested that Saul used that innocuous and polite form of address. More likely (in view of light and sound coming down from above), he meant to say, "Lord" in a worshipful way. He could never have prepared himself for the answer to his question: **I am Jesus, whom you are persecuting.** Before he could recover from that shock he received new orders to **go into the city**, the first of many commands from Christ this man would obey. In Saul's view, one of the worst aspects of Christian blasphemy had been their claim that Jesus of Nazareth was alive; now he must face this reality.

The Lord imparted to his newly-chosen one a new faith, a new interpretation of the Old Testament, a new perspective on divine redemption, a new eschatology, a new identification with followers of the Way, and a new mission for his life. To be sure, all of that would unfold in the weeks, months, and years ahead, but it began precisely at this moment on the Damascus Road.

9:7–9. Apparently Luke thought it important to emphasize the role of Paul's traveling companions. Their sharing in this experience authenticated it historically and objectively. No one could ever accuse the young Pharisee of creating a fictitious account or merely reporting some emotional trauma. Of course, emotional trauma was very much a part of the experience, for the valiant persecutor pulled himself from the ground in a state of physical, sociological, and spiritual shock. Some have suggested that the blindness was a physical outcome of pyschological stress. That might be inferred from the text, but the blindness may well have been a sign from God, a symbol of the darkness in which this man had been walking so that light to his eyes will soon coordinate with light to his soul.

In any case, Luke painted an accurate picture of a proud and ruthless man now broken and helpless. Although Saul would certainly have been familiar with fasting as a means of developing a spiritual analysis of what had happened to him, Luke does not seem to suggest that as the reason. Quite possibly he was totally devastated by this experience and unable to ingest either food or liquid.

🅱 Sanctification (vv. 10–19a)

SUPPORTING IDEA: *God not only selects and calls people who will serve him in a visible and public way, but also those who support that work behind the scenes—like the little known Ananias of Damascus.*

9:10–12. I once met a man who knew of his need for Christ and seemed quite ready to give his life to the Savior. He drove five hundred miles just to do that in a Billy Graham Crusade rather than in his home church, or in a bedroom, or even the backyard. His motives were never in doubt to me; he just had a great appreciation for Dr. Graham's ministry.

How unlike God's way of doing things that choice seems. Think of the dramatic follow-up the Sovereign Lord could have designed from the opening overture on the Damascus Road. Why not take Saul back to Jerusalem for a public declaration of faith on the steps of the temple or perhaps in front of the Sanhedrin in the very room where Stephen made his defense? Or maybe back to Tarsus, that ancient city with a significant Jewish population, likely proud of its young rabbi serving so effectively in Jerusalem. Not God. God sent Saul to the humble home of a humble servant whose name appears only twice in Acts, here and in Paul's account of this event in chapter 22.

The spotlight shifts momentarily to Ananias (obviously no connection with the Ananias of chapter 5) who lived on Straight Street. Leave it to Luke to offer a little chronological and geographical notation to carry along his history. He tells us about Saul's vision not in connection with Saul, but in God's report to Ananias. Straight Street, by the way, is still a main thoroughfare in Damascus now known as Derb Le-Mustaquim.

The dialog throughout this part of the chapter indicates that conversations with both Saul and Ananias are coming directly from Jesus, not from the Father. That becomes particularly clear in verses 14–16.

Let's not lose sight of the fact that we have no Peter and John here as we did in chapter 8. No apostles were sent scurrying from Jerusalem to connect a future apostle with their succession from the Lord. Indeed, no apostle would have greater impact for Christ in the Mediterranean world over the next few years than this blind and broken Pharisee. Still, he never formed any serious bond with the Jerusalem church. God is not in the business of religious ritual and ecclesiastical rigmarole; he focuses on regeneration and sanctification.

We call this portion of our study *sanctification* because that word means a setting apart for the purposes of God, precisely what happened in this passage.

The justification for sending Ananias seems to rest in the phrase **for he is praying**. Luke picks up on this repeatedly throughout this book, also depicting Saul as a man of prayer (16:25; 20:36; 22:17) much in the way he has already shown Jesus at prayer in his Gospel (Luke 3:21; 6:12; 9:18,28; 11:1; 22:41).

9:13–16. Ananias wasted no time in expressing reluctance. Saul's reputation had preceded him to the Christians in Damascus; they even knew his mission. We should read no rebuke nor critique of Ananias by Luke or by Jesus in this passage. This normal human response seems no more negative than that expressed by the Jerusalem church later in the chapter. Ananias did not say (like Jonah) that he wouldn't go, simply that he had a few reservations about his safety in answering this call.

Notice another fascinating development here. Whereas Saul, the unbeliever, was absolutely shocked to hear even a few words from the mouth of Jesus, Ananias seems to enter comfortably into conversation as though he were speaking to a member of his family. We can assume that in the vision he actually saw Jesus, and the dialog, though brief, took place in great reality. Interesting, too, that he refers to the believers at Jerusalem as "saints," a first reference of its kind to Christians in Acts.

Verse 15 holds the key to the chapter, for it identifies not only the fact of God's call but its intended purpose. One could argue that in one verse Luke has laid the foundation for everything he will tell us in the remaining chapters of this book. Some may think that Paul later deviated from the plan of proclaiming salvation in Jesus only to Jews when he dashed out on a mission to the Gentiles. We see here in Acts 9:15 that God himself changed the church's strategy of evangelism, and that a humble Christian by the name of

Ananias knew it before Paul had the slightest inkling of what lay ahead in his life. God had chosen a vessel (Rom. 1:1,5; 9:24; Gal. 1:15–16; Eph. 3:7–13), and that vessel would carry the name of Jesus and his message to Gentiles, as well as to Jews.

9:17–19a. Ever the obedient servant, Ananias not only went to the house on Straight Street, but he also acknowledged Saul's conversion by addressing him as **Brother Saul.** His message was brief but just as clear as a sparkling planet observed from the blackness of an Arabian Desert.

- Jesus appeared to you on the road.
- Jesus sent me here.
- Jesus will give your sight back.
- Jesus will fill you with the Holy Spirit.

After entering the city, Saul had seen a vision, and so had Ananias. The experience out on the road *was no vision*, but a direct and personal encounter with Jesus. Paul based his apostleship on the fact that he had seen and talked with the Lord (1 Cor. 9:1; 15:8). As Ananias spoke one sentence, flaky scales fell from Saul's eyes, and he received believer's baptism in the manner of all who have come to the Lord in Acts. Thereby he identified with all the Christians in Jerusalem, Samaria, Damascus, Ethiopia, and wherever else the gospel had gone. Only after his baptism did he break his fast and get back his strength. Somewhere in these few minutes (or perhaps even seconds), God filled Saul of Tarsus with the Holy Spirit, now a normative experience at the time of regeneration. The variance in Acts 8 and again in 19:1–7 represent exceptions to the biblical pattern.

An old story tells about a little boy in Sunday school whose teacher asked what part he played in his salvation. He responded that his conversion had been partly God's work and partly his own. An astounded and rather nervous teacher inquired about that strange answer until the boy replied, "I opposed God all I could, and he did the rest." Such was the experience of Saul of Tarsus. Former rabbi. Former persecutor. Former agent of the high priest. Now Luke will tell us what lies ahead.

C Proclamation (vv. 19b–25)

SUPPORTING IDEA: *The change in conversion is directly related to the distance the new believer placed between himself and God. In this case, one who had spoken publicly against the name of Jesus now proclaims it at every opportunity.*

9:19b–22. Luke's account might be a bit sketchy here because of his unique purpose for Theophilus and his awareness that believers would read Paul's various accounts of his conversion, particularly in the letter to the church at Galatia. He seems to emphasize that Paul went right to work proclaiming the Savior whom he had so recently condemned. In just a few days the center of his message developed: **Jesus is the Son of God**.

Saul was no stranger to synagogues, so they became his initial point of witness. The theme, however, is interesting, since only here in Acts do we see Jesus proclaimed as the Son of God, though Paul comes back to the theme in 13:33 by quoting from Psalm 2. Old Testament usage of this phrase usually referred to Israel (Exod. 4:22; Hos. 11:1) though the Psalm 2 passage clearly centers on the Messiah. There was no question what Saul meant by that terminology; he used it synonymously with the claim that Jesus is the Messiah (v. 22). Surely this had been a hated theme in Stephen's defense, and yet the new Christian immediately grasped its truth.

Certainly we can understand the bewilderment of the Jews in Damascus at this unexpected turn of events. They had anticipated a raging bull persecutor to clean the Christians out of their city. The Christians there were no less bewildered as they saw Saul standing with them and extolling their Savior. Though just a few days surround this account, Luke wants us to know that Saul began immediately to grow in his understanding of the Christian faith and his capability of publicly **proving that Jesus is the Christ**.

9:23–25. Most scholars believe that Luke's **many days** may have been as long as three years. We will deal with that in "Deeper Discoveries." Now the hunter became the hunted. The Jews wanted Saul dead; so they developed a conspiracy to achieve that end. In 2 Corinthians 11:32–33 we learn that Aretas IV, king of the Nabataean Arabs in Damascus, assisted the Jews in their plot and actually helped them set up the guards on the city gates.

Saul already had converts as the result of his ministry, and **his followers** helped him escape. Paul reviewed this incident in his second letter to the Corinthian church to demonstrate the humiliation he experienced for the name of Christ. The planned triumphal and powerful entrance into Damascus with the authority of the high priest ended with a Christian fugitive being lowered over the walls, just a basket case for Jesus.

Ⓓ Affiliation (vv. 26–31)

SUPPORTING IDEA: *Christians cannot and should not expect that other Christians will always agree with them and accept them, especially if their preconversion lifestyle was odious to the church.*

9:26–27. Persecuted minority movements learn caution and can be quite defensive. Surely by this time word of Saul's conversion had come back to Jerusalem; but when he tried to join that church, they wanted no part of this fearsome murderer they knew all too well. Despite the effectiveness of his message in Damascus, Saul found no welcome in Jerusalem.

Enter Barnabas. By the second mention of this good man in Acts, he has already earned the nickname "Son of Encouragement." He extended that special ministry gift of encouragement to Saul. Perhaps he just naturally befriended other believers despite their sordid pasts. From Galatians 1:17–19 we learn that Saul quickly met Peter and James, the Lord's half-brother, apparently already a leader in the Jerusalem church. We should not confuse this James with James the brother of John or any of the Twelve. We shall meet him again in chapter 15.

9:28–30. Fully accepted by both Hellenistic and Palestinian Christians in Jerusalem, Saul developed a familiarity with the believers there and continued to speak boldly in the name of the Lord. Notice in verse 29 that he picked up the work of Stephen in ministering to Hellenistic Jews; but, like those in Damascus, they, too, tried to kill him. Remember, Saul was not a Jerusalemite Jew; he was from Tarsus in modern Turkey. Perhaps he felt more comfortable among these Greek-speaking residents of the city; quite possibly this particular ministry to an ethnic minority had been neglected in recent years.

In Luke's narrative the departure from Jerusalem was contrived by the church there. Perhaps partly for his own protection and partly because they didn't want another Stephen incident, they decided to send Saul north to Philip's town, Caesarea, and then back home to Tarsus. In Acts 22:17–21, however, Paul claims that during this visit he received a vision of Jesus telling him to leave Jerusalem because God wanted to send him to the Gentiles. These are not conflicting ideas since both could have occurred somewhat simultaneously.

Saul leaves the Acts narrative for a short time. His public ministry was confined to Tarsus for nearly ten years. We can assume from what Luke tells us that this return trip (9:30) placed Paul in his native city until Barnabas went there to retrieve him in chapter 11.

9:31. Usually in Acts, *ekklesia* describes a local congregation such as Ephesus or Philippi. Here we find one of the few times where Luke uses the word *church* in the universal sense. Obviously he intended to speak of all the Christian congregations, now enjoying a respite from persecution, a time of growth, strengthening, and encouragement. This verse is a typical Lucan summary of which we have already seen several and shall see several more. Some call this break between verses 31 and 32 the end of Act II in Acts. A brief review of 5:42 indicates a similar concluding verse, suggesting there the end of Act I.

From the three thousand people who trusted Christ in 2:41, to the additional believers trusting Christ daily in 2:47, the multitude of new believers in 5:14, and the increase of disciples in 6:7, we now learn that the church still continued to grow throughout the entire land of Palestine. This is the only mention in Acts of Christians in Galilee, but their presence in that province should not surprise us. It was Jesus' home and the site of much of his ministry.

What kept Saul away from the gospel for so long? Joseph of Arimathea and Nicodemus had believed, and it's certainly not unlikely that Saul had seen and heard Jesus personally as well. We know from his own words that his deep commitment to Pharisaical Judaism caused him to choke at the mention of a Messiah from Nazareth. Beyond that, we sense in 1 Corinthians 1:18 that he simply could not get around the cross. Even if he had opportunity to observe a miracle or two and perhaps listen to Jesus' explanation of the Old Testament, which would have been impressive to an intelligent rabbi, the thought of a Messiah on the cross turned the stomachs of Jews.

Does not the same problem plague unbelievers today? Many are happy to talk about God, even a personal God who, they anticipate, will welcome them into his heaven someday. The introduction of Jesus as the virgin-born Son of Mary complicates their thinking just a bit. By the time the gospel portrays him dying on the cross for the sins of the world, many now, as then, turn away from a suffering Savior.

Restoration (vv. 32–35)

SUPPORTING IDEA: *Everything that Christians do and say centers in the name and power of Jesus Christ.*

9:32. Here we have another one of Luke's "meanwhile" passages. Did we think he had forgotten Peter now that he had begun the Pauline narrative? Certainly not. He depicts that faithful Christian as a traveling minister visiting Christians in the town of Lydda, about twenty-five miles northwest of Jerusalem. Geography is very important to Luke and very important in the study of Acts. We have already seen the gospel travel by chariot to Ethiopia and by persecutor to Damascus, so two other "foreign countries" are already involved. Furthermore, all three provinces of Palestine have congregations (v. 31), so the great commission began to move well beyond the boundaries of Jerusalem and its suburbs.

Today the international airport of Israel in Lod sits on a site very close to this ancient town. Here again we find the word **saints** which we encountered in 9:13. Paul will use it again in 26:10, but it is not a common word for Luke.

How had the gospel come to Lydda? Certainly we could assume that the persecuted Christians described at the beginning of Acts 8 took the gospel to any place we shall find it for the rest of Acts. More likely, however, this group of believers bears the fingerprint of Philip, that coastal evangelist who made his way from Gaza in the south to Caesarea in the north and therefore could very well have included Lydda when he passed through Joppa just a few miles away.

9:33. Most scholars assume Aeneas was a member of the Christian community, and the context would support that. Finding a lame man who needed healing was no novel experience for Peter, and one would guess he felt considerably more comfortable than he did back in chapter 3. This man was not only lame, however, but paralyzed.

9:34. We find no evidence that Aeneas made any request at all. Peter, acting upon the prompting of the Holy Spirit, simply says, **Jesus Christ heals you**. This verb could be rendered, "This moment, even as we speak, Jesus Christ is healing you." The additional command, **Get up** and arrange your things could refer to preparing a meal or just gathering his mat. Likely, Luke intends the latter, especially when we remember similar situations in Jesus' ministry where comparable terminology appears (Mark 2:11; Luke 5:24).

9:35. The report of this miracle spread widely. Luke tells us virtually everyone learned about it. We want to come back to Luke's use of **all**, but here we simply assume a wide report including not only the immediate city of Lydda, but on across the plain of Sharon which stretched from Joppa to Carmel and centered in Caesarea.

▣ Demonstration (vv. 36–43)

SUPPORTING IDEA: *God loves and uses ordinary Christians whose lives may seem to reflect no excitement, no travel, and no fame. Dorcas demonstrates that kind of ministry.*

9:36. "Meanwhile," in a city nearby lived a female disciple. This bears emphasis because here we find the only New Testament use of *mathetria (disciple)*, the feminine form of the word *mathetras*. Obviously, she was not the only female disciple, but this is the only time Luke so designates a woman. Luke translated her Aramaic name *(Tabitha)* into Greek *(Dorcas)* for Theophilus. Both names mean "gazelle."

This is certainly not a passage on spiritual gifts to parallel Romans 12; 1 Corinthians 12; Ephesians 4; or 1 Peter 4; but one hardly needs to stretch to see this woman utilizing her spiritual gift. Barnabas certainly had the gift of exhortation; Philip, the gift of evangelism; Saul, the gift of teaching; and here we see Dorcas practicing the gift of helps or service (Rom. 12:7). She was a "do-gooder" in the very best sense of that word, especially since she focused her ministry on the poor. If Dorcas was a single woman (the text does not tell us), we have a wonderful demonstration of a life given to service. It certainly would appear that she had special standing with the widows (v. 39) and, therefore, may well have been a widow herself.

9:37. Luke simply tells the story as it happened—**she became sick and died.** Rather than anointing her body for burial, the believers washed it and placed it in a room. Normally, no corpse would lay overnight between death and burial, but plans to call Peter may have already been in mind.

9:38. Peter was only three hours away by foot, the miracle at Lydda certainly well-known in Joppa, so why not ask that great apostle to make the trip—**at once.** We find no certainty of their expectation, but Luke's description of the appeal certainly makes it sound as though they anticipated a resurrection.

9:39. The idea of expected resurrection takes on further strength in this verse as we see Peter standing by the body, surrounded by widows weeping in their grief and holding up the garments Dorcas had made for them. The text seems to imply they simply could not let a good woman like this depart from their Christian community. She had so demonstrated godliness and servanthood, they desperately wanted her back.

Notice that this woman, so generous in life, was also devout in death. Here as always that enemy brought grief, fear, and regret. It also provided an opportunity for Dorcas to model Christian dignity, for the widows to show their love and faith, and for Peter to demonstrate God's power. Let's assume these dear ladies had also told Dorcas how much they loved her while she still lived. Whether they had or had not, that surely should be a significant lesson for us.

9:40. Raising people from the dead was hardly a common feature of any ministry, including that of Jesus. In three and a half years Jesus had only raised three people from the dead, but Peter had seen all three. Perhaps here he remembered the incident with Jarius' daughter (Mark 5:21–24,35–43). There Jesus had sent mourners out of the room and prayed. There Jesus had spoken a phrase which varied in only one letter from the Aramaic command Peter uttered here to Dorcas—Jesus' *"talitha kumi"* now becomes Peter's *"Tabitha kumi."*

As in the three resurrections Jesus performed, the raising of Dorcas was not resurrection in the technical sense of immortality. Yet our English word *resuscitation,* used commonly to describe bringing people back to consciousness, hardly seems strong enough. Dorcas died, and she would die again. Peter provided a temporary restoration to life for this lovely Christian woman at Joppa.

9:41–42. The results of this miracle? Believers rejoiced, and the unsaved believed. Every resurrection described in the Bible pictures our future. Just as Jesus' resurrection represented the final seal of God's approval on his life and work, so the resurrection of Christians whether past or future is God's ultimate approval of their faith. Like Jesus' gift of her son's life to the widow of Nain (Luke 7:15), so here Peter gave the widows back their friend and helper. Word of the risen Dorcas led many to faith in the risen Lord.

9:43. This hinge verse connects Peter on the maritime plain and Cornelius at Caesarea. Peter moves ever closer to that next episode which Luke will describe in chapter 10. A tanner's house, of course, would have been unclean to rabbis, but Peter was not over-zealous to maintain strict Jewish ritual, despite his protestation in the vision of chapter 10. Of significant importance here is the precise location, a house to which the messengers of Cornelius could be sent with some precision.

A quick glance at the map of first-century Palestine will show how God is moving Peter out of Jerusalem ever closer to Caesarea where he, not Paul, will be the first to take the gospel directly to a Gentile.

MAIN IDEA REVIEW: *God is now ready to appoint a highly trained, full-time missionary to the Gentiles. He selects Saul of Tarsus and changes his life to fit this role. Even the shorter narrative of Peter at the end of the chapter shows that very Jewish apostle taking the first step at the house of Simon, the tanner, from which God will send him also to a Gentile, Cornelius of Caesarea.*

III. CONCLUSION

God's Little People

Everyone knows Acts 9 is about the conversion of Saul. It would be inappropriate to minimize that great historical event. We should see here as well two other servants who get almost as much "press" as the rabbi from Tarsus. The hitherto unknown disciple named Ananias seems just as important in verses 10–19 as the one to whom he ministers. The final eight verses focus on Dorcas, another virtually anonymous Christian.

These stories can give us a new look at God's priorities. How caught up North American Christianity seems to be with public visibility and vocal celebrities. How megachurches and syndicated television broadcasts seem to dwarf the dogged faithfulness of people like Ananias and Dorcas or their contemporary spiritual kin. There will be ample time for Paul to thunder his gospel of grace through Asia Minor and on into Greece. Along the way, Luke makes us stop for a moment and look at the little people, the ordinary Christians who make the gospel work in their communities despite the absence of applause and recognition in the wider world.

PRINCIPLES

- God reserves the right to interrupt anyone's life whether by conversion for ministry or in death.
- The gospel must be acted upon. Hearing it, even firsthand, as Saul did from Stephen, may have no effect at all or perhaps even the opposite effect from that intended.
- Simple quiet service for God is no less important than complex public service.
- God can bring or remove persecution to his church anytime he chooses.

APPLICATIONS

- Be ready. When you least expect it, God may call on you for some very special task.
- When God has chosen a person, we have no basis to reject that one.
- When faced with a difficult ministry task, pray first.
- Sometimes God may choose to intervene in a miraculous way in order to give Christians a loved one back.

IV. LIFE APPLICATION

Satan's Strategy Session

As the story goes, Satan had called a meeting of his senior demons, a strategy session with the particular intent of devising new ways to keep people from trusting Jesus Christ for salvation. With a series of clever overhead transparencies the boss explained the dilemma—too many leaving the fold of darkness and choosing to follow the giver of light.

When he opened the meeting for discussion, he precisely asked the demons to suggest concrete ways they could act on earth to choke off these despised "conversions" in some effective way. The first volunteer proposed, "Tell them there is no God." That suggestion fell on deaf ears, for the demons knew well that many choosing to remain in the fold of darkness would never sink far enough to adopt such a ludicrous idea.

The second speaker offered, "Tell them the Bible is not true." This provoked several minutes of discussion because such a tactic had been used with some success down through the years and the idea of elevating it to a long-range strategic plan seemed to incur some favor.

Tabling the idea for a moment, the chairman heard yet a third suggestion which immediately brought a diabolic smile to all the faces at the meeting:

"Tell them it's all true, and even tell them they need to be saved—but not now." Some might believe there is no God. A greater number reject the authority of the Scripture. This delaying tactic, this intent to cause well-meaning people to procrastinate any choice on the gospel, to put off turning to Jesus until too late, this could work with untold millions.

As the story goes, the demons approved suggestion three, and the chairman declared the meeting adjourned.

Fictitious nonsense to be sure, though Satan's legions have probably used all three tactics with great success to keep people chained in darkness. Here is a chapter about light. The light of Jesus shining from heaven on Saul. The light of Ananias openly receiving his new "brother" and assisting him to faith. The light of Peter traveling to visit saints, healing and raising them as he went. The light of Dorcas caring for those who could not care for themselves.

We should see ourselves in this chapter, perhaps more than once. Some of us may have had dramatic conversion experiences. Others may feel neglected, unnoticed by fellow Christians as we try to serve God faithfully wherever he has placed us. Please notice our title again, especially the appearance of the last word in the plural. Yes, Saul was now God's chosen instrument, but so was Ananias, and Peter, and Dorcas. Christians should not try to be somebody else nor to do what God has called someone else to do. God calls and gifts us to be ourselves, even if those selves do not look much like the popular models of a particular era, place, or denomination.

V. PRAYER

God, thank you for the gifts you've given us. May we generously use them in the service of others like the brothers and sister of this chapter. Amen.

VI. DEEPER DISCOVERIES

A. Missing Phrase (v. 4)

Bible readers familiar with Paul's testimony in Acts 26:14 will notice the absence of the phrase **it is hard for you to kick against the goads** from Luke's account in Acts 9. New Testament scholars find general agreement that the phrase was added to Acts 9 on the strength of its appearance in Acts 26. The words appear in the Western Text and, therefore, in the King James Version; but the best available manuscripts do not include it in our chapter. This is a similar situation to the phrase we discussed in 8:37.

B. Gentiles (v. 15)

In the Old Testament we find Jews and Gentiles demonstrating peaceful coexistence and even intermarrying (for example, Rahab, Ruth, Bathsheba). By the New Testament era, however, hostility between Jews and Gentiles seems complete. Hundreds of years of persecution had totally embittered the nation of Israel which now hated everything Gentile and avoided contact completely. Jesus limited his own ministry to Jews with only rare exceptions (John 4:1–42; Matt. 15:21–28; John 12:20–36). Clearly, the gospel went first to the Jew and only later to the Gentiles as Paul reminds us in Romans 1. The division of all humankind into two classes—Jew and Gentile—was no longer acceptable now that the gospel had permeated the Gentile world. Paul will repeatedly write about the breaking down of that wall and the unity of all ethnic believers in Christ (Rom. 1:16; 1 Cor. 1:24; Gal. 3:28; Eph. 2:14; Col. 3:11).

C. Arabia (vv. 22–23)

In Galatians 1:17 Paul talks about a period of time spent in Arabia, and most scholars fit those three years between verses 22 and 23 of Acts 9. This was the kingdom of the Nabateans stretching east and south from Damascus. Like Moses, Saul apparently spent time in the wilderness before coming full force in his service for God. Surely we have no difficulty picturing him rethinking the Scriptures, developing the christological hermeneutic of the Old Testament for which he became so famous, receiving new revelation from the Lord, and getting his theology in general New Covenant order.

D. Luke's Use of "All" (v. 35)

Though the writing styles of the ancients were certainly considerably different from our own, they enjoyed some of the same configuration of language we still find useful today. One of these is *hyperbole*, a deliberate exaggeration to make a point. Paul used hyperbole on occasion, but Luke honed it to an art, especially in his use of the word *all* (*pas*). In fact, Luke does this so commonly that we can only select a few examples, perhaps those we have already seen.

1:19	Everyone in Jerusalem heard about this.
2:5	God-fearing Jews from every nation under heaven.
3:9	All the people saw him walking.
4:16	Everybody living in Jerusalem knows.
5:34	Gamaliel . . . was honored by all the people.
8:40	Philip preached the gospel in all the towns.

We must recognize that Luke's use of a literary style, one that we would use commonly today, in no way minimizes the integrity of the text. He is neither ignorant of the facts nor deliberately lying—he simply uses hyperbole to emphasize that these things were very wide spread. In the case of 9:35, many people saw the healed paralytic. First-century readers would not have assumed from this verse that every person living in the vast plain of Sharon had actually laid eyes on this man. Nor did Luke intend them to.

VII. TEACHING OUTLINE

A. INTRODUCTION
1. Lead story: Testimony of God's Call
2. Context: Chapter 8 ends with Philip in Caesarea, and chapter 10 will open with Cornelius in that same city. To make the connection, Luke found it necessary to introduce the conversion of Saul and the travels of Peter. The introduction of three characters since the death of Stephen (Philip, Saul, and Peter) pave the way for the drama he will unfold in the next chapter.
3. Transition: Any doubts about the life change God can produce in people should no longer plague us. Paul later claimed to be the worst of sinners. Whether he was or not, this story may well show us the best of God's grace.

B. COMMENTARY
1. Confrontation (vv. 1–9)
   a. Mission of hate (vv. 1–2)
   b. Message from heaven (vv. 3–9)
2. Sanctification (vv. 10–19a)
   a. God sends Ananias (vv. 10–16)
   b. God selects Saul (vv. 17–19a)
3. Proclamation (vv. 19b–25)
   a. Evangelism in Damascus (vv. 19–22)
   b. Escape in a basket (vv. 23–25)
4. Affiliation (vv. 26–31)
   a. A friend in Jerusalem (vv. 26–27)
   b. A visit to Tarsus (vv. 28–31)
5. Restoration (vv. 32–35)
   a. Travel of encouragement (vv. 32–33)
   b. Miracle in Lydda (vv. 34–35)
6. Demonstration (vv. 36–43)
   a. Demonstration of Christian service (v. 36)
   b. Demonstration of Christian death (vv. 37–39)
   c. Demonstration of Christian resurrection (vv. 40–43)

C. CONCLUSION: SATAN'S STRATEGY SESSION

VIII. ISSUES FOR DISCUSSION

1. Has God ever told you to wait for instructions? How do you react to having to wait on God?

2. Do your church leaders need someone like Barnabas to do the behind-the-scenes work and encourage others? What type of work would such a person do in your church? Might God be calling you to such work?

3. Who is a Dorcas role model in your church, always helping people in need? How is this role part of God's evangelism team? Is God calling you to be the Dorcas in your church?

Acts 10

No Favoritism Allowed!

I.   Introduction
Vision for the Future

II. Commentary
A verse-by-verse explanation of the chapter.

III. Conclusion
Pioneering the Gospel
An overview of the principles and applications
from the chapter.

IV. Life Application
Motivation to Go
Melding the chapter to life.

V.   Prayer
Tying the chapter to life with God.

VI. Deeper Discoveries
Historical, geographical, and grammatical enrichment
of the commentary.

VII. Teaching Outline
Suggested step-by-step group study of the chapter.

VIII. Issues for Discussion
Zeroing the chapter in on daily life.

"*The* Gospel is neither a discussion nor a debate.
It is an announcement."

Paul   S.   Rees

GEOGRAPHICAL PROFILE: CAESAREA

- Roman capital of the province of Judea
- Sixty-five miles northwest of Jerusalem
- Named in honor of Caesar Augustus
- Built by Herod the Great between 25 and 13 B.C.
- Military headquarters for Roman forces

IN A NUTSHELL

After leading up to this moment in Luke's history of the church, he drops the bombshell—the gospel will go to the Gentiles. Reason? Because God shows no favoritism; in the message of the New Covenant, whosoever will may come.

No Favoritism Allowed!

I. INTRODUCTION

Vision for the Future

In his book *A Savior for All Seasons*, William Barker describes a bishop from the east coast who visited a small midwestern religious college many years ago. While there, he stayed at the home of the president who also served on the faculty as professor of physics and chemistry.

During their stimulating after-dinner discussion, the bishop mentioned his confidence that the millennium could not be far off because just about everything about nature had been discovered and virtually anything one could imagine had been invented. What further reason could the Lord have for delaying his return?

Politely but firmly, the young college president disagreed suggesting that many more discoveries and certainly many more inventions lay around the next scientific corner. Somewhat angered, the bishop challenged the younger man to name just one invention he anticipated seeing in the future. The president replied that he was quite certain that within fifty years, men would be able to fly.

"Nonsense!" sputtered the outraged bishop, "only angels are intended to fly."

That bishop's name was Wright. At home he had two boys who loved to tinker with things and were fascinated by the sky. Two boys with significantly greater vision for the future than their father. Their names were Orville and Wilbur.

We continue to study a very "visionary" part of Acts. In chapter 9 both Saul and Ananias had visions. In chapter 10 Cornelius and Peter have visions. The use of *vision* in the broader sense is really the focus of this chapter. Acts 10:1–11:18 is the longest narrative in the book, so to understand this passage we must use the *principle of proportion*. This principle for interpreting Scripture claims that God invests longer portions of Scripture in happenings or teachings he considers highly important. In 9:32 Peter seemed quite content to travel **about the country.** He rendered significant service to believers and continued to witness to the gospel. In this narrative Peter became a visionary leader in the church. God broke into Peter's increasingly comfortable life to thrust him out beyond the boundaries of Israel, into the Roman town of Caesarea . . . right into the house of a Gentile.

We need at this point to review four considerations helpful in interpreting what lies ahead:

1. The early church resisted any acceptance of Gentiles and even efforts to evangelize among Gentiles (10:14,28; 11:2,3,8).
2. God himself introduced Gentiles into the church (10:3,11–16; 11:5–10,13,15–17).
3. Peter, not Paul, was the human instrument in reaching the first Gentile (10:23,34–43; 11:15–17).
4. The church subsequently accepted Gentiles apart from any allegiance to Judaism (11:18).

Why does this chapter hold importance for us? Because the vast majority of Christians in the world today are not Jews. This chapter treats the question of what we must do to become Christians. Even before asking that, the church had to ask, Can Gentiles come to Christ at all? We shall see this again throughout Paul's ministry and especially in Acts 15. Here is the beginning, the first foray into a genuinely Gentile world, the first step in the vision for the church's future.

II. COMMENTARY

No Favoritism Allowed!

> **MAIN IDEA:** *Anyone who trusts Jesus is welcomed into his body—the church—for God shows no favoritism in inviting people to the gospel.*

◢ The Military Target (vv. 1–8)

> **SUPPORTING IDEA:** *God is on target when he selects people for kingdom work, so we should be ready for unexpected assignments as we participate in his mission.*

10:1. Often, though not always, when God decides to extend the work of the gospel beyond its present boundaries, he targets people of influence. In Acts 6:7 **a large number of priests became obedient to the faith**. In chapter 8, the treasurer of a distant nation, cabinet member to a queen, trusted Christ. In chapter 9, God chose a persecuting rabbi and transformed him into the apostle to the Gentiles.

Here Luke introduces us to a military leader, a noncommissioned officer who had worked his way up through the ranks to the status of centurion, somewhat parallel to a captain in the American army today. He commanded a regiment, one-tenth of a legion (6,000 men). We would expect Cornelius to be in charge of three hundred to six hundred men called a *cohort*. Not everyone agrees with this analysis however, and some would apply the strict meaning of centurion, leader of one hundred. In either case, he is a man of influence in an influential city, a Gentile soldier serving a city composed dominantly of Gentiles. Caesarea experienced significant friction between that majority and the minority Jewish population.

10:2. This centurion was no ordinary Roman soldier. He was deeply religious and actually performed two out of three Jewish acts of piety—prayer and giving of alms. One commentator refers to Cornelius as a "rough Roman soldier," but nothing in the text suggests that. Probably most Roman soldiers behaved like those in Pilate's Hall. Not this one! He had been appointed to a very sophisticated post in a city committed to cultural activity and the arts. Whether there or prior to coming we do not know, he embraced the Jewish faith and supported the Jewish community. Not only that, but his entire family and all his household servants worshiped the Lord. Likely, he was not a formal proselyte to the Jewish religion, but a pious man who worshiped a monotheistic God.

10:3. We know from the text that God sent Cornelius a vision during his afternoon worship. Again, Luke's words are fascinatingly precise: **He distinctly saw an angel of God.** Commonly in Luke's writings, God uses prayer time to lead his people on to new vistas of ministry (Luke 3:21–22; 6:12–16; 9:18–22,28–31; 22:39–46; Acts 1:14; 13:1–3). As in chapter 3 where Peter and John encountered important ministry at the temple gate, we see here again that good things happen to those who worship regularly.

Luke leaves us no room to doubt that God takes total control of everything that happens in this account. Both Cornelius and Peter behave in normal ways, and God interrupts their lives with this double vision as we have already seen with Ananias and Saul, a sovereign plan to bring them together.

10:4–6. The appearance of angels whether in a vision or in person (Acts 1) tends to get one's attention. Luke uses one of his favorite words here (*atenizo*) to depict Cornelius staring at this heavenly apparition. The word appears fourteen times in the New Testament, twelve from the pen of Luke. The angel addressed him by name. His response was not dramatically different from that of Saul on the road to Damascus. He was a devout worshiper, still lost in sin and headed for hell. Yet he had enough spiritual sensitivity to treat a messenger from God with dignity and respect, a most appropriate reaction to divine revelation of any kind.

The angel's message must have been welcome—devout worship did not go unnoticed before God (Phil. 4:18; Heb. 13:15–16). God sent Cornelius a plan through his messenger—bring Peter to Caesarea. Note the precision of the plan in naming Peter, since Cornelius' messengers would find him at the home of another Simon.

10:7–8. Cornelius sent three people to Joppa, two servants and a military orderly. They went with full knowledge of the mission: A refreshing statement in a military framework where the "need to know" rule often limits personal communication. This was no covert operation to contact a spy in Palestine but overt obedience to a voice from heaven.

Luke develops a significant theological point in this chapter. People who act upon the revelation they have will be given more revelation, leading them to the truth of the gospel. Hardly some experiential or anecdotal point, this is the essence of Paul's argument in Romans 1:20: "For since the creation of the world God's invisible qualities—his eternal power and divine nature—have been clearly seen, being understood from what has been made, so that men are without excuse." Paul argued that the majority of people receiving this natural revelation and knowing God in some form "neither glorified him as God nor gave thanks to him, but their thinking became futile and their foolish hearts were darkened" (v. 21).

Cornelius provides a shining exception to that general rule of perverting God's revelation. Whatever had brought him to this point, whatever influences

God had used in his life to ready him for the gospel, Cornelius had responded correctly and now would be offered that final step, truth that leads to salvation.

🅱 The Master's Test (vv. 9–23a)

SUPPORTING IDEA: *Regardless of the religious traditions we may have behind us, we dare never turn away from anything or anyone God has selected and brought into our lives.*

10:9–13. The Cornelius contingent had nearly completed the thirty-one miles to Joppa when God appeared to Peter. Notice the apostle prays at an irregular time; but pious Jews certainly prayed more than the commanded times, and noon would have been a good choice (Ps. 55:17).

In our culture we might expect to be hungry while praying at noon, but that would not have been a normal meal time for Peter. The meal schedule would have called for a late morning breakfast and a more substantial meal mid to late afternoon. Peter, while on the roof praying at noon, became hungry. Thinking about food, **he fell into a trance**. Not imagination. Not a dream. God sent a heightened state of consciousness in preparation for the vision. Commentators play with the idea of whether **something like a large sheet** came to Peter's mind because of the awnings commonly covering the roof tops of Palestian houses in those days or perhaps from contemplating the sails of ships on the sea next to Simon's house. Such speculation, while interesting, hardly seems helpful. We are not dealing with a dream occasioned by some recent experience or thought pattern. God showed Peter a picnic spread of live animals and birds including **reptiles of the earth**! Then Peter heard a command to kill and eat from among these creatures.

Peter would have been familiar with Genesis 6:20 and even the creation account of Genesis 1:30. Even a less-than-fastidious Jew like Peter would revolt at this horrible scene, especially while his stomach growled in hunger. All this happened on the roof of a tanner's house. Even though the sea breeze may have been blowing the awful smell of Simon's work inland, Peter could hardly avoid the connection between his host's employment and the zoo picnic in his vision.

10:14–16. Did Peter recognize Jesus' voice? That is certainly possible. Whether he did or not, like Ananias, Peter seemed comfortable carrying on a conversation with heaven. Leviticus 11 was both clear and specific on dietary restrictions, and Ezekiel 4:14 dealt with the issue of eating prohibited food among the Gentiles. The voice reprimanded him, emphasizing that God had prepared the menu. Divine authority reserved the right to change or interpret any religious laws by which Peter's life was currently governed.

This happened three times before the sheet disappeared again into the heavens. Three times. We wonder whether Peter thought back to the important threes in his life. This is the third time he verbally refused God's will. Three times he had denied the Lord. In John 21, Jesus asked him three times about his love. Hardly foundation for a theological point, the numerical repetition certainly provides an interesting pattern in this apostle's experience.

During another moment in Peter's experience, he heard Jesus deal with this issue of eating and drinking. Perhaps the Lord repeated the message many times during Peter's wanderings with him. Mark recorded Jesus' statement that things which entered the body from outside (like food) did not defile a person but rather those things which came out of the heart and were expressed in speech (Mark 7:14–23). In 7:19 Mark, often thought to express Peter's viewpoint of the Christ narrative, suggests that with this kind of teaching Jesus declared all foods clean. Why this emphasis on food as preparation for ministry to the Gentiles? Polhill puts it well:

> It is simply not possible to fully accept someone with whom you are unwilling to share in the intimacy of table fellowship. The early church had to solve the problem of kosher food laws in order to launch a mission to the Gentiles. Purity distinctions and human discrimination are of a single piece (Polhill, 256).

10:17–21. Small wonder that Peter spent time **wondering about the meaning of the vision.** As he pondered the theological and behavioral significance of the sheet, the men arrived. Their presence did not change Peter's mind. Only a third revelation in our chapter did—first an angel to Cornelius, then a voice from heaven to Peter, and now the Holy Spirit telling Peter precisely what to do. In Acts, the voice of Jesus, angelic messengers, and the prompting of the Holy Spirit all convey God's Word with equal power and authority. Verse 20 uses a technical Greek term to express the comand to go without hesitation. This indicates unfettered obedience which takes no time to fret over conscience.

10:22–23a. Repetition characterizes the Cornelius story. Luke seems intent on making sure his readers grasp the divine manipulation of these events. How else can you understand Cornelius, the Gentile officer being ready to hear what Peter, the Jewish fisherman, will say? Only God's work could make Peter understand he has been sent on a preaching mission; then take the big step toward accepting Gentiles by inviting these visitors into Simon's house, presumably with his host's permission (cf. Acts 28:7; Heb. 13:2; 3 John 10).

What a night that must have been for Peter. Could he sleep? Did he spend it in prayer? Surely he sensed that God intended to change the church's methods of ministry. Surely he grasped that somehow he was the divinely chosen instrument for this change. Surely he could not forget that horrible sheet and the emotional turmoil the previous afternoon had brought.

Ⓒ The Ministry Trip (vv. 23b–33)

SUPPORTING IDEA: *Almost all ministry in Acts is done in teams, Christians working together to accomplish God's tasks on earth more effectively than any one of them could alone.*

10:23b–26. Peter took six Jewish brothers from Joppa (10:45; 11:12), a wise choice in terms of what lay ahead. These seven Jews and three Gentiles had to stay overnight somewhere, for they did not arrive until the following day (v. 24). By that time Cornelius had gathered a minicongregation of **relatives and close friends.** When Peter entered, the centurion, commander of Roman soldiers, fell at the feet of a fisherman in reverence.

Peter had seen this type of thing before (Acts 3) and immediately disclaimed any power or authority in himself. So much for Peter as the first pope or some kind of "divine man" of Greek cultural fame. This biblical and humble response was not unique to Peter. The apostle John encountered an angel who behaved the same way (Rev. 19:10; 22:8–9), and Paul and Barnabas made similar protest at Lystra (Acts 14:14–18).

10:27–29. Since Cornelius' family had practiced some form of Jewish worship, Peter correctly assumed they knew the clear position of the Jewish rabbis regarding the events of that moment. Peter was breaking the law. He publicly admitted that fact. This may have been an explanation to Cornelius of why he had come, or perhaps even a nod to the six Jewish Christians who came with him. In either case, Peter moved immediately to the main point— **God has shown me that I should not call any man impure or unclean.** Since Cornelius' invitation had not yet been made clear, Peter asked point-blank what he would like.

Peter already knew God had changed the rules. The unlawful was no longer unlawful—for whatever reason. The rationale belonged to God with Peter an obedient servant, unfettered from his previous prohibitions.

10:30–33. Again the repetition in Luke's narrative. We find here a summary of verses 3–8 with only minor variations. Verse 33 alone introduces a new idea, setting the ambience for Peter's message: **Now we are all here in the presence of God to listen to everything the Lord has commanded you to tell us.** Talk about a divinely prepared audience! What God did for Philip in a desert chariot, he did for Peter in the spacious home of a Roman officer.

How we struggle to find opportunity for witness. How guilty we feel when we fail to share the gospel with others for long periods of time. Perhaps we have neglected this important ingredient of Scripture. Perhaps we work too hard through formal church programs or other organized efforts to find anyone who will listen to our message. Maybe we should pray for God-ordained ears and God-prepared hearts to whose owners the Holy Spirit can direct us without a misstep or confusion.

Some years ago I spent several weeks in Hong Kong ministering to hundreds of Sunday school teachers, mostly men and women in their twenties. Every week they taught thousands of children on the rooftops of gigantic apartment houses in that sprawling city. My task was to encourage their ministry and perhaps impart some helpful suggestions for its enhancement.

A group of medical doctors invited me to go to dinner and answer their questions about the Christian faith. I accepted, of course, and found myself in the presence of eighteen to twenty physicians, mostly believers but some guests from outside the faith. Until nearly midnight we dialogued about God's Word and how men of science could internalize and share the Bible in their unique work environments. I could not have designed the meeting, nor could I have prepared my mind and heart to handle the intricacies of those discussions. God prepared them and me for that evening.

I've often thought when reading Acts 10:33 that this verse would make a wonderful introduction to any preacher on any occasion. Imagine a pastor introducing a guest speaker on Sunday morning or perhaps a missionary at the annual missionary conference with these wonderful words.

The Matchless Truth (vv. 34–43)

SUPPORTING IDEA: *The gospel is universal. God does not show favoritism. He invites earnest seekers from every nation to trust in Jesus Christ for eternal salvation.*

10:34–35. Luke understood the enormous impact of what he was about to write. In a few short sentences this brash disciple from Galilee, now a respected apostle from Jerusalem, would sweep away centuries of religious and racial prejudice. No longer was God only for the Jews, and no longer was Jesus only a Jewish Messiah. Here comes a new theology of remnant Christians from all nations of the world. The word for *favoritism* (*prosopolemptes*) appears only here in the New Testament, but synonyms show up in Romans 2:11, Ephesians 6:9, Colossians 3:25, and James 2:1.

We talked earlier about Mark writing Peter's version of the life of Christ. Here we have a mini-summary of the Gospel of Mark, a revolutionary message indicating that salvation does not rest in the works of some religious group. It forms the racial challenge of the gospel—God does not distinguish faces. The body of Christ reaches worldwide. Its members come from every ethnic group where the gospel has been preached (Rom. 2:11; Eph. 2:11–22; Col. 3:25; Jas. 2:1; 1 Pet. 1:17).

Like the Ethiopian treasurer before him, Cornelius followed what light God had given and now became the recipient of more light, the full light of the message of Jesus and the gospel.

10:36. Peter spoke in what some have called "broken Greek." This syntax does not reflect lack of awareness of that language on Peter's part, but rather the spontaneous flow of a man steeped in theology now explaining the Christian understanding of that theology in a language not his native tongue. He told Cornelius that God sent a message to Israel (revelation) telling good news of peace (proclamation) through Jesus who is Lord of all (glorification). The phrase "Lord of all" would be well-known to a Roman as a pagan title for deity. Christians appropriately applied it to the Son of God.

These things happened scarcely ten to fifteen years after the resurrection, so it is not at all unlikely that a sophisticated and religious man like Cornelius would have been quite familiar with the record of Jesus' life. That is precisely what Peter says next.

10:37–38. These verses likely contain a mere summary of Peter's total address. They still contain more detail than most other New Testament sermons, revealing the necessity Peter felt to explain the Jesus story more completely to Gentiles who would be familiar with the facts but not the meaning. His listeners would doubtless have known about good and evil in the world; no one living in the Roman Empire could doubt the latter, and no one worshiping the true God could doubt the former. Peter reminded them that Jesus Christ challenged the evil kingdom and delivered those **who were under the power of the devil**.

How did all this come about? Because God not only anointed Jesus of Nazareth, but he also was with him in all that he did.

10:39–43. Five times in Acts the apostles speak of witnessing the resurrection. Before he could drive home the point of the living Lord, Peter felt impelled to review the crucifixion. Evil people killed Jesus, but God raised him and showed his risen Son in public to certain chosen witnesses. This risen Lord sent Peter and his colleagues to testify that Jesus is God's appointed **judge of the living and the dead**.

Though Peter did not mention it, Cornelius surely knew the role Roman soldiers from Pilate's court played in that ugly crucifixion. How many men had he seen die this way? No, a Roman centurion needed no reminder of the cruelty of his nation's form of execution. F.F. Bruce reminds us,

> It is difficult after sixteen centuries and more during which the cross has been a sacred symbol, to realize the unspeakable horror and loathing which the very mentioning or thought of the cross provoked in Paul's day. The word *crux* was unmentionable in polite Roman society (Cicero, Pro Rabirio 16) (Bruce, *Acts*, 272).

Jesus the crucified is not only alive, but he holds the ultimate power of life and death (Acts 17:26–31; Rom. 14:9; 1 Thess. 5:9–10; 2 Tim. 4:1; 1 Pet. 4:5).

In verse 43 Peter moved to the proclamation of the universal gospel. The prophets proclaimed the Messiah, but they could not have known what Peter was now permitted to preach, namely **that everyone who believes in him receives forgiveness of sins through his name**. There! He said it. The word is now out. Not merely for an isolated proselyte like the Ethiopian eunuch or a respected urban worshiper like Cornelius. This gospel of salvation was not a one-time event; rather God declared that whosoever will may come and that will be, from this point onward, the very essence of the gospel.

⒠ The Meaningful Transition (vv. 44–48)

SUPPORTING IDEA: *Anyone who trusts in the name of Jesus for salvation receives the Holy Spirit and the privilege of baptism.*

10:44. Surely Luke intended us to understand that Peter never finished his sermon. We read no invitation and no challenge to the listeners to respond in any way. Peter is hardly in here; God decided they had heard enough because he saw that in their hearts they trusted in the one of whom Peter had been speaking.

Longenecker suggests that this phrase "struck like a thunder bolt into the consciousness of the assembled Gentiles, releasing their pent-up emotions and emboldening them to respond by faith. With the promise of forgiveness offered 'through his name' and to 'everyone who believes in him' they were given a reason for hoping beyond their fondest hopes" (Longenecker, 394).

10:45–46. Peter and his visitors witnessed what some have called "the Pentecost of the Gentile world." Luke tells us they **were astonished** (literally, "beside themselves") at the similarity between this and the Pentecost experience—instantaneous, visible, audible, it apparently affected everyone in Cornelius' household. Notice we find no laying on of hands even though an authorized apostle is present. Let's say it again—Peter did not control any of this, from the sheet in Joppa to the tongues in Caesarea. God works precisely as he chooses.

The word for **tongues** in verse 46 is precisely the same as in Acts 2, but some prefer a different translation here. Most evangelical commentators agree that the word means different languages in the Pentecost experience, but here perhaps, ecstatic utterances. Surely that is a possible interpretation in light of 1 Corinthians 12–14, and one cannot resist the common sense of the argument that foreign languages in this family room would have helped no one.

Nevertheless, we find it difficult to believe that Luke would make such a switch without some explanation, especially when in 11:15 he tells us **the Holy Spirit came on them as he had come on us at the beginning**. Whether languages or ecstatic utterance, the point of the passage is divine certification of Gentile salvation.

10:47–48. Though we have not seen precisely the same order each time, we have come to expect the firm connection between Spirit baptism and water baptism. As in the case of the eunuch (chap. 8), Spirit baptism takes places immediately upon conversion, followed by water baptism. Interesting that Peter does not offer the trinitarian formula we use today. These new Christians were **baptized in the name of Jesus Christ**. Interesting, too, that Peter did not baptize them himself, presumably delegating the task to the six brothers with him. This reminds us of Paul's caveat in 1 Corinthians 1:14–17 and Jesus' authorization of his disciples to baptize in his behalf (John 4:1–2).

What a radical breakthrough—Gentile equality with Jews in every way. Since Peter has already dined with Cornelius' three messengers, staying on with the centurion and his family for a few days no longer posed any problem for this liberated apostle.

MAIN IDEA REVIEW: *Anyone who trusts Jesus is welcomed to his body, the church, for God shows no favoritism in the invitation of the gospel.*

III. CONCLUSION

Pioneering the Gospel

Early in my ministry I served as assistant to a senior pastor who had spent many years in Africa as a missionary. How his stories of life on the field thrilled us all. I shall never forget his description of pioneering the gospel to a tribe which had never before seen a white face. They knew nothing of Jesus Christ or the Bible. As the missionary explained his purpose in coming, the tribal chief announced, "Yes, we have long been believers in your God, and we have waited for you to come; tell us more."

For those of us who live in a microchip marketplace and rarely have opportunities like this, such a story seems foreign to our world. Such events are well-known among missionaries who pioneered new peoples earlier in the twentieth century. For thousands of years the God of heaven's standard procedure has included the preparation of hearts followed by the sending of light.

Lest we think this chapter only a lesson in ancient history or even a milestone in evangelical theology, let us not lose sight of its application for today. God still prepares people, softening their hearts for the message of the gospel.

God still calls those of us who have lived in more narrow confines of dogma to broaden our thinking and recognize that God is the sovereign of the universe, not the idol of a selected few. From that day in Caesarea to the present hour, the heavenly Father who gave his Son for the salvation of all people will not allow selected Pharisees or cultic groups to live in the light of that cryptic poem,

> We are the Lord's elected few.
> Let everyone else be dammed.
> There is no room up there for you
> We don't want heaven crammed.

No. If we are to sing or recite poetry, let it be the words of Philip P. Bliss:

> Whosoever heareth shout, shout the sound!
> Spread the blessed tidings all the world around;
> Tell the joyful news wherever man is found,
> Whosoever will may come.

PRINCIPLES

- One should never argue with God, whatever the subject matter.
- People we never heard of, God has prepared for the gospel.
- God forbids any kind of racism for Christians.
- The gospel makes salvation in Jesus available to anyone who believes in him.
- Water baptism is inseparably related to Spirit baptism.

APPLICATIONS

- Look for the leading of God when you least expect it.
- When God sends you to do his work, go without hesitation.
- Never think you are too good to break bread with someone else, believer or unbeliever.
- When you go out to serve the Lord, especially on a difficult mission, take a team with you.

IV. LIFE APPLICATION

Motivation to Go

A veteran pastor served for years in a small town in northern Montana. One day the Lord called him home to heaven, and it appeared his earthly sojourn was complete. As it turned out, however, he had been brought to glory a little earlier than the heavenly schedule had designed. After making the appropriate apologies, the Lord informed the pastor he would have to return to that dreary small town and continue to serve until the actual time of his home going arrived.

Upon this announcement, an argument ensued, with the pastor actually saying, "I won't go!" and the Lord reminding him, "You must!" Finally the pastor said, "Well, Lord, I'll go back to northern Montana if you'll go with me." After the Lord pondered the offer for several minutes he finally replied, "Well, I'll go with you as far as Billings."

Silly nonsense, of course, but descriptive of Peter's early mood when that odious sheet came down. By the time the messengers arrived, he had dealt with his attitude and was quite motivated to go and accomplish whatever God wished of him. Furthermore, God went with him all the way to Caesarea and stayed with him every moment.

To be sure, the essence of this chapter, its theological epicenter, focuses on the proclamation of the gospel to Gentiles and their receipt of the Holy Spirit. Nevertheless, Peter's role as the reluctant messenger offers us significant lessons as well. Peter's first sermon upon beginning his address dealt with something he himself had just learned—**God does not show favoritism**. The specific context deals with the offer of salvation and the universal gospel, but the phrase extends itself into much more far-reaching aspects of Christian life.

God does not show favoritism . . . even though we often do. Every time we cater to wealthy people in a church and ignore those whose offerings do not enhance its ministry, we show favoritism (Jas. 2:1–9). Favoritism, says James, is sin, and one sin makes us as guilty as another no matter what artificial hierarchy of sin we may have constructed in the contemporary church.

Obviously, the opposite of positive favoritism is negative discrimination—on any basis. Solid evangelical Christians practice discrimination in ways far wider than race, age, or gender, though those common areas still present a minefield of failure. We discriminate when we don't allow sound believers of other denominations to preach in the pulpits of our denomination. We discriminate when we fail to accept baptism by another group for membership in our congregation, even though that baptism may be the same mode we practice. We constantly favor those we like and avoid those we dislike, favor those who agree with us and shun those who disagree. God does not show favoritism, and we should post in front of every evangelical church, whatever its label, and hang on the walls of every Christian home, regardless of its location, a readable and attention-grabbing sign—"NO FAVORITISM ALLOWED!"

V. PRAYER

God, thank you for universal salvation without which none of us would have ever become your children through Jesus Christ our Lord. Amen.

VI. DEEPER DISCOVERIES

A. Centurions (v. 1)

Although the Romans come in for their share of scathing denunciation in the New Testament, several notable exceptions appear in the form of centurions. A centurion in Capernaum had built a synagogue for the Jews and was so revered that they begged Jesus to heal his servant (Matt. 8:5–13; Luke 7:2–10). Of this man Jesus said, "I have not found such great faith even in Israel" (Luke 7:9). We already know the story of Cornelius as a God-fearer and newborn Christian. In Acts 27 we will meet Julius of the Augustinian band who not only was commissioned to take Paul to Rome but saved his life in the process.

We certainly dare not forget the centurion who might have become the first believer. Guarding the dying Savior at the cross, terrified by the earthquake and accompanying events, he declared with his men "Surely he was the Son of God!" (Matt. 27:54) Luke goes on to tell us that this very centurion "praised God and said, 'Surely this was a righteous man'" (Luke 23:47). The text of neither Gospel tells us that this resulted in salvation, but certainly such a declaration throughout the pages of the New Testament marked those who became genuine believers.

B. Unclean Foods (v. 14)

Jews generally identified animals by species. Any kind of sea creature (such as a shell fish without usual scales) was unclean, as were four-footed animals which did not have cloven hoofs or do not chew their cud. Obviously, pigs represent this category well. Perhaps Peter's sheet contained clean animals as well, but the ugly mixture must have scandalized him. We know of no Jewish rule indicating that the unclean animals on the sheet would have defiled the clean animals, but the voice had made no distinction whatsoever as to selecting only certain of the animals which Peter could have approved. His withdrawal and disgust indicates that either the sheet contained only unclean animals or, more likely, that it contained an indistinguishable mix which he had no intention of touching.

C. Divine Revelation (vv. 3–6, 13–15)

At this point in Acts, where we have visions occurring right and left, it might be worthwhile to note that any messenger of God holds equal weight with any other. The source of the message, not the type of messenger, is the issue. In our chapter an angel appears to Cornelius (10:3–6,22,30), a voice speaks to Peter (10:13–15), and the Spirit urges him to go to Caesarea (10:19–20). We recall an angel of the Lord and the Spirit directing Philip in chapter 8, and we'll see that connection again in 16:6–7. In every case recipients of the message clearly understood they were being contacted by God and handled the message that way.

VII. TEACHING OUTLINE

A. INTRODUCTION

1. Lead story: Vision for the Future
2. Context: Remember our literary genre in Acts—historical narrative. Luke is writing a theological history so we expect one event to flow into the next. We also expect to find meaning in the narrative as well as the speeches. With few exceptions, we see God's hand at work in the world without reading a theological treatise like Romans which builds a case carefully one point upon another.
3. Transition: We can almost sense Luke's eagerness to get to this chapter. He parks Peter at Joppa (9:43), impatient to move him the next step across God's revelational board to Caesarea. We will see this narrative continued through the first 18 verses of chapter 11 where Gentile Christians in Caesarea become Luke's basis for introducing a Gentile church at Antioch.

B. COMMENTARY

1. A Military Target (vv. 1–8)
   a. Centurion in Caesarea (vv. 1–3)
   b. Instruction from an angel (vv. 4–6)
   c. Messengers to Joppa (vv. 7–8)
2. The Master's Test (vv. 9–23a)
   a. Peter's traumatic vision (vv. 9–13)
   b. Peter's Jewish reaction (vv. 14–16)
   c. Peter's call to Caesarea (vv. 17–23a)
3. The Ministry Trip (vv. 23b–33)
   a. Reception by Cornelius (vv. 23b–26)

     b.   Request for Clarification (vv. 27–29)

     c.   Review of God's plan (vv. 30–33)

  4. The Matchless Truth (vv. 34–43)

     a.   God does not show favoritism (vv. 34–38)

     b.   Anyone who believes in Jesus receives forgiveness (vv. 39–43)

  5. The Meaningful Transition (vv. 44–48)

     a.   Baptism by the Holy Spirit (vv. 44–46)

     b.   Baptism in water (vv. 47–48)

C. CONCLUSION: MOTIVATION TO GO

VIII. ISSUES FOR DISCUSSION

1. What people has God brought unexpectedly into your congregation? How did you and your church respond? Why?

2. Are there some groups of people whom you think your church would hesitate to accept as fully participating members? How are these people different from the majority of your membership? What causes hesitancy in accepting them?

3. What are you doing to help your church avoid showing favortism in its efforts to witness for Christ and bring new members into his church?

Acts 11

Marks of a Biblical Church

I. Introduction
Is This the Best You Can Do?

II. Commentary
A verse-by-verse explanation of the chapter.

III. Conclusion
Different Ministries in a Unified Body
An overview of the principles and applications from the chapter.

IV. Life Application
Backbone of the Night
Melding the chapter to life.

V. Prayer
Tying the chapter to life with God.

VI. Deeper Discoveries
Historical, geographical, and grammatical enrichment of the commentary.

VII. Teaching Outline
Suggested step-by-step group study of the chapter.

VIII. Issues for Discussion
Zeroing the chapter in on daily life.

"*The* Christian church is the only society in
the world in which membership is based upon the
qualification that the candidate shall
be unworthy of membership."

Charles C. Morrison

GEOGRAPHICAL PROFILE: ANTIOCH

- One of sixteen cities named for the Seleucid emperor Antiochus the Great
- Three hundred miles north of Jerusalem—twenty miles east of the Mediterranean Sea
- Third largest city in the Roman Empire
- Founded 300 B.C., it was well-known for its commerce and its sin

IN A NUTSHELL

After Peter's review of his experience at Caesarea, Luke returns to the narrative of scattered Hellenists to describe the founding of the church at Antioch. This congregation became the real mother church of the New Testament from which the Christian mission went out to the Mediterranean world—to Greece and, eventually, to Rome.

Marks of a Biblical Church

I. INTRODUCTION

Is This the Best You Can Do?

In his book *The White House Years*, Henry Kissinger tells the story about a colleague at Harvard with whom he taught before joining the Nixon staff. Apparently, this professor gave an assignment, the students handed in their papers, and some days later the papers were returned.

One student looked over his paper searching in vain for some helpful comment or even a grade. The paper had no marks on it except for a question at the end of the last page: "Is this the best you can do?"

The student pondered the question and concluded the paper had not represented his best work; so he took it home and worked it over. He returned the paper to the teacher and received it back a few days later in exactly the same condition—no comments, no grade, only the haunting question at the end: "Is this the best you can do?"

"Well," thought the student, *"It's a whole lot better than the first one, but I can pump up the bibliography a bit, throw in a few more quotes, and even make it two or three pages longer."* So he did. Receiving the paper back the third time, he found exactly what he had seen twice before: "Is this the best you can do?"

As Kissinger tells the story, this went on ten times. Ten times the student handed the paper in; ten times the professor handed it back with exactly the same question. Finally, in exasperation the student approached the professor's desk, threw the paper down, and said in no uncertain terms, "Yes. This is the best I can do!" "Fine," responded the professor, "now I'll read it."

Even though I read that story years ago, I have never had the courage to try it in my own classes. It certainly makes a significant point, especially in light of the developing, growing church and the founding of a second congregation up north in the Gentile world. We sometimes confuse *excellence* with *perfection*, but they are different concepts. In living the Christian life and serving the Lord, *excellence* simply means doing the very best you can with the resources he has given.

A church of fifty with limited talent and finances may never accomplish the citywide impact which a megachurch of five or six thousand may create. Believers in that smaller church can do their work for God to the very best of their ability, perhaps even better than folks in the larger church. Luke 12:48b leaves no doubt about how the Lord's followers should handle resources— from everyone who has been given much, much will be demanded; and from the one who has been entrusted with much, much more will be asked.

In this chapter we encounter two churches, one struggling to deal with the presentation of the gospel to the Gentile Cornelius, the other exploding on the scene in God's providence. Though the chapter begins on a negative note, it ends by showing how Christians can reconcile their differences and work together—an important mark of a biblical church. Antioch offers a model (if not a pattern) for every church in every age and every place as we see the dynamic life of Christ fleshed out in this most unlikely city.

II. COMMENTARY

Marks of a Biblical Church

> **MAIN IDEA:** *When God wants to develop a work, we need only be available and willing to provide our very best efforts at his call and direction.*

A Fairness in Christian Criticism (vv. 1–18)

> **SUPPORTING IDEA:** *When God gives powerful signs to show he is developing a work, we can either join in God's work or oppose God.*

We study this large section because the narrative of the Cornelius story has been well established in chapter 10 and a good portion of chapter 11 contains Peter's review of his experience. Nevertheless, let us remember again the principle of proportion; God designs large segments of Scripture to explain things he considers important. In this case, sixty-six verses cover the conversion of Cornelius compared with thirty-one for the conversion of Saul and only thirteen for events at Pentecost. One could draw different conclusions from those numbers, but certainly this breakthrough of the gospel to a Roman was a watershed event in the early church.

11:1–3. Numerous texts in the New Testament deal with the issue of criticism among Christians. Here we have one of the best. Quite possibly Peter was accosted by this group of Jewish Christians *when he least expected it.* We have no difficulty picturing Peter returning to Jerusalem on a spiritual high. He had no time to go back to Joppa or Lydda but came right back to headquarters to tell the brothers and sisters what God had done in Caesarea.

We dare not confuse these people with the Pharisees or some other group outside the church. They clearly represented a conservative minority *within* the church, a group dedicated to protecting a Jewish perspective on Christianity. This "circumcision group" was so known not because of their own status (which would be a foregone conclusion), but because they expected any Gentiles coming to Christ would have to go through the corridor of Judaism first, and that would include circumcision.

Luke does not tell us how this news reached Jerusalem before Peter arrived. Quite possibly while he stayed in Caesarea **for a few days** (10:48), some of the ones who joined him headed to Jerusalem rather than back to Joppa. In any case, Peter's reputation as one who eats with Gentiles had preceded him, and the trap had been set.

What issue did they raise? Not the proclamation of the gospel. Not the giving of the Holy Spirit. Not baptism in the name of Jesus. Such weighty theological matters were pushed aside in order to protect a tradition of the

Jews—don't ever eat with a Gentile. They basically asked, "Whatever happened to the concept of the chosen people?" They didn't care about the particulars. They didn't want the evidence. They simply knew that a prominent church leader had done something to offend them, and they wanted to be sure he heard about it the moment he stepped into town. This group persisted in the church, and we will later find them harassing Paul and Barnabas (Acts 15:5).

11:4–14. The old Peter would have been tempted to cut off an ear or two at this point; but this is the Spirit-filled version, the man who had argued with the Lord about this very mission in question and finally submitted to God's grace. Excited as he might have been about the conversion of Cornelius, Peter was mature enough to understand why these brothers struggled with the same clean/unclean problems which plagued him in that horrible sheet.

Now Luke tells us how a mature Christian handles criticism—**Peter began and explained everything to them precisely as it had happened.** We need not comb this section in detail but merely notice the differences or perhaps the additions which Luke did not record in chapter 10.

Luke sprinkled the name of Cornelius all over the last chapter, but it does not appear here. The identity of the man was not the issue, only his race. We also learn about the six witnesses (v. 12). Then Peter moves quite quickly to the real issue in verse 14: **He will bring you a message through which you and all your household will be saved.**

One subtle difference here in chapter 11 is the matter of style. Scholars suggest that while Peter spoke to Cornelius in a version of "Jewish Greek," back home, now he is likely speaking Aramaic so the rather stilted third person style of chapter 10 turns into a fresh personal testimony in chapter 11. Of course, we have to account for Luke's literary handling of the material, but any who have taught theological matters in a second language not commonly used can certainly understand how different it would sound from the same information communicated in one's native tongue.

We have already mentioned how to handle criticism when one least expects it. Here we might add that Peter dealt with criticism *when he didn't deserve it.* He demonstrated a wonderful openness and vulnerability in simply stating what had happened with no defense whatsoever. His basic position rests in the clarity of God's will and the purity of his own motives—he acted only out of concern for the gospel and the church, and only in direct obedience to what God told him to do.

11:15–18. Beginning in verse 15 can only mean the beginning of the church at Pentecost, especially in view of the context in which Peter explained how the Holy Spirit came on the household of Cornelius. Polhill notes, "certainly for Peter it was a Gentile Pentecost" (Pohill, 267).

The warmth of verse 16 ought to make us smile. We reflect with Peter on what he felt when he saw the Holy Spirit come at Caesarea even before he finished his sermon. He tells us, **Then I remembered what the Lord had said**. That, by the way, is always a good idea. In this case he refers specifically to Acts 1:5, though this promise commonly came from the lips of John the Baptist himself (Mark 1:4–8; Luke 3:15–18).

Then the clinching argument—Peter surmised that since God was doing all of this and he has chosen to deal with Gentiles the same way he treated us Jews, **who was I to think that I could oppose God**. The argument is clear: opposition to Gentile baptism is opposition to God. Peter handled criticism when he least expected it, when he didn't deserve it, and perhaps, *when he couldn't understand it*. He trusted the Lord, he trusted his call, and he trusted the experiences God brought into his life.

The result? An immediate response of acceptance, though Acts 11:18 hardly solves this problem among New Testament Christians. In fact three nagging questions remained to be bantered about for years and then brought before the Council at Jerusalem in chapter 15.

1. What lifestyle was appropriate for Gentiles coming to Christ out of raw paganism?
2. How do these Gentile believers relate to Jewish Christians?
3. How should the Jerusalem church handle people like this?

Nevertheless, let us give these conservative brothers credit. When they heard the evidence, they offered no further objection. They not only went away silenced, but rather praised God and affirmed precisely what Peter had told them—**God has granted even the Gentiles repentance unto life**. The human and divine elements of salvation couple in this half verse: believers repented, and God granted the Spirit.

So for the moment the issue is settled. What do Gentiles have to do to become Christians? Believe in the Lord Jesus Christ—and nothing more.

Sometimes, if we respond biblically in the face of criticism, God changes people. We commend the "circumcision group" and hope that we ourselves and others in our churches will always listen to the evidence and acknowledge God's hand whenever we have questions about the behavior of other Christians.

B Founded on Aggressive Evangelism (vv. 19–21)

SUPPORTING IDEA: *Evangelism is the proclamation of the gospel, nothing less and nothing more. Results always remain in God's hand, and sometimes he astonishes us.*

11:19. We cannot proceed further in Acts 11 without linking this verse with Acts 8:4: **Those who had been scattered preached the word wherever**

they went. Luke picks up precisely on that wording and continues the story of the dispersion of Hellenistic Jewish Christians after the death of Stephen. We know what happened to Philip; now Luke wants to tell us how God is about to do a new work in a most unlikely place.

Here it is again—another "meanwhile" passage by Dr. Luke. Most of these escaping Hellenists were not as radical as some would have thought. They carefully preached the message only to Jews in three places Luke names—Phoenicia, Cyprus, and Antioch. The Phoenician plain extended seventy-five miles along the coast of middle Syria from Mt. Carmel to the Eleutheros River. Presumably, the scattered witnesses visited cities like Ptolemais, Tyre, Sidon, and even Zarepahth (cf. Acts 21:3–7).

Others took to the sea, escaping to the island of Cyprus in the eastern Mediterranean, approximately one hundred miles off the Syrian coast. All these cities (including Antioch) were steeped in Hellenistic culture, logical places for the refugees to land. They would have had no trouble explaining their faith in Christ to Hellenists like themselves. As in the early ministry of Paul, these scattered Christians first went to synagogues and preached to Jews.

11:20. Antioch was different. The word *Greeks* seems synonymous with *Gentiles* in this context, and Luke fully intends us to see the link with what has been building throughout the last three chapters. Presumably, **the men from Cyprus and Cyrene** were Hellenists who had been in Jerusalem at the time of Stephen's martyrdom. Instead of returning home, they headed north to Antioch. So Antioch developed contact with both these places (Barnabas came to Antioch from Cyprus, and one of the first missionary candidates was Lucius of Cyrene, 13:1).

This aggressive evangelism by anonymous preachers throws our heavily-programmed modern church into stark and feeble contrast. Never mind that they had been driven from their homes and scattered. Never mind that God led them to one of the most wicked cities of the Roman world. They had a message to deliver—**the good news about the Lord Jesus**. Notice they didn't preach a coming Messiah; that appropriately related to Jewish groups. Even though the Greeks in Antioch may have been proselytes, they possessed only a small portion of the zeal Jerusalemite Jews held for the coming of the Messiah.

Before we leave this verse, just a word about Cyrene. This Libyan city in North Africa lay some 2,000 feet above the Mediterranean and ten miles inland from the coast. For several hundred years it was viewed as an oasis in the desert before it became a part of Egypt in 231 B.C. The Simon who carried Jesus' cross came from Cyrene (Luke 23:26), and we know Cyrenians were present at Pentecost (2:10). The Greeks had intended to make Cyrene "the Athens of Africa," but the Romans cut short that plan.

11:21. God blessed these sincere Christians who were willing to share the gospel so that in Antioch **a great number of people believed and turned to the Lord**. The church erupted at Antioch, and a new thing happened. Both the Ethiopian eunuch and Cornelius reached out to Christians, inviting the gospel. Here Jewish Christians aggressively take the gospel to Gentiles. The church has begun to turn the world upside down. The second congregation of the New Testament comes together as the Gentile effort expands. Bock writes, "Antioch is a model community, engaging in evangelism, teaching, and ministry to brothers in need. There is no racial prejudice in the community. Only the testimony of divine reconciliation" (Bock, 76).

Fortified by Competent Leadership (vv. 22–24)

SUPPORTING IDEA: *Churches need to discover God at work and send people to encourage and help in the work God is doing.*

11:22–23. One wonders why a significant new effort like this in a Syrian city would not have called for one of the apostles. Throughout Acts, the Twelve seem quite content to serve the rapidly growing church in Jerusalem and its environs; they also might have been less than comfortable in the pagan surroundings of Antioch.

But not Barnabas. He bridged the Greek and Hebrew elements in the church. Having come from Cyprus, he was not a typical "Jerusalemite" Jew. He had already established a solid reputation for piety, generosity, and encouragement in the Jerusalem church and, after all, what do new converts need more than encouragement?

11:24. Luke liked the choice. He describes Barnabas much in the way he did Stephen and tells us that not only did he encourage new believers, but many more came to Christ after Barnabas arrived. Leadership is the name of the game in any church, but not the monarchical leadership of the Old Covenant. In the New Covenant, groups of believers serve one another. A layman, with no apparent qualification other than faithful service in another congregation, now appears to become the first senior pastor at Antioch.

Fed By Qualified Teachers (vv. 25–26)

SUPPORTING IDEA: *Biblical teaching is foundational to every congregation but especially to a newly established church consisting of Gentile converts residing in a huge pagan city.*

11:25–26. Every expanding church considers adding additional staff, and Antioch did, too. Pastor Barnabas needed an associate pastor of Christian education, someone who could help in the teaching ministry of new converts. Remember Paul had been staying pretty close to home at Tarsus for nearly ten years. Yet Luke suggests Barnabas had to search a bit to find the brilliant rabbi.

Some commentators speculate that Saul had already begun a ministry to Gentiles, preaching in the Cylician synagogues and perhaps stirring up trouble in his hometown (2 Cor. 11:23–27). Others suggest the vision of 2 Corinthians 12:1–4 fits into these years as well. Whatever difficulties Saul may have had in Tarsus seem to have dissipated in the friendly reception at Antioch, for he and Barnabas **taught great numbers of people** for a year.

The end of verse 26 offers an interesting Lucan note—**The disciples were first called Christians at Antioch**. We use that term so commonly we think it must be scattered all across the New Testament, but it appears only three times—Acts 11:26; Acts 26:28; 1 Peter 4:16. Normally in Acts, Luke refers to Christians as "believers," "disciples," or "brothers." *Christians* was an outside nickname, possibly given in derision. It means "Christ followers" or "people of Christ's party."

A new religious group had entered the New Testament scene. Up to this point we have essentially seen Jews and Gentiles. Now Christians are no longer a subset of Judaism but a distinct identity in the Mediterranean world. Longenecker suggests this was not all good for them: "The use of the name 'Christian' posed two great problems for the church. For one thing, Christians began to risk losing the protection Rome gave to a *religio licita* [i.e., a ligio (or legitimate, legally recognized) religion. . .], which they had enjoyed when considered only a sect within Judaism. Furthermore, being now in some way differentiated from Judaism, Christians were faced with how to understand their continuity with the hope of Israel and the promises of the Jewish Scriptures. As we shall see, these problems were to loom large as the Christian mission moved onto Gentile soil" (Longenecker, 402–403).

E Functioning to Meet Social Needs (vv. 27–30)

SUPPORTING IDEA: *The gospel's profound social implications sometimes seem more clear to new converts than to those of us who have been in the body for a long time.*

11:27–28. Though Antioch lay far north of Jerusalem, we commonly read the word **down** in situations like this because of the topography. The Jews didn't use *up* and *down* as we do, to refer to north and south, but rather to describe low country and high country. Enter a visitor from Jerusalem, a prophet named Agabus whom we see again in 21:10–11. We have no evidence that he was sent by the Jerusalem church; prophets in this time tended to wander about a bit. Proclaiming this message of the coming famine wherever he traveled, Agabus found his way to Antioch.

Egyptian documents indicate a major famine in certain parts of the empire around A.D. 46. As to **the entire Roman world**, we have already noted Luke's fascination with hyperbole. Luke drops chronological hints throughout this book, and we shall explore this one further in "Deeper Discoveries." Here he clearly placed emphasis upon how these young believers responded to the dire news of coming hunger among their brothers and sisters to the south.

11:29–30. The process here is very important for us today. Jerusalem did not ask for help, though they certainly had heard Agabus' message even before Antioch. Paul and Barnabas did not start a relief program with canned goods stacking up in the foyer ready for shipment to Jerusalem. The crisp and precise text provides several crucial lessons for congregational operations today:

1. The people themselves initiated the relief effort on the basis of what they learned from Agabus.
2. Apparently everyone participated.
3. Participation depended upon one's ability to give.
4. Whatever theological differences might have still existed between Jerusalem and Antioch, they posed no barrier to sharing with other Christians in a time of need.

Fascinating, too, that when Barnabas and Saul took this gift to Jerusalem, they gave it to the *elders*, not the apostles. This reminds us of Acts 6 where the Twelve delegated relief matters to seven Hellenistic leaders. Just as the office of deacon should probably not be read back into the text of Acts 6, the office of elder most likely does not stem from Acts 11.

This first mention of "elders" in Acts should not surprise us nor make us dash immediately to 1 Timothy 3. Elders were common in synagogue worship, so these Jewish Christians carried over something of that same organization to the church. We will find elders mentioned several times again in Acts (14:23; 15:2,4,6,22–23; 16:4; 20:17; 21:18).

MAIN IDEA REVIEW: *When God wants to develop a work, we need only be available and willing to provide our very best efforts at his call and direction.*

III. CONCLUSION

Different Ministries in a Unified Body

So our "marks of a biblical" church have stretched over two churches with special focus on Antioch. Jerusalem shows us how to recognize and affirm God's work even when it runs against our own traditional beliefs and practices. Antioch shows us almost every basic lesson a congregation needs to know: in a few verses Luke offers a primer on church planting.

In each case the attitude of the believers was essential. We see Peter's openness in handling criticism and the willingness of the "circumcision group" to back away when the evidence accumulated against their view. We see the agreement of Jerusalem to acknowledge Antioch as a genuine sister church and the enthusiasm of Barnabas and Luke for God's hand there. We see Saul leaving his hometown to join a less-gifted teacher in the new work at Antioch, doubtless full of enthusiasm to get his theological hands on this vast group of Gentile believers.

- Different people. Different roles. Different ministries.
- One Lord, one faith, one baptism.
- The unity of the body and the health of a biblical congregation grab center stage in this magnificent chapter. Biblical churches are marked by biblical people who accomplish God's work through his grace and power.

PRINCIPLES

- Sometimes well-meaning Christians will not agree with you.
- Belief in Jesus Christ is the only essential component for salvation.
- God uses willing laypeople in widespread ministries.
- New Christians respond well to encouragement.
- Though a derisive term at the beginning, *Christian* is a name that links us to Jesus.

APPLICATIONS

- Never ignore criticism; God may be teaching you a great lesson.
- When others criticize you, review your obedience to God and your motives.
- Before you respond to criticism, review Proverbs 15:1.
- Encourage other Christians at every opportunity.
- Look for people in need, and ask God what you can do to help them.

IV. LIFE APPLICATION

Backbone of the Night

One of the most demanding ministry experiences of my life was a six and a half week lecture tour to the nation of South Africa. I visited every part of that country, preaching in Soweto, Zululand, and up near the Kruger National Park, known throughout South Africa as "The Game Reserve." Just north of there stretches the Kalahari Desert of Botswana, populated by small people called the !Kung Bushmen, so-called because they punctuate their language with clicking sounds.

Standing on the sands of the Kalahari and looking up at the night sky, one can see thousands of heavenly lights and see them more clearly. What we call the "Milky Way" stands out, of course, but such terminology would have no significance at all to the Bushmen. I learned, however, that they had their own name for that vast cluster of stars. They call it "The Backbone of the Night." When asked why they have chosen such a title, they say, "Those stars hold the night together. If it were not for the Backbone of the Night, great chunks of darkness would fall down upon us and kill us all."

Limited astronomical accuracy to be sure, but a magnificent picture of the church. Jesus is the light of the world, and in his image we are lights in the world. How did Paul put it in Philippians? "Do everything without complaining or arguing, so that you may become blameless and pure, children of God without fault in a crooked and depraved generation, in which you shine like stars in the universe as you hold out the word of life." (Phil. 2:14–16a).

Antioch became such a congregation. The darkness of that city now surrendered to the light of the gospel. Not only that, but this starry and stellar group of Christians would soon send that light around the Mediterranean world, something Jerusalem never seemed quite interested in doing. Mother church? No one can doubt the significance of Jerusalem in the early chapters of Acts; but now things are different. The mother church for the Gentile world, the home base for the rest of Acts, will not be Jerusalem, but Antioch, a congregation which bore *the marks of a biblical church.*

V. PRAYER

God, help us be more like the believers at Antioch. Help us to encourage one another, to share the gospel fervently, and to care for other Christians in need. As the church in the darkened world of our own day, may we indeed be "the backbone of the night." Amen.

VI. DEEPER DISCOVERIES

A. Household Salvation (v. 14)

It seems apparent that all the members of Cornelius' family (and likely his servants as well) trusted Christ (10:44–48; 11:14). In this case, we have every reason to believe that Cornelius merely gathered them and they each voluntarily opened their hearts to the gospel and trusted Christ. Of greater difficulty is the passage in Acts 16:31 where Paul promised that if the Philippian jailer believed he would be saved **and your household**. Even there, the text mitigates that collective prophecy when Luke tells us that Paul and Silas **spoke the word of the Lord to him and to all the others in his house** (v. 32).

On this passage Marshall observes, "The New Testament takes the unity of the family seriously, and when salvation is offered to the head of the household, it is as a matter of course made available to the rest of the family group (including dependents and servants) as well. . . . It is, however, offered to them on the same terms: they too have to hear the Word (16:31), believe, and be baptized; the jailer's own faith does not cover them" (Marshall, 273).

B. Antioch (v. 20)

The brief profile offered earlier hardly does justice to this remarkable city. At the link of the Lebanon and Toras Mountain ranges, right where the Orontes River breaks through those hills and flows to the sea, sat a significant urban center sometimes called "Antioch-by-Daphne" since that celebrated temple of Apollo was nearby. Other appellations included "Antioch-on-the-Orontes," "Antioch the Great," "Antioch the Beautiful," and even "The Queen of the East."

Modern Antakyah, a poor city of about 35,000 located in southeast Turkey, apparently never recovered from its sack by the Persians in A.D. 540. First-century Antioch was a genuine melting pot. Its 500,000 inhabitants joined western and eastern cultures, Greek and Roman cultures, Semitic Arab and Persian influences. The city contained a large Jewish population, perhaps as much as one-seventh of the total.

Amid sophistication and commerce, Antioch indulged itself as a highly visible representation of Roman vice. The pleasure park of Daphne offered moral depravity of every kind. Juvenal, the Roman satirist, complained that the sewage of the Orontes flowed up the Tiber, bringing into the imperial city the superstition and sin of the east.

What would we consider a modern counterpart? Obviously major North American cities would be considerably greater in size, but what about influence and reputation? New York? Chicago? Los Angeles? Toronto? Perhaps all would qualify on most counts and, thank God, in each we would find thriving communities of Christians spreading the light today as did these new converts in Antioch almost two thousand years ago.

C. Christian Prophets (vv. 27–28)

As the gift of prophecy takes shape in the Pauline epistles, it seems to center on proclaiming and explaining God's written revelation. At this point in the history of the church, however, prophets were still predicting the future. We have already noted that Agabus appears again in chapter 21 and that Luke mentions other Christian prophets in Acts 13:1 and 15:32. We dare not forget Philip's prophesying daughters (21:9).

Traditional Jews believed prophecy ceased during the exile but expected its return at the coming of Messiah. Peter's quotation from Joel at Pentecost clearly linked prophecy with Christianity and demonstrated to some extent that the Jews were right—prophecy did come back dramatically with the coming of Messiah. Notable exceptions occurred even prior to Pentecost—John the Baptist and Jesus himself, both clearly recognized by the New Testament as prophets.

Perhaps the most important issue here is to recognize the transitional nature of Acts. We should not be surprised to see the visionary foretelling of Agabus replaced by the explanatory forthtelling of Paul and others (1 Cor. 14).

D. Reign of Claudius (v. 28)

Verses like this help us date the events in Acts. The reign of Claudius took place from A.D. 41–54, and Roman historians refer to a string of bad harvests and famines during that reign. Most scholars place the Judean famine about A.D. 46 so we should find our place here in Acts 11 just prior to that. If we place the death and resurrection of Christ in A.D. 30, we can place the founding of the church at Antioch approximately fifteen years later. Since events in Acts cover a period of about thirty years, we are approximately halfway through the historical time period Luke intends to cover in this book.

VII. TEACHING OUTLINE

A. INTRODUCTION

1. Lead story: Is This the Best You Can Do?
2. Context: Contextually, this is a divided chapter with the first eighteen verses clearly linked to chapter 10 and the rest of the chapter laying the groundwork for chapter 13 and the rest of Acts. The fact that Luke only gives twelve verses to the founding of the church at Antioch should not leave us wondering about the principle of proportion. He will return to this church repeatedly in future chapters and tell us a great deal more about how it served the wider purposes of Christ's kingdom in the world.
3. Transition: Reading Acts 11 seems like looking in a mirror, perhaps the one James described in his candid epistle. First we see criticism and how to handle it. Then we see how anybody, even laypeople on the run, can serve as God's agents in undertaking important tasks for him.

B. COMMENTARY
1. Fairness in Christian Criticism (vv. 1–18)
    a. When you least expect it (vv. 1–3)
    b. When you don't deserve it (vv. 4–14)
    c. When you can't understand it (vv. 15–18)
2. Founded on Aggressive Evangelism (vv. 19–21)
    a. Travels of the persecuted Hellenists (vv. 19–20a)
    b. Founding of the church at Antioch (vv. 20b–21)
3. Fortified by Competent Leadership (vv. 22–24)
    a. The sending of Barnabas to Antioch (vv. 22–23)
    b. The success of Barnabas in Antioch (v. 24)
4. Fed by Qualified Teachers (vv. 25–26)
    a. Saul comes to help (vv. 25–26a)
    b. Disciples called Christians (v. 26b)
5. Functioning to Meet Social Needs (vv. 27–30)
    a. Prophecy of Agabus (vv. 27–28)
    b. Aid for Judea (vv. 29–30)

C. CONCLUSION: BACKBONE OF THE NIGHT

VIII. ISSUES FOR DISCUSSION

1. How long has it been since your church discovered God developing a new work? How did you respond?
2. What can your church do to be sure it is alert to what God is developing? What role does prayer, Bible study, and church fellowship have in this?
3. How does God use hard times and troubles to develop new work? Do you expect your troubles to lead to opportunities to join God in new work?

Acts 12

❧❧

Adventures
of a Prison Escapee

I. **Introduction**
Good People . . . Gone!

II. **Commentary**
A verse-by-verse explanation of the chapter.

III. **Conclusion**
Grab Your Coat and Thongs
An overview of the principles and applications from the chapter.

IV. **Life Application**
Rescue Rejection
Melding the chapter to life.

V. **Prayer**
Tying the chapter to life with God.

VI. **Deeper Discoveries**
Historical, geographical, and grammatical enrichment of the commentary.

VII. **Teaching Outline**
Suggested step-by-step group study of the chapter.

VIII. **Issues for Discussion**
Zeroing the chapter in on daily life.

❧❧

"*G*od is not greater if you reverence Him, but you are greater if you serve Him."

A u g u s t i n e

CHARACTER PROFILE: JOHN MARK

- Mentioned by name ten times in the New Testament
- Native of Jerusalem where his mother was hostess of a Christian congregation
- Missionary intern on the first missionary journey
- Cousin to Barnabas
- Author of the second Gospel

GEOGRAPHICAL PROFILE: TYRE AND SIDON

- Ancient seaports on the Phoenician coast
- Mentioned as early as Joshua and also in 2 Samuel and Isaiah
- The art of glassblowing first discovered at Sidon in the first century B.C.
- Cities were visited by Christ (Matt. 15:21; Mark 7:24–31)

IN A NUTSHELL

*F*ew chapters in Scripture show us God's total providence over human life. James dies, but Peter is released with no human reason given in either case. As the chapter ends with Herod's death, we see God's control even in the affairs of secular politicians. Meanwhile, one constant positive theme runs throughout the chapter—the vibrancy of the church.

Adventures
of a Prison Escapee

I. INTRODUCTION

Good People . . . Gone!

About 1975 I left the faculty of Trinity Evangelical Divinity School to serve as president of Miami Christian College in Florida. One of my Trinity colleagues was Paul Little, still world famous for his evangelism among university students and his books *Know What You Believe, Know Why You Believe,* and *How to Give Away Your Faith.* During the Trinity years I frequently ministered at a Bible conference in Ontario, a hundred miles or so north of Toronto and just south of the famous Muskoka Lakes region. On a highway I often traveled while in that area, Paul Little met a sudden and ferocious death in a head-on automobile accident. In our tears, we who knew him wondered why.

About five years later God took home another friend, another Christian leader whose service we considered so crucial in God's work. Missionary statesman Phil Armstrong, executive director of what was then called The Evangelical Alliance Mission (now SEND, International), lost his life in a plane crash in Alaska. Again in our tears, we who knew him wondered why.

Many times I've wondered at God's design in taking these men from us. How privileged I was to have known them personally, to have their lives touch mine in ways that imprinted my own ministry. Yet how inconsequential my work compared to theirs, how seemingly secondary in light of eternal values. Why these men? Why at their prime? We have so few sterling Christian leaders to serve the kingdom in such a desperate age. Why did God find it necessary to populate heaven's millions with these two more?

Such questions, of course, have no answer, nor even any value. God knows what he is doing, and *he* is doing it—we call it *sovereignty.* He works with the broad plan of the ages well in mind, for he drew up the plan. We deal with one infinitesimal chronological and geographical dimension of that plan; yet how often we want to second-guess how God works in his world among his people.

Chapter 12 pictures for us Christians already suffering from famine and now having to suffer escalated persecution. Luke seems to contrast the warm care of Antiochan believers with the cold, cruelty of Herod. Earlier problems pitted the church against the nation's religious authority—Pharisees and

Sadducees in the Sanhedrin. Now we see the first exhibit of church-state relationships. The story is not pretty—not for the church and, as it turned out, not for Herod.

Luke tells the story in a delightful narrative, one of the most interesting and even amusing in all of Acts. He seems to want us to grasp at least two central concepts in this chapter: the cruelty of the Jewish state and how God dealt with it; and the total sovereignty of God in dealing with his servants in any way he chooses.

Perhaps both these lessons can be transferred to our modern lives with little difficulty. Few Christians in North America are dragged off to prison and certainly not beheaded, though that fate certainly still awaits God's servants elsewhere in the world. On the other hand, however, one can hardly say that civil government is a friend of the gospel.

As to God's control, we see that every servant is dispensable; every leader must be ready to see heaven. For any of us who belong to the Lord, this day might be the last—or it might be the first of thousands more.

II. COMMENTARY

Adventures of A Prison Escapee

MAIN IDEA: *God watches over his church and carries out his plan even when immediate events seem beyond our explanation.*

A Powerful King and a Praying Church (vv. 1–5)

SUPPORTING IDEA: *Persecution and trouble call a church to prayer.*

12:1. Saul had deserted to the other side, so Herod took the role of chief persecutor. Luke tells his readers **It was about this time**, certainly referring to the famine described in the previous paragraph. Bible historians put the approximate date at A.D. 44, probably in the spring of that year. Quite possibly, these events happened before the famine hit, since Luke likely concluded the Antioch narrative before moving back to Jerusalem. The masses generally hated the king and the entire Herodian family (see further description in "Deeper Discoveries"), so Agrippa made special efforts to win Jewish affection. He decided to persecute Christians as one way to elevate his own reputation among the Jews.

Herod's favor with Rome depended, as did all other territorial monarchs, on his ability to keep the *Pax Romana* ("the peace of Rome"). In Israel that meant advancing the majority and suppressing minorities, especially disruptive groups like this growing band of Christians. In one sense he behaved much like Pilate, governed only by what Rome would think, though he bore even greater blame than the governor. Pilate was a Roman who knew nothing about Hebrew theology and only acted upon the case of Jesus when he had to. Herod, on the other hand, had every reason to understand the background of messianic expectation yet deliberately initiated these attacks against the Christians.

12:2. Luke further defines the narrative. Apparently chief among those arrested was James, one of the Lord's original apostles. How interesting! Two brothers (James and John) inseparable throughout the Gospels—one died first, and the other became the last of the apostles to see the ascended Lord. Scholars are not fully decided on the meaning of **put to death with the sword** since the Romans preferred crucifixion or beheading, but Jewish execution would call for the sword to be thrust through the body. Given Herod's efforts to curry favor with Rome, beheading would seem the likely choice here, though one could hardly be dogmatic.

We hear often about the martyrdom of Peter and Paul; but, in fact, this chapter records the only apostolic death the New Testament describes. Martyrdom was still quite new to these Christians. Perhaps they understood Stephen's death a bit better because of his Hellenistic connections and his fiery oratory. James, however, was a Galilean, a purebred Jew now killed by the king of the Jews for political purposes.

12:3. Inflated by his success murdering James, Herod grabbed the apparent leader of the Jerusalemite Christians, a man who had already been in trouble with the Sanhedrin more than once. Luke even tells us when this happened—**during the Feast of Unleavened Bread**. This seven-day celebration, one of three annual feasts, began the day after Passover each spring. Mosaic law required all males in Israel to attend at Jerusalem. Luke may be telling us the city would have been teeming with thousands of worshiping visitors, a perfect time for a crooked politician to grandstand for the crowds.

Both Peter and James had walked with the Lord. James, whom Jesus surnamed "Boanerges" (Son of Thunder), had joined his brother John in asking whether they might sit at Jesus' right and left hands in glory (Mark 10:35–45). Jesus told them they had no idea what they were asking and talked about the cup that he would drink and the baptism with which he would be baptized. Of course, they agreed that would be no problem; but they could not grasp what he meant or what they volunteered for. Perhaps now John, and Peter as well, remembered those words.

12:4. To murder someone during the feast would be untoward even for a vicious king like Herod, so he threw Peter into prison. Herod had no intention of losing this victim, so three shifts of four guards watched him constantly. Verse 6 tells us he was actually chained between two soldiers, an unnecessary and pretentious overkill. Luke uses the term **Passover** to cover the entire period of the Passover proper and the seven additional days given to the Feast of Unleavened Bread. Religious celebration continued at the time of the arrest. When it was over, the execution could take place.

Not only did Herod gain political capital by making Peter a spectacle of the state; he may have been tipped off by the Sanhedrin and so have sought to avoid repeating their embarrassing experience with this former fisherman (5:19). Peter may well have thought that night of Jesus' words in John 21:18, though their complete fulfillment certainly awaited a future day.

12:5. Another Lucan contrast. A church leader in prison and a congregation **earnestly praying to God for him**. Of course, this was their only available weapon (2 Cor. 10:4). Criswell described their intercession with characteristic color.

> Did you know that prayer is the real battle field of the world? The whole universe looks down upon that little group interceding for the life of their chief apostle. God looks down upon it. The angels look down upon it. The hosts of heaven look down upon it. The powers that be, the ages look down upon it. The real battle field where the decisive events of time and history are decided is in the faithful group of followers of the Lord who are down on their knees, praying without ceasing to God (Criswell, 384–385).

Luke repeatedly reminds us how seriously the early believers took their privilege and responsibility of prayer (1:14,24; 2:42; 4:24–31; 6:4,6; 9:40; 10:2,4,9,31; 12:12; 13:3; 14:23; 16:25; 22:17; 28:8). Calm Christians pray during a crisis in their lives. Such behavior led to John Wesley's salvation. When Wesley first went to the colonies, he was not born-again. During the return trip to England he endured hours of dark brooding over the failure of his missionary work in Georgia. The little ship on which he sailed hit a terrifying Atlantic storm; Wesley feared for his life. On that ship he heard a group of Moravians singing through the storm and concluded, "I have not been saved." Upon returning to England in 1738, Wesley wrote, "I went to America to convert the Indians; but, oh, who shall convert me?" On May 24, 1738, largely through the influence of Moravian Peter Poehler, Wesley felt his heart "strangely warmed" at a meeting in Aldersgate Street. Then the founder of Methodism became a genuine evangelist and proclaimer of scriptural holiness.

The persecution had now become universal in Israel or at least in Jerusalem, but this group of believers apparently considered no marches, sit-ins, or protests to demand their rights as a minority group. They did the one thing earnest Christians have always done—they prayed.

B An Awful King and an Awkward Church (vv. 6–19a)

SUPPORTING IDEA: *God's sovereignty in protecting his work in the world is not limited by our ability to understand it, to interpret it, or to act on it intelligently.*

12:6. Luke again tells us about the heavy prison guard but observes that on this night before the proposed trial and execution **Peter was sleeping**. Like Daniel in the lion's den, this New Testament servant had learned to trust his God. What else could he do? He had already experienced one miraculous escape from prison, so he knew God could do that if he chose. If not, he had no intention of accommodating Herod's violence by making a scene on what could have been the last night of his life.

How interesting that Satan and his earthly henchmen take such great pains to protect their work when they think they have seized a victory. The dead and broken body of Jesus was placed in the tomb, covered with a stone, and certified with a Roman seal. Roman guards protected the tomb from a motley crew of followers too afraid to show up for the crucifixion.

12:7. Miracle time again. The sleeping Peter needed to be awakened, so God could get on with his plan. As he arose, the **chains fell off his wrists**. The apostle was "touched by an angel," and he didn't even know it. Next, the cell filled with light, but Peter had no idea what to do. A well-known dreamer, Peter went through the motions as though he were dreaming again. We use the word *escape*, but God provided genuine deliverance; Peter had nothing to do with it. The phrase **angel of the Lord** comes from the Septuagint (Exod. 3:2,4,7) and clearly designates God's personal involvement.

12:8–10. The amazing "vision" continues and, unlike the unpleasantness of the sheet in chapter 10, this story line must have been much to Peter's liking. The angel and the prisoner stride right past two gates and two guards and finally come to the gigantic gate **leading to the city**. Here Luke uses a fascinating word (*automate*) from which we get our English word *automatic*. The door opened *automatically*. God does not always use earthquakes or voices from heaven to accomplish his will on earth. This ancient iron gate swung open as though the departing pair had triggered its action by passing through an electric eye beam. For Peter, on this particular night, God demonstrated his heavenly "open-door policy." The angel walked with him one more block and then left. His work was done.

12:11–12. The cool night air hit Peter, and he **came to himself**. Fully awake, Peter talked to himself, convincing himself that he had experienced a double deliverance, from both civil and religious oppression. No time to stop and ponder the past. Prison escapees need to stay on the move, and Peter knew exactly where to go. By the time Luke wrote, of course, Mark was better known than his mother, so he identifies the place in that way. At this time, however, she hosted one of the many Jerusalem congregations and owned the home where God now directed Peter. This is the first introduction of John Mark in the narrative of Acts, but we shall see him again in chapters 13 and 15, as well as other places in the New Testament (Col. 4:10; Phlm. 24; 1 Pet. 5:13). Notice that supernatural deliverance does not preclude common sense. From the minute he walked out that iron gate, Peter was "on the lam." Hiding became as important as announcing his deliverance to the church.

12:13–14. Luke offers us several tender and humorous moments. We find one here. **Many people** were in prayer at Mary's home as Peter knocked at the outer entrance, probably a courtyard in front of the main door. A servant girl named Rhoda (meaning "rose") was thrilled to see Peter, so thrilled she left him standing outside while she rushed back in with the news of his arrival.

12:15. The response of the Christians sounds so normal, so like us, it makes us want to laugh and cry at the same time. They had been praying, quite possibly for days, that God would release Peter and send their beloved leader back to them. Now God had done precisely that, and they were too stunned to believe it. They called the poor girl a "maniac" (*maine*) since she had obviously taken leave of her senses, perhaps overcome by the emotion of the prayer meeting. In the face of her persistence they finally yielded to the idea that she must have seen something—**it must be his angel**.

What a fascinating idea. Ancient Jews and many modern Christians believe that each person has a guardian angel, though that idea is hardly supported with great weight in the pages of the New Testament. Some years after the New Testament was written, this concept developed into the view that these guardian angels also bore the image of the persons they protected and often appeared immediately after that person's death. Although we certainly do not want to read postbiblical literature back into our interpretation of Acts, it is not difficult to see that notion among these early believers. Did they believe Peter had been delivered and now waited outside in the street? No. They *could* believe, however, he had died and gone to heaven and his look-alike angel stood there!

With all due respect to these sincere praying Christians, it may be worthwhile noting again that *the danger when people do not believe the truth is not that they will believe nothing, but that they will believe anything.*

12:16–17. Meanwhile, Peter, perhaps glancing over his shoulder to see if the prison detail had picked up his scent yet, kept knocking. They finally went as a group, opened the door, and actually saw him. Still, they were astonished. Apparently a mood of celebration set in somewhat noisily because Peter had to tone them down to explain what happened. One can understand how noise would be a bad idea with soldiers all over the streets.

After he told the story to the group at Mary's house, Peter wanted it relayed to **James and the brothers.** Then he took off for somewhere else, possibly Antioch (Gal. 2:11–21). Apparently James, the brother of Jesus, had already begun to emerge in the church. Later Paul would describe him as one of three pillars in the Jerusalem church (Gal. 2:9), along with John and Peter himself. James may already have held some significant administrative post as early as the mid-30s, but that ended with his martyrdom in A.D. 62 (see "Deeper Discoveries").

Peter only appears in the narrative of Acts one more time, at the Council of Jerusalem in chapter 15. We assume, of course, that he continued his ministry, perhaps outside Judea where, for some time at least, he was still a fugitive.

12:18–19a. Herod's fearsome revenge cost sixteen innocent lives. Whom should we blame? Peter? Certainly not. The deliverance depended on him not at all. God? The guards were very much alive when his angel left Peter on a Jerusalem street. A current slogan demands, "Guns don't kill people; people kill people." Whatever one's view of gun control, the fact remains that people *do* kill people. Herod, because of sin in the world and in his heart, caused the deaths of these sixteen men.

Roman justice required guards whose prisoners escaped to receive the judgment that had been levied against the escapees (Acts 16:27). Nevertheless, Herod was a Jewish king, not a Roman governor. He could have shown some clemency, but that was not his nature, as Luke has been consistently reminding us.

A Dead King and a Dynamic Church (vv. 19b–25)

SUPPORTING IDEA: *God may allow the death of saints and cause the death of sinners. Human mortality has little to do with the ongoing work of his kingdom in the world.*

12:19b–20. Herod couldn't be bothered any more with the Peter incident. He rushed to Caesarea to put out another political fire. Apparently in worse famine conditions than those in Herod's kingdom, the people of Tyre and Sidon depended on Judea for food. The audience with Herod, gained through the mediator Blastus, took place during a public festival (Josephus tells us about athletic contests in honor of the emperor). This occurred nearly a year after Peter's release, but Luke connects the two events.

12:21–23. Taking advantage of the occasion, Herod delivered a public address, common Roman behavior but not much in character for a Jewish king—except this one. The people's response (whether sincere or not, Luke does not tells us) ascribed deity to this wicked man. Luke implies he had the opportunity to deny it and, failing to do so, was struck down by God's angel.

Josephus reported that Herod lived in pain for five more days and died at the age of fifty-four (Antiq. XIX, 343–50, vii.2). Scholars cannot agree on the disease which killed Herod, but speculation seems to center on round worms, which is precisely what Luke says. Herod could very well have recited in his dying days a poem Lord Byron wrote centuries later:

> My days are in the yellow leaf;
> The flower and fruits of love are gone;
> The worm, the canker, and the grief are mine alone.

So God's angel strikes twice in this chapter, once for deliverance and the second time for death.

12:24–25. Luke comes to the end of Act III; all is still well with the church, perhaps even better with wicked Herod Agrippa in his grave. Interestingly, Luke returns to the narrative we read at the end of chapter 11 to make connection again with Antioch and move into the material of 13:1–5. He also takes us away from Jerusalem, to return again only in chapter 15 for the Council. From now on, all the action will begin and end at Antioch. The work continued strong at Jerusalem, however, and Luke does not wish to belittle its importance. This final summary of the Jerusalem church from Luke's pen sounds very much like 6:7 and 9:31. Luke has clearly established the proclamation of the gospel throughout Judea and in Samaria. Now he will give the rest of his book to **the ends of the earth**.

MAIN IDEA REVIEW: *God watches over his church and carries out his plan even when immediate events seem beyond our explanation.*

III. CONCLUSION

Grab Your Coat and Thongs

In our family, we practiced a sharing of leadership for family worship. We struggled to create some kind of interesting worship time for our children and finally decided on a few minutes after dinner each evening. We agreed to place a different family member in charge each of the four nights we worshiped together. Our four-year-old daughter proved herself the most creative worship leader in the clan. On one occasion she "passed the hat" and (we are quite sure) took the money to Sunday school with her the next time she went.

I shall never forget her rendering of Acts 12. Apparently, she had heard the story in Sunday school and, unable to read, asked Dad to read the story, after which she retold it in four-year old imaginative style. Upon arriving at verse 8 she said (and after nearly three decades I can still quote it) "And the angel said, 'Peter, grab your coat and grab your thongs; we're getting out of here.'" God's delivering hand sometimes rescues from danger, sometimes from death—but only at his choice and in his timing.

Can you imagine the early Christians telling this story over and over? Certainly they loved the part about the angel, the chains falling off, and the door opening automatically. What a knee-slapper over Pepsi and popcorn to recall how they told Rhoda she was crazy if she thought Peter was actually standing out on the street!

As we read the Bible, we must see real people praying real prayers, struggling with real doubt, and living out real lives for Christ. They were like us and we are like them.

PRINCIPLES

- Governmental power is no match for God's power.
- God's angel can act for deliverance or for death.
- God is sovereign in all his dealings with humanity.

APPLICATIONS

- We say prayer changes things, but actually God changes things— and not all things.
- The present world is full of injustice and pain, and we should expect it.
- The early Christians were real people with real problems—like us.
- When you can't do anything else, pray. When you can do something else, pray first.

IV. LIFE APPLICATION

Rescue Rejection

I think the story first surfaced during the Mississippi floods back in the 80s and then resurfaced during the terrible midwestern floods in the early 90s. A man whose house lay in the path of oncoming water stood out on his front porch when National Guardsmen came by in a jeep. "Get in," they said, "the big water is headed this way." The man replied, "God will help me. I'm staying right here." As the water began to rise, he went up to the second story and looked out at a boat, again intent on rescue. He responded the same way: "God will help me. I'm staying right here."

Finally, the rising floods drove him to the roof where a passing rescue helicopter spotted him and shouted over the loud speaker, "Your whole house will soon be covered. We'll drop a rope ladder, and you can climb up to safety." Again the man shouted up to his would-be deliverers, "God will help me. I'm staying right here."

As the story goes, the man drowned and went to heaven where, after an appropriate wait, he was granted an audience with God. He complained in no uncertain terms that his faith had been real; he had expected God's miraculous deliverance in some way. Why had God let him down? Letting the man unload his whole story, God finally replied, "What do you mean I let you down? First, I sent you a jeep; then I sent you a boat; then I sent you a helicopter, and you turned them all down."

God works through natural means as well as supernatural. Many places in the Bible, we see a situation changing without the distinct characterization of a miracle. Where the text clearly describes a miracle, we should not shy away from claiming a miracle happened. When an angel appears in light, chains fall off, and a large iron gate opens automatically, we can probably chalk it up to a miracle, not intervention of natural causes.

The key lesson of this chapter certainly focuses on the sovereignty of God. He chose and designed the fascinating miracle which caused Peter's deliverance. At the same time he did not ignore James. For reasons known only to him, God determined that James' ministry on earth was finished. No matter how much the believers may have thought his presence necessary. No matter that James himself may have considered and expected a significantly longer term of service.

We have seen it before in Luke, and we shall see it again. The Sovereign Lord to whom the believers prayed clearly carried out his will, in his timing, and in his way.

V. PRAYER

God, protect your people through your gracious hand. Deliver especially those who serve in dangerous places, and help us always to trust your judgment in everything that happens in our lives and our churches. Amen.

VI. DEEPER DISCOVERIES

A. Herod (v. 1)

Born 10 B.C., grandson of Herod the Great and the son of Aristobulus, Herod Agrippa I grew up in Rome where he had been sent in 7 B.C. after his father's execution. He lived his youth as something of a playboy, assisted with a pension from Herod Antipas, his uncle. In A.D. 36 he returned to Rome but offended Tiberius and ended up in prison until Caligula released him after the death of Tiberius about a year later.

He began his rule over the northernmost Palestinian tetrarchies. When Herod Antipas was banished in A.D. 39, Agrippa received his tetrarchy also. In A.D. 41 the Emperor Claudius, an old friend from Agrippa's days in Rome, added Judea and Samaria which restored the entire kingdom of his grandfather, Herod the Great. By then he had truly become the "King of the Jews," reigning over Judea, Samaria, Galilee, Trans-Jordan, and the Decapolis.

Scholars trust Josephus' description of Herodian politics which depicts Agrippa as very Jewish in the presence of Jews and very Roman when with Romans. He moved the seat of government from Caesarea to Jerusalem, elevating that city in the eyes of the world. He even began rebuilding the city's northern wall. Many Jews considered these days a better era, even though Rome still ruled the world.

Let's run by those Herods once again. Herod Antipas murdered John the Baptist, and Herod the Great was on the throne during Jesus' birth. Herod Agrippa I of Acts 12 was the nephew of Antipas and the grandson of Herod the Great. It was an ugly family! James and Peter would not be the last of God's people to feel their power. At the end of Acts, Herod Agrippa II listened to Paul (Acts 26:28); there seems to be no significant evidence that the cruelty of his father passed on to him.

B. "About this Time" (v. 1)

Scholars are unsure of the chronology Luke followed at this point in the book. We have already suggested that the arrival of Barnabas and Saul in Jerusalem may have followed the persecution of chapter 12. Since we know the date of Herod's death was A.D. 44, the events of chapter 12 would have occurred in the spring of A.D. 43. In this view, the famine described in 11:28 occurred a year or two later, perhaps A.D. 46. This seems to juggle events a bit, but also fits in nicely with Galatians 2:1–10, linking that visit with the famine visit of chapter 11.

In any case, while Luke wants to keep the flow going as a legitimate historian, he has no intention of writing in the strict chronology of the western world. In general the events in Acts occur from about A.D. 30 to 60, but Luke will tell his story in ways that accomplish his purpose without regard to chronological exactness.

C. Work of Angels (vv. 7–10,15,23)

Luke scattered the word *angel* all over this chapter. He shows us three different facets of these special beings. The first is the *deliverance angel* of verses 7–10, the second the imagined *guardian angel* of verse 15, and the third the *death angel* of verse 23. As messengers of God, angels were present at the foundation of the world and the birth of Jesus (Luke 2:13–15). They are God's ministers (Ps. 103:21) who serve him quickly and fervently. They control the forces of nature (Rev. 7:1; 16:3) and bring judgment upon God's enemies (Gen. 19:1,12–13; Ps. 78:49).

An angel rolled the stone away from the tomb at the time of the resurrection (Matt. 28:2). Two angels announced the ascension in Acts 1:10–11. They watch over the affairs of the redeemed (1 Cor. 4:9; 11:10; 1 Tim 5:21). Theologian Robert Lightner reminds us, "We do not know all the specific ways God's angels minister to the child of God. However, this should not deter us from believing that they do indeed minister" (Lightner, 141).

D. James in Acts (vv. 2,17)

Multiple men named James appear in our chapter. Verse 2, as we have already noticed, refers to the brother of John, son of Zebedee, whom we know well from the Gospel accounts. The James of verse 17, however, enters the narrative of Acts without introduction. He is James, the Lord's brother and administrative leader in the Jerusalem church (Gal. 1:19; 2:9). Later, we will see him presiding at the Jerusalem Council of A.D. 49 (15:13–21). Acts 21:18 stronly implies that he was the head of the Jerusalem church.

James, the Lord's brother, is mentioned in Matthew 13:55 as the son of Joseph and Mary, not just Mary alone as Jesus was. This James wrote the epistle in the New Testament which bears his name even though he didn't become a believer until after the resurrection. During the Lord's life on earth James had challenged Jesus, along with the other half-brothers (John 7:2–5); but now, like Paul, he had been born again, selected by God for leadership in the church. He had seen Christ after the resurrection (1 Cor. 15:7). By the time Jude wrote his epistle, James was so well-known Jude could call himself simply **a brother of James** (Jude 1).

VII. TEACHING OUTLINE

A. INTRODUCTION

1. Lead story: Good People . . . Gone
2. Context: Much of what we have said about the chronology of the passage speaks to the question of context. Luke is itching to get to chapter 13, to unleash the missionaries across Asia Minor. First he must bring to closure the situation in the Jerusalem church. Apparently the death of Herod accomplished that. The last verses of chapters 11 and 12 indicate how parenthetic this Jerusalem story is in the Lucan narrative.
3. Transition: In our own spiritual growth through Acts, Luke has thrown at us again and again the dominant control God maintains over his church. From the ascension to the death of Herod, his

people merely watch as the Sovereign Lord guides human history to achieve his purposes.

B. COMMENTARY

1. Powerful King and a Praying Church (vv. 1–5)
    a. Death of James (vv. 1–2)
    b. Fate of Peter (vv. 3–4)
    c. Prayer of the church (v. 5)
2. An Awful King and an Awkward Church (vv. 6–19a)
    a. Release from prison (vv. 6–11)
    b. Reaction from the church (vv. 12–17)
    c. Revenge from Herod (vv. 18–19a)
3. A Dead King and a Dynamic Church (vv. 19b–25)
    a. Opportunity for truth (vv. 19b–20)
    b. Judgment for pride (vv. 21–23)
    c. Impetuous for the gospel (vv. 24–25)

C. CONCLUSION: RESCUE REJECTION

VIII. ISSUES FOR DISCUSSION

1. Is your church aware of the great persecution the church is facing worldwide today? What actions is your church taking in light of these persecutions?
2. How do you and your church demonstrate that you expect God to answer your prayers?
3. How has God answered the prayers of your church? Has the church used the experience to help the Word of God increase and spread?

Acts 13

How to Send Out Missionaries

I. Introduction
Hidden Peoples and the Third Millennium

II. Commentary
A verse-by-verse explanation of the chapter.

III. Conclusion
The Task Is So Small
An overview of the principles and applications from the chapter.

IV. Life Application
The Day the Disciples Carried Stones
Melding the chapter to life.

V. Prayer
Tying the chapter to life with God.

VI. Deeper Discoveries
Historical, geographical, and grammatical enrichment of the commentary.

VII. Teaching Outline
Suggested step-by-step group study of the chapter.

VIII. Issues for Discussion
Zeroing the chapter in on daily life

"*The* Spirit of Christ is the spirit of missions, and the nearer we get to Him the more intensely missionary we must become."

H e n r y   M a r t y n

GEOGRAPHICAL PROFILE: CYPRUS

- Island in the eastern Mediterranean Sea off the coast of Syria —148 miles long, 40 miles wide
- Greeks considered it the birthplace of Zeus
- Old Testament refers to it in Ezekiel 27:6
- It housed a large colony of Jews during the first century A.D.

GEOGRAPHICAL PROFILE: PAPHOS

- Capital of Cyprus
- Roman city built by Augustus lying ten miles north of old Greek Paphos
- Located on the extreme west end of the island
- Likely contained a large Jewish population

GEOGRAPHICAL PROFILE: PAMPHYLIA

- A small province of southern Asia Minor extending along the Mediterranean coast for about seventy-five miles and inland thirty miles to the Troas Mountains
- Only became a part of the Roman provincial system in the first century A.D.
- Sent representatives to Jerusalem at the time of Pentecost (Acts 2:10)
- Inhabitants of this area were considered backward and illiterate

cts 13 and 14 describe Paul's first missionary journey. Of particular importance here is the way the Antioch church chose its missionaries and sent them out. Luke then records the journey from Antioch to Iconium.

How to Send Out Missionaries

I. INTRODUCTION

Hidden Peoples and the Third Millennium

ccording to Peter Wagner, "Missiologists are suggesting for the first time in history that there appears to be light at the end of the Great Commission tunnel!" (Wagner, *Spreading the Fire, Acts One Trhought Eight,* 68). In context he refers to the U.S. Center for World Mission (USCWM) and its aggressive work to make the gospel available to all people groups by the year 2000. The center's director, Ralph D. Winter, identifies 17,000 "hidden peoples" who represent 17,000 mission fields. The 2.5 million Bible-believing congregations in the world offer a ratio of approximately 150 congregations per mission field. The center also speaks of 70 million evangelicals in America (an interesting but dubious figure), 17.5 million of whom are aged 18–35. As we enter the third millennium, we need about 100,000 new missionaries in preparation during this decade, only one-half of one percent of the young people available.

What about financial resources? The question is commitment, not availability. The USCWM estimates that American evangelicals control an annual disposable income of about $850 billion. One-fifth of one percent of that amount would support 12,000 church-planting teams around the world. While we bemoan the depravity and cynicism of our continent, God continues to work around the world. Early in 1996 the USCWM reported, "All of the types of statistics fall to the ground before the simple fact that, across the centuries, the number of humble people committed to God have continuously grown faster than the general population. Today, 600 million out of 5.7

billion people in the world are Bible-believing Christians. With the rapid increase in world population, many people cannot believe that the Kingdom of Christ is expanding even faster at over three times the rate of world population growth."

According to Dr. David Barrett, author of the *World Christian Encyclopedia*, the ratio of Christians to total world population was 1:99 in A.D. 1430 and has dropped to 1:8 in 1995. We often hear that Islam is the world's fastest growing religion, and the nightly news seems to support that. Not so, says USCWM: "Christianity is by far the fastest growing global religion—if what is measured is Christianity's most significant type of growth—the growth in the number of those truly believing" (*Mission Frontiers* Jan/Feb. 1996, 5).

What staggering statistics as we stare down the turn of a millennium. What a fascinating comparison for the first missionaries back in the middle of the first century A.D. Look what started—at Antioch!

This watershed chapter in our book shows several major shifts in Luke's history of the early church. The spotlight moves from Jerusalem to Antioch, from Peter to Paul, from Jews to Gentiles, and from Palestine to the Mediterranean world. The Christians at Antioch apparently took literally and prophetically Isaiah's words, "I will also make you a light for the Gentiles, that you may bring my salvation to the ends of the earth" (49:6).

To say that 70 million evangelicals and $850 billion are available means nothing about actually achieving the Great Commission. In this chapter we find only five people and virtually no mention of money. Still, Luke shows us a total willingness to be used of God in moving out to proclaim the gospel wherever he would send his servants. We must recapture that in our day! Thank God for all the resources we have at our disposal, all the modern technology that makes penetrating unreached people groups a much greater possibility than it was fifty years ago. The secret is to develop in our congregations the mentality of global Christianity, a mentality so thoroughly demonstrated by the church of Antioch.

II. COMMENTARY

How to Send Out Missionaries

MAIN IDEA: *God-called missionaries, supported by a strong home congregation, can take the gospel anywhere and see God bring pagan peoples to himself.*

Ⓐ Send Called People (vv. 1–5)

SUPPORTING IDEA: *God leads his church to call out and commission missionaries for the work he is developing in this world.*

13:1. Luke begins by telling us about the leadership resources of the Antioch congregation. Five men are named, and two spiritual gifts come into focus—prophecy and teaching. We should not be surprised to see Barnabas named first, since he was apparently serving as "senior pastor" in the Antioch congregation.

We know nothing of Simon Niger except that his first name was Jewish and his other name Latin rather than Greek. Since *Niger* means "dark-complexioned" (or black), some have speculated that he may have come from African descent. Some believe he may have been the Simon of Cyrene (Luke 23:26) who carried Jesus' cross and whose sons Alexandria and Rufus were Christians in the church at Rome (Mark 15:21; cf. Rom. 16:13).

Much speculation surrounds Lucius of Cyrene, but the point is that we have no further information than what appears here. Luke tells us that Manaen had been brought up with Herod and uses the word *syntrophos* (indicating a foster brother or intimate friend) referring to Herod Antipas. Saul we know as a regenerated persecutor, now the chief teacher of the Antioch church.

Today we would call these men "missionary candidates." Is there a distinction in this group between prophets and teachers? Some suggest that the Greek text allows for this, but the more simple reading of the verse seems to indicate in general that all five possessed and used these gifts. It is not impossible, and perhaps even probable, that they all had the opportunity to at least see and hear Jesus in his earthly ministry. Perhaps none of them were believers until after the resurrection, but the Son of God, whose message they would now proclaim, would have been known to them as eyewitnesses.

13:2. Pronouns are crucial throughout these early verses of our chapter. Does the word **they** refer to the five candidates or to the entire congregation? There is no way to fix that conclusion grammatically, but we certainly understand the Holy Spirit speaks to the entire congregation when he calls for two of the five candidates to be selected for the mission. The word *called,* transliterated *proskaleo,* clearly indicates a divine call.

Notice the climate in the congregation—worship and fasting. Not frantic activity with programs burning out everybody in the congregation. In an attitude of worship and fasting they understood the Spirit to select missionaries for God's **work**. An interesting little word, so common in the Greek language and in English as well, yet in this case designating the missionary effort as a whole. It appears in the same context again in 14:26 at the conclusion of this first journey.

During this process of selection no one in the Antioch church, including the candidates, knew what lay ahead. We read these verses in the light of the entire chapter, and we know exactly where God's will intends to take them. They offered themselves to the Lord for whatever he wished and wherever he wished to send them. This verse strongly emphasizes *call* at two points—the Holy Spirit sets the candidates apart and announces that God has called them for a special work.

13:3. The congregation continued fasting. Here Luke introduces praying (though surely they had been doing this all along). They commissioned the chosen two with the laying on of hands and **sent them off**, an interesting word (*apelysan*) which means "to release them from their duties" at Antioch. What a joyous passage. Willing workers released by a worshiping congregation through a wise procedure. No apostles were present—the sending of the first missionaries was a people project.

In verse 3 we have less problem with the antecedent of **they**. Clearly by now Luke is talking about the entire congregation (a strong likelihood throughout both verses 2 and 3), for the candidates would hardly lay hands on themselves. This missionary commissioning service demonstrates a planned and orderly congregational project and shows that, to a large extent, early missions was a lay movement. Luke makes it plain throughout the rest of Acts that Barnabas and Saul always felt themselves under the authority of the congregation at Antioch which had commissioned (not ordained) them for this specific missionary project.

One can hardly overemphasize the significance of lay leaders, congregational involvement, and ministry teams throughout Acts. The church is not, and never has been, buildings, programs, and property. God's church consists of people, and the emphasis always falls on them in Luke's record. Criswell tells an interesting story emphasizing this tone of Acts:

> Some years ago a famous radio entertainer delivered his version of Lincoln's Gettysburg Address. His presentation was so different that he was deluged with mail after he delivered the address. You see, the entertainer did some research and found that when Lincoln delivered that address, he put an emphasis upon one word in that dedication. We always say: "The government *of* the people, *by* the people, and *for* the people should not perish from the earth." The entertainer discovered that when Lincoln delivered his speech he said, "That government of the *people*, by the *people*, and for the *people* should not perish from the earth." Lincoln emphasized not a preposition, but the *people*. He was moved by the people. That is the emphasis that

ought to be in our work and in our assignments. Our work concerns people. It concerns human souls (Criswell, 400).

13:4. Seleucia lies north and a bit west of Antioch, a sixteen-mile journey on foot. There the new missionaries boarded a boat and sailed for Cyprus, Barnabas' home island. Though Luke does not tell us, we can safely assume that the Antioch congregation continued to pray for the missionaries and to thank God for selecting them, even though they had lost the two most prominent members of their pastoral staff.

As we leave the Antioch church along with Barnabas and Saul, let's take a quick glance ahead 350 years. After the fall of Jerusalem in A.D. 70, Antioch became the world center of Christianity. By A.D. 400, one hundred thousand Christians lived in that city.

We may also assume that the church provided whatever they needed to at least begin this project. Cyprus was not untouched with the gospel (11:19), and Barnabas certainly had appropriate connection there to get the ministry started. The island was a senatorial, not an imperial, province since it remained under the leadership of a proconsul (v. 7) rather than a governor like Pilate.

13:5. Landing at the closest seaport on the eastern shore of the island, they immediately went into the synagogue which, as we know from other texts in Acts, demonstrated a basic plan for missionary ministry in the New Testament. Basically three things emerge in this short verse to be fleshed out in Luke's expanding narrative across following chapters. In no small way they form a missionary strategy.

1. Go to the cities.
2. Go to the synagogues first (Rom. 1:16–17); but if they don't listen, proclaim the gospel to the Gentiles.
3. Carry out all ministry as a team (the only exception arising in Acts 17, Paul's spontaneous speech on the Areopagus).

Informal strategy to be sure, but strategy none the less. The first missionary team consisted of three members since John Mark went along as a *hyperetes*, a helper or servant. He was a rookie, an intern, not unlike a college student going out on short-term missionary service for the summer months, or perhaps even for an entire year.

How did the preaching mission fare in Salamis? Amazingly, Luke does not tell us. Assuming Christians were already there, however, this was not a pioneer effort. The focus could well have been upon confirming Cypriot Jews already committed to Christ.

B Expect Mixed Results (vv. 6–12)

SUPPORTING IDEA: *When the gospel is preached, some accept it, and some reject. Sometime the rejecters become major stumbling blocks Satan places in the path of those trying to understand the truth.*

13:6–7. The missionaries headed west across the island and finally arrived at Paphos, the western port city. Here Luke introduces just two characters in one of his famous contrast passages. Stylistically, this account reminds us of Luke's description of Simon Magus in chapter 8. Here there is no pretense of accepting the gospel and wanting more truth; even before we see his name, we learn Bar-Jesus (son of Jesus) was **a Jewish sorcerer and false prophet.** Like Simon, Bar-Jesus was a *magos.* Sorcery and magic had been banned in Judaism, but its practice continued (Luke 11:19; Acts 19:13–16). The word *Elymas* means "sorcerer," as Luke tells us in verse 8; but there seems to be no connection between that and Bar-Jesus. We can only conclude that Luke is connecting Elymas with *magos* rather than the proper name Bar-Jesus.

This man served as an attendant of the Roman proconsul, Sergius Paulus, whom Luke describes as **intelligent,** sufficiently interested in theology and Jewish history to call these itinerant "professors" to his quarters for a discussion. Polhill notes:

> One should not be all together surprised that a Roman official could be hoodwinked by such a figure. Romans put great stock in powers of divination and even had their own sacred oracles. Charlatans like Bar-Jesus were usually smooth and highly knowledgeable, practicing a sort of pseudo-science. His Jewish credentials did not hurt him either. The Jews had a reputation among the Romans for their antiquity and depth of religious knowledge (Polhill, 293).

Whatever his motive, Sergius received the ultimate approbation from Luke—**he wanted to hear the word of God.**

13:8–9. Luke does not leave Elymas' motives to imagination: he tried to turn the proconsul from the faith proclaimed by his guests. We should view this in terms of diverting rather than turning back. Sergius Paulus had not yet trusted Christ; that occurs in verse 12.

Elymas obviously saw some interest, and it troubled him. Perhaps job security all of a sudden seemed shaky, so he debated with the missionaries in an attempt to keep the proconsul in pagan darkness. Bad choice. Luke tells us that **Saul, who was also called Paul, filled with the Holy Spirit, looked straight at Elymas,** similar to the way Peter stared down Simon. In both cases the overarching power of the Holy Spirit directed in the encounter.

We should not be thrown by the name change in verse 9. Paul is not a Christian name, as some have suggested, but a Roman name. Up to this point Saul of Tarsus has been nothing but a Hebrew born of Hebrew parents (Phil. 3:5). His work has been exclusively with Jewish congregations even though not in Jerusalem. Here, we have a completely Roman setting, a Gentile context for the gospel which would largely characterize Paul's ministry for the rest of his days. He had carried these two names all his life. Luke, fully understanding the changing context, adopts the name Paul for the rest of Acts.

13:10–11. In very theological language, Paul described the treachery of Elymas and called down the hand of the Lord in blindness. His name was Bar-Jesus, "son of the Savior"; but Paul called him **child of the devil**, a wordplay even Sergius Paulus could have grasped. This apostate Jew constantly perverted the way of the Lord (Jer. 5:26–27). A trickster and a fake, he was about to experience the power of the true God in stark and frightening contrast to the petty little magical games he had played.

The blindness was temporary (v. 11). Perhaps Paul remembered his own experience, but we can be sure the Holy Spirit had revealed this fact to him. Could God have been giving Elymas an opportunity to repent and return not only to righteous Judaism but also to Christian faith? The question is moot, for he showed no indication whatsoever of repentance, only an effort to deal with his new disability.

13:12. The blindness of one became light for another: when Sergius saw this miracle, **he believed**. Because baptism is not mentioned, although Luke commonly included it in earlier accounts, some scholars have suggested this was not a genuine conversion. One even says "This may suggest that the conversion was not a lasting one" (Marshall, 220). Those views do not take into consideration the broader context of Acts. Luke uses the same word *(believe)* in 14:1; 17:34; 19:18, also without any mention of baptism. In every case the context strongly suggests that we should understand a genuine salvation experience. The intelligent proconsul had "put it together," precisely what the word *synetos* means. This striking incident of blinded Jew and believing Gentile launched the missionaries, and particularly Paul, into a new career—proclaiming the gospel to Gentiles.

Luke has taken us on a journey across an island to record one conversion. In so doing he has also introduced us to a new ministry philosophy signaled by the switch in Paul's Roman name from the Hebrew name Saul.

Proclaim a Historical Foundation (vv. 13–25)

SUPPORTING IDEA: *As the missionaries moved on to Pisidian Antioch, they found opportunity for Paul's first recorded sermon. It, like Stephen's, centers on the historical foundation Christianity finds in the Old Testament record of how God dealt with Israel.*

13:13. Up to now Barnabas has led the missionary team. Luke dramatically indicates something happened in Paphos to change that order. Rather than saying **Paul and Barnabas** (13:42,46), he tells us that **Paul and his companions sailed to Perga in Pamphylia.** The ship would land at the port of Attalia, and the passengers would travel five miles on foot to Perga. Later they preached at Perga (14:25), but this time it was just a stopping point.

This verse offers a brief line which needs further clarification—**John left them to return to Jerusalem.** Luke does not tell the reason for the young man's departure, but 15:37–39 makes it clear that a genuine falling out occurred on the team. This would seem to eliminate speculation that illness or fear of danger alone created the problem. Some have suggested Mark's dissatisfaction at seeing the leadership of the team switch from his cousin's hands to those of Paul. Others note that a Jerusalemite Christian like Mark would have been stunned by the conversion of a Roman aristocrat and may well have headed home on that note alone.

A discussion after the Sergius Paulus event may well have determined that what seemed to be a visitation of synagogues when they started out now would become a direct mission to Gentiles. Again, that could have been an unpalatable plan for the young man. All we know for sure is that Mark's reasons for leaving seemed invalid to Paul and, in the apostle's mind, disqualified Mark from further involvement in missionary service (15:36–40).

13:14–15. This formal synagogue service probably included the Shema, additional prayers, and the Torah reading. The invitation indicates that the synagogue rulers recognized the distinguished and learned character of their guests, and that they anticipated from the text of the day a **message of encouragement.** Since Antioch was the most important city in southern Galatia, this represented no mean invitation. Some have suggested Paul may have worn his official pharisaical robes to the service and therefore been recognized immediately as one who could contribute. I have no idea what text Paul built upon that day (though scholars speculate freely), but we do know from established synagogue practice that he tied together passages from the Pentateuch and the prophets and that the theme, as we have already noted, centered on encouragement.

13:16–20a. Addressing both ethnic Jews and Gentile proselytes, Paul rushed past the patriarchs and started in Egypt. He moved quickly over the Exodus and the desert. By the end of the first paragraph, he had covered 450 years and brought the nation to Canaan. In his historical review, Paul seems to emphasize that God sent Moses. No need to elaborate these points; synagogue worshipers would have known all the particulars.

The basic thrust at the beginning establishes God's control of history and the unique place of Israel in that history. The verbs attributed to God are crucial in the entire sermon: God chose, God prospered, God led, God endured,

God overthrew, and God gave. The theme of God's sovereignty continues not only from the pen of Luke, but in the ministry of those he describes.

13:20b–22. Moving rapidly onward, Paul touched on the judges, Samuel, Saul, and landed on David, the diving board he would use to plunge into the gospel pool about Jesus. Having told his listeners that God sent Moses, he now reminds them he also sent David. After establishing God's control of history, Paul wanted to define the line of Messiah. He chose to do so with apparent emphasis on 2 Samuel 7:6–16.

With the theme of sovereignty Paul coupled the theme of grace. God in his graciousness has done all these things. Perhaps the most gracious act of the Old Testament (apart from the deliverance from Egypt) was raising up David as a king after God's own heart. This called up 2 Samuel 7:14, and Paul would make the sonship connection very shortly. As Longenecker puts it:

> By anchoring Israel's kerygma in the messianically relevant 'son' passage of 2 Samuel 7, Paul has begun to build a textual bridge for the Christian kerygma—which kerygma he will root in the messianic 'son' passage of Psalm 2:7. By drawing these two passages together . . . , he will draw together Israel's confession and the church's confession, thereby demonstrating both continuity and fulfillment (Longenecker, 425).

13:23–25. God sent Moses, God sent David, and God sent Jesus. Now Paul establishes the true identity of the Savior by moving to the facticity of the resurrection. This is clearly a surprise proposition linked to Isaiah 9–11. No confusing terminology! Paul has said Jesus is the Messiah. John was the last of the Old Testament prophets, commissioned to proclaim repentance and baptism. That work ended when the actual Savior came on the scene, and John himself was the first to acknowledge that (Matt. 3:11; Mark 1:7; Luke 3:15–16; John 1:27).

D Offered Universal Gospel (vv. 26–37)

SUPPORTING IDEA: As David was Jesse's son, Jesus is God's Son, so Paul's sermon pressed on to crucifixion, burial, resurrection, and eyewitness reports to affirm the truth and meaning of the gospel.

13:26–27. For the second time in his speech, Paul addressed his hearers as **brothers**. He moved now to a distinct offer of salvation. He has begun to universalize the gospel but will complete that in verse 46. Throughout this section Paul presents a fourfold Christian confession not unlike that which appears in 1 Corinthians 15:3–5:

1. Jesus was crucified.
2. He was buried in a tomb.

3. God raised him from the dead.

4. He was seen by many witnesses.

In condemning Jesus, the people of Jerusalem fulfilled the words of the prophets read every Sabbath in the synagogues. There is no question about Paul's "Jew first" policy here. He spoke to children of Abraham and **God-fearing Gentiles** and said that the message of God's Messiah, Jesus, came directly to them.

These verses lay a foundation for Paul's letter to the Romans: "A man is not a Jew if he is only one outwardly, nor is circumcision merely outward and physical. No, a man is a Jew if he is one inwardly; and circumcision is circumcision of the heart, by the Spirit, not by the written code. Such a man's praise is not from men, but from God" (Rom. 2:28–29).

13:28–31. Paul rehearsed the essential gospel and ended with a phrase with which we have become accustomed in this book: those who knew Jesus and the events surrounding his life, death, and resurrection **are now his witnesses to our people.** No question about his death; he was actually buried. No question about his resurrection; **for many days he was seen.** We already know from 1:3 that those **many days** were forty in number.

The antecedent for the frequent use of **they** in this paragraph takes our eyes directly back to **the people of Jerusalem and their rulers** (v. 27). Sometimes people who emphasize the Jewish role in the death of Christ are called anti-Semitic. The preachers in Acts tend to relieve Pilate of responsibility as Paul, a Jew, does here.

G. Campbell Morgan emphasizes the grace of this passage. How, despite all the setbacks of history and the rejection God knew his Son would meet, he still sent the Savior into the dark world.

> That is the infinite music of the Gospel. When He brought the Savior into darkness and blindness even among the people of His own choice and exaltation and government they did not know Him. They read the law and the prophets, which led up to, and promised this great Saviour; but when He came, they were blind, and did not understand Him. There is no more wonderfully illuminating word, revealing at once the Divine government and the Divine grace, than that in which the apostle declared that God compelled the folly and sin of these people to fulfill His purpose. They fulfilled the Scriptures they did not understand, by condemning Him Who stood in their midst, according to the purpose of God (Morgan, 329).

So to the offer of salvation Paul has added the purchase of salvation and the evidence of the completion of salvation's work. Substitutionary atonement put Jesus on the tree. To put it another way, the resurrection proves the cross (Rom. 1:1–6).

Oh can it be upon a tree,
The Savior died for me.
My soul is thrilled,
My heart is filled,
To think it was for me.
(John Newton, 1779; c 1917, 1944 by G. J. Excell Loftus; owned
by Hope Publishing Company).

13:32–37. In basic New Testament homiletics, Paul stays with the resurrection theme and goes on to quote Psalm 2:7; Isaiah 55:3; and Psalm 16:10. God kept his promise; the gospel has come, and the signature of that promise rests in the resurrection. How was this a message of encouragement (v. 15)? The Father had provided for his children. He had delivered on a promise made hundreds of years earlier to their forefathers. Notice how Paul included himself in the group of witnesses though he was not a Galilee-to-Jerusalem disciple. Paul's purpose in the use of the Old Testament here is not immediately obvious except for Psalm 16:10 in verse 35.

The *NIV Study Bible* handles verse 33 by saying in a marginal note, "'Today I have become your Father' here refers to the resurrection of Jesus" (p. 2121). How does Isaiah 55:3 relate to God raising Jesus from the dead, never to decay? We can find an answer only by linking verses 34 and 35 and then joining them to Paul's words in verses 22 and 23.

God's promises of resurrection to David had been fulfilled in Jesus his greater Son. David was dead, and everyone in the Pisidian Antioch synagogue knew that. Rather than waiting for some future resurrection day when David along with righteous Jews would be raised from the dead, these specific promises from Old Testament texts have already been fulfilled in the resurrection of Jesus.

Explain Biblical Forgiveness (vv. 38–43)

SUPPORTING IDEA: *Resurrection not only settles God's promise, it also sends God's forgiveness and shows God's grace.*

13:38–39. With the third reference to his **brothers** Paul brought his sermon to a close—something Stephen never had an opportunity to do. What did all this mean? What should these people do with the information that Jesus and his resurrection fulfilled the messianic promises of the Old Testament? How does one react to this kind of "good news"?

Paul left no fuzziness in his message. Forgiveness comes through faith in Jesus, and that produces justification impossible by the law of Moses. This is pure Pauline gospel which we shall encounter everywhere in his New

Testament letters as well as his preaching in the Book of Acts. Justification is a legal term describing the standing of the believer before God.

Might the strange construction of these verses suggest that the law could justify from some things but only the gospel could take care of the rest? Hardly. Everything we know about Pauline theology militates against that kind of view. Paul preached grace alone; and Luke, the careful historian, himself no sloppy theologian, could never stumble into that kind of interpretation.

13:40–41. With the invitation came a warning, a caveat that the prophets not only promised resurrection but also predicted scoffers who would perish through unbelief. Paul quoted Habakkuk 1:5 to let his audience know that faith would bring forgiveness and justification but rejection would bring punishment. In the Old Testament context of Habakkuk, the nation of Israel had failed to see the rise of Babylon and the implications of that awesome enemy on the horizon. Paul used the text here to describe any who refused to accept the gospel.

13:42–43. Paul was finished. He and Barnabas left the building amid invitations to return next week and continue. Not only that, but both Jews and proselytes were fascinated with this gospel and talked with Paul and Barnabas about it. At this point, it surely appeared to Paul and Barnabas that things went so well in the synagogue that such ministry could go on indefinitely. That was hardly the case as we shall see.

What did Paul and Barnabas mean when they urged the inquirers **to continue in the grace of God**? Were these people already Christians, and Paul was attempting to strengthen their faith? Were they devout Jews on the verge of recognizing the reality of the Messiah Jesus and encouragement aimed at their progress toward that goal? Since Luke gives us not the slightest hint of conversions in the synagogue and since we have no reason to believe any Christian Jews lived in Pisidian Antioch at this time, the latter interpretation may be our best choice, though one should not be dogmatic in affirming it.

Marshall combines the views by suggesting that:

> This phraseology . . . suggests that these people already trusted in the grace of God, as they had come to know of it through the Old Testament, and were now being urged to continue in that basic attitude by believing in Jesus as the one through whom God's promises were being brought to fulfillment (Marshall, 229).

▤ Move on to Receptive Gentiles (vv. 44–52)

SUPPORTING IDEA: *Whenever the gospel is preached, we should expect a mixed reaction. Some will believe; some will reject and turn away; still others will reject and stir up some kind of opposition.*

13:44–45. Doubtless Paul and Barnabas spent most of that week talking about the gospel with whomever was interested. They must have answered hundreds of questions. The whole city was stirred up and interested enough to show up at the synagogue **to hear the word of the Lord**. Notice that the opposition in these verses had nothing to do with the message but rather sprang from envy at the popularity of the missionaries.

We can imagine the Jews upset that their synagogue was being crowded by Gentiles like some secular meeting hall. Then they must have been even more incensed that Paul and Barnabas showed no hesitation in speaking to this mixed multitude. The NIV uses **talked abusively** to translate *blasphemountes*. These Jews blasphemed Paul's message and therefore, certainly in Luke's eyes, blasphemed Paul's Savior as well.

13:46–47. We can almost hear Paul turn to Barnabas and whisper, "I was afraid of this." In just one sentence he acknowledged that his duty to proclaim the gospel first to Jews has been finished. They rejected it and chose not to accept the Life of the Ages. Now it's Gentile time at the old city, and to affirm it Paul quotes Isaiah 49:6 (cf. Luke 2:28–32).

Notice that turning to the Gentiles was not a once-for-all decision but applied only to the local situation. As Paul moved on, we discover him following this formula in every city—first to the Jews, then to the Gentiles.

The phrase **do not consider yourselves worthy** is not only interesting, but curious. One can hardly imagine synagogue Jews thinking of themselves as unworthy of eternal life. Perhaps we should see here just a bit of Pauline irony which might be paraphrased, "You Jews, who always consider yourselves righteous, now apparently do not think you are sufficiently righteous to take advantage of God's gift; so we'll offer it to the Gentiles and see what they say." The idea of inherent self-righteousness driving out God's righteousness is hardly new; this common spiritual disease afflicted the Pharisees.

Luke made an interesting transition and application in the use of Isaiah 49:6. Israel was to be the light for the Gentiles; but, since it never fulfilled that role, God sent Jesus to become his real servant and carry out that mission. Now Paul and Barnabas, servants of Jesus, have inherited the mantle and become the light (Luke 1:78–79; 2:29–32; 2 Cor. 4:3–6).

13:48–49. Luke wastes no time telling us how the Gentiles responded to this amazing turn of events. He avoids his tendency at hyperbole (we saw it again in verse 34) to make sure his readers understand that only those appointed for eternal life believed. Whatever one's view on election for salvation, it is impossible to avoid this doctrine in the pages in the New Testament. As we have noticed earlier, it runs hand in hand with the doctrine of free will. The harmonization of those two seemingly conflicting views exists only in the mind of a gracious God. Somehow, God chooses us while at the same time (from our point of view) we trust him. The gospel then spread through the whole region (presumably southern Galatia), not only by the apostles' continuing visits to other towns but by the witness of new Gentile believers.

13:50–52. How interesting! The Jews incited their most influential women along with **the leading men of the city** to stir up persecution against the missionaries and throw them out of the area. Longenecker suggests that the **God-fearing women** were the Jewish wives of the city magistrates induced to convince their husbands that Paul and Barnabas needed to get out (Longenecker, 430). This is no mob violence nor a religious reaction like the Sanhedrin's stoning of Stephen. Apparently the Jews convinced the Roman authorities that Paul's illegal message could upset the *Pax Romana* and that would be enough to get them expelled.

For their part, Paul and Barnabas simply followed the directions Jesus gave for dealing with unreceptive listeners—they symbolically shook off the dust of the city as they left town (Luke 10:11). Nor was this departure traumatic or negative. As Paul and Barnabas traveled the great Via Sebaste on its southeast leg to Iconium eighty miles away, the new believers at Pisidian Antioch whom Luke already calls disciples **were filled with joy and the Holy Spirit.**

MAIN IDEA REVIEW: *God-called missionaries, supported by a strong home congregation, can take the gospel anywhere and see God bring pagan peoples to himself.*

III. CONCLUSION

The Task Is So Small

I have heard it said that Billy Graham was at Lausanne during the now famous and historic moon shot of earth when the cameras in the space capsule aimed back at that beautiful blue sphere. Since then, the picture has appeared in thousands of places. We have grown accustomed to seeing ourselves as part of the solar system in what could almost be called an out-of-planet perspective. Seeing it for the first time thrilled all of us, and those present with Billy by the television set that day said he responded by saying, "God, it's so small; let's just reach out and take it."

I'm unable to verify the story, but the response certainly sounds like Billy and every aggressive missionary from the first century to the twenty-first. From our perspective in any given locale on the globe, the task looks enormous. We think about language school, deputation, acculturation, and a thousand other problems that we face in sending out missionaries. All of them are real, challenging problems!

Somehow the global vision must be seen from above—from God's perspective. It is, after all, his world; and we are, as Paul so clearly put it, his light to the people who live on the globe. Surely he can overcome all the obstacles we face in sharing his grace with the lost. Oh that God would give us greater vision, broader horizons of ministry. That he would enable us to say with Billy, "God it's so small; let's just reach out and take it."

PRINCIPLES

- Only people called of God to serve can be effective in his work.
- Praying congregations support those who represent them around the world.
- When the gospel is proclaimed, we should always expect mixed results.
- When the gospel is proclaimed, the people God has called to himself will believe.

APPLICATIONS

- Be available for whatever God wants you to do and wherever he wants you to go.
- Reflect the spirit of Antioch, and be a global Christian.
- Pray for willing workers for today's harvest, and help send them out.
- Understand the gospel clearly, and be able to present it with no confusion.
- Recognize that God's sovereign grace prevails in all human activity.

IV. LIFE APPLICATION

The Day the Disciples Carried Stones

Elizabeth Elliott, herself a missionary of the highest stature, tells a story, a fable, about the day Jesus asked the disciples to carry stones. In the morning he told them to find a stone which they would carry all day. We can imagine them selecting the lightest and smallest they could find.

As the story unfolds, that night Jesus and the disciples made camp. At mealtime the disciples asked what to do with the stones. Jesus told them, "I'm glad you asked. I will now turn those stones to bread, and that will be your evening meal." As the disciples ate the few bites they had carried throughout the day, they pledged never to be caught in such a dilemma again.

Sure enough, the next day Jesus asked them in the morning to pick up stones and carry them all day. What a day! Lugging heavy boulders from place to place with the happy anticipation of a full meal that night.

When they made camp, the disciples asked the same question, but this time the Lord's answer was different. "The stones? Just place them over there in a pile. We don't need them anymore." When the protestations and complaining had died down, Jesus had only one question for the disciple band: "For whom did you carry your stone today?"

Certainly I have taken some liberties in retelling the story, but the basic idea remains the same. Effective missionaries, pastors, deacons, elders, Sunday school teachers, and disciples of all kinds do what they do for the glory of Christ, not for their own benefit. In this chapter Paul and Barnabas left home to travel for Jesus' sake. They entered into confrontation with a wild-eyed sorcerer for Jesus' sake. They proclaimed the gospel to hesitant Jews for Jesus' sake. They endured persecution at Pisidian Antioch for Jesus' sake. The result was not pain and complaining, but rather rejoicing—even at the difficulty.

We may very well ask ourselves the same question about difficulties in our lives: "For whom did you carry your stone today?" Only when we see Christ at the center of everything we do; only when our motives center on how best to please him; only when we allow the Holy Spirit to fill us as he did Paul and Barnabas will we really be able to say in genuine honesty, "I carried my stone for Jesus."

V. PRAYER

God, grant us the willingness to serve you wherever you send us, in total dependence upon your power and grace to enable us to speak the gospel well and to trust God with the results.

VI. DEEPER DISCOVERIES

A. Fasting (v. 2)

Voluntary abstinence from food was not necessarily a practice of the early church, but we do see it from time to time (Matt. 6:16; Acts 14:23). The believers at Antioch apparently felt it necessary to seek God's will in this important matter so strenuously that they fasted to concentrate on prayer. We should not think of fasting as demonstrating greater spiritual sincerity and certainly not as a way to impress the Lord. Like these Christians, those who practice fasting today should do so voluntarily with the purpose of focusing more fully on some phase of the Lord's work.

B. Four Hundred Fifty Years (v. 20)

Commentators ponder where these 450 years fit in. Some argue for the Egyptian sojourn, the conquest, and the distribution of the land. Others connect the phrase to the rest of verse 20 and include the period of judges as well. This seems to be in conflict with 1 Kings 6:1. According to Marshall, "It seems best to take it of the sojourn in Egypt (400 years), the wilderness wanderings (40 years verse 18), and the occupation of the land (10 years)" (Marshall, 223). At any rate, in round numbers Luke is clearly within range no matter how one calculates the precise statistics.

C. Appointed (v. 48)

Though some commentators move rapidly over this phrase, Luke clearly intends us to grasp its full significance. I suggested earlier that salvation includes both human faith and divine appointment. I retain that view here with further detail. Paul tells us Christ chose us before God formed the world (Eph. 1:4). In Romans 8:29–30 he reinforces the idea dramatically: "For those God foreknew he also predestined to be conformed to the likeness of his Son, that he might be the firstborn among many brothers. And those he predestined, he also called; those he called, he also justified; those he justified, he also glorified." Other verses demostrate the same truth:

John 6:44—"No one can come to me unless the Father who sent me draws him."

Matthew 11:28—"Come to me, all you who are weary and burdened, and I will give you rest."

John 3:16—"For God so loved the world that he gave his one and only Son, that whoever believes in him shall not perish but have eternal life."

1 Timothy 2:1,3,4—"I urge, then, first of all, that requests, prayers, intercession and thanksgiving be made for everyone. . . . This is good, and pleases God our Savior, who wants all men to be saved and to come to a knowledge of the truth."

2 Peter 3:9—"The Lord . . . is not wanting anyone to perish, but everyone to come to repentance."

Barnhouse calls the theme of sovereignty in the Bible "a Wagnerian *leitmotif*." He says:

God is sovereign, in absolute control of all things. If this were not so, man would have abolished Him long ago. Nothing in all the universe can happen without either God's direction or permission. In Acts 2:23 we saw the plain teaching that the crucifixion of Jesus Christ was under the direct supervision of God Almighty. This event was planned from all eternity. Christ was the **Lamb slain from the foundation of the world** (Rev. 13:8). Yes, it was man who sentenced Him to die. It was man who drove in the nails. But it was God who ordered it. **It pleased the Lord to bruise Him; He has put Him to grief** (Isa. 53:10). Here we see the wonderful way in which there is harmony of the divine decree and human free agency (Barnhouse, 122–123).

Whenever the Bible presents seemingly irreconcilable information (such as the option of choosing salvation over against the idea that God has already chosen us), the best course is not to gravitate to one extreme or the other but to try to understand the two as antinomies. An antinomy is simply an apparent contradiction between two equally valid principles, and that is exactly what we have here. The truths seem mutually exclusive, yet Bible-believing Christians should hold them simultaneously even though that defies human reason, believing that, if we understood everything as God does, there would be no contradiction.

Many have stumbled on this point, arguing that God would not give us biblical truth which runs counter to intellectual processes he created. Where did we get the idea that we must think like God? What else might Isaiah have meant when he wrote "As the heavens are higher than the earth, so are my ways higher than your ways, and my thoughts than your thoughts" (Isa. 55:9)?

As a seminary student I desperately struggled with this. I watched classmates come down on both sides. Some declared an absolute determinism, while others indicated their preference for free will. Our theology professor, Dr. Alva J. McLain, offered us a very helpful illustration one day to demonstrate that interpretation of this difficult dilemma depends on perspective.

He described a gate into the garden of salvation. Over the outside portal one reads the words **Whosoever will may come**. Responding to this gracious invitation, we walk through, assuming the choice has been made voluntarily. Nothing outside the garden hinted we *must* go in nor that anyone had preordained our entrance. From this perspective it appears to be exclusively our own choice—free will.

As we begin to make our way through the flowers and shrubs, we glance back, hoping to get one more glance of that beautiful invitation. What shock to discover that the words on the inside portal are different: **Chosen in him**

from the foundation of the world. Now we realize both are true. From our perspective, we have chosen Christ; we have believed the gospel and trusted him for salvation. From God's perspective, however, he has made possible everything that led up to that salvation choice. There is an old hymn which puts this doctrine so well.

> I sought the Lord, and afterward I knew
> He moved my soul to seek him, seeking me;
> It was not I that found, O Savior true;
> No, I was found of Thee.

VII. TEACHING OUTLINE

A. INTRODUCTION

1. Lead Story: Hidden Peoples and the Third Millennium
2. Context: Jerusalem is behind us, and the world lies before. God's missionaries walk and sail around the Mediterranean to proclaim the gospel. This activity will continue through most of the rest of Acts. We begin the chapter in Antioch with the beautiful commissioning of the first missionaries. Now we leave Paul and Barnabas only temporarily in Iconium where we will find them again at the beginning of chapter 14.
3. Transition: We dare not get so caught up in the geography or even the theology of our chapter (and many to follow) that we fail to look into the mirror of God's Word for today. Missionaries are desperately needed right now, and congregations ought to be praying, yes and maybe even fasting, to focus on our global task. Never have we had greater resources in the church to carry out the Great Commission than today. Can we find the tenacious visionary faith of Antioch once again?

B. COMMENTARY

1. Send Called People (vv. 1–5)
   a. Willing workers (v. 1)
   b. Worshiping congregation (v. 2)
   c. Wise procedure (vv. 3–5)
2. Expect Mixed Results (vv. 6–12)
   a. Opposition to the gospel (vv. 6–8)
   b. Punishment from God (vv. 9–11)
   c. Faith in the truth (v. 12)
3. Proclaim a Historical Foundation (vv. 13–25)
   a. God prepared Paul (vv. 13–15)

b. God sent Moses (vv. 16–20)
c. God sent David (vv. 21–22)
d. God sent Jesus (vv. 23–25)
4. Offer a Universal Gospel (vv. 26–37)
   a. Jesus' coming was prophesied (vv. 26–27)
   b. Jesus' death came because of rejection (vv. 28–29)
   c. Jesus' resurrection forms the foundation of the gospel (vv. 30–37)
5. Explain Biblical Forgiveness (vv. 38–43)
   a. Forgiveness leads to justification (vv. 38–39)
   b. Rejection leads to perishing (vv. 40–41)
   c. The sermon leads to positive discussion (vv. 42–43)
6. Move on to Receptive Gentiles (vv. 44–52)
   a. Open hostility (vv. 44–45)
   b. Ready believers (vv. 46–48)
   c. Official persecution (vv. 49–52)

C. **CONCLUSION: THE DAY THE DISCIPLES CARRIED STONES**

VIII. ISSUES FOR DISCUSSION

1. Is God calling people from your church to become missionaries? How is the church encouraging people to listen to and respond to God's call? How is the church responding to those who answer the call?
2. What resources and people is Satan using to attack the work of your church? How are you recognizing and combatting these attacks?
3. Is your church proclaiming the good news to people who have never heard it? If not, why not? Are people responding to the gospel in your church?

Acts 14

Things Are Tough All Over

I. **Introduction**
No One Ever Talks to Us This Way

II. **Commentary**
A verse-by-verse explanation of the chapter.

III. **Conclusion**
Worth all the Trouble
An overview of the principles and applications from the chapter.

IV. **Life Application**
The Single Starfish
Melding the chapter to life.

V. **Prayer**
Tying the chapter to life with God.

VI. **Deeper Discoveries**
Historical, geographical, and grammatical enrichment of the commentary.

VII. **Teaching Outline**
Suggested step-by-step group study of the chapter.

VIII. **Issues for Discussion**
Zeroing the chapter in on daily life.

Q u o t e

*"To get through the hardest journey
we need take only one step at a time,
but we must keep on stepping."*

M e g i d d o   M e s s a g e

GEOGRAPHICAL PROFILE: ICONIUM

- Located on the border between Pisidia and Lycaonia
- Flourishing agricultural area surrounded by desert
- Important commercial center whose industries centered in produce and wool
- Lies 90 miles southeast of Antioch on the Via Sebaste

GEOGRAPHICAL PROFILE: LYSTRA

- Small country town in the hill country
- Roman military outpost
- Granted the status of a colony in 6 B.C.
- Located 100 miles southeast of Pisidian Antioch
- Populated primarily by uneducated Lycaonians from a small Anatolian tribe

GEOGRAPHICAL PROFILE: DERBE

- Located 45 miles south of Iconium
- Formed the eastern boundary of the Roman Empire in first-century Asia Minor
- Site only recently discovered in the mid-twentieth century, now known as Kerti Huyuk in modern Turkey

GEOGRAPHICAL PROFILE: ATTALIA

- Main port town of Pamphylia located on the Gulf of Adalia
- Founded by and named for Attalus Philadelpus, king of Pergamum from 159–138 B.C.

I N   A   N U T S H E L L

*A*cts 14 concludes the first missionary journey, picking up the missionaries in Iconium and returning them by the end of the chapter to Antioch of Syria. This chapter represents the first foray of the gospel into raw pagan territory where superstition and superstituous behavior prevailed.

Things Are Tough All Over

I. INTRODUCTION

No One Ever Talks to Us This Way

*O*ne of my faculty colleagues served several terms as a missionary in Latin America and is totally fluent in Spanish. Concerned as well with intercultural ministry in the major cities of America, he habitually travels in a Dallas City Police patrol car through the inner-city streets inhabited largely by a minority population.

On one night time trip, the officers encountered a 14-year-old boy lying in his own blood, surrounded by a crowd of relatives and neighbors. Hubbub and confusion reigned everywhere. People were shouting, crying, and waving their arms. Since no one in the crowd spoke English and neither officer spoke Spanish, Mike became the interpreter.

After calming the group and getting the basic information, the officers got the boy off to the hospital; and the crowd began to disperse. An elderly gentleman, however, lingered for a moment, came up to Mike, and said, "I want to thank you for talking to us like this. Nobody ever talks to us this way."

He expressed not only appreciation for the opportunity to speak to someone who understood his language and who was able to do something practical about his grandson's dilemma, but also gratefulness for the kindness and gentleness with which Mike spoke with distressed family members. They were accustomed to brusque orders, raised voices, and hostile tones. All of a sudden, here stood a man who spoke to them as a friend and offered help in time of need.

In the chapter before us, Paul and Barnabas, sophisticated Jews with strong backgrounds in Old Testament theology, plunge like pioneer missionaries into new territory. Iconium was not greatly different from the city of Pamphylia, but Lystra and Derbe represented virgin fields for the gospel. No synagogues there, no Jewish population familiar with messianic promises to whom they could proclaim the message of the risen Christ. Here the gospel plunges into raw heathenism, the like of which these missionaries certainly never before saw in such primitive form. Surely their residence in Antioch displayed all the wickedness available anywhere in the civilized world. Still, the difference between Antioch and Lystra could be compared to the difference between a capital city like Lima, Peru, and the jungle tribes living two or three hundred miles inland.

Though the pagan peoples of Lystra may have acted differently than the Latin population of inner-city Dallas, they responded for the same reason—"no one ever talks to us this way." To Romans, Greeks, and Jews alike, these cities represented people beyond the periphery of any kind of civilization or culture. Yes, they had to be governed because they were part of the empire. They didn't have to be liked and certainly did not have to be ministered to in any fashion—except by Christian missionaries commissioned to take the gospel **to the ends of the earth**.

II. COMMENTARY

Things Are Tough All Over

MAIN IDEA: *In God's plan, every human being should have an opportunity to hear the gospel, not just those who live in civilized areas where modern communication is available.*

A Rejection in Iconium (vv. 1–7)

SUPPORTING IDEA: *God often uses opposition to the gospel to create new opportunities to preach the gospel.*

14:1. For all practical purposes, this ancient Phrygian town had been transformed by the Greeks into a city-state. Located on a plateau above the surrounding desert, it enjoyed the best of both worlds, the forest and plains to the south and the mountains to the north. Historians tell us that Iconium remained somewhat resistant to Roman influence and culture, preferring rather the temperament and flavor of Greek civilization. Indeed, it was governed by an assembly of citizens called the *Demos,* and its public documents were written in Greek, not Latin. Because of its beauty and prosperity, William Ramsay called Iconium the "Damascus of Asia Minor" (Ramsay, *Cities of St. Paul*, Grand Rapids: Baker, 1979, 317–319).

Here the missionaries followed their basic plan and headed right for the synagogue. They had followed the same pattern in Pisidian Antioch, with the same results. Don't miss an important idea here: *Paul had not given up on the Jews.* His words in 13:46, as we noted there, did not indicate a final turning away from God's people of the Old Covenant but rather turning away from the rejecters in Pisidian Antioch. Here again, he starts fresh in Iconium and wins converts among both Jews and Gentiles.

14:2. As in Pisidian Antioch, the opposition came not from Gentiles but from unbelieving Jews. Luke uses poignant language to describe what happened—stirring up the Gentiles, the Jews **poisoned their minds**, literally "caused their minds to think evil." Not only against Paul and Barnabas, but against all believers there (**the brothers**).

14:3. This time, rather than shaking off the dust of the city, Paul and Barnabas evidently decided that the persecution actually gave them a good reason to stay a **considerable time** in Iconium. They spoke boldly for the Lord (Luke surely intends us to understand "Jesus" here), and he confirmed the message through miracles (*semeia kai terata*).

All this took place in Galatia, so we can understand this ministry in light of the Galatian letter. There Paul tells us that these mighty works of the Spirit certified that God approved his gospel (Gal. 3:4–5). Luke uses an interesting phrase—**the message of his grace**—to describe the gospel. The linking of the message with the accompanying miracle reminds us of Hebrews 2:1–4.

Signs and wonders in Acts remind us of the transitional nature of this book. Barnhouse puts it well:

> These signs and wonders were specially given to the apostles and early Christian church workers because there was no written New Testament as yet. Not a line of the New Testament had been written at this point, and there was no solid authority to which the apostles could point and say, "See, we're preaching truth. You can check it in the Word of God!" There was no completed Word of God. So God enabled the apostles to perform wonders and signs to authenticate their ministry, but these wonders and signs would fade as God's Word came into being (Barnhouse, 126).

14:4–5. Acts 14:4,14 contain the only use of the term *apostles* in this book. Certainly, Luke refers to Paul and Barnabas in context, thereby broadening the word beyond the common understanding of the Twelve which included neither (1 Cor. 9:4–6). The word for **plot** indicates a spontaneous reaction uncontrolled by reason and planning. Three groups aligned themselves against the apostles—Jews, Gentiles, and **leaders**. The grammar of the text seems less precise regarding this latter word, but perhaps we should take it in reference to both Jews and Gentiles, quite possibly a reference to civil authorities.

14:6–7. The pilgrim and stranger motif throughout the New Testament begins to take incarnate form in these missionaries, now driven out of the second city on this trip. Rejected disciples who proclaimed a rejected Lord represented the New Testament standard. They stand in refreshing stark contrast to the contemporary prosperity gospel in which Christianity wants to be popular, large, influential, and wealthy. No kingdom politics or civil religion here, just the basic gospel proclaimed wherever people will listen.

As the apostles made their way to Lystra, they proclaimed God's Word **to the surrounding country**, a probable reference to small towns and villages, perhaps even isolated settlements along the way. This flight was more than just geographical; it was political in terms of boundary. Paul and Barnabas literally crossed from one political region to another; these verses emphasize that transition.

B Rebellion in Lystra (vv. 8–20)

SUPPORTING IDEA: *God rarely asks Christians to seek physical abuse for the cause of the gospel, but in the providence of God, sometimes such abuse and persecution cannot be avoided.*

14:8–10. Paul and Barnabas escaped both Pisidian Antioch and Iconium without physical harm, but literal persecution caught up with them in Lystra. Surely Paul's wide education had prepared him to know he was entering pagan darkness. Lystra represented primitive idolatry, people who knew neither Hebrew religion nor Greek philosophy. Essentially, Lystra's population consisted of Roman military veterans, a "retirement center" for that vast army.

With no synagogue, God gave them a different place to start their ministry, an account quite reminiscent of Peter and John healing the lame man in chapter 3. We should notice the text carefully; Paul had already preached before the miracle took place. In that fact, this account differs significantly from chapter 3. Furthermore, this man chose not to jump around and hold on to his healers but simply began to exercise his new ability to walk.

Today we talk about the "contextualization of the gospel" as the focus of modern missions. That means we seek to put the gospel message in the framework of the particular people's understanding. That is precisely what these missionaries did as they traveled from one place to another. Speaking to synagogue Jews in Pisidian Antioch or Iconium offered a vastly different challenge than speaking to ignorant pagans in Lystra. Both of those contexts stood in stark contrast to what Paul found in the Vienna of the ancient world, Athens.

14:11–13. The miracle produced a reaction as yet unseen by Christian missionaries. Yet the behavior would be perfectly normal for people accustomed to worshiping false gods. Notice Luke tells us right away that these people spoke their own local language, indecipherable to Paul and Barnabas. This accounts for their slow reaction to the proceedings described in these verses. In Lystra we see a significant contrast with Acts 3, where Peter could immediately discern that the Aramaic speakers around him intended to give him and John credit for the healing. None of Paul's Hebrew, Greek, Aramaic, or Latin was useful on this unusual occasion.

Zeus was the main god of the Greeks; and Hermes, his chief speaker. (For more, see "Deeper Discoveries.") Interestingly, Luke tells us why they linked Paul with Hermes, but why call Barnabas the main god? One possible explanation is physical appearance. If Barnabas was large and strong and exhibited a certain inherent dignity, they might very well conclude that Zeus was with them allowing his chief spokesman to carry his message. The text contains no hint that the Lycaonians had any idea of Barnabas' home area, though again we have a fascinating parallel since Zeus reportedly came from Cyprus.

More likely these primitive people knew the common legend of the area which accounts not only for their naming the apostles, but for their celebrative behavior. Longenecker summarizes it succinctly:

> According to the legend, Zeus and Hermes once came to "the Phrygian hill country" disguised as mortals seeking lodging. Though they asked at a thousand homes, none took them in. Finally, at a humble cottage of straw and reeds, an elderly couple, Philemon and Baucis, freely welcomed them with a banquet that strained their poor resources. In appreciation, the gods transformed the cottage into a temple with a golden roof and marble columns. Philemon and Baucis, they appointed priest and priestess of the temple, who, instead of dying, became an oak and a linden tree. As for the inhospitable people, the gods destroyed their houses (Longenecker, 435).

Among the Christians of the day, certainly Barnabas and Paul were rather free-thinking leaders, but this sacrilege far exceeded Peter's sheet. Sacrificial bulls draped in woolen wreathes were led to the temple of Zeus outside the city to become sacrifices to these visiting deities. Once the apostles caught on (either through grasping visually the flow of events or by the translation of some local words into Greek), they jumped into action. Memories of Herod's worms surely haunted any first-century public figure who stood in danger of being worshiped instead of God.

14:14–18. How does one stop pagan worship in one's behalf? Luke tells us **they tore their clothes and rushed into the crowd** insisting on their humanity. In Joshua 7:6 tearing clothes demonstrates distress, and in Mark 14:63 it protests perceived blasphemy. Doubtless both occurred on this occasion. Romans 1:20 will not allow that conclusion. In fact, the whole point of emphasizing God's "testimony" establishes accountability to respond to natural revelation.

Given more time, Paul might well have developed in Lystra a message somewhat in the same pattern of his magnificent speech on the Areopagus (Acts 17). Luke suggests the crowd had already lost control; the best they could achieve was to stop the sacrifice.

Perhaps most important in this passage is the exclusivity of the gospel. Even without mention of Jesus, the cross, and the empty tomb, Paul had rendered practicing polytheism **worthless** and called the Lycaonians to the **living God**. We shall continue to see in Acts the early Christians' unwillingness to compromise the "one-way" gospel they preached. The generous Romans made room for everybody else's religion within the vast ideology of the empire. The Greeks lined up gods one right after another and even built altars to unknown gods, just in case they might have missed one. Christians preached Jesus only. As Criswell put it, "You do not stitch the Christian faith to some old dirty rag of paganism or heathenism or atheism. Christianity is a seamless robe. You do not add to it, you do not take away from it, and you do not rend it. It is woven one throughout" (Criswell, 439–440).

14:19–20. Wherever the early missionaries went, the bad guys in the black hats weren't far behind. Stalking Paul and Barnabas right into this stronghold of paganism marched antagonistic Jews from both Pisidian Antioch and Iconium. They easily convinced the fickle crowd that these two were not gods. Rather, they were obviously impostors. Since Paul had been doing all the talking, he alone felt the brunt of their wrath and their stones. The text seems clear regarding Paul's physical condition because Luke tells us they *thought* he was dead.

Luke leaves us with many questions as Paul and Barnabas leave for Derbe. Might Timothy have been present on this occasion? Did Paul's rising constitute some form of miracle? Was the deliverance from the angry Lycaonians and Paul's reentry to the city a miracle in itself? What other New Testament passages shed light on this event?

To the first three questions we can find no clear answers in the text. Paul mentions the stoning in 2 Corinthians 11:25. Some have even found Lystra in 2 Corinthians 12:7 where Paul alludes to the thorn in the flesh. Barnhouse asks us to stretch our thinking just a bit further and consider whether Paul might have undergone a near death, out-of-body experience on this very occasion which he describes in 2 Corinthians 12:1–4.

Paul there refers to himself in the third person—**a man in Christ**—who went to heaven and **heard things that cannot be told, which man may not utter**. This was more than a vision. It was a definite transport into heaven. I'm suggesting that it was at this point in his missionary career, described in Acts 14, that Paul went to heaven. The few moments during which his body laid inert on the ground and his friends stood by helplessly, thinking him dead and wondering what to do about the matter, he may well have left the body and then returned following his experience of 2 Corinthians 12 (Barnhouse, 129–130).

Maybe. Luke certainly makes no effort to link the two events, nor does Paul in the 2 Corinthians account. It seems best to assume that Paul was badly beaten up but quite alive when the disciples gathered around him outside Lystra that day.

Review in Galatia (vv. 21–25)

SUPPORTING IDEA: *New converts need encouragement. Missionaries who bring them the gospel or people who lead others to Christ bear some responsibility for the strengthening, discipling process.*

14:21a. Journeying sixty miles southeast, Paul and Barnabas reached Derbe, preached the gospel there, and **won a large number of disciples**. Wait a minute! Were there no believers left behind at Lystra? Not yet. That awaits a future visit. Why would Luke so hurriedly mention ministry in a town where the results were so obviously significant? Probably because he knows he will revisit this town in his accounts of the second and third journeys and give it more press at that time.

Longenecker suggests Luke is simply a man of his times, more interested in the larger cities, the central target of most of the missionary activity in Acts. He does offer a suggestion of importance for Lystra and Derbe, however, and an applicational note worth reproducing here:

> Probably the larger and more influential churches were in Antioch and Iconium as well, though the congregations in the smaller and more rural towns seem to have contributed more young men as candidates for the missionary endeavor (e.g., Timothy from Lystra—16:1–3; Gaius from Derbe 20:4)—a pattern not all together different from today, where the larger churches often capture the headlines and the smaller congregations provide much of the personnel (Longenecker, 438).

14:21b–22. In Derbe the missionaries could very well have headed southeast 150 miles to Tarsus and then easily returned to Syrian Antioch, but it was not yet time to go home. The churches of southern Galatia needed encouragement in their time of suffering, so they returned to the cities where they knew opposition awaited in order to tell the Christians, **We must go through many hardships to enter the kingdom of God.** These churches of southern Galatia were the likely recipients of the epistle to the Galatians written between the end of the first journey and the Jerusalem Council. When we read Galatians, therefore, we might think about these believers and remember how they came to Christ, enduring opposition from both Jews and Gentiles in the earliest days of their faith.

We wonder why Luke doesn't tell us about renewed opposition in these three cities which had treated the missionaries so badly. Perhaps we should conclude that on the return trip they confined their ministry exclusively to small groups of believers and therefore did not offend synagogue leaders or influential people in either Gentile or Jewish communities of those cities.

Let's not try to find a theology of suffering in the latter part of verse 22. Some popular religions today argue that people must find salvation through suffering. I have watched faithful followers of Catholicism plod forward on bleeding knees at the shrine of Lourdes in Portugal. I have seen flagalantes beat their backs bloody in the Philippines to earn favor with God. No, salvation does not come through suffering, nor were the missionaries talking here about salvation since their encouragement came to people already in the family of God. Rather, they reflected the word of the Lord Jesus about sharing his sufferings along the way to heaven (Rom. 8:17; Phil. 3:10–11; Col. 1:24).

14:23. The appointing of elders to new congregations affords sufficient consequence to give further space to it in "Deeper Discoveries." Here we notice only that a different word appears, *cheirotonesantes*, rather than the usual *presbyteroi* or *episkopoi*, the latter two used interchangeably in the New Testament. The NIV offers two marginal notes as options to the main text: "Barnabas ordained elders," or "Barnabas had elders elected." We should recognize the nature of these fledging churches. The manner of selecting leadership in established congregations like Jerusalem (Acts 6) would of necessity have been a very different process than that used with church planting efforts in the Gentile world of Asia Minor.

14:24–25. This time the apostles had the opportunity to preach at Perga, the chief city of the province of Pamphylia, something that apparently eluded them on their first visit (13:13). Attalia seems to have been nothing more than an embarkation point for the trip back to Antioch.

Report in Antioch (vv. 26–28)

SUPPORTING IDEA: *When a congregation sends out workers for ministry and supports them in that effort, it deserves a full report of what God has done through his servants.*

14:26. Luke leaves no question in our minds about Antioch as the genuine mother church for the Gentile ministry. There Paul and Barnabas **had been committed to the grace of God**, and the work they had been commissioned to do was now complete. Though we know that two more journeys will follow, we cannot read that information into chapter 14. As far as the missionaries or the sending congregation understood, the work had ended. They had no plans for additional activity in Asia Minor at that time. The first missionary journey covered about 1,400 miles by land and sea.

14:27. What was the central essence of the report to Antioch? God opened the door of faith to the Gentiles (Acts 15:4,9,11–12; 9:15–16). The word **church** is singular, though surely there must have been numerous congregations meeting all over the vast metropolis of Antioch. When they came together, they met as one, emphasizing strong unity in the community of believers. Perhaps Luke's phraseology once again introduces his next chapter, for he addresses the very point of the Jerusalem Council debate: under what conditions should this **door of faith to the Gentiles** be opened.

14:28. The first missionary trip took just over a year. Luke's **long time** suggests about the same period of time. Some find in Luke's phraseology the implication that the missionaries will go out again and that their stay at Antioch was temporary. Doubtless, it was temporary, but we dare not infer what the Christians thought at that time.

What did the missionaries do during this year? Certainly we do not stretch our understanding of scriptural narrative if we picture them enjoying some much needed rest and renewed fellowship with the brothers and sisters at Antioch, as well as continuing their former teaching ministry in that congregation. We also know that during this year Paul very likely wrote Galatians. By the time he and Barnabas appeared before the Jerusalem Council in chapter 15, he had not only experienced a year of evangelism among Gentiles but also declared his understanding of Christian soteriology. Today we might say he was already "in print" on this very important subject.

MAIN IDEA REVIEW: *In God's plan, every human being should have an opportunity to hear the gospel, not just those who live in civilized areas where modern communication is available.*

III. CONCLUSION

Worth All the Trouble

Was it worth it? All those miles. All that time. The persecution! the stoning! the humiliation! We haven't the slightest hesitation recognizing that Paul and Barnabas thought every moment of their first missionary journey extremely valuable by heaven's standards. They functioned "with eternity's values in view"; and, as Paul repeatedly explained in his letters, all the hostility and opposition meant nothing if he could fulfill God's plan for his life and ministry.

It was also worth it to the church at Antioch. Picture Paul as a modern missionary showing slides from Pisidian Antioch, Iconium, and Lystra! Imagine the gasps in that darkened room in Antioch as he flips in a new tray and shines up on the white wall pictures of the Lycaonians dragging out the bulls and wreaths to worship the missionaries. Imagine the tears when the believers see the pictures Barnabas took of Paul lying near death outside the Lystra gates. See the harbor at Attalia and the mountains north of Iconium. We "ooh" and "ahh" with the audience at the magnificent sunset shots taken from the back end of the ship on the way home to Antioch.

Mainly, Paul wants us to see the pictures of the new converts. Look at this small group. Here's one more. Look at those two there. Here we see a man and his wife who both trusted Christ on the same day. Was it worth it? Was it worth it to the people who responded to the gospel?

PRINCIPLES

- The gospel almost always receives varied response.
- The gospel places its primary emphasis on God's grace.
- Christians are pilgrims and strangers in this world.
- The gospel always confronts evil and darkness—then and now.
- The gospel builds upon common grace and natural revelation.

APPLICATIONS

- Things are tough all over—but not impossible.
- Things are tough all over—but God knows our problems.
- Things are tough all over—but we can be faithful to our commitments.
- Things are tough all over—but we rejoice in the midst of our problems.
- Things are tough all over—but people are praying for us and want to hear reports of our victories.

IV. LIFE APPLICATION

The Single Starfish

Walking along a beach one day, a boy saw a man pick up a starfish and throw it back into the water. "Why did you do that, mister?" asked the boy.

"Because the tide is going out, and the starfish would be stranded here and dry out. In all likelihood, he would be long dead before the tide comes in again," responded the man.

"What difference could it make? Surely there are thousands and thousands of starfish in that ocean. What difference would it make if you throw just one back in the water so it can live?"

"It makes a great deal of difference to this one" smiled the man as he walked on down the beach, perhaps to find another starfish.

What difference does it make if we hand out a gospel tract to a filling station attendant or a bellman at a hotel? What difference could it make if we precisely outlined the gospel in a Sunday school class on a day when we know two unsaved visitors are present? What difference would it make if we sacrifice a bit in order to send missionaries to those hidden peoples of the world we talked about at the beginning of chapter 13? Like the lame man Paul healed at Lystra, it makes a great deal of difference to each one as an individual.

People don't trust Christ in huge groups; that became the second and third century way of "making Christians." People trust Christ one by one and, like the starfish thrown back to the sea, receive opportunity for life by hearing the gospel.

V. PRAYER

God, make us willing to accept persecution, embarrassment, humiliation, or whatever else is necessary to be your faithful witnesses to people around us who desperately need the gospel no less than the Jews at Pisidian Antioch, the sophisticated Gentiles at Iconium, or the raw pagans at Lystra. Amen.

VI. DEEPER DISCOVERIES

A. Great Pairs in Acts

We notice repeatedly how the ministry in Acts is carried out in teams. Sometimes the teams number three (Barnabas, Saul, and John Mark); sometimes, larger; but often, two. At least seven prominent couples in Acts form a study all their own.

- Peter and John (Acts 3; 4:13; 8:14)
- Barnabas and Saul (Acts 11:25–26; 12:25; 13:2)
- Paul and Barnabas (Acts 13:43,46,50; 14:1; 15:2,12,22,35)

- Judas and Silas (15:32)
- Barnabas and Mark (15:39)
- Paul and Silas (15:40; 16:19,25; 17:4,10)
- Silas and Timothy (Acts 17:14–15; 18:5)

B. Zeus and Hermes (v. 12)

Two inscriptions discovered by archaeologists near Lystra identify the Greek gods Zeus and Hermes as worshiped in the Lycaonian portion of Galatia. One reflects the dedication to Zeus of a statue of Hermes, and the other refers to a "priest of Zeus." Longenecker's recitation of the legend (as told earlier in our study) may very well have basis in fact.

As chief of the Olympian gods, Zeus was the Greek equivalent of the Roman Jupiter. In Greek fantasy religion, Saturn married Rhea. They became "father and mother of the gods" and gave birth to Zeus. He, in turn, through various marriages and illicit unions, became the father of most of the greater gods of the pantheon. Hermes parallels the Roman Mercury, known both as the messenger of the gods and their chief spokesperson.

As we noted earlier, the Romans generally accepted the gods of conquered peoples and added them to their collection. In addition to gods of their own which paralleled Greek deities, they worshiped Athena, Isis of the Egyptians, and, had the early Christians let them, might very well have added Jesus along with the worthless gods in the pantheon.

C. Common Grace (v. 17)

Common grace is a theological phrase which describes God's bounty poured out on all men and women regardless of their faith or righteousness. In our present passage it describes God's gifts of rain and grain, both of which come into the hands of the saved and the unsaved (Ps. 145:9; Matt. 5:45; Luke 6:35). We also see common grace in the Spirit's restraint of sin in the world. Without common grace Satan's activity would run rampant over a wicked society all too ready to embrace his cause (Gen. 6:3).

In a more specific dimension, common grace can refer to the Holy Spirit's conviction of sin in the world. In John 16:7–11 Jesus promised that the Holy Spirit would come to convince the world of sin, righteousness, and judgment. Through common grace the Holy Spirit enlightens the minds of unbelievers so they can understand the gospel; through *special grace* the Spirit regenerates the heart and brings the believer to salvation.

Common grace also explains why unsaved people can be so pleasant and kind, sometimes even more gentle than members of God's family. That is because God's common grace curbs the devastating effects of sin in the world so it does not reach its fullest extent. Osterhaven offers a useful definition:

Common grace is understood to be the unmerited favor of God toward all men whereby 1) he restrains sin so that order is maintained, and culture and civil righteousness are promoted; and 2) he gives them rain and fruitful seasons, food and gladness, and other blessings in the measure that seems to him to be good (Osterhaven, 172).

D. Elders (v. 23)

The Bible identifies two church offices by name—elders and deacons. The primary passage is 1 Timothy 3:1–13, where Paul discusses the qualifications of both at some length. We find comparable material in Titus 1:5–9. Elders are also associated with deacons in Philippians 1:1. At Thessalonica elders "ruled" or led the church (1 Thess. 5:12), a situation not unlike that at Rome (Rom. 12:8). The English words *elder* and *bishop* translate *presbyteros* and *episkopos* and are used quite synonymously in the New Testament (Acts 20:17,28; Titus 1:5–7).

If "pastor" is an office, it inseparably relates to elder ministry where Acts 20 details the shepherding duties of the elders (1 Pet. 5:2). Congregational responsibilities toward elders are described in 1 Timothy 5:1,17–19 and 1 Thessalonians 5:13. Rewards await elders who have served well and consist of such things as "a crown of glory" (1 Pet. 5:4) and "a crown of righteousness" (2 Tim. 4:7–8).

Different denominations structure churches in different ways, and the New Testament certainly allows freedom for that. The Scriptures establish the offices of elder and deacon but hardly demand that every congregation utilize both or must use certain terminology to designate church leaders.

Of greater importance than titles and structure is allegiance to biblical qualifications. Francis Schaeffer, in his insufficiently heralded book *The Church at the End of the 20th Century*, writes:

> Not only does the Bible set forth the offices of the church but it also describes the kind of men who should hold these offices. The qualifications for elders and deacons are given in two places —1 Timothy 3:1–13 and Titus 1:5–9. These give what the elders and deacons should be like. The church has no right to diminish these standards for the officers of the church, nor does it have any right to elevate any others as though they are then equal to these which are commanded by God himself. These and only these stand as absolute (Schaeffer, 65).

VII. TEACHING OUTLINE

A. INTRODUCTION
1. Lead Story: No One Ever Talks to Us This Way

2. Context: We travel with Luke through Asia Minor from Iconium to Derbe and back along the same route until the first missionaries return to Antioch and tell their story. Since the three missionary journeys constitute a significant portion of Luke's book, this first precedent holds significant importance for us.

3. Transition: At various points in the chapter we see ourselves in the text. Like Paul and Barnabas we want to speak boldly for the Lord (v. 3). Like the crowd at Lystra, we are grateful for God's common grace (v. 17). Like the new believers at Iconium and Antioch, we hear Paul reminding us how we must endure hardship before we enter the kingdom (v. 22). With the Antioch church we rejoice at the return of missionaries and the report of how God has worked through their ministry (v. 27).

B. COMMENTARY

1. Rejection in Iconium (vv. 1–7)
   a. Conversion to the gospel (v. 1)
   b. Opposition from the Jews (vv. 2–4)
   c. Danger to the missionaries (vv. 5–7)
2. Rebellion in Lystra (vv. 8–20)
   a. The initial miracle (vv. 8–10)
   b. The pagan worship (vv. 11–13)
   c. The message from Paul (vv. 14–18)
   d. The persecution and departure (vv. 19–20)
3. Review in Galatia (vv. 21–25)
   a. Evangelism in Derbe (v. 21a)
   b. Encouragement in Iconium and Antioch (vv. 21b–23)
   c. Exit from Asia Minor (vv. 24–25)
4. Report in Antioch (vv. 26–28)
   a. Return to Antioch (v. 26)
   b. Report in Antioch (v. 27)
   c. Rest in Antioch (v. 28)

C. CONCLUSION: THE SINGLE STARFISH

VIII. ISSUES FOR DISCUSSION

1. How do city churches and rural churches in your area cooperate to make sure that every person has a chance to hear and respond to the gospel? Is there something you could do to help the churches do this in a better way?

2. What reputation does your church have in the community? What are you doing to improve the image of the church so more people will be drawn to it and through it to Jesus?

3. What kind of ongoing program does your church have to strengthen and encourage its members in discipleship growth?

Acts 15

Church Business Meetings Can Work!

I. **Introduction**
Tradition

II. **Commentary**
A verse-by-verse explanation of the chapter.

III. **Conclusion**
Freedom of theGospel of Grace
An overview of the principles and applications from the chapter.

IV. **Life Application**
God Is Watching the Apples
Melding the chapter to life.

V. **Prayer**
Tying the chapter to life with God.

VI. **Deeper Discoveries**
Historical, geographical, and grammatical enrichment of the commentary.

VII. **Teaching Outline**
Suggested step-by-step group study of the chapter.

VIII. **Issues for Discussion**
Zeroing the chapter in on daily life.

"*Sometimes* I get the feeling that the two biggest problems in American today are making ends meet—and making meetings end."

R o b e r t   O r b e n

BIOGRAPHICAL PROFILE: SILAS

- Possibly the Aramaic form of the name-Saul
- Silas appears only in the Book of Acts
- A prominent member of the Jerusalem church and a Roman citizen
- Paul's companion on the second and third missionary journeys
- The name Silvanus, the Latin equivalent of the Greek *Silas* of Acts, appears repeatedly throughout the New Testament: Acts 15:22, 40; 2 Corinthians 1:19; Acts 16:38; 17:10; 18:5; 1 Thessalonians 1:1; 2 Thessalonians 1:1; and 1 Peter 5:12

GEOGRAPHICAL PROFILE: CILICIA

- First inhabited by the Hittites, then later by Sumerians and Phoenicians
- Located in the southeast portion of Asia Minor
- Tarsus was the eastern city of Cilicia's eastern plain
- From 51–50 B.C., Cilicia was governed by the orator Cicero

BIOGRAPHICAL PROFILE: JUDAS

- Leader in the church at Jerusalem
- May have been the brother of Joseph Barsabbas (Acts 1:23)
- Luke calls him a prophet
- He accompanied Silas to Antioch to deliver the report of the Jerusalem Council

After serving the church at Antioch for a year or so, Paul and Barnabas found it necessary to return to Jerusalem to counter an uprising among legalistic Christian Jews still focused on the question, "What must Gentiles do to be saved?"

Church Business Meetings Can Work!

I. INTRODUCTION

Tradition

*W*ho can forget the opening scene of *Fiddler on the Roof* as Tevye rolls his wheelbarrow onto the stage and addresses the audience in the now-famous song, "Tradition." He explains life set against Czarist Russia in the little town of Anatevka, populated largely by hard-working Jewish families. The year is 1905. The Russian Revolution is about to begin. In the village of Anatevka, a pious Jew, who raises his five daughters with the aid of quotations from the Bible (many of which he invents himself), explains that their village has chosen guidelines unrelated to the Czar or the Revolution. The peasant dairyman and his friends acknowledge that age-old laws of tradition govern their lives. Their traditions give order to their lives and stability to their community. Without their traditions the good citizens of Anatevka would be as shaky as a "fiddler on the roof."

In the church we have many traditions, too. Some of them, such as the special ways in which a congregation celebrates Christmas or Easter, help us draw closer to God even though we may not be able to define or support the practices from Scripture. By using the words *traditional* and *contemporary* to talk about types of worship, we acknowledge that a good bit of what we do has developed from years of practice.

One tradition often maligned in church work is the role of boards and committees. People regularly say things like, "An elephant is a horse put together by a committee." Even leadership books, ignoring the strong evidence of recent research favoring group decision-making, keep insisting that groups may discuss, but individuals make decisions. In other words tradition tells us to put up with committees, to tolerate business meetings, simply because no better way exists to get the church's work done.

In the chapter before us we have an example of a church business meeting. As we follow it through its processes, we shall see a group of believers thoroughly involved in a very significant issue of theological importance. The way we evangelize and do mission work today is still dependent on what was decided by the Jerusalem congregation in this chapter. It should not escape our attention that they carried out this work without complaining or criticizing the necessary process. These good people show us something we often seem reluctant to admit: "Church business meetings can work!"

II. COMMENTARY

Church Business Meetings Can Work!

> **MAIN IDEA:** *The salvation of Gentiles occurs precisely the same way as does salvation of Jews—through faith in Jesus Christ because of God's grace.*

A Motion (vv. 1–5)

> **SUPPORTING IDEA:** *God's people may try to add rituals and rites to the requirements for salvation, but God never does.*

15:1. The year is approximately A.D. 49. The church at Antioch faced its first crisis. Legalists from Judea, possibly still smarting from Peter's visit to Cornelius and now totally thrown off balance by the results of the first missionary journey, decide they will head for Antioch and straighten out the liberalism Paul and Barnabas were teaching there. This group, known as "Judaizers," and others of their persuasion also carried influence in Galatia at this time. Some have suggested that they operated with the full blessing of James and Peter, but certainly no evidence in this chapter or anywhere else supports that view.

Mark went back to Jerusalem (13:13) and may have incited ill will against the missionary team with his account of the conversion of Sergius Paulus. Nor should we miss the fact that when Paul and Barnabas returned from the first journey they stopped at Antioch, apparently making no effort to go back to Jerusalem with some kind of report.

The Judaizers had tradition on their side. Jews had been welcoming Gentiles into the faith for hundreds of years; the procedure was well fixed. Since Christianity was just a messianic branch of Judaism at this time, why should the rules change? Why should they back away from requiring circumcision and the keeping of the Mosaic law? After all, if they couldn't hold on to the traditions, the fledging church could become as shaky as a fiddler on the roof.

The Judaizers failed to realize (or refused to see) that God had changed the rules. At this point in the history of the church, the large and growing church at Antioch provided the best display of people living according to the new guidelines. If these legalists wanted to stop Paul's "antinomian (against the law) tendencies" before they got completely out of hand, Antioch was the place to start.

15:2. Unless a reader has just joined the Acts narrative in chapter 15, the debate offers no surprise. After what the missionary evangelists had been through and what they had seen God do, they could hardly have allowed the Judaizers to convince Gentile Christians at Antioch, or anywhere else, that they must be involved in circumcision and law-keeping.

Who sent Paul and Barnabas? From everything we already know about the Antioch church, we can only assume that all the representatives to Jerusalem were appointed by the entire congregation. That's the way the missionaries had been sent out in the first place, and we have no evidence to indicate any hierarchy had grown up at Antioch since that time.

The representative group went to Jerusalem to meet with **the apostles and elders**, so apparently a structure of elders had developed at the original church. As the drama unfolds, James seems to serve as the chairman or moderator of the meeting.

15:3–4. Having to travel approximately 250 miles, the Antioch party headed south. They may very well have taken a month as they made a leisurely journey, interrupted by visits to groups of Christians along the way. We should remember the Christians in Phoenicia and Samaria largely resulted from the Hellenistic evangelistic efforts (11:19) and would hardly be a part of the strong traditionalist core Paul and Barnabas would combat at the meeting.

Luke does not suggest that they discussed the forthcoming meeting along the way, though they may well have done that. The main conversation reviewed the first missionary journey and the stories Paul and Barnabas had to tell brought joy at every stop. Upon arriving in Jerusalem, they reported again **everything God had done through them**. We should probably see this as a general meeting open to everyone and designed to hear the different viewpoints.

15:5. Luke tells us the major premise of the debate, the formal motion for the meeting. How interesting to read that the issue was raised by **some of the believers who belonged to the party of the Pharisees**. Interesting, but not surprising. From everything we know about the Pharisees both in the

Gospels and so far in Acts, they were interested in the messianic message of Christianity; some became believers quite early. We also know that their commitment to ritual and tradition could very well have carried over into their Christian lives and made them a separate subgroup within the church known as the party of the Pharisees.

We dare not confuse the Ten Commandments with **the law of Moses**. From our perspective we often view those two as one, but they were not. The New Testament never argues that Christians should not pay attention to the Ten Commandments, though certainly they will never lead to salvation. This argument was not about that. It dealt with the ritualistic practices of the Jews which set them apart from other people—circumcision, food laws, and other guidelines for living.

Furthermore, we should not be surprised that the Pharisees spoke up in defense of their oral traditions. This commitment to oral tradition rather than the written Scriptures brought both Jesus and Paul into conflict with the Pharisees on numerous occasions.

Notice how the statement of verse 5 sounds a bit different than the one we saw in verse 1. The chapter begins by talking about what Gentiles had to do to become Christians, but here we seem to face the question of what Gentile Christians must do to retain their status. That kind of distinction may be useful in light of the Book of Galatians. That entire epistle seems to deal with the question of what people need to do to gain favor with God *after* they had been saved by grace.

Having understood that distinction however, let's recognize that the broad issue of the Jerusalem Council dealt with how Gentiles should relate to the issues of Judaism when they come to faith. It is hard to imagine that even Pharisees who had been born again would argue that circumcision or law-keeping saves anyone. Such heresy should not have been perpetrated by anybody in the congregation. But the meeting goes on.

Ⓑ Discussion (vv. 6–11)

SUPPORTING IDEA: *The bottom line in any discussion about salvation must sound very much like Peter's words in verse 11:* **It is through the grace of our Lord Jesus that we are saved.**

15:6–9. Luke apparently describes a meeting within a meeting as the apostles and elders convene under advisement to deal with this momentous issue. When we hold verses 6–11 up to verse 12 however, it would appear that if a separate meeting actually took place, it probably occurred in the general meeting hall and perhaps even within the hearing of the wider assembly. In any case, as the primary speaker at this point, Peter used his time to rehearse the Cornelius incident. He was not in charge of the meeting and spoke as a missionary apostle, not as a church administrator.

Peter's story hadn't changed since he offered it to the Judaizers at the beginning of chapter 11. This is not some heretical deviation dreamed up by Paul or by Peter himself. Luke records precise language: **God made a choice**; **God . . . accepted them**; **by giving the Holy Spirit to them**; **. . . he made no distinction.**

15:10–11. Apparently Peter's patience began to wear thin on this issue, for he accused the Judaizing Pharisees of tying up Gentile believers and trying to make them do something no one in the Jewish nation had ever been able to do. This reference to law as a yoke was not original with Peter (Matt. 23:4; 11:29–30).

Informative also is Peter's language about testing God. Acts condemns all tests of God (Acts 5:9). If anyone in the group had doubts about Peter's position, those doubts would have been removed with his humble statement of verse 11 which even put the Gentiles first in explaining salvation by grace. Prideful word order which protected Jewish primacy would have said "that they are saved, just as we are." Marshall captures Peter's argument succinctly:

> The point here is not the burdensomeness or oppressiveness of the law, but rather the inability of the Jews to gain salvation through it, and hence its irrelevance as far as salvation is concerned. . . . Since Peter is talking about the kind of *faith in God* that leads to salvation (cf. v. 7), if both Jews and Gentiles are saved in this way, clearly obedience to the law is not required of Gentiles. Nor, may we add, is obedience to the law demanded of Jews as a means of salvation (Gal. 5:6; Marshall, 250).

Shouldn't the Jews then just abandon law-keeping all together? That evades the point. Whether they did or not had nothing to do with Gentile salvation, the only agenda at this meeting. Paul countered this issue throughout his ministry. In his letter to the Galatian churches he treated the error which Judaizers had planted there:

> It is for freedom that Christ has set us free. Stand firm, then, and do not let yourselves be burdened again by a yoke of slavery. Mark my words! I, Paul, tell you that if you let yourselves be circumcised, Christ will be of no value to you at all. Again I declare to every man who lets himself be circumcised that he is obligated to obey the whole law. You who are trying to be justified by law have been alienated from Christ; you have fallen away from grace. But by faith we eagerly await through the Spirit the righteousness for which we

hope. For in Christ Jesus neither circumcision nor uncircumcision has any value. The only thing that counts is faith expressing itself through love (Gal. 5:1–6).

Ⓒ Action (vv. 12–21)

SUPPORTING IDEA: *In a church business meeting, people representing different points of view need to be heard. When that happens, it is often useful to summarize the proceedings before a decision is reached.*

15:12. This verse seems redundant in the light of verse 5 except that Luke specifies the miracle aspect of the first missionary journey. Notice how Paul never entered into debate on this occasion. Both times he spoke he merely told what God had done. Peter handled the defense of the grace position quite admirably (sounding very much like Paul), so the missionaries now just add more documentation. We read with interest the changed order of names—**Barnabas and Paul**. Presumably, this is Luke's way of telling us that Barnabas still held the predominant position in the Judean churches.

15:13–18. We have heard from the missionaries; we have heard from the apostolic representative; and now the ruling elder takes charge of the meeting which, as the text clearly indicates, had settled down and was proceeding quite smoothly. Verse 13 gives us another hint that Luke recognizes his hero is in a completely Jewish setting—the use of Peter's Jewish name by James. The terminology **a people for himself** has been used heretofore only of Israel. James thoroughly adopted Peter's view that God had been manipulating all these events. To clinch the case, James quoted Amos 9:11–12.

Rather than allowing the question "How did those Gentiles get in?" James insists rather on pressing the question "What is God doing?" He does not even mention Barnabas and Paul, a wise choice in that Jewish context. Since no Old Testament prophet had ever said that Gentiles had to become Jews to know God's blessing, and since Peter (one of our own) demonstrated by personal experience that God wants to bring Gentiles directly to himself through grace, then let's just go with Amos and settle this thing.

Two groups emerge in the quoted passage: the fallen house of David (Israel) and the rest of mankind (Gentiles). The whole missionary model is at stake here. The Pharisees and other Judaizers wanted to carry out the proselytizing model, traditionally accepted and utilized by Israel. Peter described a new model, and James affirmed it as a prophetic model.

Just as Peter's quotation of Joel in chapter 2 represented a direct New Testament statement about fulfilled Old Testament prophecy, so here James said, "This is that"—the words of Amos are being fulfilled in the salvation of

Gentiles right now. We will treat James' quotation of Amos in "Deeper Discoveries." Suffice it here to say James intended to show that neither the Council nor any other Christian group should oppose God's fulfillment of prophecy so aptly demonstrated in what the Council had heard that day. As Polhill puts it, "From the beginning the Jewish Christians had realized that the promises to David were fulfilled in Christ. But they were now beginning to see, and what James saw foretold in Amos, was that these promises included the Gentiles" (Polhill, 330).

15:19–21. James begins by saying what the group should not do. Whatever else happens, they would not lay the yoke of the law on the backs of the Gentiles. Incidentally, if the New Testament intended to convey that baptism is some sort of "Christian circumcision," the initiatory rite into the faith, this would have been the place to say it. James did not say it, nor did Paul write it in either Galatians or Romans; that analogy has no solid basis in Scripture.

We learn four "guidelines" which many have taken to be a compromise on the part of James. In fact these restrictions have little to do with the central issue of the Council and seem more sociological than theological. They fall under the "no offense" principle every Christian should live by. Most places where Gentile believers then practiced Christianity also had sizable Jewish communities. Seeking not to alienate either group, the Council asked Jewish Christians to accept Gentiles without discussions of law-keeping while asking Gentile believers to refrain from those things which would have been odious to devout Jews. In no case do these four restrictions relate to salvation.

We might parallel this to rules in the student handbook at a Christian college. A college may have curfew, a time by which students need to be in the dormitories. Or perhaps drinking and smoking are prohibited on campus. Not many years ago some colleges disallowed beards because of a possible association with certain types of lifestyles in the world. None of these are biblical issues, and none of them have a nickel's worth of relevance with respect to salvation. Yet we would all argue that a Christian college has the right to set certain standards so that other segments of the Christian community (local churches, donors, parents) would not be offended by campus behavior. As long as we do not pretend that the presence or absence of rules creates righteousness, we can understand Acts 15. Essentially verse 21 emphasizes the presence of Jews and Gentiles worshiping together.

Perhaps it would be useful to sum up these four regulations in our modern understanding: no idolatry, no immorality, no murder, and no eating meat offered to idols. For further information review Leviticus 17 and 18.

One could wish that this conclusion had united the Jewish and Gentile factions of the church permanently, but in historic fact, by A.D. 100 they worshiped almost totally apart from one another. What did result, however, was freedom to continue the Gentile mission. That answered Luke's concern and quite possibly James' as well.

So the Council was not a one-agenda-item meeting after all. They dispensed with the initial "motion" quickly (v. 19). Then James introduced a second motion which had to do with how Christians avoid offending one another and live together in harmony. That became the written "minutes" of the meeting.

Implementation (vv. 22–29)

SUPPORTING IDEA: *Churches must make and implement policies and procedures to ensure that everyone receives the opportunity to receive the gospel without any strings attached.*

Every church needs to protect its integrity at all times. The Jerusalem church did that by sending written notification to the churches in the hands of two trusted Jerusalemite Christians.

15:22. Whether we can find congregational government in this verse is certainly open to question. We certainly see group decision making and the general approval of James' conclusion. In view of Luke's hyperbole, one wonders whether we should take him literally when he says **the whole church**. Did his judgment really silence the Pharisees? Did the Judaizers agree with this plan? Presumably, whatever they may have felt in their hearts, they went along with the general body and agreed to notify the Gentiles of the conclusion.

Quite likely, Judas, the son of Barsabbas, and Silas functioned as elders in the Jerusalem church, though Luke does not use the term in this passage. *Silas* is a Greek name; *Silvanus,* the Latin equivalent. Almost all scholars agree the New Testament records of these two names refer to the same person (15:40; 1 Thess. 1:1; 2 Cor. 1:19; 1 Pet. 5:12).

Obviously, Paul and Barnabas would return to Antioch. Just as obviously, they could have carried this letter with them, but they represented one side of the issue. Had James given them the letter and asked that they read and interpret it to the Christians at Antioch, the Pharisees might have been justified in complaining about a one-sided conference.

15:23–24. This was no ordinary memo, but rather a formal letter of great import. Clement of Alexandria living at the end of the second century referred to this paragraph as "the Catholic epistle of all the apostles." It begins with a formal greeting (cf. Acts 23:26; Jas. 1:1) and ends with a formal farewell. The Greek text of verses 24–26 consists of one sentence not unlike Luke 1:1–4. The letter contains an apology for the trouble Judaizers may have caused in Antioch, clearly indicating that the church at large did not agree with their point of view.

15:25–27. The letter commends Barnabas and Paul and introduces Judas and Silas, even indicating the purpose of their trip: **to confirm by word of mouth what we are writing.** These two would provide not only an eyewitness account but a "Jerusalem interpretation" of the letter. They would answer any questions the Gentile believers might ask regarding what the letter really means. Notice that the expected reading audience was wider than just Antioch, including all of Syria and Cilicia.

15:28–29. The letter removes any doubt as to its origin or authority by claiming that the Holy Spirit induced the "following requirements." The letter also acknowledges that the requirements would be burdensome to Gentiles accustomed to living more freely than these few guidelines suggested. The wording differs ever so slightly from verse 20, but the intention and content remain the same.

Many have wondered why Paul never cites this letter in his epistles. Being present at the Council and present again when the letter was read to the Antiochan Christians, he surely would have had its impact well in mind throughout his ministry. Two suggestions help us. First, Paul does mention these issues without any special quotation at various points such as his treatment of sexual immorality in 1 Corinthians 5–7 and food sacrificed to idols in chapters 8–10. Second, Paul was a missionary evangelist, not a local pastor. These provisions dealt with the social behavior which would accommodate fellowship between Jews and Gentiles in the church. Since they had nothing to do with salvation (and that was Paul's constant central theme), presumably he thought it unnecessary to rehash what everyone already knew.

Application (vv. 30–35)

SUPPORTING IDEA: *Important decisions affecting the life of any church must be communicated clearly if we expect people to apply them in their lives.*

15:30–32. The messengers arrived and read the letter. The people rejoiced! All was quiet on the northern front of the church. Judas and Silas, obviously possessing the gift of prophecy and possibly exhortation, enjoyed themselves so much they decided to stay and continue their ministry at Antioch rather than go back to Jerusalem.

15:33, 35. After some time Judas and Silas returned to Jerusalem, sent on their way **with the blessing of peace.** Whatever caused the rupture, relations between Antioch and Jerusalem were restored. The letter had freed the gospel from entanglement with Judaism and had laid a foundation for freedom in Gentile evangelization. In the wider context of the New Testament we can also see that attitudes toward Paul were probably polarized, and many Jews permanently antagonized. Two factions would forever remain in the church, but not because James and the others in Jerusalem had not made a genuine effort at unity.

The better manuscripts omit verse 34 which appears in the NIV marginal note: **But Silas decided to remain there**. Most scholars concede that some later scribe felt a necessity to keep Silas in Antioch so he would be available for a second missionary journey (v. 40). Luke's wording in verse 33 is quite clearly plural, and since the Paul/Barnabas debate over Mark occurred sometime later, Silas had ample time to return to Jerusalem at this point and come back to Antioch again at some subsequent time.

Meanwhile, Paul and Barnabas came back home to do what they loved among people they loved. Furthermore, they ministered in a clear understanding that nothing would hamper their proclamation of grace to the Gentiles. As Polhill puts it:

> The Jewish Christian leadership showed a concern for the world mission of the church that overshadowed their own special interests. They took a step that was absolutely essential if the Gentile mission was to be a success. To have required circumcision and the law would have severely limited the appeal to Gentiles, perhaps even killed it (Polhill, 337).

Disagreement (vv. 36–41)

SUPPORTING IDEA: *Christians disagree, and even separate at times, but ultimately God works everything out for his own purposes.*

15:36. We have observed the history of the early church to the year A.D. 50. Luke will now begin a new section in his account. He sets it off with the words *meta tinas hemeras* ("after some days"), used with some frequency to note a time division and transition to a new section of his work. Notice Paul does not intend a second journey for missionary evangelism, though that is precisely what God will do with this proposed trip. His initial motivation, however, was just to go back to towns where they had been to check on the believers and encourage them.

15:37–39a. Barnabas hesitates not a moment in welcoming Paul's proposal and assumes they will also take Mark along. At first, it would seem, the difference is merely in discussion, Paul taking the position that he did not want "to have this one with them continually." Luke doesn't hesitate to tell us the reason for Paul's concern—Mark had deserted them.

Here we have a classic confrontation: the choice between disqualifying a person who has made a major blunder or seeking to restore that person to a ministry role. Did Mark still seem unrepentant about his behavior earlier? Did Paul feel Mark might water down the new freedom of the Jerusalem Council decision? Was the anger of the Judaizers at Jerusalem aroused by Mark and his reports from Pamphylia? Luke does not tell us. He does tell us that this difference, this obvious disagreement, became a *paroxysm*, a blowup between these two dear friends. The only other New Testament use of this word appears in Hebrews 10:24, where the writer used it in the positive sense of provoking good behavior in others.

15:39b–41. Certainly these good men could have solved their problems by agreeing that one or both of them would stay in Antioch, maybe call off the whole idea as a bad plan. But God intended two missionary teams instead of one, and so Barnabas **took Mark and sailed for Cyprus** while Paul appointed Silas to replace Barnabas and headed north and west through Syria and into Asia Minor.

Why Silas? Certainly Paul must have recognized outstanding qualities in this young man at Jerusalem, on the way back to Antioch, and in his time at the Antioch church. Furthermore, it couldn't hurt to have a leader from the Jerusalem congregation traveling through Gentile territory and affirming the Council's decision. Unlike Barnabas, he was a Roman citizen which, as we shall see, could come in handy (16:37).

MAIN IDEA REVIEW: *The salvation of Gentiles occurs precisely the same way as does salvation of Jews—through faith in Jesus Christ because of God's grace.*

III. CONCLUSION

Freedom of the Gospel of Grace

In this chapter we have watched the church struggle with a major problem and emerge unified. We have seen two outstanding Christian leaders struggle with personal conflict and emerge victoriously to carry on God's work in the world. Most important, we have seen, and ourselves enjoyed, the freedom of the gospel of grace to provide salvation. Let no one believe nor teach that to be a Christian one must trust Jesus, be circumcised, join the church, be baptized, live a moral life, keep the Sabbath, or anything else. Salvation comes by God's grace through faith in the Savior—that alone and nothing else. Philip Bliss put it this way back in the nineteeth century:

> Free from the law—O happy condition!
> Jesus hath bled, and there is remission;
> Cursed by the law and bruised by the fall,

Grace hath redeemed us once for all.
Now we are free—there's no condemnation;
Jesus provides a perfection salvation:
"Come unto me," O hear His sweet call,
Come, and He saves us once for all.

PRINCIPLES

- When you have a problem in the church, let all interested groups have a say.
- Church meetings should be calm and orderly.
- Church controversies should always seek conformity with the Word of God and the will of God.
- Churches must protect the integrity of their witness in the world.

APPLICATIONS

- Church decisions are not always unanimously applauded.
- Salvation comes by grace alone plus nothing.
- The Christian life is lived by grace, not by human effort.
- The gospel is available to anyone regardless of ethnic or religious background.

IV. LIFE APPLICATION

God Is Watching the Apples

David Seamans, author and professor at Asbury Seminary, tells a story about the campus where the seminary shared cafeteria facilities with Asbury College in Wilmore, Kentucky. On one occasion, students moving through the cafeteria line found near the beginning a large basket of bright red apples. The cafeteria staff had placed a sign above the basket, quite appropriate for a Christian college campus, "Take one only please—God is watching."

As students made their way through the line selecting meat loaf or taco salad, and peaches or chocolate mousse, they found at the other end a large box of broken cookies which the staff had put out. Attached to the box was a piece of notebook paper containing a note obviously scrawled by a student. It read, "Take as many as you want; God is watching the apples."

Yes, God watches the apples. God watches the cookies, too. God watches the pastor. God also watches the Sunday school teachers, the ushers, and the custodial staff as well. God is present in the deacons' meeting. God is likewise present in that little home Bible study where three or four ladies meet over coffee.

Luke will not let us forget how God controlled and designed all the events of the early church. Seven times this chapter refers to Gentile salvation, but the key line comes from Peter: **God made a choice among you that the Gentiles might hear from my lips the message of the gospel and believe.**

How we should praise God for Acts 15. The vast majority of Christians in the world today have no Jewish blood and no contact with the Jewish religion. Most of us are Gentiles from races and backgrounds totally unrelated to the people of Old Testament promise. We are children of the New Covenant, the result of missionary efforts which began in the first century with the work of Paul and Barnabas throughout Asia Minor.

This chapter affirms what we already know—that our salvation comes from God and that our ability to live in righteousness before him depends totally upon his grace and the power of his Holy Spirit. It acknowledges all the moral pollution around us, not at all unlike environments of those early Christians in Antioch, Syria, and Cilicia.

We also see that God can put together pieces of our fragmented human efforts to bring glory to himself. We owe Luke a deep debt of gratitude for not covering up the details of struggle among these early believers. Paul and Barnabas—heroes of the faith, pioneer missionaries, church leaders, mentors, and disciplers—break their relationship arguing over whether another Christian should or should not accompany them on a ministry trip! Obviously it was no petty matter to either of them, but an issue of deep concern. So we learn that Christians do quarrel and, in the long run, it probably doesn't matter who was right or wrong, but whether peace can be achieved and the work of God can continue unhindered.

Yes, God watches the apples. God watches the broken cookies. It matters not whether we perceive of ourselves in the basket or the box—God is watching us.

V. PRAYER

God of grace and mercy, we thank you that you give us salvation just because you want to, just because it is the way you are, the God of grace. Forgive us when we try to add something to the gospel as we tell it to other people. Teach us to appreciate the freedom of your grace and to share it freely.

VI. DEEPER DISCOVERIES

A. Acts 15 and Galatians 2

Commentators cannot agree on whether the key passage in Galatians 2:1–10 describes the visit of Paul and Barnabas to Jerusalem here in Acts 15 or the earlier visit at the end of chapter 13. One cannot prove either, but evidence seems to favor a coordination of the Galatians passage with the earlier visit. For one thing, the issue in Galatians is circumcision and the Gentile mission, not table fellowship with Gentiles. Furthermore, Galatians 2 describes a private meeting, whereas this chapter depicts a totally public council. Galatians 2 lacks any mention of the letter or conditions of Acts 15, and one surely would expect Paul to raise the issue if he wrote subsequent to the Jerusalem Council.

Marshall, Longenecker, Polhill, and Bruce all adopt the connection of Galatians 2 with 11:30 even though one encounters some problems defending that position. If we place the writing of Galatians at the end of the first journey and before the Jerusalem Council, obviously we cannot fit Galatians 2 into Acts 15. Again, most evangelical scholars prefer the dating of Galatians in Antioch before the Council and, for the reasons identified above, see Acts 15 as Paul's third visit to Jerusalem, not his second.

B. James' Quote (vv. 16–18)

James' use of the Amos 9:11–12 quote has troubled commentators ever since Luke wrote this book. For one thing, it seems to follow the Septuagint (a Greek translation of the Old Testament), but one can hardly picture James using the Septuagint in the Aramaic-speaking Jerusalem Council, especially on the issue of Gentile salvation. For that reason, some argue this does not come from James at all, but rather was inserted by Luke. One solution suggests that James may have used a Hebrew variant of the text rather than the Septuagint, a variant popular in the first century when Greek influence would have dominated Hebrew communities.

Special attention focuses on verse 18 which Longenecker calls "notoriously difficult." He concludes:

> It is perhaps best to interpret the words here as a comment by James to this effect: We cannot be in opposition to the express will of God, as evidenced by Peter's testimony and the prophets' words—but only God himself knows for certain how everything fits together and is to be fully understood! (Longenecker, 447).

C. New Testament Prophets (v. 31)

The word *propheteia* comes from *prophemi* which means "to speak forth." When defining any word of Scripture, we must take into consideration two extremely important factors: *etymology* (the basic derivation of the word) and *use*. Sometimes they differ greatly, and most scholars agree that use at the time of the word's appearance takes precedence in determining its meaning.

In this case, however, we find no great difference between the derivation of the word and its use. The idea of speaking forth, particularly speaking forth the Word of God, is common wherever the word appears. The problem comes when we link New Testament with Old Testament usage. Old Testament prophets were primarily forthtellers, who spoke God's word of warning or hope to the day in which they lived. They also at times served as foretellers whose task and ministry proclaimed future events. This foretelling became the focus for New Testament usage of Old Testament prophecy. This foretelling aspect of the word does not disappear from New Testament usage; but, as Gerhard Friedrich suggests, the idea of prediction in the word is really a "special sense," and one which "occurs chiefly in Revelation" (TDNT, 6:830).

In the New Testament we see that prophecy occurs primarily among believers (1 Cor. 14), but it can appear in evangelistic settings as well. Some New Testament prophets were women (Acts 21:8–9), and multiple prophets could appear in any given congregation (1 Cor. 14:24,29).

In my book *Unwrap Your Spiritual Gifts*, I conclude the chapter on prophecy with this paragraph:

> Results of properly using the gift of prophecy in the modern congregation will not be greatly different from those in the first century. The local church will reflect order, peace, encouragement, consolation, conviction, spiritual awareness, and learning. Above all, exercising the gift of prophecy results in spiritual upbuilding—the primary task of the church (Gangel, 44).

D. Disappearance of Barnabas (v. 39)

After Paul and Barnabas parted company, Barnabas never appears again in Acts. Some see this as some kind of punishment and have drawn inferences that one should never quarrel with a senior leader ("lift not up your hand against the Lord's anointed"). Such a view only reinforces imperial styles of leadership quite contrary to the New Testament text. In fact, Luke simply carries through the story with a focus on his hero (Paul) since he wants to explain to Theophilus how the gospel spread across the Roman Empire. Paul names Barnabas in 1 Corinthians 9:6 as a noble example, one who poured himself into ministry.

The chief significance of Barnabas occurs in the influence he had in his cousin's life. Mark surfaces dramatically (after about ten years) to associate with Peter (1 Pet. 5:13) and become a member of Paul's team once again (Col. 4:10; Phlm. 24). Not only that, but Mark's maturity in ministry continued to develop so that toward the end of Paul's life he asked Timothy to bring Mark to the Mamertine prison in Rome (2 Tim. 4:11).

This affords a marvelous example for us. God will call some into public ministry. These may travel far and wide; their names may appear in bulletins and reports all around the country, or even around the world. God will call others to take one person—a John Mark—and work with that fledgling leader to mentor him or her to the place of profit in ministry. Neither calling is greater nor lesser in the eyes of God. Paul's vast ministry among the Gentiles is a marvelous example of missionary evangelism. Barnabas's personal ministry with Mark is also a marvelous example of pastoral mentoring. Both are essential. Both serve eternal values. Both carry equal weight in the eyes of the God who assigned them.

VII. TEACHING OUTLINE

A. INTRODUCTION

1. Lead Story: Tradition
2. Context: Acts 15 represents the center point in the book and a bridge into full-scale Gentile evangelism as Paul and Silas take the gospel all the way to Rome. It also forms a theological high water mark with the clear-cut affirmation by Peter (supported by the entire Council) that **it is through the grace of our Lord Jesus that we are saved**.
3. Transition: Only here in our book do all the principal characters of Acts appear in the same place at the same time. Luke centers on the gospel to the Gentiles, salvation by faith, dialog as a means of solving church problems, and the launching pad from Antioch for the next missionary journey.

B. COMMENTARY

1. Motion (vv. 1–5)
   a. Major premise (v. 1)
   b. Trip to Jerusalem (vv. 2–3)
   c. Conflict with the Pharisees (vv. 4–5)
2. Discussion (vv. 6–11)
   a. God made a choice (vv. 6–7)
   b. God accepted the Gentiles (vv. 8–9)
   c. God gives salvation through grace (vv. 10–11)
3. Action (vv. 12–21)

      a.   Report from Barnabas and Paul (v. 12)

      b.   Citation from Amos (vv. 13–18)

      c.   Conclusion by James (vv. 19–21)

  4. Implementation (vv. 22–29)

      a.   Decision affirmed (v. 22a)

      b.   Messengers appointed (v. 22b)

      c.   Letter prepared (vv. 23–29)

  5. Application (vv. 30–35)

      a.   Return to Antioch (vv. 30–31)

      b.   Ministry in Antioch (vv. 32–35)

  6. Disagreement (vv. 36–41)

      a.   The basic issue (vv. 36–37)

      b.   The apostolic argument (vv. 38–39a)

      c.   The divine solution (vv. 39b–41)

C. CONCLUSION: GOD IS WATCHING THE APPLES

VIII. ISSUES FOR DISCUSSION

1.   What issues or problems threaten the unity of your church? What are you doing to settle the issue and preserve the unity?

2.   What is your church tempted to add to the conditions for salvation and church membership? Are you willing to accept all people who apply for membership under the same conditions?

3.   What people in your church deserve thanks and commendation for the way they have helped your church maintain its unity and its focus on Christ's mission? What can you do to encourage and recognize them?

Acts 16

Singing in Our Struggles

I. **Introduction**
Now We Will Win

II. **Commentary**
A verse-by-verse explanation of the chapter.

III. **Conclusion**
The Joy of the Lord
An overview of the principles and applications from the chapter.

IV. **Life Application**
One Man's Carelessness
Melding the chapter to life.

V. **Prayer**
Tying the chapter to life with God.

VI. **Deeper Discoveries**
Historical, geographical, and grammatical enrichment of the commentary.

VII. **Teaching Outline**
Suggested step-by-step group study of the chapter.

VIII. **Issues for Discussion**
Zeroing the chapter in on daily life.

"*Happiness* comes not from having much to live
on but having much to live for."

anonoymous

BIOGRAPHICAL PROFILE: TIMOTHY

- Resident of Lystra
- Child of a mixed marriage—Greek Gentile and devout Jew
- Paul's spiritual son and fellow-missionary
- Leader of the church at Ephesus

GEOGRAPHICAL PROFILE: BITHYNIA

- Section of the northern part of Asia Minor bordering the Black Sea, the Bosphorus and the Sea of Marmora
- A Christian community existed there (1 Pet. 1:1)
- An ancient area whose history goes back beyond 600 B.C.
- Today a part of modern Turkey

CITY PROFILE: TROAS

- Northwestern corner of Asia Minor on the Aegean Sea
- Entrance to the Dardanelles
- Located about ten miles from the site of ancient Troy
- Roman colony and one of the most important cities in northwest Asia

CITY PROFILE: NEAPOLIS

- Seaport for the city of Philippi
- Located on the Via Ignatia which connected the Adriatic and Black Seas
- Though archaeologists are unsure, the site is probably close to modern Kaballa

CITY PROFILE: PHILIPPI

- Named for Philip II, father of Alexander
- Site of Mark Antony's defeat of Brutus and Cassius
- Location of a professional school of medicine
- The first European city to hear a Christian missionary

I N   A   N U T S H E L L

*L*uke tells us, as the second missionary journey got underway, how the gospel went to Europe, and particularly to Philippi, his own home city. A highlight of the chapter is the conversion of the Philippian jailer and the founding of the church there.

Singing in Our Struggles

I. INTRODUCTION

Now We Will Win

*O*n December 7, 1941, the Japanese Air Force launched a surprise attack on Pearl Harbor and forced the United States into World War II. Vice Admiral Chuichi Nagumo led a thirty-three ship strike force which steamed under cover of darkness to within two hundred miles of Oahu. His carriers launched 360 airplanes against the American Pacific Fleet. The first bombs fell on Pearl Harbor about 7:55 A.M. Eighteen U.S. ships were sunk or severely damaged, some 170 planes destroyed, and American forces suffered about 3,700 casualties. President Roosevelt described it as "a day which will live in infamy," and the motto "Remember Pearl Harbor!" became a rallying cry for the rest of World War II.

In Great Britain, Prime Minister Winston Churchill received the news of Pearl Harbor differently. Though deeply sympathetic with American losses, he understood that this fatal mistake by the Japanese in underestimating American resolve would now force full-scale U.S. involvement in the war. Upon grasping this enormous consequence, Churchill reportedly said, "Now we will win."

Throughout the course of human events we find such history changing moments, decisions which move things in a different direction. Such is the case with the chapter before us today. God's plan to take the gospel west into Europe rather than north into Asia changed the face of global evangelism and the march of the church for hundreds of years. When we think of Zwingli, Luther, Calvin, we remember Europeans ultimately influenced by the decision Paul made to follow God's leading against his own personal preferences.

God still changes history in directing the efforts of his people. Not many years ago, we thought the Berlin Wall impregnable and expected the Cold War to go on forever. Who could have predicted in 1985 a united Germany and frenetic missionary activity all across eastern Europe, especially throughout the old Soviet Bloc countries?

God's timing often differs from what we would have planned and often makes little sense to us. Of course, our reasoning, so dimmed by sin and the limitations of mortality, has no way to grasp the historic impact of immediate decisions. Like Paul, we must trust the leading of God's Spirit day by day in living our lives, raising our children, making decisions for a business or ministry. In every arena of life we must serve him with a constant alertness to the Holy Spirit's leading.

II. COMMENTARY

Singing in Our Struggles

MAIN IDEA: *God's people can sing in their struggles when they know he leads and blesses in each step of their lives no matter how difficult and dark some days may be.*

A A Song of Believers in Growth (vv. 1–5)

Supporting Idea: *Reports of church decisions encourage local congregations and help them grow.*

16:1–2. In chapter 14 we saw Paul and Barnabas visit Iconium, Lystra, and Derbe on their swing from west to east. Now the journey takes them in the reverse order. Having rounded the bend of the Mediterranean (where Syria meets Cilicia) to visit Derbe, they came to Lystra. Here they found Timothy, evidently one of the converts from the first journey. Luke tells us young Timothy had a good reputation in the city of Lystra and that he was the product of a mixed marriage, an important point in understanding the circumcision of verse 3.

16:3. Acts 16:3 with its demand for circumcision amazes us, following so quickly the decision of the Jerusalem Council. Why would Paul want to force circumcision on any one? First, we must ask, why would a Jew have married a Greek? Quite likely because of the small size of the Jewish community in Lystra, a city the Greeks dominated. In Jewish law a child took the religion of its mother, but in Greek law the father dominated the home (2 Tim. 1:5). If Jews held little influence, why was Timothy's mother allowed to raise him in her devout faith? Most scholars suggest that Timothy's mother was a single parent, his father having died some years earlier. That cannot be proven in the text, of course, though the tense of the verb **was**, at the end of verse 3, seems to suggest this.

Even the small Jewish community in Lystra would have considered an uncircumcised child of a Jewish mother an apostate. Paul obviously wanted to continue his mission to Jews as well as Gentiles. He could not have done that by ignoring Timothy's situation. Here we must distinguish clearly between proclaiming the gospel to Gentiles and proclaiming it to Jews. The issue in the Jerusalem Council dealt exclusively with Gentiles who, for all practical purposes, considered Timothy a Jew. Paul refused to impose Jewish law on Gentile converts, but he continued to live as a Jew himself. Being a good Christian certainly did not require being a bad Jew according to New Testament standards.

Luke tells us in verse 1 that Timothy was already a believer. *This circumcision had absolutely nothing to do with salvation.* Paul wanted to remove the stigma from the young man's status in the eyes of the Jewish community in Lystra. Assuming he already planned to take Timothy along to replace John Mark, Paul could foresee Jews in every city he would visit raising the circumcision issue.

Timothy would become a major player on the missionary team. He participated in six of Paul's epistles (2 Cor. 1:1; Phil. 1:1; Col. 1:1; 1 Thess. 1:1; 2 Thess. 1:1; Phlm. 1) and received two more. Paul calls him a son (1 Cor. 4:17; 1 Tim. 1:2), a fellow worker (Rom. 16:21; 1 Cor. 16:10), and includes Timothy whenever possible in his itinerant ministry before ultimately placing him in a leadership role at Ephesus. To be accepted in ministry to Jews, Timothy had to affirm his Jewish heritage and be circumcised.

16:4–5. With their newly acquired assistant, Paul and Silas headed north to Iconium and west again to Cilicia, announcing the decision of the Jerusalem Council and strengthening the converts from the first journey. Luke ends Act IV in his history by stating again the health of the church in general and particularly the churches of Asia Minor which **were strengthened in the faith and grew daily in numbers.**

Though the Jerusalem Council letter was written only to churches as far as Antioch, we should probably conclude that Paul shared its message all over southern Galatia. If we assume the early date of the writing of Galatians (after the first journey), the Jerusalem Council would be a logical and necessary follow-up for any believers who had read Paul's letter. Furthermore, the decision of the Council served not merely the purpose of answering a single question for a specific church (Antioch), but became a principle by which first-century evangelism was conducted.

Quite abruptly Luke's primary purpose for the second journey comes to a conclusion. In 15:36, Paul suggested to Barnabas that they **go back and visit the brothers in all the towns where we preached the word of the Lord** and see how they are doing. That effort receives five verses, most of which are given to the specific discussion of Timothy. Paul had a plan, but God changed it to redirect the force of the gospel.

🄱 A Song of Believers in Obedience (vv. 6–10)

SUPPORTING IDEA: *In thinking through the future of our lives, we must always be sensitive to the Holy Spirit's leading and God's call to stay or go.*

16:6. Luke tells us that the missionary trio continued north and west through Phrygia and Galatia. In some way, the Holy Spirit kept them from preaching the Word **in the province of Asia.** Geography grabs the utmost importance in studying Acts, and especially the missionary journeys. Here we must make a distinction between northern and southern Galatia.

Southern Galatia, including the towns of Antioch, Iconium, Lystra, and Derbe, received the letter to the Galatians. Northern Galatia was made up of Celtic people (who later immigrated to the British Isles). The Roman province of Asia (not to be confused with the continent to which we ascribe that name today) was located west of Antioch and contained principal cities along the Aegean Sea. The Holy Spirit directed Paul away from that area and sent him instead north and then west on a course for Troas.

It is useless to ponder how the Holy Spirit conveyed this message. From what we already know in Acts, it could have been through a vision, an inner understanding of God's will, or even the prophetic utterance of a local Christian somewhere along the way.

16:7. Paul hit another wall and was again redirected in his travel plans. With all these starts and stops along the way, it is virtually impossible to dogmatically trace the missionaries' route. Polhill (345) suggests that this second change in direction occurred near Dorylaeum. That affords as good a guess as any.

The new travel directions came by the **Spirit of Jesus.** Again, Luke does not tell us how the message came, but the theological link of the Holy Spirit in verse 6 with the Spirit of Jesus in verse 7 offers an important affirmation of deity for the third person of the Trinity. Furthermore, Paul links both of these with God in verse 10, so we have a full trinitarian involvement in this Macedonian call.

16:8–9. In obedience to the heavenly message, the trio abandoned plans to head north and probably east which would have taken them along the Black Sea to cities connected by an elaborate Roman road system. Had they continued north out of Galatia, they would have eventually arrived in the modern areas of Romania and Bulgaria, moving ever further away from

Europe and its cultural center, Athens. They finally came to Troas. There Paul received a vision from a Macedonian begging him to come to Greece.

Here the missionaries stood at the pivotal port between two significant land masses of the ancient world—Asia Minor and Europe. They faced two gigantic waterways—the Aegean and Black Seas. Commentators speculate on the nature of the vision and the identity of the man, but all such imaginative meandering seems useless. Luke emphasizes neither geography nor personalities in this paragraph but rather the absolute God-directed plan and route of this missionary trip.

We did not include Macedonia in the geographical profiles at the beginning of this chapter because of its crucial importance in the flow of the text. Named for Philip of Macedon, it had become a Roman province in 148 B.C. Formerly a Greek kingdom, Macedonia came under strong Athenian influence as early as five hundred years before Christ. There Aristotle came to tutor Alexander the Great after the death of Plato. No less an orator than Demosthenes verbally attacked "the Macedonian menace." Indeed, the army created by Philip of Macedon later followed his son Alexander all the way to the Ganges, overthrowing the Persians on the way.

The Bible records several Macedonian Christians such as Gaius, Aristarchus, Secundus, Sopater, and Epaphroditus and their enthusiastic support for Paul (Acts 17:11; 19:29; 20:4; Phil. 4:10–19; 1 Thess. 2:8,17–20; 3:10). It is also likely Luke himself came from Philippi in Macedonia.

16:10. The missionaries wasted no time in following God's obedience but got ready **at once** (*eutheos*, which could also be translated "immediately") to cross the sea to a waiting Europe. Here Luke introduces the first of several "we" sections in Acts, Luke's way of showing when he joins the missionary party (20:5–15; 21:1–18; 27:1–28:16). At other times he tells the narrative in third person. The purpose of this voyage is clear—**to preach the gospel** to Greeks in their own country.

G. Campbell Morgan captures the spirit of the obedient Christians and the excitement that must have been in those four missionary hearts as they sailed west across the Aegean.

> Oh, to go, not where I may choose, even by my love of the Lord, but where I am driven by the Lord's command. Circumstances of difficulty are opportunities for faith, and the measure of our perplexity in service and in Christian life is the measure of our opportunity. Let us follow the gleam, though the darkness threaten to envelop. Let us be true to the inward monitor, and if in being true, suddenly illness prevent, and we cannot follow, then rest in the Lord in the darkness, and know that God's shortest way to Troas may be athwart our

inclinations and purposes. It is better to go to Troas with God, than anywhere else without Him (Morgan, 377).

 A Song of Believers in Fellowship (vv. 11–15)

SUPPORTING IDEA: *Women have always been important in God's work on earth, from Sarah and Deborah to Dorcas and Lydia. Amazing! The "man from Macedonia" turns out to be a woman.*

16:11–12. Troas to Philippi was a 130-mile journey broken up by two stops. Samothrace, an island in the northeastern Aegean was the location of a mystery religion worshiping the god Cabiri. Greeks called Samothrace "Poseidon's Island." In their view this ancient Greek god of waters, earthquakes, and horses stood atop Mount Fengari (a site higher than the city of Denver) and surveyed the plains of Troy. Arrival at Neapolis the next day (see Profile) indicates that the wind favored the travelers on a westward route; the return trip (20:6) took five days.

Philippi must have been an exciting stop for a city-dweller like Paul. With its enviable history, its important agricultural industry, and strategic commercial location, its gold mines and its famous school of medicine—this qualified as a sophisticated metropolis. Luke calls it the "leading city of that district of Macedonia," though the wisdom of the times would have assigned that approbation to Amphipolis. Scholars engage in a great deal of exegetical squabbling over what Luke actually said here, but when the dust settles, perhaps the NIV rendering is the best. Luke expresses pride in his own city (a common attitude both then and now), not the general viewpoint held across Greece about Philippi.

How interesting that the missionary team didn't plunge immediately into frenetic ministry. After all, they had a visionary call to this place; why waste time before proclaiming the gospel? Luke simply tells us (and remember, we now have an eyewitness account) they **stayed there several days**.

16:13. In cities where no Jewish synagogue existed, believers gathered under the sky and near water so other Christians knew where to find them. In Jewish law a synagogue could not be started with fewer than ten male heads of households to form the congregation. Since we have some clue as to the very limited influence of Jews in Philippi, Luke fascinates us with this tranquil scene which probably unfolded on the banks of the Gangites, just over a mile outside the city. Twenty years after Pentecost and hundreds of miles from Antioch, Paul and his companions quietly sat with the women and discussed spiritual matters. Luke finds no need to tell us they explained the gospel; by this time he assumes we understand that.

16:14. The first convert in Europe was a Jewish **worshiper of God**, a Gentile who worshiped with the Jewish women by the river. Lydia was not only a Gentile and a proselyte, but also a businesswoman. Interestingly, the Hellenistic district of Lydia had garnered fame for its dying industry, especially royal purple. We cannot assume her name derived from that area, but it offers an interesting parallel.

The text tells us **the Lord opened her heart**—what a beautiful way to describe receptivity to the gospel. Paul told the Corinthians that people rejected the gospel because their minds had been darkened (2 Cor. 4:4). The light of truth cuts through the darkness; and when God chooses to open hearts (as here), people enter the eternal kingdom of his Son. Perhaps Lydia had affiliated with the Jewish synagogue at Thyatira and, having moved her business to Philippi, continued to worship with faithful Jews there.

16:15. What a clever way to ascertain whether the evangelist who proclaimed the gospel to you believes that your faith is genuine and effective. Lydia makes their acceptance of her hospitality a conditional demonstration of her conversion. Here again, as in the case of Cornelius, members of her household also hear and believe. We have every indication that the church began to meet at her home.

Let's remember too the generosity of the Philippian congregation in the ministry of Paul (Phil. 4:14–19). We have reason to believe that Lydia became a major contributor not only to the ongoing work in Philippi, but to the missionary activity of Paul.

A Song of Believers in Persecution (vv. 16–28)

SUPPORTING IDEA: *Sometimes, just when things seem to be going great, the bottom drops out. In those times, too, we trust God and sing in the midst of our struggles.*

16:16–18. The python, a mythical serpent of the Greeks, guarded the temple of Apollo. By A.D. 50, they used the word *python* to describe a possessed person through whom the python gave prophecy. Pagan generals would commonly consult people with a "pythian spirit" before marching off to war; owning such a python-possessed slave girl would be a gold mine for her master.

The term "pythian spirit" also was used in that day to speak of ventriloquists, so Paul and his friends encountered a most unusual demonic scene. The slave girl followed them day after day, speaking in strange voices yet telling the truth about their ministry. Since she was demon-possessed, we should hardly be surprised that the demon(s) recognized truth (Luke 4:34, 41; 8:28). The term **Most High God** would be understood by pagan Greeks to refer to Zeus, but the phrase could also acknowledge the Hebrew *Yahweh* (Num. 24:16; Ps. 78:35; Isa. 14:14; Dan. 3:26; 4:32; 5:18,21).

Since she told the truth, why not appreciate such valuable public relations? Probably because the shouting of the possessed slave girl attracted more attention than the gospel itself. Paul feared his audience would lose track of their priorities, so he practiced a basic New Testament exorcism in familiar words. Some have supposed that the girl immediately became a Christian and part of the embryonic church at Philippi. Luke does not tell us that since his interest centers primarily on what happened to Paul and Silas as a result of the exorcism.

16:19–21. Like the owners whose pigs Jesus sent over the cliff (Mark 5:16–17), the slave girl's masters became angered at this loss of income. The charge was perpetrating an illegal religion and thereby upsetting the *Pax Romana*, but the opening line is instructive—**These men are Jews.** That may very well account for the jailing of Paul and Silas but not Luke and Timothy.

In many ways our own culture parallels the ancient Roman Empire. Here is another example—the ugly face of anti-Semitism waiting to arise at any moment. Was there an uproar? Did the missionaries advocate customs unlawful for Romans? Both charges seem doubtful, but by this time New Testament Christians were accustomed to being imprisoned on false charges.

We often think of fascism as originating with Hitler and demonstrated most obviously in his Third Reich. As Polhill reminds us, the word is essentially Roman and tied to the **magistrates** of verse 20:

> They were the enforcement officers. Their symbol of office was a
> bundle of rods with an ax protruding from the middle, tied together
> with a red band called the *fasces*. (This symbol was revived in mod-
> ern times by Mussolini for his "fascist" movement; Polhill, 352.)

16:22–24. Of course the crowd joined the complaints of local merchants against a couple of strangers, especially Jews. Now Paul and Silas got their first taste of Roman justice. With no trial, no hearing, and no opportunity to defend themselves, they were beaten with a wooden rod and thrown into the inner cell (*esotera*) of the prison with their feet placed in stocks. Perhaps Luke emphasizes the extra security to highlight the deliverance miracle coming in the next paragraph. In any case, Paul never forgot this experience and wrote about it to the Christians at Corinth (2 Cor. 11:23, 25).

16:25–28. Here Luke gives us one of the most beautiful scenes in Scripture. Beaten, bleeding missionaries, their feet in stocks, literally turn this prison into Sing-Sing—that grim state facility in Ossining, New York. It bears no connection whatsoever to this account, but the fascinating name helps form our picture. Not only did they sing and pray, but the rest of the prisoners listened to them!

Then God visited Philippi with another one of his open-door miracles. This time, rather than the quiet angel of chapter 12, we see a violent earthquake. **All the prison doors flew open, and everybody's chains came loose**.

As we recall 12:19, we understand the behavior of the jailer. If his prisoners escaped, it would be his life anyhow. Why not do the deed now and save beatings and suffering along the way? Accustomed as we are to prison breaks in Acts, this time the account differs. Rather than escape, Paul and Silas stayed right in their cell and somehow persuaded the rest of the prisoners to do so as well. God's intent on this occasion was not the physical deliverance of his servants, but the spiritual deliverance of the jailer and his family.

E A Song of Believers in Faith (vv. 29–34)

SUPPORTING IDEA: *The message of salvation by grace through faith, once proclaimed by Peter to a Centurion in Caesarea, now comes to another member of the Roman army in a dark and broken prison in his dark and broken city.*

16:29–30. We have no trouble understanding why the jailer showed gratitude to Paul and Silas; they had literally saved his life by not leading a mass exodus of prisoners. What could he possibly have meant by his now-familiar question, **what must I do to be saved?** Was it the earthquake, a clear demonstration of the power of the God these men served? Had he been told of the words of the slave girl so he would know why these men were in his prison? Had he listened to the hymns and heard the gospel proclaimed in song and prayer? Luke does not tell us, though quite possibly all these factors were involved. In any event, the jailer demonstrated three attitudes needed for salvation—recognition of his need, awareness of a Savior, and response to the gospel.

16:31–34. Whatever the jailer intended, Paul and Silas directed his focus immediately to Jesus and offered a response still heard on the lips of Christians proclaiming the gospel around the world. The missionaries further explained God's message not only to the jailer, but to others in his house. Luke carefully reminds us that the faith of the jailer would not automatically transfer to the rest of the household. The promise of salvation depended upon the individual response of everyone who heard the message (see "Deeper Discoveries" in chapter 10).

Those who glibly use the quotation of verse 31 should not ignore the emphasis of verse 32. We don't know how long Paul and Silas explained the message of salvation to these people, but obviously that explanation was essential for them to make sense of the initial answer. Furthermore, proclamation of the Word held priority over their physical condition and comfort.

First, the jailer and his family were reconciled to God, then to their former enemies—these two most unusual prisoners.

⒡ A Song of Believers in Freedom (vv. 35–40)

SUPPORTING IDEA: *Sometimes one must confront the enemies of Christ to gain some measure of justice. Christians should use every legal and biblical means to keep themselves and the gospel free from restraint.*

16:35–36. Unlike the other two prisoner release scenes we have read in Acts, this time the authorities saw no connection between God's earthquake and the prisoners. After all, everyone was still present and accounted for, and word of the jailer's conversion had probably not yet reached his superiors. We can be sure that the last three words of verse 36 came from the heart of the jailer and were not a part of his orders from higher up. Quite possibly the magistrates only intended to keep Paul and Silas in prison overnight and then release them, assuming the beating and jailing would be sufficient to keep them from disturbing the peace any further.

16:37. Speaking to the officers (not the jailer), Paul raised the issue of Roman citizenship and vowed to stay right in prison until the magistrates themselves personally escorted them out. Roman citizens could travel anywhere without liability to prosecution by local laws. He could always appeal to Caesar (as Paul did later in his ministry). Then no one less than the Emperor could touch him. This was no small matter with Paul (22:25–28). On this occasion it certainly didn't hurt to have a fellow Roman citizen like Silas standing by his side.

16:38–39. To their credit, the magistrates understood their mistake and rectified it publicly. The problem of the angry mob remained a potential threat to the peace of the city, so they requested that Paul and Silas leave. Again, Polhill:

> Paul may have seemed a bit huffy in his demand for a formal apology from the magistrates, but that is not the point. It was essential that the young Christian community have a good reputation among the authorities if its witness was to flourish. Christians broke none of the Roman laws. Luke was at pains to show this. It would continue to be a major emphasis in Acts. In this instance Paul and Silas were totally innocent of any wrong-doing. It was important that the magistrates acknowledge their innocence and set the record straight. This was why Paul made such a major point of it (Polhill, 358).

16:40. Yes, they would leave—but not until they made one more visit to the fledgling church. What a congregation! Since the "we" sections end at verse 17, most commentators believe Luke stayed on in Philippi and would therefore have been a leader of the church until his next outing with the missionaries. We assume the church met in Lydia's home, and it seems safe to conclude that the jailer and his family became a part of the congregation as well.

The slave girl offers a bit of a question. The text gives no specific word about her salvation, so I feel a bit reluctant to add her to the group, though some scholars do so. No apostles present, no elders ordained, this fascinating group of believers became a responsible congregation taking upon themselves mutual edification and the expansion of evangelism in Philippi. We need not wonder how they fared, for we have Paul's letter to the church (Philippians) to demonstrate his great joy and confidence in God's work there.

MAIN IDEA REVIEW: *God's people can sing in their struggles when they know he leads and blesses each step of their lives no matter how difficult and dark some days may be.*

III. CONCLUSION

The Joy of the Lord

The second missionary journey still had a long way to go, but Luke would have few stories as exciting as this. We should learn from this fascinating chapter that it does not take a sweeping massive effort of evangelism to plant the church of Jesus Christ. We may read about thousands coming to the Savior in Acts 2, but here a seemingly pitiful handful form the nucleus of a New Testament congregation. People enthralled with megachurches and megaprograms may snicker at the meager beginnings of Philippi. Those who have been involved in church-planting efforts, who have struggled with a handful of people over a long period of time, understand precisely what God was doing here.

We've seen the gladness of Lydia and the joy of the jailer and his family. We have sensed the dependence upon God felt by this group of people with whom Paul and Silas met before leaving town. A. B. Simpson, founder of the Christian and Missionary Alliance, once penned these words:

> The joy of the Lord is the strength of His people,
> The sunshine that banishes sadness and gloom,
> The fountain that bursts in the desert of sorrow,
> And sheds o'er the wilderness gladness and bloom.

The joy of the Lord is our strength for life's burdens.
It gives to each duty a heavenly zest.
It sets to sweet music the task of the toiler,
And softens the couch of the laborer's rest.

PRINCIPLES

- A spiritual son very often comes from a spiritual mother.
- When God sends us somewhere to minister, he has someone ready to listen.
- God's people can rejoice in the ugliest and most painful circum stances.
- The size of a congregation is irrelevant in measuring God's work in a city or town.

APPLICATIONS

- Raise spiritual children at home, and don't forget the grandparent influence.
- Find somebody else's spiritual orphan to adopt if necessary.
- Visit other groups of believers when you travel.
- Sing and pray in the most difficult moments of your life.
- Be ready to explain the gospel to anyone, anytime, anywhere.

IV. LIFE APPLICATION

One Man's Carelessness

They called it unsinkable. They claimed it was the safest ship afloat. As the night of April 14 yielded to the early morning of April 15 in 1912, the *Titanic*, a British steamer of the White Star Line, hit an iceberg during its first voyage from England to New York City. Some 1,600 miles northeast of New York City, the collision tore a 300-foot gash in the hull. Since lifeboats had room for less than half the approximately 2,200 persons on board, only 705 survived, mostly women and children. The great ship sank in about two and a half hours.

Experts discovered that a wireless operator took his earphones off and went to sleep, quite possibly for just a few minutes. The U.S. ship *California* sailed just twelve miles away at the moment of impact, but no one was at the radio to make contact until too late. On that dreadful night, 1,625 people died due to one man's irresponsibility.

Christians should be responsible people. God holds us responsible to gather for worship, fellowship, and edification as the women did by the river in Philippi. He holds us responsible to proclaim his Word effectively as the missionaries did in the pagan city of Philippi. He holds us responsible to keep our spirits up by his grace when life crumbles all around us. He holds us responsible to explain the gospel at every opportunity he puts in our paths.

As he did with the small group of believers at Philippi, so he holds us responsible to be lights in darkness, witnesses of the resurrection and of the Savior's grace both as individuals and as the collective body of Christ. What a wonderful thing if a church leader could write to your congregation what Paul later wrote to the church at Philippi:

> Paul and Timothy, servants of Christ Jesus, To all the saints in Christ Jesus at Philippi, together with the overseers and deacons: Grace and peace to you from God our Father and the Lord Jesus Christ. I thank my God every time I remember you. In all my prayers for all of you, I always pray with joy because of your partnership in the gospel from the first day until now, being confident of this, that he who began a good work in you will carry it on to completion until the day of Christ Jesus (Phil. 1:1–6).

V. PRAYER

God, we thank you for this wonderful story of grace and courage. We thank you for the church at Philippi and for the missionaries who founded it. May our lives reflect the unity and humility of these early believers.

VI. DEEPER DISCOVERIES

A. Circumcision (v. 3)

We dealt with the circumcision of Timothy in our commentary on this verse, but we need to set that event with Paul's decision regarding Titus. In Galatians 2, Paul talked about going to Jerusalem with Barnabas and Titus. This was a private visit in which he wanted to explain the Gentile mission again to the leaders of the church. He wrote:

> Yet not even Titus, who was with me, was compelled to be circumcised, even though he was a Greek. This matter arose because some false brothers had infiltrated our ranks to spy on the freedom we have in Christ Jesus and to make us slaves. We did not give in to them for a moment, so that the truth of the gospel might remain with you (vv. 3–5).

The situations, of course, are totally different in every way. If Paul wanted to be effective in the synagogue ministry he had chosen to pursue or among Jews anywhere he would find them (especially in Timothy's case in Lystra), he would have to maintain his own Jewishness and insist that others do so. Even a son of a mixed marriage like Timothy came under the law of circumcision, not for salvation, but to fulfill the customs and traditions of the Jews (1 Cor. 9:16–23).

Titus was not a Jew. As a Gentile, his circumcision would have broken the guidelines of the Jerusalem Council and militated against everything Paul preached with respect to God's grace to the Gentiles. Paul had no reason whatsoever to circumcise a Gentile apart from making that a step toward becoming a Christian. Since the Jerusalem Council had agreed there were no steps between paganism and Christianity, circumcising Gentiles was at best a useless procedure, and at worst a deliberate violation of the gospel of grace.

B. "We" Sections (v. 17)

Though commentators cannot agree, some evidence suggests that Luke participated in the missionary travels somewhat intermittently. The famous "we" sections end at 16:17 and begin again in 20:5 which describes a departure from Philippi. It seems quite safe to conclude that Luke spent that intervening time in Philippi and joined the missionary team again at that later point.

Polhill rejects the idea of a Lucan residence in Philippi and doubts that Philippi was even Luke's home city. Marshall and Longenecker, however, believe Luke stayed and that the "we" sections of Acts are very much intended to identify his joining and leaving the missionary team. Longenecker argues, "To judge by the way the 'we' sections in 16:10–17 and 20:5–15 focus on Paul's visits to Philippi, it may be that Luke had some part in the founding and growth of the church there" (Longenecker, 459). Longenecker also argues that the combination of the "we" section passages with Luke's strong emphasis on Philippi (30 verses) leads us to "reasonably suppose that the use of 'we' points to a resident of Philippi who traveled from Troas to Philippi with Paul and Silas and that this person was Luke himself" (Longenecker, 458).

VII. TEACHING OUTLINE

A. INTRODUCTION
1. Lead Story: Now We Will Win
2. Context: Acts 16 describes the beginning of the second missionary journey with special attention to the Macedonian Call which diverted the gospel westward instead of northward and took the missionaries to Europe. Luke gives almost the entire chapter to

events in Philippi and ends with the missionaries leaving that city and journeying deeper into Macedonia, indeed, all the way to Athens.

3. Transition: This chapter helps us understand the different ways in which people can come to Christ; not different truths of the gospel but different surroundings and circumstances. Lydia, the proselyte, already worshiped the Lord by a peaceful river. The jailer was at the point of suicide with nowhere to turn but to the Jesus Paul preached. We have seen and will continue to see other circumstances which bring people face to face with the eternal choice.

B. COMMENTARY

1. A Song of Believers in Growth (vv. 1–5)
   a. Introduction of Timothy (vv. 1–2)
   b. Circumcision of Timothy (v. 3)
   c. Ministry of Timothy with the team (vv. 4–5)
2. A Song of Believers in Obedience (vv. 6–10)
   a. Divine diversion (vv. 6–7)
   b. Divine direction (vv. 8–10)
3. A Song of Believers in Fellowship (vv. 11–15)
   a. Trip to Philippi (vv. 11–12)
   b. Joy by the river (vv. 13–14)
   c. Beginning of the church (v. 15)
4. A Song of Believers in Persecution (vv. 16–28)
   a. The slave girl (vv. 16–21)
   b. The stocks (vv. 22–24)
   c. The shakeup (vv. 25–28)
5. A Song of Believers in Faith (vv. 29–34)
   a. Desperate quest (vv. 29–30)
   b. Personal regeneration (vv. 31–33)
   c. Family commitment (v. 34)
6. A Song of Believers in Freedom (vv. 35–40)
   a. Official release (vv. 35–36)
   b. Legal recourse (vv. 37–38)
   c. Civil request (v. 39)
   d. Friendly departure (v. 40)

C. CONCLUSION: ONE MAN'S CARELESSNESS

VIII. ISSUES FOR DISCUSSION

1. What struggles and situations tend to make these days dark and troubled ones for your church? What do you see God doing to bring light and hope to your church?

2. Has the Holy Spirit put up a stop sign on some program or plan of your church? How would your church recognize such a sign from the Spirit? What would your church do about it?
3. In what ways is your church reaching out to people where they are instead of expecting them to come to your church building? What evangelistic results is your church having? How are you celebrating what God is doing among you?

Acts 17

The Gospel and the Greeks

I. **Introduction**
Interruptions in History

II. **Commentary**
A verse-by-verse explanation of the chapter.

III. **Conclusion**
Unchanging Resistance
An overview of the principles and applications from the chapter.

IV. **Life Application**
The Power of the Book
Melding the chapter to life.

V. **Prayer**
Tying the chapter to life with God.

VI. **Deeper Discoveries**
Historical, geographical, and grammatical enrichment of the commentary.

VII. **Teaching Outline**
Suggested step-by-step group study of the chapter.

VIII. **Issues for Discussion**
Zeroing the chapter in on daily life.

"Good philosophy must exist . . . because bad philosophy needs to be answered."

C . S .   L e w i s

CITY PROFILE: AMPHIPOLIS

- Thirty-three miles southwest of Philippi
- Once the capital of the northern district of Macedonia
- Located on the east bank of the Strymon River
- Controlled access to the Hellespont and the Black Sea

CITY PROFILE: THESSALONICA

- Cicero said this city was "situated in the bosom of our domain"
- Founded by Cassander in 315 B.C.
- Capital of Macedonia
- Population of nearly two hundred thousand
- Today the modern city of Salonika

CITY PROFILE: BEREA

- Fifty miles southwest of Thessalonica
- Located in the foothills of the Olympian Range
- Cicero referred to it as "off the beaten track"
- Located on a tributary of the Haliacmon

CITY PROFILE: ATHENS

- Named in honor of the goddess Athena
- Its naval fleet formed the basis of the Greek maritime empire
- Cultural and educational center of the Greek world, a status which continued under the Romans after they conquered the city in 146 B.C.
- At this time, it was a city of nearly ten thousand but its historic reputation remained

GEOGRAPHICAL PROFILE: VIA IGNATIA

- Roman highway beginning in Neapolis
- Ran west across Macedonia
- Ended at Adriatic Coast where ships would leave for Italy

I N   A   N U T S H E L L

his chapter contains an outstanding demonstration of cultural adaptation of the gospel. We saw some of it in chapter 14 where Paul preached common grace to the mob at Lystra, but Acts 17 represents the Bible's most dramatic demonstration of how to explain Christian truth to intelligent unbelievers.

The Gospel and the Greeks

I. INTRODUCTION

Interruptions in History

"*Do* you remember what you were doing when John F. Kennedy was shot?" is a frequent query by Americans old enough to recall. That assassination, so public, so violent, and so unexpected, somehow indelibly placed its mark in the minds of Americans that fateful day in November of 1963. I remember the moment precisely. I was teaching a class in an undergraduate college in Kansas City when a student rushed in and shouted in the middle of the lecture, "The president has been shot."

British novelist David Lodge remembers, too. He sat in a London theater watching a satirical review he had helped write. One sketch called for a character to show an attitude of carelessness during an interview by holding a transistor radio to his ear. To capture a touch of realism, the transistor was always tuned to a real station.

On that fateful day, the announcer broke in to tell the listening audience what had happened across the Atlantic. The actor frantically turned off the radio . . . but it was too late—reality had interrupted fantasy; death had put an end to comedy.

At various times God interrupts history. He did so at the incarnation, at the crucifixion, at the resurrection, at Pentecost, and again in this chapter as he sent the gospel to the cultural and educational capital of the Greco-Roman world. This is one of Paul's major points in this impromptu speech (v. 30). In the past God put up with ignorance from the heathen. Now that he has sent his Son to die and has bought our salvation through the resurrection, **he**

commands all people everywhere to repent. Not only that, but in the future God will again interrupt history with a day of judgment presided over by Jesus, his resurrected and glorified Son.

I love the book of Acts so much I find it extremely difficult to identify a favorite chapter. Again and again I find myself coming back to this wonderful confrontation between pagan idolatry and Christian theism. Let's not forget the important ministries at Thessalonica and Berea before Paul even reached Athens. This exciting chapter recites for us again what happened when the gospel came to the Greeks on their home turf.

II. COMMENTARY

The Gospel and the Greeks

> **MAIN IDEA:** *The central message of the new covenant gospel centers on Jesus Christil and his resurrection.*

Ⓐ Proclamation in Thessalonica (vv. 1–4)

> **SUPPORTING IDEA:** *Jesus' suffering, death, and resurrection should not surprise anyone, for they fulfill God's Old Testament promises.*

17:1. For a long while Paul was unable to practice his basic missionary strategy of preaching first in a synagogue. Thessalonica offered him another opportunity. At this significant city (see Profile) which dominated Macedonian government and commerce, the diverse population would have included a significant Jewish component (1 Thess. 2:14–16). From the beginning it appears Paul selected this site as the base for Balkan evangelism (1 Thess. 1:7–8).

Surely they had endured a difficult three days walking here from Philippi despite the continuing pain from their beatings. Covering about thirty-three miles a day along the Via Ignatia, the missionary team must have been exhausted upon arrival. As usual, Luke leaves us with a lot of questions. Why no ministry in Amphipolis and Apollonia? Or was there ministry, and he just didn't tell us about it because Thessalonica would become an important center for the gospel? Did the missionaries have access to horses which eased the journey, or did they possibly amble through several more towns than Luke names, perhaps walking as long as a week to make the trip from Philippi? Luke cares for none of that because he wants to get Paul into that synagogue as quickly as possible.

17:2–3. Despite their experiences in pagan territory where no synagogue existed, the missionary policy had not changed—"To the Jews first, but also to the Gentiles." Paul stayed at least three weeks, for he went on the Sabbath three times to reason (*dielexato*), explain (*dianoigon*), prove (*paratithemenos*), and proclaim (*kathangello*). This was Paul's forté, his area of greatest expertise. On familiar ground in a synagogue, the former rabbi could now develop a carefully-developed messianic Christology based on a host of Old Testament texts. Today we would talk about a Christian hermeneutic, finding Jesus in key passages throughout the law, the writings, and the prophets (Luke 24:26, 46; Acts 3:18; 26:22–23; 1 Cor. 15:3–4; 1 Pet. 1:11).

17:4. A familiar strategy utilized a familiar message and drew a familiar response. A **large number** of Jews and proselytes believed. Luke uses the word **persuaded** (*apeisthesan*), an appropriate corollary to the words he has used to describe the way Paul presented the gospel.

Interesting that Luke should mention they **joined Paul and Silas**. Silas had been in the background for most of this second journey but came into prominence again here in a Jewish setting. Perhaps we should remember that he represented Paul's seal of approval from Jerusalem in proclaiming the gospel to the Gentiles without saddling them with Jewish rituals and restrictions in their quest to come to faith.

B Persecution by the Jews (vv. 5–9)

SUPPORTING IDEA: *In Acts we have seen numerous motivations for persecution; jealousy, however, is not that common. Apparently, the Jews felt quite comfortable rejecting Christ, but they couldn't stomach the **large number** of Gentile proselytes who embraced the gospel. What does one do when one is unhappy with another's choice of religion? The Jews followed a standard operating procedure: find some riffraff, form a mob, start a riot.*

17:5. "Bad characters" (*agoraios*) are crude people who hung around the marketplace because they had nothing else to do. All of a sudden Luke introduces Jason as though we already knew that Paul and Silas were quartered at his home. His name would have been the Greek equivalent of Jesus or Joshua. Some have concluded he was therefore a Jew. Certainly he was a believer, perhaps having trusted Christ as part of the group mentioned in verse 4. We might also conclude that Aristarchus and Secundus mentioned in 20:4 may have been converted at this time.

Luke repeats an important lesson here; so will we. A strategy emerges here, not just a mindless mob. The Jews wanted to demonstrate that these two outsiders were disturbing the *Pax Romana*, the one thing Rome could not tolerate. If the Jews could have demonstrated that Paul and Silas ultimately caused the riot, they could have made their case stick.

17:6–7. Apparently Jason had hidden the missionaries, so they dragged him and a few other Christians before the magistrates (*politarches*).

Remember, we are beyond A.D. 50 here so the officials at Thessalonica would surely know of the Edict of Claudius, dated about that time, expelling all Christians from Rome because of constant riots.

Their complaint? **These men who have caused trouble all over the world have now come here.** Here we have more Lucan hyperbole, though of course he may be recording exactly what they said in their wild exaggeration of the truth. Not only have these troublemakers come, but Jason has shown them hospitality. Look out. Here comes the *coup de grace*—they defy Caesar's decrees and claim that Jesus is their king. What a familiar sound. We can see Jesus in Pilate's hall (Luke 23:2,4; John 19:12,15). We can hear the frantic multitudes in Jerusalem screaming, "We have no king but Caesar!"

Smart plan: accuse your enemies of disturbing the peace and claim they spoke out against Caesar. Roman officials would spring into action in no time. Longenecker suggests that this constant hassle over Jesus and Caesar as king led to Paul's avoidance of the words "kingdom" and "king" in his letters (Longenecker, 469).

17:8-9. The plan worked, upsetting both people and magistrates. Their main concern was law and order, not punishment. For one thing, the perpetrators remained in hiding, and it hardly seemed useful to punish their host, probably an upstanding citizen of the city. Their final ruling was a bond which acted in the reverse way we use it today. In our legal system, one posts bond to guarantee his availability in the city of accusation. In this case, Jason guaranteed the missionaries' departure. Paul saw in this the act of Satan shutting down the ministry in Thessalonica (1 Thess. 2:18). Nevertheless, the church there grew and prospered as we learn from Paul's letters to that congregation (1 Thess. 3:6-10).

Ⓒ Perseverance in Berea (vv. 10-15)

SUPPORTING IDEA: *Never trust somebody else's explanation of the Scripture until you have studied it for yourself and allowed the Holy Spirit to confirm the truth of what you hear.*

17:10-12. The missionaries were on the road again. In the cover of darkness they continued the fifty miles west to Berea. Much to their delight, they found a synagogue. Sneaking off to Berea had solid precedent in the Roman world. Cicero (106-43 B.C.) had written that Roman authorities were so unpopular in Thessalonica that when he visited that city on government business he sometimes found it necessary to head off to Berea to escape the heat. Perhaps Paul had the same thing in mind. Hang out for awhile in Berea; when things died down, go back inside the beltway to continue his witness.

Paul may not have been prepared for the reception God set up for him in this foothill town. Luke leaves his objective narrative to offer an opinion about the Bereans which has etched them in Christian recognition for two thousand years. How many churches have a "Berean" Sunday school class which, one would hope, attempts to model itself after these open-minded people who personally checked out Paul's arguments in the Scriptures? Luke seems to be telling us that if recipients of the gospel can put religious, political, and social prejudice out of the way for a bit, they will understand how logical and biblical the message about Jesus really is. Luke's reference to Greek men and women in verse 12 indicates that Greek Gentiles as well as Jews and proselytes came to faith in Berea.

17:13–15. The Thessalonian troubles followed Paul to Berea and apparently created such a commotion that the lives of missionaries were in danger there as well. Now Luke introduces a number of personnel shifts as members of the missionary team move about. As nearly as we can piece together the story, Silas and Timothy rejoined Paul at Athens (1 Thess. 3:1). Even though Timothy has not been mentioned since the early verses of chapter 16, we have to assume he remained a part of the missionary team throughout the trip.

The point here is to get Paul away safely, for he seemed to be the major target of the attack. Silas and Timothy stayed temporarily at Berea after which Timothy rejoined Paul in Athens only to be sent back to Thessalonica (1 Thess. 3:2). Silas went from Athens back to Macedonia (18:5), and Paul left Athens for Corinth. So the missionary team split up for security reasons, and also to diversify the ministry a bit. They will regather at Corinth.

Preaching in the Agora (vv. 16–21)

SUPPORTING IDEA: *When ministering to intellectuals, don't use "church language," but reason from as much common ground as you can find. Make your way as quickly as possible to Jesus and the resurrection.*

17:16–17. Athens! The ancient parallel of modern Vienna, Paris, Rome, or New York. Not in population to be sure, but in cultural influence on a nation and in the case of Athens, an empire. The intellectual capital was also the idolatry capital, a city which contained more idols than people! Here Socrates, Plato, Aristotle, Epicurus, and Zeno had lived and taught. True, the heyday was now behind this formerly glorious city, but the past lived on in its temples and statuary.

Luke began this portion of his narrative by focusing not on the city, but on the missionary team. Up to this point in Acts, every ministry we have studied has been group-centered. Team leadership dominates this book. Luke almost feels compelled to explain why Paul would have ministered alone in this strategic city. His explanation centers in Paul's inability to control his emotions in the midst of such raw paganism. Like Jeremiah of old, he could not quell the fire in his bones and was infuriated with the idolatry all around him.

Here also the basic strategy changes. Paul did not wait for rejection in the synagogue but rather divided his time daily between synagogue Jews and proselytes and the pagans in the Agora (marketplace).

17:18–19. In his marketplace ministry, Paul encountered a group of Epicurean and Stoic philosophers (see "Deeper Discoveries"). The nature of their philosophy hardly captures Luke's primary attention: simply two secular schools of thought trying to make sense out of life apart from biblical revelation. We could substitute pragmatism, utilitarianism, atheism, agnosticism, communism, or a host of other more modern philosophies.

As they engaged in dialog with Paul, they called him a **babbler** (*spermologos*), less a term of derision than a description of his philosophy. Though hardly philosophical allies, Epicureans and Stoics at least attributed some order and design to each other's system of thought. Paul seemed to be a "seed-picker," a word used to describe birds picking up grain or even poor farmers finding seed in the marketplace, taking it home, sowing it without separating the types, and, therefore, reaping a field of mixed grain. These sophisticated thinkers saw Paul as somebody who had picked up bits and pieces of philosophy with no coherent system. In other words, he was eclectic.

Other critics saw the distinctive theological thread in Paul's preaching and correctly analyzed his emphasis on a God other than the many they worshiped in Athens. Perhaps they saw Jesus as the new God and resurrection (*anastasis*) as his chief goddess.

Since the Areopagus is both a hill and the formal name of a court which often met on that hill, scholars are divided as to the meaning of verse 19. The NIV clearly implies a formal hearing, though hardly a trial. Longenecker says, "We should doubtless understand Paul's appearance before the Athenian Council of Ares as being for the purpose of explaining his message before those in control of affairs in the city so that he might either receive the freedom of the city to preach or be censored and silenced" (Longenecker, 474).

If the Council met on that gigantic flat rock (it sometimes met in the royal portico in the northwest corner of the Agora), the sight was spectacular. The Parthenon stood just off to the right if he addressed the group facing down to the Agora. Today, in ruins, the splendor and aura of the place still excite the visitor familiar with this narrative. Today Areopagus is the name of the Greek Supreme Court and still fascinates Christians when they hear the term.

17:20–21. Luke merely repeats the standard assessment of the Athenians, not necessarily a critical remark. This city had given itself over to discussion of ideas and cared for little else. This marketplace preacher had advocated **some strange ideas**, so they wanted an opportunity to evaluate his views. Marshall says of Luke, "His tone is distinctly sarcastic" (Marshall, 285), but that is not necessarily the case if he is merely reflecting what all Macedonians believed about Athens. Perhaps he wanted to draw a contrast between the charge of the Epicureans and Stoics that Paul was philosophically confused, and suggested that they themselves suffered this intellectual disease.

🅱 The Persuasion on the Areopagus (vv. 22–31)

SUPPORTING IDEA: *Sometimes God provides launching pads for the gospel—an inquiry, an incident, or even an idol. Then it's our job to make our way from that opportunity to the truth of God's Word.*

17:22–23. Although the KJV renders the phrase in a critical tone ("too superstitious"), Paul probably began with a commendation. One would not capture the ears and hearts of proud Athenian philosophers by condemning them in one's first sentence. The word in question is *deisidaimonesteros* which could be translated, "to revere the spirits firmly."

As in Lystra, so in Athens, it would have been futile to begin with the God of the Old Testament choosing a certain people, sending prophets, and promising a Messiah. That was a message for synagogues or Jews gathering by a river. Paul began with the doctrine of God and launched his message with a local object lesson, the altar to *agnosto theo*.

Whether his audience picked up on it or not, Paul certainly seemed to intend an irony here. The Greeks erected altars to unknown gods to make sure all religious bases were covered. Now the missionary apostle wants to introduce them to a God completely unknown to them.

We know about the existence of such altars, and we need not wonder if either Paul or Luke created fictional narrative here. Even though most of the evidence indicates a plural designation ("to unknown gods"), Paul might very well have adapted that typical Greek polytheism to the monotheism he was about to proclaim. They worshiped in ignorance; Paul dispelled that ignorance by explaining the self-revealed God of the Bible.

17:24–28. From the doctrine of God Paul moved on to the doctrine of creation. We hear echoes of Stephen as Paul launched into an explanation of **The God who made the world and everything in it**. Virtually every line contradicts the religious views of his audience. There was only one God, not many; he does not live in temples like these standing all around us; he is not served by human effort; he knows no special people (like the Jews or the Greeks) since all were made by God; God purposes to draw humanity to himself.

The Athenians believed they had originated from the soil of their homeland and were different than other peoples. Paul pointed to the common ancestor (Adam) and indicated that the times and boundaries of peoples are in God's hands. To this point the Greeks would have had little difficulty following Paul and would have found a good bit of agreement in what he said. His meaning, of course taken directly from biblical sources, ran far beyond their humanistic pantheism.

Some have taken verse 26 to erect discriminatory boundaries between races, but, of course, that was hardly Paul's intent. In the words of Barnhouse, "What Paul is saying here is that it is God who determines how long a nation shall exist—the time of its ascendancy, popularity, and decline. No nation decides this by itself; God is in control. Like Daniel said, 'He (God) removes kings and sets up kings' (Dan. 2:21). God decides not only how long a nation stays on the map, but also how far it will reach before it is sent into decline by God. *He* determined how far the Roman Empire, or the British Empire, or Hitler's Third Reich would go before it came to an end. This is what Paul had in mind" (Barnhouse, 151).

Quite a message for philosophers who understood only too well the history of their own city's decline. They could well have agreed that the gods played a major role in what had happened to Greece and especially to Athens. To attribute all this to the providential hand of a single deity would have been beyond their imagination.

In this amazing balance of presuppositional and common ground apologetics, Paul made his way to the whole purpose of creation, namely, worship of the one true God. Knowing that God and worshiping him was possible, for even some Greek poets had tapped into the truth. The first part of verse 28 comes from *Cretica* by Epimenides, and the second part of the verse from *Hymn to Zeus*, written by the Cilician poet Aratus. To be sure, both of these lines were directed at Zeus in Greek literature, but Paul applied them to the Creator of whom he spoke. So in five short verses Paul affirmed that God made the world; God gave all people life; God controlled the nations; and God revealed himself so people would seek him, a result quite possible for he is both transcendent and imminent.

17:29–31. Moving in logical sequence from his quotes, Paul emphasized a personal relationship with God. Idolatry was wrong; God could not possibly be like gold or silver or stone. God makes people—people do not make God. Ignorance must end because God had revealed himself not only in Old Testament Scripture, but also in the life and death of his Son. Universalism is a lie. God will *not* eventually find some way to bring all people to himself.

Paul told the mob at Lystra (14:16) the same thing. Pagans are lost because of natural revelation (Rom. 1 and 2). Perhaps in the past people could complain about excuses (though God would not accept such as valid);

but now judgment was coming, and the resurrection proved that no one will be exempt from the authority of Jesus. From the doctrine of God to the doctrine of creation to the doctrine of repentance, Paul preached the gospel on Mars Hill.

Paul assumed the fact of the resurrection and emphasized more its meaning. In reality, the *fact* of the resurrection saves no one; it is precisely the *meaning:* Jesus arose for our justification that makes the difference. All of a sudden in verses 30 and 31, Paul left the familiar domain in which he had been working and dealt with subjects foreign to these philosophers. Polhill says:

> The concept of repentance must have sounded strange to the Athenians. Even stranger was Paul's warning of God's coming day of judgment (v. 31). Strangest of all was his reference to the resurrection of Christ. . . . Just as Peter had pointed to the resurrection as proof to the Jews that Jesus is Messiah, so to the Gentiles Paul pointed to the resurrection as proof that he is the coming judge of all humanity (Polhill, 377).

Many have criticized Paul for not quoting Scripture and talking about the cross that day (see "Deeper Discoveries"), but his contextualization of the gospel in the heart of Greek culture provides a brilliant model of communication and adaptation. Glasser reminds us:

> Paul did not combat religious systems or philosophical systems. Instead, he addressed men. He reached out after the hungry-hearted, the groping—those who like blind men confessed their blindness as they fumbled to find the latch of the door. The altar and its inscription revealed to Paul the ultimate agony of idolatry, but it was the one hopeful sign he could find in all Athens. In seizing on it, he accepted the validity of the universal religious consciousness of man and the universal ethical concern of man. Were he among us today he would say, "Don't preach to Buddhists, to Muslims, to Hindus. Just preach to men. Reach out to men in the tragedy of their need and you will win them to Christ" (Glasser, 11–12).

The Greeks, steeped in philosophy and religion, had a very poor sense of history. Since God is the key to history, Paul worked his way through creation and sovereignty to end up at the door of repentance and resurrection. Makito emphasizes:

> The Bible is the only answer to history. It is the only book which asserts that the universe has its own purpose, because it is God who sponsors the whole universe. It has a beginning and a definite end.

Like a good producer of a program, God holds the universe every second. Not one minute of the course of history is out of God's controlling hands (Makito, 80).

F Perception of the Message (vv. 32–34)

SUPPORTING IDEA: *As usual, the gospel received a mixed response, and the missionaries assessed the effect of the Areopagus address.*

17:32. The Greeks would have had no problem at all with the immortality of the soul, but bodily resurrection was beyond their grasp. So Luke tells us **some of them sneered**, but others willingly listened further. Some take this as general politeness or the constant inquisitiveness of the Athenian philosophers, but we see no good reason for accepting their response as anything less than sincere. This shocking news about bodily resurrection needed much further explanation. Apparently, however, the scoffers outnumbered the serious. Paul saw that an opportunity to speak freely in the city would not be forthcoming.

17:33–34. Nevertheless, **A few men became followers of Paul and believed.** Luke names Dionysius, a member of the council, and a woman named Damaris. Apart from some fascinating traditional accounts, we know nothing further about either of these people, nor does Luke tell us that a church formed in Athens. Most scholars believe that did not happen. Today a flag on the Parthenon is lowered to half mast on Good Friday and raised again on Easter. It may be a small matter, but Christians familiar with Acts 17 can hardly forget that this brave and brilliant missionary proclaimed the gospel just a few yards away from that flag.

Luke certainly does not portray the Areopagus address as a failure. Anytime people believe and are saved, regardless of the number, the ministry has been effective. Furthermore, Paul's speech contained all the basic elements of the gospel: it condemned idolatry and sin (v. 29); it showed need for repentance (v. 30); it argued the certainty of judgment (v. 31a); and it offered salvation through Christ's resurrection (v. 31b).

MAIN IDEA REVIEW: *The central message of the new covenant gospel centers on Jesus Christ and his resurrection.*

III. CONCLUSION

Unchanging Resistance

An old story tells about a missionary with a microscope who showed an Indian the dirty water of the Ganges. The lens provided undeniable proof; the filthy river used by people for bathing and laundry, by animals for every possible purpose, and by everyone as a dumping ground was not fit to drink under any circumstances.

After lifting his eye from the microscope, the Indian asked a curious question: "Are there any other things like this around the area?" Upon being assured by the pioneer missionary that this microscope was the only one he might ever see, the Indian grabbed the scientific instrument, smashed it on a rock, and continued drinking from the Ganges.

So it was with twenty-nine of the thirty Areopagus Council members. Paul had introduced them to the God they did not know and and had shown them there was no other. With the exception of Dionysius, their response was to deny Paul's God and return to their pantheon of worthless idols.

Unbelievers do that today—worshiping the idols of riches and wealth (the Greek god Mammon); wine, alcohol and drugs (Bacchus); immorality and lust (Astarte and Aphrodite); political power and terrorism (Mars); and health and strength (Hercules). Things haven't changed much since Paul stood on the hill that day in Athens.

All this reminds us of James' words to Christians:

> Anyone who listens to the word but does not do what it says is like a man who looks at his face in a mirror and, after looking at himself, goes away and immediately forgets what he looks like. But the man who looks intently into the perfect law that gives freedom, and continues to do this, not forgetting what he has heard, but doing it—he will be blessed in what he does (Jas. 1:23–25).

Luke has shown us three reactions to the gospel in this magnificent chapter. The Thessalonians chose persecution (though many believed); the Bereans chose to investigate the Scriptures themselves; and the Greeks chose to deny or delay. Such is the reaction to the gospel then and now. Gospel truth does not change. The day will come when God will judge the world through Jesus Christ, and "he has given proof of this to all men by raising him from the dead" (Acts 17:31b).

PRINCIPLES

- The Romans were right about one thing—monarchy is better than anarchy.
- Christians should study the Bible devoutly and regularly.
- Wherever the gospel goes, it will always encounter false gods of some kind.
- Idolatry of any kind should be detestable to believers in the one true God.

APPLICATIONS

- Know how to explain the gospel using the Scriptures.
- Read your Bible at home, and take it to church with you every time you go.
- Don't be thrown off base by secular philosophies; they are all empty of life's answers.
- Stand courageously for your faith in Christ—even when you have to stand alone.

IV. LIFE APPLICATION
The Power of the Book

In this rich chapter of God's Word we have seen two totally different approaches to communicating the gospel. In Athens, Paul approached the philosophers with common-ground apologetics, quoting Greek poets and launching his message from an idol. As we have observed, in that setting citations from the Old Testament Scriptures would have been totally meaningless. Nevertheless, he made his way to repentance and resurrection, both very clear even in Luke's brief synopsis of what Paul must have said that day.

The Bereans were quite anxious not only to hear the Scripture, but to search Scripture for themselves. This ought to be a pattern among Christians and can serve us as a model even today when witnessing the gospel to Jews. Christians do not worship the Bible, but extol it as the source of special revelation, the infallible, inerrant repository of God's special revelation. Great American leaders have often emphasized the significance of the Bible in life and society:

"It is impossible to rightly govern the world without God and the Bible" (George Washington).

"I believe the Bible is the best gift God has ever given to man. All the good from the Savior of the world is communicated to us through this Book" (Abraham Lincoln).

"That book sir, is the rock on which our Republic stands" (Andrew Jackson).

"Believe me, sir, never a night goes by, be I ever so tired, but I read the Word of God before I go to bed" (Douglas MacArthur).

"To read the Bible is to take a trip to a fair land where the spirit is strengthened and faith renewed" (Dwight Eisenhower).

Sir Walter Scott obtained Lord Byron's Bible after the death of that great literary figure. Just inside the front cover Scott found these words:

> Within that awful volume lies
> The mystery of mysteries!
> Happiest they of human race
> To whom our God has granted grace
> To read, to fear, to hope, to pray,
> To lift the latch, and force the way;
> But better had they not been born
> Who read to doubt or read to scorn (Robertson, 17).

V. PRAYER

God, thank you for your Holy Word. Help us to be faithful students of the Scriptures and knowledgeable teachers of your truth whenever you provide those opportunities. Amen.

VI. DEEPER DISCOVERIES

A. Proving the Resurrection (v. 3)

How would you go about proving the resurrection if an unsaved friend asked you to do that? Of course, you cannot—and neither could Paul. The resurrection was a historical event, certainly more easily argued in the first century than the twentieth. Paul's ministry in Thessalonica did not center on overwhelming his listeners with what today would be called "proof." The word for *proof* is based on the verb *paratithemi* which appears several times in the New Testament. In Matthew 13:24,31, the NIV translates it with the simple word *told*. In Luke 9:16 concerning the feeding of the five thousand, our word is rendered in English, *set before*. The word appears again in Acts 14:23 as Paul and Barnabas appoint elders and commit them **to the Lord**. The same idea appears in 1 Timothy 1:18; 2 Timothy 2:2; and 1 Peter 4:19.

In Acts 17:3, the KJV uses the word "alleging;" NLB chooses "pointing out," and RSV selects the same words as the NIV. The weight of evidence certainly suggests words like "propound," "set forth," "affirm," "commit," or "commend" as preferable to "prove," especially when applied to the resurrection.

In the synagogue setting at Thessalonica, Paul demonstrated that Old Testament Scriptures clearly provided sufficient evidence of Christ's messiahship; his death and resurrection could be squared with the theology devout Jews believed.

B. Women in Acts

Twice Luke emphasizes influential women in the Macedonian congregations (16:14; 17:12). Part of this is just Luke's way of handling these materials. As a Greek, he would have been considerably more open to emphasizing the importance of women than would a Palestinian Jew. However, we must also take into consideration the strong role women played in Greek culture. It is probably incorrect for us to view the women only as having importance because they were the wives of key officials. Sufficient evidence suggests their independent role in the Greco-Roman world. The word *gune* can be translated either "woman" or "wife." Luke uses it nineteen times in Acts, most frequently with honor (1:14; 5:14; 8:12; 13:50; 16:14; 17:4; 17:12; 17:34).

C. Epicureans and Stoics (v. 18)

The Epicurean school of philosophy, named after its founder Epicurus (342–270 B.C.), held that pleasure, particularly a life free from pain, passion, superstition and anxiety, was the chief end and the highest good. Epicureans were essentially deists, denying life after death and taking a rather detached view of deity, certainly to the point of denying any divine providence.

Stoicism was founded by Zeno (340–265 B.C.) and took its name from the "painted stoa," a colonnade in the Athenian Agora where Zeno commonly taught. Stoicism stressed living harmoniously with nature, using the rational abilities one possesses, and depending only on oneself for needs. God, to the Stoics, was some kind of world soul; their theology radiated pantheism.

Both philosophies, different as they were, demonstrated the secular alternatives for dealing with life's problems and issues. Perhaps the Stoics placed even more emphasis on reason than did the Epicureans, and Paul's Areopagus address would certainly have picked up on that.

D. Areopagus

Areopagus means "Hill of Ares," the Greek god of war. The Romans knew this god as Mars, which explains why we find "Mars Hill" in the KJV of 17:22. As one makes one's way from the Agora up to the Acropolis, the Areopagus is located just between. Even in the ruins of today, it is a most distinctive site. In Paul's day, the whole scene would have been dominated by the Parthenon located up in the Acropolis. Since the Areopagus lay just west of the Acropolis, if Paul faced north or east he would have looked respectively to the marketplace or the Parthenon, in either case a dramatic view.

VII. TEACHING OUTLINE

A. INTRODUCTION
1. Lead Story: Interruptions in History
2. Context: Acts 17 is the middle chapter of three which deal with the second missionary journey. Its treatment of three evangelism missions however, clearly focuses on Athens where, for the first time in Scripture, the message of the one true God confronted the society of many gods.
3. Transition: North American cities today are much more like Athens than Jerusalem. Centers of education and culture, sophisticated cities house people too caught up in themselves to pay much attention to God's truth. Yet in all these major modern population centers we find strong congregations of believers speaking God's truth to society just as Paul did in Athens hundreds of years ago.

B. COMMENTARY
1. Proclamation in Thessalonica (vv. 1–4)
   a. Familiar strategy (v. 1)
   b. Familiar message (vv. 2–3)
   c. Familiar response (v. 4)
2. Persecution by the Jews (vv. 5–9)
   a. By intimidation (vv. 5–6)
   b. By lies (vv. 7–9)
3. Perseverance in Berea (vv. 10–15)
   a. Perseverance of the believers (vv. 10–12)
   b. Perseverance of the troublemakers (v. 13)
   c. Perseverance of the missionaries (vv. 14–15)
4. Preaching in the Agora (vv. 16–21)
   a. From synagogue to marketplace (vv. 16–17)
   b. From theology to philosophy (vv. 18–19)
   c. From the familiar to the unfamiliar (vv. 20–21)
5. Persuasion on the Areopagus (vv. 22–31)
   a. Doctrine of God (vv. 22–23)
   b. Doctrine of creation (vv. 24–28)
   c. Doctrine of repentance (vv. 29–31)

6. Perception of the Message (vv. 32–34)
   a. Some sneered (v. 32a)
   b. Some delayed (vv. 32b–33)
   c. Some believed (v. 34)

C. **CONCLUSION: THE POWER OF THE BOOK**

VIII. ISSUES FOR DISCUSSION

1. Is your church more like the people in Thessalonica or those in Berea? What is the evidence for your conclusion here?
2. Who are the agitators against the church today? What is the church doing to cause people to stir up trouble against the church? How does your church face opposition to it?
3. Do you know of people who have never heard about God before? What strategy and message would you use to approach these people and introduce them to Jesus? Are you willing to begin using such strategy today?

Acts 18

Corinth!

I. **Introduction**
Serving the City

II. **Commentary**
A verse-by-verse explanation of the chapter.

III. **Conclusion**
The Importance of the Local Church
An overview of the principles and applications from the chapter.

IV. **Life Application**
Alexandria!
Melding the chapter to life.

V. **Prayer**
Tying the chapter to life with God.

VI. **Deeper Discoveries**
Historical, geographical, and grammatical enrichment of the commentary.

VII. **Teaching Outline**
Suggested step-by-step group study of the chapter.

VIII. **Issues for Discussion**
Zeroing the chapter in on daily life.

Q u o t e

"The church's mightiest influence is felt when she is different from the world in which she lives."

A .   W .   T o z e r

GEOGRAPHICAL PROFILE: ACHAIA

- A Roman province including the Peloponnesus in northern Greece south of Macedonia
- A senatorial province, not an imperial province
- Corinth was the capital
- To speak of Achaia in Macedonia was to speak of all of Greece

CITY PROFILE: CENCHREA

- The eastern harbor of Corinth in the little town of the same name
- Home of Phoebe (Rom. 16:1)
- Site of Paul's famous haircut

BIOGRAPHICAL PROFILE: GALLIO

- Full name—Junius Annaeus Gallio
- Proconsul of Achaia about A.D. 50
- Born in Spain but adopted by the Roman orator, Lucius Junius Gallio
- Of him Seneca once said, "No mortal was ever so sweet to one as Gallio was to all"

I N   A   N U T S H E L L

Though Ephesus is mentioned briefly, this chapter focuses on Corinth. It also deals with cooperative ministry, eloquence in evangelism, and the incomplete way in which God's truth is sometimes proclaimed. Paul's ministry in Corinth took place about A.D. 51.

Corinth!

I. INTRODUCTION

Serving the City

Imagine yourself boarding a plane at Boston's Logan Airport. Although departing nearly forty-five minutes late, your plane has now reached its cruising altitude of 35,000 feet. You are well on your way to covering the three thousand air miles to San Francisco. The sun has begun to set as you touch down at the city by the bay. An experienced traveler, you realize you have entered a world very different from the one you just left. You are cultural light years out of the New England aura, the historic staid ambiance that settles over Boston, much in the way a morning fog rolls into San Francisco. The cities are vastly different in social style, attitude, and almost every other way.

That also describes Athens and Corinth. With minimal mileage between them, the cultural distance loomed vast. Like Boston, Athens was the older city; and Corinth, relatively new. When Paul entered the Corinthian gates, he could see no major building over one hundred years old. With a population of nearly two hundred thousand, it was the largest city in Greece. From what we learn in Acts and in the two long epistles to the Corinthian church, we can conclude this city provided Paul with his greatest challenge. We should not be surprised that he spent approximately a year and a half there.

Set on a plateau overlooking the isthmus connecting central Greece and the Peloponnesus, Corinth had been built just north of Acrocorinth, a rocky hill rising to 1,886 feet and affording an almost impregnable fortress. The port of Lechaeum faced the Adriatic Sea on the west, and Cenchrea opened to the Aegean Sea on the east. Corinth dated to about 800 B.C., but Lucius Mummius leveled it to the ground in 146 B.C. Julius Caesar rebuilt it in 46 B.C. So the city was both old and new.

The population also deceives us a bit. More than twenty times larger than Athens, Corinth officially counted only its free citizens—Greeks, Italians, Roman army veterans, business and commerce people, and Orientals including a large number of Jews. Corinth was also home to nearly a half million slaves, bringing its overall population to about 700,000.

Along with its commerce, Corinth was famous for its immorality. For nearly five hundred years the Greek verb *korinthiazesthai* ("to Corinthianize") referred to sexual immorality, a condition at its height in Paul's day. The city worshiped the usual pantheon of Greek gods with a special focus on Aphrodite, her temple, and one thousand sacred prostitutes.

It also boasted temples to Malicertes, Apollo, and Asclepius, the god of healing.

I have visited Corinth with the aid of a Greek official who showed me a portion of the tombs not open to tourists. There, clay replicas of human body parts showed the kinds of diseases most commonly brought before Asclepius for his healing. Sexual organs abounded in the collection, indicating that various kinds of sexually transmitted diseases probably ran rampant through Corinth. Into this city came the apostle, fresh from his debate on the Areopagus. Here God called him to plant a new Christian community. Little did he know it would become one of the most diverse and difficult groups of the first-century church, coping with all the problems transformed pagans could bring into a congregation.

Today, the church of Jesus Christ once again faces the challenge of decaying cities. Every sin known to humankind not only plagues urban sprawl, but thrives there. Furthermore, that's where people live. Lots of people. Most people. In the country of Austria, large in land area by European standards, one-third of all the population lives in the city of Vienna. Mexico City alone has a population greater than all of Canada. Of course, we dare not forget tribal missions and rural ministry, but to make an impact of dramatic proportions for God, the church must understand how to serve the city.

II. COMMENTARY

Corinth!

MAIN IDEA: *Christians working together can present an effective and long-lasting ministry in cities as long as they focus on the redeeming power of Jesus Christ and his Word.*

A Tentmakers in the City (vv. 1–4)

SUPPORTING IDEA: *People with similar interests and occupations can cooperate together to forward the progress of the gospel.*

18:1–2. Paul found a fascinating couple in the city. We already know about the decree of Claudius (A.D. 49–50) driving Jews from Rome, so we know that this couple had not been in Corinth very long. Aquila, a Jew, came from Pontus, a province in the northeastern region of Asia Minor along the Black Sea between Bythynia and Armenia (2:9). His wife Priscilla *(Prisca)* was likely a Roman citizen. Like Paul, they worked as tentmakers. Longenecker speculates that, "Together, perhaps through Aquila's craftsmanship and Priscilla's money and contacts, they owned a tentmaking and leather-working firm, with branches of the business at Rome, Corinth, and

Ephesus (cf. 18:2, 18–19,26; Rom. 16:3; 1 Cor. 16:19; 2 Tim. 4:19)" (Longenecker, 481).

Priscilla stands out as one of the great ladies of the New Testament, always depicted in team ministry with her husband. Of the six times the Bible mentions them, four times it names Priscilla first. From everything we know about Priscilla and Aquila, they represent mature Christians whose service to the kingdom swept far beyond their contact with Paul. Clearly, they were already believers by the time he met them in Corinth, probably having come to faith in Rome.

Luke tells us, **Paul went to see them,** but he does not tell us why. Had their reputation reached the apostle in Macedonia? Did he know them professionally through the tentmaking trade? Did he just wander into that portion of the marketplace and meet them, thereby receiving an invitation to their home? Luke indicates only that their profession and their faith brought them together in a bond that would last Paul's lifetime.

18:3. Paul wrote often about his "secular occupation" and seemed to take a good bit of healthy pride in his self-support (1 Cor. 4:12; 1 Thess. 2:9; 2 Cor. 11:7). Only here, however, does the Bible tell us Paul was a tentmaker, working either in leather or cilicium, cloth woven from goat's hair. Willingness to work to support oneself while proclaiming the gospel served as a life principle for Paul. Perhaps this came from his rabbinic days when students were required to adopt a trade so they need not depend upon teaching for a livelihood. The wisdom of the ages haunts us today. Many teachers still wonder whether one can make a living at such a task, and many college and seminary students struggle with the potential of "tentmaking" as a means of ministry.

In today's selfish society, such a practice runs against the grain, but we cannot escape its biblical precedent, not only in Paul who apparently practiced it part-time with the primary focus on preaching, but also in Priscilla and Aquila who never left their full-time work to carry out vocational ministry. A major principle surfaces here: *there is no secular duty for a Christian*; everything we take on, from changing diapers to governing a state, becomes a form of service to Christ (Col. 3:23–25).

If we put together the New Testament information on the public ministry of Priscilla and Aquila, the following time chart seems to indicate their whereabouts:

A.D. 50–53	Corinth
A.D. 53–57	Ephesus
A.D. 57–62	Rome

This couple will return again before our chapter ends. Before we leave them here, notice the Bible never indicates anything about Paul's ministry *to them*, only about their ministry *to him*. In three different cities over some sixteen years he depended upon them, not they on him. It takes very little imagination to see the three of them in Corinth after a day in the marketplace, sitting by the fire as this wonderful couple kept the apostle spellbound with their stories about Rome.

18:4. Probably conforming to the pattern already laid by Priscilla and Aquila, Paul seems to have gone to the synagogue for ministry only on the Sabbath, presumably working full-time during the week. Indeed, Luke seems to make a distinct contrast between verses 4 and 5, primarily aimed at showing again how we accomplish biblical ministry through a team rather than through an individual. Only after Silas and Timothy arrived did Paul give himself completely to preaching. Meanwhile, he dialoged with Jews and proselytes, trying to persuade them to accept the Christian message.

🄱 Witness to the City (vv. 5–11)

SUPPORTING IDEA: *In the providence of God, the foolishness of preaching leads to faith in the gospel and the development of the church.*

18:5–6. How God blessed Paul in Corinth! Not only did he enjoy the fellowship of Priscilla and Aquila, but now his teammates rejoined him and brought with them money from the congregation of Philippi (2 Cor. 11:9; Phil. 4:14–15). News from Thessalonica also encouraged him (1 Thess. 3:7–10). What more could a missionary evangelist want—sound reports of effectiveness at a previous stop, a solid base on which to begin evangelism in the city, and substantial funds to free him up to give full-time to the gospel.

We can go clear back to Pisidian Antioch (13:46–52) to see this pattern of ministry—preaching in the synagogue, rejection, direct contact with Gentiles. In response to the opposition and abuse, Paul adopted a typical Jewish symbol and shook out his clothes (Acts 13:51). He had fulfilled his responsibility as a Jew. Their rejection and the ultimate judgment for rejection would be on their heads (Ezek. 33:4; Matt. 23:35; 27:25; Acts 5:28). As in Pisidian Antioch, Paul did not go to the Gentiles permanently, even though the language at the end of verse 6 seems to suggest that. He turned from Jews to Gentiles in Corinth, but he would repeatedly go back to the Jews and their synagogues in future ministry.

18:7–8. The first Corinthian congregation met in the house of Titius Justus, also called Gaius Titius Justus in 1 Corinthians 1:14 and sometimes linked with the Gaius of Romans 16:23. He was a God-fearer before Paul came to town. Now he became a Christian, as did Crispus, the synagogue ruler, and **his entire household**. Crispus was not the first believer in Corinth, but quite likely became the most prominent.

We marvel at God's movement in this city. When Paul had to leave the synagogue, God not only provided a home for his ministry but one located directly next to the synagogue. In this prime location **many of the Corinthians who heard him believed and were baptized**. We know two of those converts from this passage and yet another name from Romans 16:23—Erastus, the director of public works.

Though Christians do not need external sources to confirm their confidence in Scripture, it is always interesting to see what archaeologists unearth. Polhill observes, "An inscription has been excavated in a plaza adjacent to the theater at Corinth. It mentions Erastus as the treasurer (*aedile*) of the city who provided the funds for the plaza" (Polhill, 385).

18:9–11. We have become quite accustomed to visions in Acts. Here is another one. This time the vision came in the midst of spiritual prosperity in the growing church. We should not forget that Paul said he came to Corinth with fear and trembling (1 Cor. 2:3). We may also assume ongoing opposition from the Jews headquartered right next door to the house-church. Unlike the Macedonian vision which moved Paul geographically in a different direction, here the Lord simply assured him of his safety and affirmed the mission already underway. In response, Paul continued in Corinth for a period of eighteen months **teaching them the word of God**. "The Lord" inevitably refers to Jesus in Acts (23:11), precisely whom Paul had already seen on the Damascus Road.

We should not move too quickly over the phrase **I have many people in this city** (v. 10). Does this mean people already converted like Elijah's seven thousand who had not bowed the knee to Baal? Or is the Lord projecting the vast number of believers who would make up the rather large Corinthian congregation before Paul left the city? Marshall suggests, "The saying indicates divine foreknowledge for the success of the gospel in Corinth (cf. 13:48). Fortified by this message, Paul could look forward to its double fulfillment in his safekeeping from persecution (18:12–17) and in successful evangelism (18:11)" (Marshall, 296). Morgan, in typical eloquence, expands the concept of the phrase.

> So the Lord speaks of every great city long before the people to whom he refers are manifest to others. Do not put this out of its historic relation. This word was not said when the church had been formed. This was not said of those whom we call saints in Corinth. It was said at the point when this man seemed to be at the end of his work, and was filled with fear, and with trembling of soul, even though there had been a measure of success. . . . I think from that moment as this man passed through the streets, or talked in the house of Titus Justus, or looked at the curious crowd who came to

him, he was forevermore looking, hoping that he might see beneath the exterior that repelled him, because it was so unlike his Lord, those whom his Lord numbered among his own. "I have much people in this city." What an inspiration for the Christian worker in a great city given over to corruption (Morgan, 429–430).

Ⓒ Protection from the City (vv. 12–17)

SUPPORTING IDEA: *When Christians face trouble and even danger, God can raise up support from the most unlikely places or the most unlikely people.*

18:12–13. We can fairly well estimate that Paul had been in Corinth since the autumn of A.D. 50 and remained there until the spring of 52. Gallio became proconsul of Achaia on July 1, A.D. 51. Apparently, the Corinthian Jews decided it was worth another crack at the renegade rabbi, and they brought him into the court (*bema*, 2 Cor. 5:10). On what charge? The usual one—acting against Roman law. Since the *bema* was located in a city square, this would have been a very public discussion. The outcome fixed the attitude of Rome toward Paul's ministry.

Was the charge directed against the breaking of Roman law or Jewish law? Certainly a Roman official would be more interested in any case regarding Roman law. The completely disinterested Gallio may tip us that the Corinthian Jews, however unwisely, complained that Paul broke their own Jewish laws. Still, a third possibility suggests that the Jews intended Gallio to understand that Paul had broken Roman law. His interpretation threw the case right back to them since he could find no Roman law violated by Paul's preaching in Corinth.

18:14–17. In typical form, Paul seems quite ready to answer the charge, whether Roman or Jewish law; he could deal with either one. On this occasion he had no opportunity to open his mouth; Gallio didn't want to hear the defendant, since he considered the charge to center only on **questions about words and names and your own law**. Bock is helpful here.

> The claim is that Paul leads others to worship God in a manner different from the Law. What is probably meant here is that Judaism was recognized as an official religion in the empire, but they are challenging that Christianity is not. . . . though it seems to be anachronistic to mention the *religio licita* concept. Bruce speaks more carefully of a *collegium licitum*. The issue involves a request to force Paul to leave us (the Jews) alone. Note the issue is stated in terms of worshiping God in the singular. This may show that the concern is Jewish practice, though others question the accuracy of their remarks

because of this detail, expecting a plural reference to a pagan ruler about what Paul is saying to all men, including Gentiles. But it is Jews making the complaint, so a singular is appropriate. They are seeking a "restraining order" of sorts as far as Jews are concerned (Bock, 122–123).

In any case, Gallio seems not the least bit interested in Jewish theology. He stated flatly, **I will not be a judge of such things.** When he threw them out of the *bema*, they took it out on Sosthenes, beating him on the spot. Gallio still considered their behavior an internal problem of a minority group, unworthy of Rome's intervention.

We have a problem here. In verse 8 Luke calls Crispus the ruler of the synagogue. In verse 16 it is Sosthenes. We dare not forget that as much as a year had passed, and Crispus surely resigned his post when the Christian congregation began its meetings at his home. Presumably Sosthenes became his successor.

That doesn't answer the question of why he was beaten. Part of the problem stems from the fact that Luke gives us no antecedent for "they" at the beginning of verse 17. Did the Greeks beat Sosthenes, taking advantage of Gallio's treatment of the Jews to express their ever-present anti-Semitism? Or does Luke intend us to understand that Sosthenes had become a Christian, or at least a Christian sympathizer, and the angry Jews beat him in frustration over Gallio's judgment? Different scholars take different approaches on this, and we cannot know for sure from the text. We note with interest that a "Sosthenes" mentioned in 1 Corinthians 1:1 was Paul's assistant in writing that letter, though we have no concrete evidence to link the two.

Absence from the City (vv. 18–23)

SUPPORTING IDEA: *We must always follow God's leading, even when it takes us out of places which have become somewhat comfortable. In looking at the future we must always say that our plans depend on God's will.*

18:18. Paul stayed in Corinth until the spring of A.D. 52, then headed for Syria along with Priscilla and Aquila. We must watch the geography closely here, for Luke clearly summarizes the end of the second journey and without sequence. Even at the end of this verse, Luke backtracks to tell us about Paul's vow and haircut (see "Deeper Discoveries"), a matter of no small disagreement among Bible scholars down through the years. Very likely Paul had in mind heading for Jerusalem from the moment of the Cenchrean haircut, but Luke never tips the text in that direction. Surely we must take Syria as Paul's ending destination, specifically, the church at Antioch. Along the way he made several important stops, not the least of which took him to the Port of Ephesus in western Asia.

18:19–21. Ephesus did not appear as a "Profile" at the beginning of this chapter, for it does not enter the spotlight until Acts 19. On this quick trip Paul **went into the synagogue and reasoned with the Jews**, but apparently carried out no protracted ministry on this occasion. Despite scholarly squabble over Luke's account here, it seems best to take him at his word and find Paul making a hasty trip to the synagogue before his ship continued across the Mediterranean to Caesarea. Paul promised a return to Ephesus. He made good his word on the third journey.

The ministry of Priscilla and Aquila took them to Ephesus for the next five years. Quite possibly, they moved there for business purposes. Still, two questions remain. What happened to Silas and Timothy? We simply do not know. Perhaps they remained at Corinth, or they could have gone to Jerusalem with Paul and continued with him on the third journey. Interestingly, Silas disappears from Luke's account after Acts 18, leaving us to our own conjecture where he went. The other question has to do with Paul's rush through Ephesus. Surely the best explanation is that he planned the trip to celebrate a Jewish feast and also faced the closing of sea traffic for the impending winter.

18:22. Upon landing on the Phoenician coast, Paul traveled the sixty-five miles southeast of Jerusalem and then up to Antioch. In scarcely more than a whisper Luke has brought the second journey to a close; just as swiftly, he will begin the third.

18:23. Paul probably remained at Antioch from the late summer of A.D. 52 through the spring of 53. Then he set his sights for Ephesus, fifteen hundred miles to the west. Along the way he visited the churches we have come to know, most likely including Tarsus, Derbe, Lystra, Iconium, Pisidian Antioch, and perhaps some Luke has not told us about **throughout the region of Galatia and Phrygia**. This ministry across Asia Minor was not new evangelism, but encouragement and establishment of existing congregations.

🅴 Testimony to the City (vv. 24–28)

SUPPORTING IDEA: *Sometimes eloquence and zeal tend to mask a rather shallow message.*

18:24. Another Lucan **meanwhile**, this time with the actual word inserted. We need to know what happened in Ephesus before Paul arrived, so Luke breaks into the narrative of Paul's ministry to tell us about a new character— Apollos. A native of Alexandria (see "Life Application"), he was well-educated and well-versed in the Old Testament text. He had become a Christian evangelist and zealously proclaimed everything he knew about the gospel.

How he came to faith and why he came to Ephesus, Luke does not tell us. Since Luke has repeatedly emphasized God's control over all events related to his people, he probably expects readers to understand Apollos' visit to Ephesus and his encounter with Priscilla and Aquila as very much a part of the divine plan.

18:25. Apollos understood the way of the Lord, spoke with great zeal, and curiously, **taught about Jesus accurately**; yet he only knew about the baptism of John (see "Deeper Discoveries"). Presumably, Luke wants us to understand that Apollos' knowledge of the gospel and the messianic truth about Jesus came through disciples of John the Baptist, thereby limiting his understanding to pre-Pentecost Christian theology.

18:26. Like many preachers, what Apollos said was quite true. What he *left out* demonstrated his inadequate understanding of Christian truth. We may assume that he had no idea about the coming of the Holy Spirit, the founding of the church, and certainly the now extensive mission to the Gentiles. Who better to pick up on that deficiency than these stable and mature Christians, Priscilla and Aquila. Together they invited him home, and together they taught him the Word of God. We can only imagine the astonishment and joy with which Apollos received this new information.

18:27–28. Priscilla and Aquila would have been full of stories about the work in Corinth, the decision of Gallio, and the lengthy ministry of Paul in that city. Whatever the motivation, Apollos decided to leave Ephesus, where the ministry seemed clearly to be in capable hands. Carrying letters of recommendation (from Priscilla and Aquila?), he headed for Corinth, where **he was a great help to those who by grace had believed**.

This skilled debater appears again in the early chapters of 1 Corinthians, showing the appreciation of the Corinthian congregation for his ministry. We are not surprised by that, for the constant conflict between Christians and Jews in that city offered a great platform for someone who could eloquently demonstrate messianic Christology from the pages of the Old Testament Scriptures.

Some call Apollos the first Christian apologist, but surely that title must be reserved for Stephen. Others indicate that Apollos may very well have written Hebrews. Though the text of that book may reflect both the content and eloquence evident in this man's public ministry, we have no overt evidence of that authorship.

MAIN IDEA REVIEW: *Christians working together can present an effective and long-lasting ministry in cities as long as they focus on the redeeming power of Jesus Christ and his Word.*

III. CONCLUSION

The Importance of the Local Church

Ministry in the cities of this chapter (Corinth and Ephesus) centers in the faithfulness of a local congregation and the way believers related themselves to it. Faithfulness to a local congregation ought to be standard lifestyle for believers because we need it ourselves, the congregation needs us (Rom. 12:5), and the Lord works through local churches to accomplish the task of the universal body and the expansion of God's kingdom on earth.

Every character in our chapter demonstrates faithfulness to local groups of believers—Paul, Silas, Timothy, Priscilla, Aquila, Titius Justus, Crispus, Apollos, and of course, Luke. When believers gather, the edification and encouragement of our mutual involvement with Christ makes possible evangelism in the community and expansion of the mission around the world.

W. A. Criswell, former pastor of First Baptist Church, Dallas, Texas, tells the story of a woman who had lived her life in rural north Georgia. She had been faithful to a little country church there. Later, she and her husband moved to Atlanta and raised two sons. Both boys gave their hearts to the Lord in that city and wanted to be baptized and join the church, even asking their mother to join with them. She couldn't tear her membership or her heart away from the rural church where she had been baptized, and the issue was never resolved.

As the boys grew into men, they became leading businessmen in Atlanta. As Criswell tells it, "Down the aisle that mother came, placing her life in that church and asking prayer for her two sons. The pastor said that the mother went to those two boys and pleaded with them, but the boys smiled and said, "'Mother, we understand, but we have found another life'" (Criswell, 610–611).

We find it hard to imagine how modern-day Christians could overdo faithfulness to and ministry in a local congregation where people love Jesus Christ and where the Word of God is faithfully taught from pulpit and in classrooms. Overcommitment and burnout characterized earlier decades, and could certainly happen again; but careless lack of interest seems a greater problem in our day.

PRINCIPLES

- Christians do not have to give up their jobs to be effective in God's service.
- The local church maintained a high priority among devoted believers in the New Testament world.

- Hospitality is a proven and biblical way to serve God in holy stewardship.
- Women are very important in the church, including their roles in teaching Christian doctrine directly.
- God can encourage his people through visions or through the lives and encouragement of other believers.
- God will not allow his church and his work to be controlled by government or politics.

APPLICATIONS

- Practice a biblical work ethic—not capitalism, but stewardship.
- Acknowledge that work is a gift from God, not the result of sin.
- Encourage pastors and church leaders, and correct them (privately) when they are wrong.
- Be faithful to your commitments, and leave the problems to God.
- Prepare yourself well, but don't be afraid to change.
- Be faithful to your church.

IV. LIFE APPLICATION

Alexandria!

We began with a city, and we end in a different one. This time to Alexandria, the home of Apollos, great cultural center, and grain port on the coast of North Africa where the Nile meets the Mediterranean. During the first century it was the second largest city in the Roman Empire and home to a great university modeled after Athens itself. Alexandria shipped 150,000 tons of grain annually to Rome.

It was also a city of no minor religious and philosophical significance. The birthplace of the Septuagint, it housed Clement, Origin, and Athanasius. Founded by Alexander the Great in 332 B.C., its merchant ships, the largest and finest of the day, sailed all across the Mediterranean. Its university was especially noted for the study of mathematics, astronomy, medicine, and poetry. The Alexandrian library became the largest and best known in the world, reportedly housing from 400,000 to 900,000 books and scrolls.

The population consisted of Jews, Greeks, and Egyptians. Unlike other places in the empire, Jews enjoyed equal privileges with the Greeks. Though the philosophical thought of Alexandria seems inconsequential for the first-century church, it certainly impacted subsequent generations. The theological center there adopted the allegorical method, derived initially from Philo and developed in Christian theology by Clement and Origin. Perhaps Apollos carried such thought with him, though we have no signal in the text that his theology had developed that well; his life predated the full development of Christian theology in that great city.

Years ago, George Sweeting, then president of Moody Bible Institute, wrote about ministry to cities (*The City*, Moody Press, 1972). At the beginning of the second chapter he reminds us,

> The city is here to stay. We cannot ignore, deplore, or flee it forever. At the present time 90 percent of the earth's inhabitants live in five percent of the earth's area. Within the next century it is claimed that 30 billion people may live in a universal city that covers the globe. Already the United States is a metropolitan society, with at least 60 percent of its population clustered in the cities. But in the urban areas the masses of coming generations will work out their destinies. In the cities the future of America will be decided for better or for worse (Sweeting, 19).

Surely Luke does not minimize the Derbes and Lystras of Paul's day when he emphasizes urban congregations like Antioch, Corinth, and Ephesus, to say nothing of Jerusalem. This follows the missionary plan from the beginning, a plan continued in contemporary missionary strategy.

V. PRAYER

God, give us a new vision of the cities of our world. May we serve, pray for and support those willing to continue and extend urban ministry in these desperately needy centers of population. Amen.

VI. DEEPER DISCOVERIES

A. Edict of Claudius (v. 2)

Though we have discussed this briefly before, it may be useful to visit it again here. During the ninth year of the reign of Emperor Claudius, sometime between January 25 A.D. 49 and January 24 A.D. 50, Claudius was compelled to deal with riots regularly arising in the Jewish community in Rome. Suetonius tells us in *Vita Claudius* 25.4 that these riots occurred "at the instigation of *Chrestus*." At this distance we have no guarantee that Chrestus was not some local agitator, but most scholars agree Suetonius was really describing conflict between Gentiles and Jews in Rome, or more properly, between Christian and non-Christian Jews, and that Chrestus was really a way of saying Christ. Ramsay tells us:

In the earliest stages of Christian history in Rome, such a mistake was quite natural; and Suetonius reproduces the words which he found in a document of the period. As Dion Cassius mentions, it was found so difficult to keep the Jews out of Rome on account of their numbers, that the Emperor did not actually expel them, but made stricter regulations about their conduct. It would therefore appear that the edict was found unworkable in practice; but Suetonius is a perfect authority that it was tried, and it is quite probable that some Jews obeyed it, and among them Aquila (Ramsay, 254).

B. Report from Thessalonica (v. 5)

Most likely 1 Thessalonians formed Paul's response to the report Silas and Timothy brought from Thessalonica to Corinth. That bright epistle commends the growth of the church, encourages its steadfastness, defends the apostle's motives, instructs them about the coming of the Lord (apparently a major doctrinal confusion at Thessalonica), and calls the congregation to patience.

While still at Corinth, Paul wrote 2 Thessalonians which focuses even more thoroughly on the second coming of Christ and how believers should live in the present world in anticipation of that great event. Both books stress that Christ's coming is near, but they emphasize constant attention to right living rather than some kind of cultic expectation of immediacy. In 2 Thessalonians, eighteen out of forty-seven verses (38 percent) deal with end-time events.

C. Gallio's Decision (v. 15)

Whatever the Jews intended with their accusations, Gallio clearly considered the complaint outside the boundaries of Roman authority, a theological dispute of intramural proportions in the Jewish community. His responsibility as Rome's official presence in Corinth was to judge civil and criminal cases, not theological squabbles. The Roman proconsul saw Christianity as a subset of Judaism, not some new kind of religion which required approval of the courts. This is precisely what the apostles taught as evidenced by their constant pattern of going first to Jews in the synagogue and proclaiming that the Messiah had come.

Longenecker stresses the importance of this judgment by a Roman authority.

The importance of Gallio's decision was profound. Luke highlights it in his account of Paul's ministry at Corinth and makes it the apex from an apologetic perspective of all that took place on Paul's second missionary journey. There had been no vindication from

Roman authorities of Christianity's claim to share in the *religio licita* (legally recognized religion) status of Judaism in Macedonia, and the issue had been left entirely unresolved at Athens. If Gallio had accepted the Jewish charge and found Paul guilty of the alleged offense, provincial governors everywhere would have had a precedent, and Paul's ministry would have been severely restricted. As it was, Gallio's refusal to act in the matter was tantamount to the recognition of Christianity as a *religio licita*; and the decision of so eminent a Roman proconsul would carry weight wherever the issue arose again and give pause to those who might want to oppose the Christian movement (Longenecker, 486).

D. Paul's Vow (v. 18)

This simple notation by Luke has caused no minor riot among commentators and theologians for hundreds of years. Barnhouse does not mince words:

> Here, Paul was definitely out of the will of the Lord. He had no right to take this vow, or to have his head shaved as a symbol of it. This was deliberate sin on his part. Since God puts everything in Scripture, I believe he allows us to see this episode so that we can realize that Paul was fallible in some things (Barnhouse, 168–169).

Barnhouse assumes Paul involved himself in some kind of law-keeping, thereby violating the grace principle laid down by the Jerusalem Council. In fact, this act had absolutely nothing to do with salvation or the preaching of the gospel of faith in Jesus. We do not know why or when Paul took a vow, but it certainly might have been during the dark hours of Jewish persecution in Corinth, perhaps in a deep night of prayer for God's intervention, which he clearly received (18:9–10).

If this was a Nazirite vow (not all agree it was), it involved abstinence from alcohol and allowing one's hair to grow until some point in the future, obviously Paul's arrival at Cenchrea in this case. Then the head would be shaved and the hair offered as a burnt offering at the temple in Jerusalem (Num. 6:1–21; Acts 23:21–26). Paul never claimed to be anything but a Jew saved by grace so this practice of a Jewish custom should hardly be surprising.

Normally, the head would be shaved at Jerusalem, and the hair disposed of immediately. The law did not restrict doing it earlier and carrying the hair to Jerusalem for completion of the ritual. Certainly, the practice seems strange to us, but in the boundaries of Paul's oriental world, this would be a very normal behavior. Polhill says:

In any event, the significance of the vow is that it shows Paul to have been a loyal, practicing Jew. In his mission to the Gentiles, he did not abandon his own Jewishness. He was still a 'Jew to the Jews' and still continued his witness in the synagogues. Interestingly, on Paul's final visit to Jerusalem, when James wanted him to demonstrate his Jewish loyalty before the more legally zealous Jewish Christians, participation in a similar vow was chosen as the means to accomplish this (21:20–24) (Polhill, 390).

VII. TEACHING OUTLINE

A. INTRODUCTION
1. Lead Story: Serving the City
2. Context: Acts 18 is of singular importance in our book not only because of the decision of Gallio but because of the elongated ministry in Corinth. Since we have two lengthy New Testament epistles to this church, our understanding of those two books is greatly heightened by this chapter in which Luke shows us the foundational beginnings of the Corinthian congregation.
3. Transition: As we walk across Asia with the missionary team, we find ourselves plunged from the intellectual idolatry of Athens to the immoral idolatry of Corinth, and we see that the gospel can bear its witness of truth and righteousness in any environment. As always, God produces the results when his servants stay faithful to his Word.

B. COMMENTARY
1. Tentmakers in the City (vv. 1–4)
   a. Friendship with Priscilla and Aquila (vv. 1–2)
   b. Employment with Priscilla and Aquila (v. 3)
   c. Ministry with Priscilla and Aquila (v. 4)
2. Witness to the City (vv. 5–11)
   a. Proclamation in the synagogue (vv. 5–6)
   b. Converts in Corinth (vv. 7–8)
   c. Vision from the Lord (vv. 9–11)
3. Protection from the City (vv. 12–17)
   a. Complaint of the Jews (vv. 12–13)
   b. Decision by Gallio (vv. 14–16)
   c. Beating of Sosthenes (v. 17)
4. Departure from the City (vv. 18–23)
   a. The vow at Cenchrea (v. 18)
   b. Visit to Ephesus (vv. 19–20)

       c.   Trip to Jerusalem (vv. 21–22)

       d.   Ministry at Antioch (v. 23)

    5.   Testimony to the City (vv. 24–28)

       a.   Description of Apollos (vv. 24–25)

       b.   Instruction of Apollos (v. 26)

       c.   Departure of Apollos for Corinth (vv. 27–28)

C.   CONCLUSION: ALEXANDRIA!

VIII. ISSUES FOR DISCUSSION

1. Do you have special friends with whom you share common hobbies and interests? Can you find a way to use those common hobbies and interests in God's work?

2. Do you know a young Christian with enthusiasm and zeal who needs more training in the basics of Christian faith? Are you willing to help train that young person?

3. What do you say when people try to prove that the gospel is wrong and Jesus is not the only way to salvation?

Acts 19

Invading the Kingdom of Diana

I. **Introduction**
The Exorcist

II. **Commentary**
A verse-by-verse explanation of the chapter.

III. **Conclusion**
Spirit against Spirit
An overview of the principles and applications from the chapter.

IV. **Life Application**
Demons in Haiti
Melding the chapter to life.

V. **Prayer**
Tying the chapter to life with God.

VI. **Deeper Discoveries**
Historical, geographical, and grammatical enrichment of the commentary.

VII. **Teaching Outline**
Suggested step-by-step group study of the chapter.

VIII. **Issues for Discussion**
Zeroing the chapter in on daily life.

"No church or other association truly thrives unless struggles and differences are alive in it."

G .   M .   T r e v e l y a n

GEOGRAPHIC PROFILE: EPHESUS

- Major religious center—focus of the worship of Diana (Artemis)
- Leading commercial city of Asia Minor
- Population estimated at 300,000
- A beautiful city, very sophisticated, wealthy, and pagan

BIOGRAPHICAL PROFILE: ERASTUS

- Treasurer of the city of Corinth
- Mentioned in Romans 16:23
- Member of the missionary team
- Probably the same person named in 2 Timothy 4:20

BIOGRAPHICAL PROFILE: GAIUS

- A Macedonian member of the third journey missionary team
- Not to be confused with others in the New Testament by the same name but designated by geographical location as follows: Gaius of Derbe (Acts 20:4); Gaius of Corinth (1 Cor. 1:14); Gaius the convert of John (3 John 1,5–8)

BIOGRAPHICAL PROFILE: ARTISTARCHUS

- Macedonian member of the missionary team
- Convert from Judaism
- Fellow prisoner of the apostle Paul
- Mentioned in Acts 19:29; 20:4; 27:2; Col. 4:10; Philemon 24

I N   A   N U T S H E L L

Acts 19 is about Ephesus—its paganism, the ministry of Paul, the reaction, and the riot. The Ephesian ministry took place approximately from A.D. 53 to 56.

Invading the Kingdom of Diana

I. INTRODUCTION

The Exorcist

A controversial movie, *The Exorcist,* soon became a cult film and a precursor to many other movies about evil spirits and demonism. Most Christians understand that this is no area for "meddling." Even the viewing of films or playing of games related to Satan's domain could be dangerous.

It's easy to slough off such an attitude in the sophisticated Western world where most of us have never seen a case of demon-possession and have little understanding how evil spirits control a person or even a society. Many missionaries in Third World countries can testify how they encounter demon possession with regularity and are often forced to deal with it directly, becoming "exorcists" themselves. Occasionally, even in North America, a pastor called to a frantic household may find family members gathered around someone with behavior so completely irrational and so medically inexplicable that demon possession must be considered a possibility.

The Bible is no stranger to the reality of demons. Merrill Unger once wrote:

> The Old Testament is replete with demonological phenomena because since the fall of man in the Garden of Eden, God's saints have been the object of Satanic attack (cf. Gen. 4:1–6; 6:1–10). Israel was surrounded by pagan nations which manifested the whole gamut of demonological practices and beliefs and clashed with Israel's monotheistic faith. Enlightened Israelites regarded idols as demons worshiped by man (Unger, 9).

These evil spirits manifested themselves over and over again, even in Israel.

Certainly in Ephesus we should not be the least surprised that Satan held a strong foothold and that his demons manifested themselves with regularity. At the time of Paul's visit, Ephesus had begun to fade as a commercial center and looked more and more for its popularity and stability to the worship of Diana, a multi-breasted goddess of fertility. One of the seven wonders of the ancient world, her temple was almost four times the size of the Parthenon at Athens. It stood 400 feet by 200 feet and took 220 years to build. The temple itself was surrounded by 127 white marble columns, each 60 feet high. This tourist attraction of no small proportions attracted evil spirits and demonism of every kind. Into this center of darkness came Paul leading his missionary team. He discovered, quite possibly for the first time in his ministry, that he must also become an exorcist.

II. COMMENTARY

Invading the Kingdom of Diana

MAIN IDEA: *When the gospel of Jesus Christ invades the domain of Satan, spiritual warfare is bound to occur.*

Confusion at Ephesus (vv. 1–7)

SUPPORTING IDEA: *Salvation in Jesus brings the obligation to testify to him through baptism and the gift of the Holy Spirit.*

19:1–2. By the summer of A.D. 53, the third missionary journey had already begun (18:23). Paul had promised the Ephesians he would return. On his arrival he found **some disciples** and asked them a strange question. The text does not tell us whose disciples they were, and Bible scholars by no means agree. Some consider them unbelievers who appeared to be disciples; but, since Paul wasn't sure, he asked them about the Holy Spirit. Their answer stuns us. Even John had talked about the Holy Spirit (Luke 3:16), and one would certainly expect his followers to respond differently. From what we know in this brief account, these men were even less advanced than Apollos, placing their singular focus on John the Baptist.

We know Luke uses the word *disciples* in contexts other than a description of Christians (Luke 5:33; 7:18), and we have already seen him refer to Simon the Sorcerer as a believer (Acts 8:13). Perhaps our best interpretation acknowledges these twelve (v. 7) as genuine disciples of John, but incomplete in their understanding of all he had taught. Clearly, they did not worship with other Jews in the synagogue Paul visited earlier (18:19–21), but in a city the size of Ephesus that should not be surprising. God's providence led

Paul to find these sincere followers of John and to take them the next step into full recognition of the messiahship of Jesus, his death and resurrection, and the acknowledging and reception of the Holy Spirit.

One further thought. Some believe Paul taught a subsequent receipt of the Holy Spirit, unconnected with initial regeneration. They have then built a doctrine of salvation around such a view, making the question read, "Did you receive the Holy Spirit after you believed?" We have repeatedly seen in Acts that the wider New Testament message of salvation emphasizes the correlation of repentance, faith, and regeneration with the residence of the Holy Spirit in the life of the new believer. Since these men had no idea what happened at Pentecost, they had not taken that step. The separation between their initial faith (whatever that was) and the present time was due to ignorance, not any direct response to New Testament theology. In other words, *Acts 19 is the exception that emphasizes the rule of instantaneous Spirit-indwelling at the time of regeneration.*

19:3–4. For the fifth time in Acts, Luke records the connection between the baptism of John and that of Jesus (1:5; 11:16; 13:25; 18:25; 19:4). Since these disciples had already been baptized to repentance and expectation of the Messiah, Paul proclaimed the remainder of the Christian message. Luke assumes we understand they received it and were born again.

Can we call these men justified believers, caught in a transitional period of the first century? Their sincerity certainly made them prime candidates for Paul's completed message. If they had not believed before he came (which I believe is likely), they certainly came to faith in Jesus that day.

According to Clement, followers of John the Baptist were still alive in the second century. We should certainly expect, as in any such similar case, that his original teaching would have been corrupted through generations of oral transmission.

19:5–7. This is the only "rebaptism" in Acts, and Paul probably would not have considered it that. These believers accepted John's baptism as a step toward their acknowledgment of Jesus, and there seems to be no effort to rebaptize such people (Apollos is probably our best example). These Ephesians seem to have been several steps behind that point; baptism **into the name of the Lord Jesus** was essential in their case. Furthermore, God sent a replicated mini-Pentecost with tongues and prophecy.

This very special case should not be used as the basis of any New Testament theology. Speaking of the baptism, Marshall says:

> This was necessary in the case of the Samaritan converts in chapter 8 to make it quite clear that they were accepted fully into the Jewish church centered on Jerusalem; and it was necessary in the present instance to make it clear to these members of a semi-Christian

group that they were now becoming part of the universal church (Marshall, 308).

This passage affords such an extraordinary case that we may want to review several observations before we leave these verses:

1. The coming of the Holy Spirit to a believer occurs at the time of regeneration and is not some subsequent event.
2. Two baptisms are most uncommon for Christians and perhaps occur here because these men had not yet believed in Christ.
3. Luke does not commonly associate the laying on of hands with baptism; in fact, in Acts we find it only here.
4. The manifestation of tongues may certainly be given by God in connection with Spirit baptism, but does not commonly appear that way in Acts.
5. The number of the men (twelve) seems interesting, but it should not be taken in any kind of symbolic sense.

B Ministry at Ephesus (vv. 8–12)

SUPPORTING IDEA: *God chooses when and where to use his servants and what gifts or signs will or will not accompany their ministry.*

19:8. The business with the disciples of John over, Paul, following his normal pattern of ministry, went to the synagogue. This time he stayed for three months without running into trouble—a record to date in his ministry. This teaching stint fulfilled the invitation and acceptance we found in chapter 18. Preaching in synagogues about the kingdom was not only Paul's stock in trade, but also followed the example of his Master (Luke 4:43).

19:9. When opposition arose, it did not immediately take the form of persecution, just stubbornness in a refusal to believe. Not only that, but some Jews from the synagogue **publicly maligned the Way.** Rather than put up with this constant impediment, Paul left the synagogue, taking with him the Jewish Christians (the word *disciples* does not likely refer back to v. 1), and set up shop in the lecture hall of Tyrannus ("The Tyrant").

Luke doesn't tell us whether Paul worked at tentmaking in Ephesus and paid Tyrannus rent for the hall. Perhaps the hall was vacant during the early afternoon, and Paul could use it without charge. Certainly we do the text no harm to assume that Priscilla and Aquila picked up the charges enabling Paul's ministry to continue.

19:10. Remember our discussion about Luke's use of hyperbole? Here we find it again. During the two years that followed **all the Jews and Greeks who lived in the province of Asia heard the word of the Lord.** Luke did not count noses, nor should we take that word *all* literally. Our author intends to demonstrate that the evangelism at Ephesus spread much wider than the city itself. During this time the missionary team founded churches in Colosse, Laodicea, and Hierapolis, commonly known as the churches of the Lycus Valley.

During these three years Paul wrote a letter to the Corinthian church which we do not have, but to which he refers in 1 Corinthians 5:9–10 and 2 Corinthians 6:14–7:1. Here also, upon receiving word from Corinth about the various problems in that church, he penned 1 Corinthians.

19:11–12. These verses represent a most unusual passage in Acts and the entire New Testament. Luke even introduces this point by talking about "extraordinary miracles" (*dynameis outastychousas*). All miracles are extraordinary—that's what makes them miracles. But Luke wants us to know these were no common healings, such as Peter and John reaching out to the lame man in chapter 3. Here, God used inanimate, intermediary objects to carry healing power from Paul to the sick. This resulted not only in healing, but the casting out of evil spirits. The word translated **handkerchiefs** we might today call "sweat towels," and the word for **apron** would describe the typical cover worn by someone in trades which required protection of outer clothing.

Whether these were initially Paul's possessions passed around among those who needed healing or whether people brought their own towels and aprons for Paul to touch, we do not know from the text. Many commentators seem uncomfortable with this passage and suggest Luke has recorded some fanciful imaginings or that he deliberately wants us to know Paul did not sanction this kind of activity.

All that fails to take into consideration the cultural context—Ephesus. Longenecker makes the point well:

> So it need not be thought unnatural that just as Paul met his audiences at a point of common ground ideologically in order to lead them on to the Good News of salvation in Christ, so at Ephesus he acted in the way here depicted. The virtue, of course, lay not in the materials themselves but in the power of God and the faith of the recipients (Longenecker, 496).

It may also help us to remember that in Jesus' day some were healed by touching his garments (Luke 8:44). Earlier in Luke's record God even healed people when the shadow of Peter passed over them (Acts 5:15).

Let's not miss Luke's cursory handling of this unusual activity. *Miracles never form the center of evangelism; they only serve as a means to the end of proclaiming faith in Christ.* That held true in the ministry of Jesus and certainly throughout Acts. That such a passage as this should form a basis for people seeking healing through sending cloths through the mail or touching television sets at a certain time is indicative of how like Ephesus our dark and superstitious culture has become.

Sorcery at Ephesus (vv. 13–22)

SUPPORTING IDEA: *When the Spirit of truth clashes with the spirit of evil, there is no contest—God will always win.*

19:13–14. In this most difficult of chapters in Acts, readers find themselves with a "John the Baptist Cult," healing through sweat towels, and now the bizarre account of the seven sons of Sceva. No less a conservative scholar than Ramsay chokes right at this point. He dismisses the entire section by saying:

> In this Ephesian description one feels the character, not of weighed and reasoned history, but of popular fancy; and I cannot explain it on the level of most of the narrative. The writer is here rather a picker-up of current gossip, like Herodotus, than a real historian. The puzzle becomes still more difficult when we go on to v. 23 and find ourselves again on the same level as the finest parts of *Acts* (Ramsay, 273).

This was Ephesus after all, where the bizarre seems normal. We have already seen Simon Magus and Bar-Jesus; the sons of Sceva belong in the same camp. Here the environment encouraged wild incantations to deliver the demon-possessed, and Jewish exorcists were quite popular throughout Asia in the first century.

Obviously, after watching Paul's miracles, these popular magicians picked up on the idea of carrying out their business in the name of Jesus. Syncretism has always been popular when heathenism confronts Christian truth; why not blend the much more compatible elements of Hebrew mysticism with Christian miracles? We wonder, too, what kind of "chief priest" Sceva might have been. He does not appear in lists provided by Josephus. Likely, Luke did not intend to place him in some official position but either to describe what these charlatans called themselves, or to indicate that Sceva may have come from a prominent priestly family.

19:15–16. Apparently the exorcism business can be rather dangerous, especially when one starts using Jesus' name without being controlled by his Spirit. Upon hearing this newly designed incantation, the evil spirit in one victim offered a most interesting rejoinder: **Jesus I know, and I know about Paul, but who are you?** First, let's notice Luke uses two different words for **know** when he refers to Jesus and Paul. The demon said he *knew* Jesus personally, i.e., by experience (*ginosko*), and he had *heard about* Paul (*epistomai*). Those who have read James 2:19 or even remembered the contact of

Jesus with demons will not be surprised that these demons knew divine truth. They are, after all, fallen angels, hardly ignorant of intentions God has for and in his world.

Furthermore, Paul had to say or do nothing. The demon overpowered all seven charlatans, beating them so badly they ran out of the house naked. Christianity has nothing to do with magic, especially a religious perversion of truth that somehow connects the name of Jesus with quackery. Marshall captures the appropriateness of the situation.

> In a situation where people were gripped by superstition, per-
> haps the only way for Christianity to spread was by the demonstra-
> tion that the power of Jesus was superior to that of the demons, even
> if those who came to believe in Jesus were tempted to think of his
> power and person in ways that were still conditioned by their prim-
> itive categories of thought; it took time for the church to purify its
> concept of God from pagan ways of thinking, and the tendency to let
> our ideas of God be influenced by contemporary, and sometimes mis-
> leading, trends of philosophical and scientific thinking is one that
> still confronts the church (Marshall, 312).

19:17–19. The Sceva incident brought fear (*phobas*) on Jews and Gentiles alike; people thought twice before using the name of Jesus inappropriately. Even Christians openly confessed evil deeds. Some of them had previously been sorcerers, so they brought their magic materials for a public burning. Luke, who loved this kind of detail, tells us that they burned 137 years worth of salary in collective sorcery scrolls!

Two things grab our attention here. First, magic had been a part of life for these people before trusting Christ (probably hundreds of people dabbled in various kinds of magic and sorcery). Until the Sceva incident, new Christians did not necessarily consider their former behavior to be that evil. Now, seeing how they should revere the name of Jesus, and how his people should avoid contact with the occult and anything that has connection with demons, they gladly rid themselves of the past.

Second, this act of what we would call today "separation" was not enforced by the church in any legalistic way. We find no mention of it what-soever by Paul or anyone else. These believers decided on their own, prompt-ed by the way they understood God's will for their lives. For Christians, sep-aration from sin ought to be an obvious norm of behavior.

19:20. Apparently, this incident was only one of many like it. Luke tells us that "in this way" the Lord's word spread and grew in power. Luke ends Act V of Acts with another brief summary of the health of the Lord's work. We have seen this in 6:7 and 12:24, but this time Luke refers to the dark cul-ture of western Asia Minor where, for the first time, the gospel confronted the common activity of demons. Truth has invaded the kingdom of Diana and is winning the battle.

19:21. Almost abruptly Luke tells us Paul had decided to leave the Lycus Valley and head back to Jerusalem—by going in the opposite direction. Obviously, he wanted to revisit the churches in Macedonia and Achaia, and then he would head for Rome. Why go back to Jerusalem when he was already hundreds of miles on the way to Rome? Luke does not tell us, but Romans 15 explains that he needed to take a collection back to the Jerusalemite Christians (vv. 25–31). That collection presumably came from churches in Greece rather than Ephesus. Luke was not finished with the Ephesian narrative, but he set the tone here for what will drive the rest of this book—on to Rome.

19:22. Typically, missionary evangelism requires preparation, so Timothy and Erastus headed into Greece while Paul stayed at Ephesus a while longer. This is the first mention of Erastus though he appears in 2 Timothy 4:20 as a team member and friend of Paul with a special interest in the Corinthian congregation.

Whether or not this person connects with the Erastus of Romans 16:23 cannot be known. Certainly, Silas might still have been available, though we have not heard about him since chapter 18. We should not trouble ourselves by such omissions since Luke focuses on the central figure of his narrative with a supporting cast that enters and exits various scenes without announcement.

Paul would go to Rome, of course, but in chains. He could not have known that when making the announcement at Ephesus any more than you and I can see what lies ahead. As Barnhouse puts it, "Probably many of us would not be able to cope with what is in store for us if we knew it in advance" (Barnhouse, 179).

𝔻 Riot at Ephesus (vv. 23–34)

SUPPORTING IDEA: *When God and Satan clash, entire cities can be thrown into an uproar, and the outcome is often unpredictable.*

19:23–24. What about the Ephesian account prompted Luke to refer to Christianity as **the Way** throughout this narrative (18:26; 19:9; 19:23)? Perhaps this early designation of the gospel seemed appropriate in the primitive conditions at Ephesus. Or maybe Luke wanted his readers to understand that the riot account he will now unfold was directed against all believers, not just Paul.

In any case, the issue centered on economics, no small point of contention at Ephesus where the temple of Artemis was, in Polhill's words, "the principal financial institution of Asia, receiving deposits and making loans"

(Polhill, 409). Thousands of pilgrims and tourists came to Ephesus to visit the temple and, as in any situation throughout the history of civilization, dealers in religious artifacts surrounded such a valuable site. Since the preaching of the gospel had turned many away from the hideous cult, local silversmiths and their union organizer, Demetrius, decided to counterattack.

19:25–27. As much as we would like to find Demetrius the villain in this account, he reacts in the same way secular businessmen would today. We see strikes turn into riots all the time.

Furthermore, Demetrius was right on target. His complaint that Paul preached that **man-made gods are no gods at all** represented the apostle's message quite accurately. He had said precisely that in Athens, in Corinth, and certainly in Ephesus. If increasing numbers of people believed him, the silversmiths would indeed be out of business. Demetrius knew the value of those scrolls and could picture such an economic disaster hitting him and his fellow statue-makers. Since their livelihood depended upon the popularity of Diana (Artemis), the best way to defend it was to elevate and promote the goddess.

19:28–31. Beginning on an economic note, Demetrius now had the crowd stirred up at the religious level. Devotion or patriotism sells better than greed any day, so the whole city was excited. In the absence of Paul, Gaius and Aristarchus became victims of the crowd which rushed into the massive theater, the largest public building in Ephesus. Located on the western slope of Mount Pion, the open-air amphitheater held approximately 25,000 people.

Ever the optimist, Paul wanted to face that screaming mob, but the believers restrained him. Luke adds, **some of the officials of the province** also begged him to stay out of the theater. This refers to Asiarchs, members of wealthy Roman families which stressed loyalty to the Emperor (see "Deeper Discoveries").

19:32–34. The word **assembly** in verse 32 translates *ekklesia* which we have come to recognize as the New Testament word for *church*. Here it simply means a group of called-out ones, in this case a crowd dedicated to anarchy and riot. A typical mob—screaming whatever came into their heads and many (Luke says **most**) having no idea what they were doing in the theater.

For some reason that Luke does not tell us, the Jews **pushed Alexander to the front.** Perhaps he intended to explain that all this fuss was not caused by the Jews; they had raised no complaint about Artemis worship before this Christian evangelist came to town. Since Jews were as odious to the pagan Ephesians as Christians, they took up their chant **in unison for about two hours.** It seems useless to identify Alexander with the person of the same name identified in 1 Timothy 1:19–20 or 2 Timothy 4:14. A connection is certainly possible. But the name appeared so commonly that any final judgment seems futile.

ⅅ Order at Ephesus (vv. 35–41)

SUPPORTING IDEA: *The Scripture always condemns mob rule and anarchy. Government officials, even those who oppose Christianity, are to be obeyed by the Lord's people.*

19:35–36. Luke introduces an unlikely and anonymous hero who became the secular counterpart to Gamaliel of the Sanhedrin. The city clerk was probably a record-keeper of some type, though some suggest he would have been the chief executive officer of the city, perhaps parallel to a modern-day mayor. He recognized immediately that Roman officials could interpret this riot as a violation of *Pax Romana* and Ephesus might be in danger of losing self-governing privileges.

The **image which fell from heaven** scholars generally identify as a meteorite since such a stone formed the center of worship at one of the other sites of Artemis worship (Roman world contained thirty-three).

19:37–39. How could a few gospel preachers really threaten the vast worship of Diana? True, a handful had stopped coming to the temple, but no one in their number had robbed any temples in the city nor even blasphemed the great goddess. So what was the right way to handle this? *Sue.* North Americans should feel right at home in this passage. The word **assembly** in verse 39 again translates *ekklesia*, this time a reference to the formal legal group which met three times a month. In short, there was no public issue at stake here and, therefore, no reason for this large public assembly. If Demetrius had a private matter to settle with anyone else in the city, let him do it in a court of law.

19:40–41. We should not view the city clerk's actions as a defense of Christianity in any form. His task was to restore order and settle this mob before it got completely out of control—and he handled the situation very well.

We have not answered the question of why Luke would devote such a large amount of his work to this episode which features no preaching, no conversion, and the appearance of no major characters in Acts. Most likely, he wanted to emphasize again the fact that the preaching of the gospel and the behavior of Christians broke no civil laws in the Roman Empire. We have already seen this in the Gallio decision (chap. 18), and Luke will repeat it several more times before the book ends. From the viewpoint of Greco-Roman authorities all around the Mediterranean world, Christianity was a subset of a legal religion (Judaism) and deserved no punishment as an illegal cult.

In his inimitable way, Morgan expresses dissatisfaction with the behavior of the town clerk because it represented secular support for the church. In his own words,

> Let us be very careful that we do not waste our energy, and miss the meaning of our high calling, by any rejoicing in the patronage of the world. It is by the friction of persecution that the fine gold of character is made to flash and gleam with glory. The Church persecuted has always been the Church pure, and therefore the Church powerful. The Church patronized has always been the Church in peril, and very often the Church paralyzed (Morgan, 465).

III. CONCLUSION

Spirit against Spirit

What a chapter! Luke has taken us from a group of twelve "disciples" who had not heard that the Holy Spirit had come (even though Pentecost occurred over two decades earlier) through healings brought about by sweat towels touched by Paul, past the naked and bleeding seven sons of Sceva to a city riot in the great theater of Diana. What a chapter! And what a city!

Paul had spent nearly three years here, but now it was time to leave. Yet we know from his later letter to this church how deep and genuine their faith had become. That letter stresses spiritual blessings in Christ and the need to live a lifestyle which reflects those blessings. Only when we see that in context of this chapter can we appreciate what it must have been like to be a believer in the fledgling church at Ephesus.

This chapter has pitted spirit against spirit, evil spirits against the Spirit of God. Surely by the end of Paul's ministry there, the Ephesian believers had grasped the enormous significance of God's power active in them as a defense and antidote to the darkness all around them. If they could have had access to the words, they might well have sung the grand old hymn refrain:

> Blessed quietness, holy quietness,
> What assurance in my soul!
> On the stormy sea
> He speaks peace to me,
> How the billows cease to roll!
> (Manie P. Ferguson)

PRINCIPLES

- Christians receive the Holy Spirit at the time they believe, and he indwells them from that point on.
- Evil spirits (demons) are very real, both in the ancient world and today.
- Christians must renounce all forms of the occult and spiritism.
- Separation from obvious sin is a biblical norm.
- Mob rule and anarchy are always unbiblical.

APPLICATIONS

- Trust God's Spirit to deliver you from confusion, error, and rebellion.
- Separate yourself from anything that has connections with evil spirits or demonism.
- Submit to properly constituted authority, and avoid all riots and mobs.
- Expect that God will provide deliverance even though it may come from a most unusual source.

IV. LIFE APPLICATION

Demons in Haiti

One of my colleagues for the past fifteen years of ministry has been Walt Baker, former missionary to Haiti and for over twenty years an associate professor of missions at Dallas Seminary. Almost every summer, Walt and his wife Dottie take a group of students back to Haiti for intensive, short-term missionary activity.

While the team ministered in that country during the summer of 1987, a witch doctor trusted Christ and agreed to set a date for the burning of his devil house and all the implements of his craft. Walt arrived on the appointed day only to find the man drugged by his wife and sister who refused to surrender his body since they wanted to use it for further demon worship.

For nearly two hours Walt debated with the women outside the house, but to no avail. Legal right to the body was theirs of course; and failing to convince them otherwise, he had no choice but to leave. At the time of his departure, he literally banged his sandals against the house in the manner of the prophets and apostles and committed it to the curse of God, never to have contact with it again.

Christians tend to be too soft on issues of spiritism and demon worship. True, we don't encounter the overt practices common to first-century life in

Ephesus, but our culture is full of movies, video games, board games, astrology, ouija boards, and other paraphernalia which have distinctive connection with ancient demonism.

When we belong to Christ, he indwells us by his Spirit; and we go to war with Satan's demon forces. Any yielding to their power sets up a dangerous point of vulnerability for those who want to live victoriously in Christ. Perhaps, like the godly Ephesian Christians, we should "burn our scrolls," at least symbolically, and draw a very sharp line between God and Satan in our lives, our homes, our churches, and our society.

V. PRAYER

God, we thank you for the faithful Christians at Ephesus, and we pray that our lives will be more like theirs, devoted to Jesus even though evil controls the culture all around us.

VI. DEEPER DISCOVERIES

A. Baptism of John (v. 3)

This strange group of twelve men Paul found at Ephesus had probably been baptized in the way John taught, certainly not likely baptized by John himself. As second or third generation followers of the Baptist, they would have known something about Jesus but not the distinctive Christian message. Furthermore, they would have known about the Holy Spirit but not that God had already fulfilled the promise John alluded to.

Clearly Apollos was a step ahead of this group, and that should not surprise us. The eloquent young preacher lived in one of the largest and most sophisticated cities of the realm (Alexandria) and also traveled about. We have every reason to believe that the twelve in our chapter lived a secluded life as a minority religious group buried in pagan Ephesus.

I have taken the position that these men came to faith in Christ when Paul explained the gospel and at that time received the Holy Spirit. It was essential for baptism to follow since they had known only "John's baptism" up to that point. As Ryrie puts it:

> These twelve men, who had been baptized by John the Baptist, were rebaptized by Paul after they believed the Christian message. This furnishes an example for counseling those who today were baptized either as unbelieving infants, adolescents, or adults and who then came to faith in Christ. It also serves as an argument against infant baptism, for why baptize an infant if later, after he personally receives Christ, he must be baptized again? (Ryrie, 423).

B. Demons (vv. 13–16)

The words *demons* and *evil spirits* both apply to that same group of fallen angels expelled from heaven along with Satan when he fell (Matt. 25:41; 12:24; 17:14–18). There is only one devil, but he commands legions of demons who do his will and work. Apparently, some are already chained (2 Pet. 2:4; Jude 6), while others roam the earth to carry out the nefarious work of their leader (Eph. 6:11–12).

Modern-day Christians confronted with this tricky issue face a two-sided problem. On the one hand, we must resist the tendency to ignore or downplay the reality of demons and their work just because we don't confront it in everyday life. On the other, it is probably equally unwise to overplay the role of evil spirits and make spiritual warfare the central task of the Christian life. Lightner puts it well:

> Demons and demonic activity should not be ignored, but neither should they be given such prominence in our thinking that we find them everywhere and excuse ourselves from responsibility for our own sin. We do indeed face a spiritual and supernatural foe (Eph. 6:12). But as children of God we have been delivered from Satan's kingdom of darkness and have been translated into the kingdom of God's dear Son (Col. 1:13). We must wage battle against evil supernaturalism with the armor of divine supernaturalism (Lightner, 145).

C. Artemis Worship

Artemis of Ephesus (Diana) bore only vague similarity to the huntress goddess of Greek mythology. Instead, the grotesque, multibreasted image represented a Near Eastern mother-goddess of fertility, probably centering in worship of a meteorite vaguely resembling that image. Worship of Diana held center stage in Ephesus. The huge, brilliantly-colored temple contained an altar twenty feet square with a massive image of Diana covered with animals, birds, and multiple breasts from waist to neck. Conybeare and Howson describe the temple in detail.

> The scale on which the Temple was erected was magnificently extensive. It was 425 feet in length and 220 in breadth, and the columns were 60 feet high. The number of columns was 127, each of them the gift of a king; and 36 of them were enriched with ornament and color. The folding-doors were of cyprus-wood; the part which was not open to the sky was roofed over with cedar; and the staircase was formed of the wood of one single vine from the island of Cyprus. The value and fame of the Temple were enhanced by its being the treasury where a large portion of the wealth of Western Asia was

stored up. It is probable that there was no religious building in the world in which was concentrated a greater amount of admiration, enthusiasm, and superstition (Conybeare, 465–466).

D. Asiarchs (v. 31)

The headquarters of this emperor cult centered at Pergamum, where the major temple was built in about 29 B.C. Annually, one Asiarch was elected to serve the entire province; and others, for each city containing a temple (Smyrna and Ephesus). Since this was a lifetime appointment, there could well have been several, perhaps even many, Asiarchs at Ephesus during Paul's visit there. Their attitude toward Paul illustrates Luke's emphasis in repeatedly reminding Theophilus that civil authorities treated Christians and Christianity with greater respect than did the Jews.

VII. TEACHING OUTLINE

A. INTRODUCTION

1. Lead Story: The Exorcist
2. Context: Luke focuses the third journey in Ephesus with only the slightest mention of the trip out (18:23; 19:1) and the trip back (21:1–19). Events of chapter 19 set up the pastoral counsel of chapter 20 when Paul met the Ephesian elders at Miletus.
3. Transition: We have journeyed with Paul and his companions to the pagan darkness of Ephesus, and we shall see the brilliant light of the gospel shining forth from that city. We meet the church leaders in chapter 20 and read the epistle to the Ephesians later in the New Testament.

B. COMMENTARY

1. Confusion at Ephesus (vv. 1–7)
   a. Report of John's baptism (vv. 1–3)
   b. Receipt of the Holy Spirit (vv. 4–7)
2. Ministry at Ephesus (vv. 8–12)
   a. Biblical preaching (vv. 8–10)
   b. Miraculous healing (vv. 11–12)
3. Sorcery at Ephesus (vv. 13–22)
   a. The sons of Sceva (vv. 13–16)
   b. The scrolls of Diana (vv. 17–20)
   c. The strategy for Rome (vv. 21–22)
4. Riot at Ephesus (vv. 23–34)
   a. Speech of Demetrius (vv. 23–27)
   b. Mobs in the streets (vv. 28–31)
   c. Riot in the temple (vv. 32–34)

5. Order at Ephesus (vv. 35–41)
   a. Dismissal of the charges (vv. 35–37)
   b. Dismissal of the behavior (vv. 38–40)
   c. Dismissal of the assembly (v. 41)

C. CONCLUSION: DEMONS IN HAITI

VIII. ISSUES FOR DISCUSSION

1. Recall the experience of your own baptism. What did it mean to you? What did it mean to those who observed it? Did you consciously receive the Holy Spirit at that time?
2. How would you explain evil spirits to another person? Do you think evil spirits are active today? What evidence of this activity do you see? What actions do you then take?
3. What forms of sorcery are practiced today? How do you explain to a young person why sorcery does not work?

Acts 20

How to Lead in the Church

I. **Introduction**
Wanted: Followers

II. **Commentary**
A verse-by-verse explanation of the chapter.

III. **Conclusion**
Nonexistent Leadership
An overview of the principles and applications from the chapter.

IV. **Life Application**
Augustine's Dream
Melding the chapter to life.

V. **Prayer**
Tying the chapter to life with God.

VI. **Deeper Discoveries**
Historical, geographical, and grammatical enrichment of the commentary.

VII. **Teaching Outline**
Suggested step-by-step group study of the chapter.

VIII. **Issues for Discussion**
Zeroing the chapter in on daily life.

| Q u o t e |

"We will only be weak and stumbling believers
and a crippled church unless
and until we truly apply God's Word—
that is, until we truly love Him and act on that love."

C h a r l e s   C o l s o n

BIOGRAPHICAL PROFILE: ARISTARCHUS

- Name means "the best ruler"
- A Greek from Thessalonica
- Member of Paul's missionary team
- Paul's "fellow-prisoner"
- Mentioned in Acts 19:29; 20:4; 27:2; Col. 4:10; Phlm. 24

BIOGRAPHICAL PROFILE: TROPHIMUS

- Gentile Christian from Ephesus (Acts 21:29)
- Paul's traveling companion (Acts 20:4)
- Unjustly accused of entering the temple in Jerusalem (Acts 21:29)
- Name means "nourishing"

BIOGRAPHICAL PROFILE: TYCHICUS

- Paul's close friend and valued helper
- An Asian, possibly from Ephesus (Acts 20:4)
- Sailed to Jerusalem with Paul to take the collection from the Macedonian churches
- Carried letters to Ephesus (Eph. 6:21) and Colossae (Col. 4:7–9)
- Stayed with Paul during his second Roman imprisonment (2 Tim. 4:12)

GEOGRAPHICAL PROFILE: SAMOS

- An island off western Asian Minor
- Inhabited since about 1100 B.C.
- Famous for metal work, woolen products, and pottery
- Home of the poet Aesop and the astronomer Conon

GEOGRAPHICAL PROFILE: MILETUS

- Southernmost of the Greek cities in Asia Minor
- Significant outpost of Greek colonization
- Leader of the Ionian Revolt in 499 B.C.
- Home of Thales—philosopher, physicist, and astronomer
- A silting harbor has now placed the city ten miles from the sea it once bordered

I N   A   N U T S H E L L

This chapter contains the emotional message to the leaders of the Ephesian church but also serves as a general farewell to all the mission churches as Paul heads back to Jerusalem and then on to Rome.

How to Lead in the Church

I. INTRODUCTION

Wanted: Followers

The application form of a certain college contained the question, "Are you a leader?" One student pondered the question for a long time in view of her high school record which contained no athletic or scholarly achievements and no student offices. She honestly answered the inquiry— "No." During the waiting period which always accompanies an application process, the young woman wondered often whether she should have "adjusted" the facts slightly and answered the question differently.

Much to her amazement, a letter arrived from the registrar's office with the following message: "Welcome to our college. A study of our application forms for next year shows that we have 1,452 leaders in the freshman class, and they will certainly need at least one follower."

In his book *Rediscovering the Soul of Leadership*, Eugene Habecker emphasizes the essential connection between leading and following: "Whenever I talk about leaders throughout the course of this book, I do so in the context of the leader as being one who can both follow and lead. Whenever I discuss followers, I mean a follower who can both lead and follow" (Habecker, 17).

Habecker goes on to develop an entire chapter on "Followership" and concludes that unit of the book with the following paragraph:

> The relationship between leaders and followers is an interactive and mutually dependent one. And both roles, not just that of the leader, must be carefully attended to. Without good leaders the organization, most likely, will not experience growth and development. Without good followers holding leadership accountable, the organization may lose its collective soul and commitment to mission. When leaders and followers, who both follow and lead, work together, each recognizing biblical claims and each striving to understand the organizational dimensions of what it means to "honor Christ and put others first," then there is the likelihood that tremendous and dynamic organizational development will occur (Habecker, 119–120).

This chapter deals with leading and following. The leaders of the church at Ephesus were followers of both Paul and Christ. Still, as elders they took responsibility for leading spiritual growth in congregational life at Ephesus. Apart from the Timothian epistles, this chapter may offer the most important information in Scripture dealing with how church leaders function and relate to a congregation. Rarely do we get a more thorough and poignant picture of what elders do than in this loving, yet painful, challenge from an apostle whose traveling ministry now nears its end.

II. COMMENTARY

How to Lead in the Church

MAIN IDEA: *Biblical church leadership is multiple, and the duties of elders center on caring for and nurturing the flock of God.*

Personal Encouragement (vv. 1–6)

SUPPORTING IDEA: *Church leaders encourage the members to remain faithful to God and to their calling to minister.*

20:1–3a. We have now reached late A.D. 56 and early 57. This rather extensive ministry in Greece is summarized briefly by Luke though insights from 2 Corinthians, and Romans provide us with a slightly expanded picture. The key word of this portion appears twice in the text, once in each of these first two verses.

After the riot at the Temple of Diana, Paul encouraged believers in Ephesus and then traveled through western Asia Minor, continuing to encourage and edify Christians throughout the area. This already announced departure (19:21–22) had several very clear objectives: to leave the trouble at Ephesus behind; to encourage believers in the province of Asia and throughout Greece; to meet Titus in Troas (2 Cor. 2:12–13); and to collect offerings for Judea (1 Cor. 16:1–4; 2 Cor. 8:1–15; Rom. 15:25–28).

Paul did not find Titus in Troas and hastily crossed the Hellespont to make his way down to Corinth. He met his friend in Macedonia (2 Cor. 7:5–16). In response to the young man's report from Corinth, Paul wrote 2 Corinthians. We cannot know for sure, but experts estimate that the ministry in Macedonia lasted for over a year. The gospel spread across the Balkan Peninsula at this time, quite possibly as far as Illyricum (Rom. 15:19).

From Macedonia Paul went on to Achaia (Greece) and spent three months at Corinth, where he wrote Romans in the winter of A.D. 57–58. Throughout this time, the collection for the Judean Christians occupied the forefront of Paul's mind. All the epistles written on the third missionary journey mention the offering for the saints (Gal. 2:10; 2 Cor. 8 and 9; Rom. 15:25–32). It is not unthinkable that Paul would have gone on from Greece to Rome and then Spain had he not felt an enormous compulsion to personally take the offering from the Gentile churches back to Jerusalem.

20:3b–4. Because of a Jewish plot, Paul abandoned plans to sail from Corinth. Instead he headed back north through Macedonia, taking with him an interesting array of associates to whom Luke links geographical identification: Sopater from Berea (probably same as Sosipater in Rom. 16:21); Aristarchus and Secundus from Thessalonica; Gaius from Derbe; Timothy from Lystra; Tychicus and Trophimus from Asia; and Luke from Philippi (the "we" section begins again in verse 5).

The text does not mention a representative from Corinth, and commentators have pondered that omission. Perhaps Paul himself spoke for the Corinthian church. In any case, this large group of companions provided safety for the funds Paul carried and also would represent a stunning array of young Gentile church leadership to display in Jerusalem (1 Cor. 16:3; 2 Cor. 8:16–24).

20:5–6. We should notice that the last "we" section ended in Philippi (16:10–17). That is precisely where Paul picks up Luke again. The Asians went on to Troas, but Luke and Paul (and perhaps others) stayed at Philippi for celebration of the Feast of Unleavened Bread. Some suggest that they may have observed the "Christian Passover," i.e., Easter, with the church at

Philippi (1 Cor. 5:7f.) though that is not a widely held view. After the feast, Paul, Luke, and whoever else still remained in their group joined those who had gone ahead. This time the journey by ship took five days contrasted with the two recorded in 16:11.

ⓑ Personal Ministry (vv. 7–12)

SUPPORTING IDEA: *Attend church regularly—especially on Sunday—and try not to fall asleep.*

20:7. Here we find one of many New Testament references for Sunday worship. The missionary team stayed a week in Troas (presumably waiting for their ship). On Sunday, as Luke emphasizes, they not only came together to worship but also to "break bread." Interestingly, it was a Sunday evening service. These believers could well have included Jews and Gentiles, both of whom would have been working on Sunday, so an evening service made good sense. In light of 1 Corinthians 10:16–17; 11:17–24, we should probably interpret "break bread" (*klasai arton*) as the celebration of the Lord's Supper.

20:8–9. Leave it to Luke to add a bit of local color, a fascinating incident which he personally observed. The service was long; the lamps may have cut off some oxygen flow; Eutychus may have worked an extra shift. For whatever reason, the young man fell asleep in a third-story open window and fell to his death. The name Eutychus means "good luck." We notice nothing unusual about this incident until we get to the next three verses.

20:10–12. Apparently others outraced Paul down the stairs where he found them holding the young corpse. The miracle reminds us of Elijah and Elisha (1 Kgs. 17:21; 2 Kgs. 4:34–35) and certainly of the ministry of Jesus. The second reference to "breaking bread" seems to take that phrase beyond the Lord's Supper and describes what could well be called a midnight snack. The excitement of the fall, the resurrection, and the nourishment of the snack rejuvenated both preacher and audience, so Paul preached on until daylight. The comfort theme of verse 12 links very nicely with the encouragement motif of verses 1 and 2. Indeed, Luke uses the same word (*parakaleo*). At every stop on this last leg of the third journey, people were built up and encouraged in their faith.

ⓒ Personal Testimony (vv. 13–24)

SUPPORTING IDEA: *When one comes to the end of ministry and life, one ought to be able to rehearse the integrity with which both have been conducted.*

20:13–16. Luke offers the mandatory geographical notes to get the group from Troas to Miletus, where the next major event will take place. For some unknown reason, Paul stayed at Troas while his companions sailed around Cape Lectum. He walked the 20 miles from Troas to Assos along the coastal road and met the ship there. After stops at Mitylene, Kios, and Samos, they arrived at Miletus, a port at the mouth of the Meander River, approximately thirty miles south of Ephesus. Paul did not make a personal visit to Ephesus because he determined to get to Jerusalem in time for the feast of Pentecost.

We encounter a minor problem here. If Paul had gone immediately to Ephesus and immediately back, he could have made the journey in less time than it would take for a messenger to go to Ephesus, gather the elders, and bring them back to Miletus. We can conjecture other factors such as travel weariness or the hesitancy to enter again into the problems at Ephesus, but Luke seems quite precise. Presumably in the wider picture we should envision Paul's estimate that he could not have torn himself away from Ephesus for many days and therefore chose this means of communicating with the church.

20:17–18. Throughout Acts, Luke records Paul's speeches to non-Christians. Paul's epistles on the other hand are written exclusively to believers. This section of chapter 20, therefore, is the closest text in Acts to a Pauline epistle and, as we should expect, abounds in theology. Paul would have waited at Miletus at least three days and possibly as long as five for the **elders** to arrive.

Here, elders (*presbuteros*) certainly refers to church officers rather than a group of older Christians. Obviously, the church knew whom to send. When they arrived, Paul talked about his life as a model before them (1 Thess. 2:1–5). The first testimony to integrity targeted not his ministry, but his *life*. We may assume that the Jews in Ephesus continued to poison the atmosphere there with attacks on Paul; so this farewell address to the elders begins by establishing his credibility first of all in behavior.

20:19. From life, Paul moves on to *service* and focuses on humility and suffering. Three times in this section Luke mentions tears (20:31,37). When we compare this chapter with Paul's epistles, we see him expressing to the elders exactly how he felt about his own ministry and emphasizing qualities which he believed best reflected Christian leadership.

The elders would surely have known about the many **plots of the Jews** which had tested Paul—at their city, in Antioch, Iconium, Lystra, Thessalonica, Berea, and Corinth. Humility and servitude, though very common themes in Paul's writings, receive far too little press in the modern church (2 Cor. 10:1; 11:7; 1 Thess. 2:6; Phil. 2:3–11; Col. 3:12; Eph. 4:2).

20:20. Life—service—*preaching*. In public meetings such as the Hall of Tyrannus, and privately from house to house, Paul taught anything and everything he thought might be helpful to the new believers. At Corinth he was attacked by advocates of "another gospel" (2 Cor. 11:4), and at Ephesus he knew the church would be constantly besieged by the most blatant immorality and idolatry. Believers living in such an environment desperately need all the truth they can grasp to withstand evil and grow in the Lord.

20:21. The word for **declared** (*diamarturomai*) occurs also in verse 23 **warns** and 24 **testifying**, as Paul solemnly charged his hearers that the only access to God comes through repentance and faith, two themes we have seen with regularity in Acts. Many wonder why Paul seems defensive in this opening paragraph. If we think back on the difficulties he had faced from city to city, and especially at Ephesus, we can certainly understand why he wanted to review the solidarity of the message which brought the Ephesians to faith. Furthermore, this address would culminate in a challenge. We could very well see this opening paragraph as a focus on example rather than a defense of Paul's own behavior.

20:22-24. Not only has Paul lived, served, preached and *declared* faithfully, but he will finish the race. He repeats the inner witness of the Spirit which drives him to Jerusalem (20:22) and now adds that the same Spirit who took him to that city has warned him that he will face **prison and hardships** everywhere.

Would these difficulties eventually take his life? Apparently the Spirit has given no firm witness on that, but Paul left no question that he was quite prepared to pay that price. This attitude characterized Paul's ministry throughout his Christian life (2 Cor. 4:7–5:10; 6:4–10; 12:9; Phil. 1:19–26; 2:17; 3:8; Col. 1:24). The ultimate record, of course, appears in 2 Timothy 4:6–8 where Paul no longer needs to look toward the future of the race but actually can declare it completed. Along the way, he had a singular goal, a central mission in all that he did—*to testify to the gospel of God's grace.*

D Personal Responsibility (vv. 25–31)

SUPPORTING IDEA: *The duty of lay leaders, particularly church officers, is to guard the flock.*

20:25-28a. Whether Paul had in mind his death (of which he had just spoken), or the fact that his future ministry plans did not include a return to the Aegean, Luke does not tell us. For whatever reason, the apostle was quite convinced he would not see the Ephesian leaders again. The possibility exists that Paul actually did return to Asia after the first Roman imprisonment (2 Tim. 4), but even if that is an accurate conclusion, it does not change what Paul felt and said on this occasion.

Like Ezekiel as watchman (Ezek. 33:1–6), Paul sounded the alarm and thereby delivered himself from any responsibility for those who have heard his gospel. He has proclaimed **the whole will of God**, an interesting phrase which probably includes the basic message of the gospel and additional teaching by which Paul sought to build up believers in the faith.

Now these overseers (*episkopoi*), these bishops, have a responsibility to *guard* themselves and *the flock*. Most scholars hold the words *presbuteros* and *episkopos* to be synonymous in the New Testament, making elder and bishop (overseer) the same office. Polhill, however, sees a distinction in this particular context: "The Ephesian leaders were not designated as bishops but rather as elders who functioned to 'watch over the flock of God.' This image of the leaders as shepherds of God's flock permeates all of vv. 28–30 and is a common biblical theme" (Polhill, 427). Some have suggested that the term "elder" focuses on dignity, whereas the term "overseer" emphasizes duty, but such distinctions seem unnecessary.

20:28b–30. Not only do the elders guard the flock; they *shepherd the church of God*. The metaphor of a sheepfold appears often in Scripture (Jer. 23:2; Ezek. 34:12–16; Zech. 10:3; 11:4–17; John 10:1–18; 21:15–17; 1 Pet. 2:25; 5:2).

The second part of verse 28 uses a very curious expression which seems to indicate that the Father bought the redemption of the church with his own blood. Since the trinitarian Godhead is a unity, one could argue that the blood of the Father is the same as the blood of the Son, but that would be a very unusual New Testament expression. Grammatically, we can possibly render the last phrase "which he bought with the blood of his own," thereby emphasizing the "beloved son" motif of John.

Acts has emphasized the resurrection, not the cross, but this verse makes it clear that the atonement never strayed far from the minds of Paul or Luke. Enemies of the gospel will arise from both outside and inside the congregation, a prediction which quite literally came true (1 Tim. 1:3; 2 Tim. 1:15; Rev. 2:1–7).

20:31. Guard the flock; shepherd the flock; *warn the flock*. The church can resist false teaching in direct proportion to its knowledge of and dedication to the Scripture. Paul had constantly warned against false doctrine, and now that responsibility would fall to the elders. Polhill writes:

> By the second century Asia was a virtual seedbed for Christian heresy. Paul's warning was thus timely and essential. It is not by chance that this section both opens and closes with an exhortation to vigilance (vv. 28, 31), and Paul's reference to his three-year ministry with the Ephesians was not just a reminder of his warnings but also an appeal to be faithful to the sound teachings he had brought them (cf. 20:20f.) (Polhill, 428).

E Personal Example (vv. 32–38)

SUPPORTING IDEA: *When Christians part, especially when it may be for the last time, they must commit each other to God and trust "the tie that binds."*

20:32. Three major themes surface in this one brief verse: *grace* which appears everywhere in Paul's writings; *Christian nurture* (1 Cor. 8:1; 10:23; 14:4, 17; 1 Thess. 5:11); and the *inheritance* (Rom. 8:17; Gal. 3:18; Eph. 1:14; 5:5; Col. 3:24). We should not miss the strong statement that church leaders stand under the Word of God and not over it. God's Word, not the personalities of human leaders builds, up God's people.

20:33–35. Like Paul, the Ephesian elders should not covet material things nor expect such from the congregation. One can only assume that these were hardly full-time vocational pastors but lay leaders who served others through hard work. Paul's concern for the weak and the needy is well documented in his epistles (Rom. 15:1; 1 Thess. 5:14; Eph. 4:28; Gal. 6:2). He particularly turns to this theme in dealing with the elders (1 Tim. 3:3, 8; Titus 1:7, 11), perhaps because false teachers in Asia so frequently acted in greed and love of material things.

Would God that modern church leaders, many of whom live in opulence far exceeding that of their parishioners and constituents, would pay heed to this simple teaching from Miletus. The greed against which Paul warned the Ephesian elders seems to be an assumed trait of many popular figures in the modern church.

20:36–38. What a touching scene, this tearful prayer meeting and farewell at Miletus. The obvious love between Paul and the elders stands as a model for us today, which Francis Schaeffer so often called the mark of the church. Marshall captures the scene.

> The display of emotion with tears and kisses would be natural enough in the culture of that time. The kiss is here a sign of affection rather than the more formal "holy kiss" of Christian worship. The last impression left by the scene is the conviction that Paul will not be able to see them again. There is a finality about his ensuing journey to Jerusalem. We may well see a certain parallel between Jesus, setting his face to go to Jerusalem to certain death, and Paul, conscious that he was going to imprisonment and not expecting to see his friends again (Marshall, 337).

MAIN IDEA REVIEW: *Biblical church leadership is multiple, and the duties of elders center on caring for and nurturing the flock of God.*

III. CONCLUSION

Nonexistent Leadership

We began our study of this chapter by talking about leadership. We do well to end the commentary there as well. An old Chinese proverb traditionally attributed to Dao Teh Ching says, "A leader is best when people barely know that he exists. Not so good when people obey and acclaim him. Worse when they despise him. Fail to honor people—they fail to honor you. But of a good leader, who talks little when his work is done, his aim fulfilled, they will all say, 'We did this ourselves.'"

Ephesian elders harbored no doubts about Paul's leadership. The passage leaves no doubt that Paul intended them to lead as he did. Paul may be Luke's hero for the narrative of Acts; but the strength of the churches rested on the faithfulness of team leaders like the Ephesian elders, and we should never forget that.

This passage centers in God's Word and the teaching of God's truth providing a foundation for salvation and holy living. We do not find it difficult to end our study of Acts 20 and open the hymn book to sing:

> How firm a foundation, ye saints of the Lord.
> Is laid for your faith in His excellent Word!
> What more can He say than to you He hath said,
> To you who for refuge to Jesus have fled?

PRINCIPLES

- Sunday worship is well attested by the resurrection and the practice of the New Testament church.
- Every leader bears a responsibility for serving the Lord humbly and faithfully.
- Church officers have a special duty to shepherd God's people.
- Greed should never enter our motives in Christian service.

APPLICATIONS

- Love your church because Jesus bought Christians with his own blood.
- Be patient with people slow to grow and help them mature in the Lord.
- Encourage other believers every opportunity God gives you.

- Be willing to pray and, when appropriate, cry with other Christians.
- Determine to finish your own race and complete the task the Lord has given you.

IV. LIFE APPLICATION

Augustine's Dream

St. Augustine, we are told, once dreamed that he approached the gates of heaven. An angel stopped him before he could enter and asked, "Who are you?" He responded, "*Christianus ego sum*"—I am a Christian. "No," said the angel, "you are a Ciceronian. Here we judge people by what interests them, and you have interest only in the classics." Augustine claims that as a result of the dream, he changed his habits and devoted much more attention to the Scriptures and holy living.

Such focus of life becomes the centerpiece of our chapter—Paul's challenge to the Ephesian church leaders. Through them, the Holy Spirit and the Word speak to us as well, raising questions about our values, our focus in life.

How easy in our hectic world to value the temporary and ignore the eternal. Paul commended these brothers **to God and to the word of his grace, which can build you up and give you an inheritance among all those who are sanctified** (v. 32).

This chapter ought to call us back to the basics, back to the priorities of Christian faith to which Paul gave his life. The twenty-fourth verse of Acts 20 could well be a life verse for serious Christians intentionally wanting to be the Lord's disciples: **However, I consider my life worth nothing to me, if only I may finish the race and complete the task the Lord Jesus has given me—the task of testifying to the gospel of God's grace.**

V. PRAYER

God, please allow us to be your disciples in the fullest biblical sense. Make us communicators of your grace and caring friends of other brothers and sisters in the faith. Amen.

VI. DEEPER DISCOVERIES

A. Three Months in Greece (v. 2)

This probably refers to a visit to Corinth, the capital of Achaia. During the winter months, ships did not sail regularly; and Paul had occasion to visit the Corinthian church, strengthen its theology and faith, and most likely, write the Book of Romans. Paul's work in the eastern Mediterranean had nearly finished, and Rome was very much on his mind. Instead of making the personal visit he really wanted, he had to content himself with a letter. The elaborate theological makeup of Romans suggests both his awareness that he addressed a church which had never heard an apostle before and likely reflects the theological struggles he had to deal with in Corinth at that time.

B. Feast of Unleavened Bread (v. 6)

Since all the earliest Christians were Jews, Jewish feasts regularly carried over into the worship of the church. Essentially, this feast and the Feast of Passover had become interchangeable events by New Testament times. Actually, the two formed a double festival which began on the 14th of Nisan (March-April) and commemorated the deliverance of the Jews from Egypt and God's creation of the nation. The Feast of Unleavened Bread began the day after Passover and lasted seven additional days (Lev. 25:5–8). All male Jews physically able and ceremonially clean were to attend this feast, the Feast of Pentecost, or the Feast of Tabernacles. On these special pilgrimage festivals sacrifices were offered at Jerusalem (Num. 28–29).

No evidence indicates that early Christians connected Passover with Easter until the second century. Schaller writes:

> This form and interpretation of the Passover festival disappeared early in the history of the church. During the 2nd cent. the celebration of Easter on a Sunday became general, with its emphasis on remembering the sacrificial death of Jesus, the true Passover lamb. This process gives clear expression both to the break between Judaism and Christianity and to the decline of eschatological expectation within the early Christian church (Schaller, 634).

C. Feast of Pentecost (v. 16)

Occurring the fiftieth day after Passover, this second great pilgrim festival also called pilgrims to Jerusalem and explains Paul's desire to get there, especially since he had missed Passover. This feast, originally the festival of firstfruits of grain harvest (Exod. 23:16; Lev. 23:17–22; Num. 28:26–31), was also called the Feast of Weeks because it followed seven weeks of harvesting after Passover. By the time of our text it commemorated the anniversary of the giving of the law at Mount Sinai and a renewal of the Mosaic Covenant.

D. Elders (v. 17)

Though one cannot argue firmly that the use of the words *presbuteros* and *episkopos* in this chapter indicates the establishment of the office at Ephesus, neither could one argue the reverse. Certainly the Bible places elders at

Ephesus (1 Tim. 3), and we assume that elders along with deacons comprise the two offices of the church. Some talk about "ruling elders"; others, "teaching elders"; but this chapter focuses on "caring elders." In all likelihood they both ruled and taught, but the emphasis of the passage certainly centers on their shepherding role (Phil. 1:1; Titus 1:7).

The word *episkopos* appears only five times as a noun (Phil. 1:1; 1 Tim. 3:1; 1 Tim. 3:2; Titus 1:7; 1 Pet. 2:25), but thirteen times as a verb. Yet in discussing ecclesiology we tend to focus only on those noun forms because of our infatuation with organization and offices. The verb forms (*episkeptomai/episkopeo*) pick up the tone of Acts 20. In Matthew 25:36,43, the word refers to looking after others. In Luke 1:6–8; 7:16, we find God coming to help his people; in Acts 15:14, God shows his concern; and in verse 36 Paul decides to visit the churches. James uses it to talk about looking after orphans and widows (1:27). Without diminishing the importance of 1 Timothy 3, perhaps Acts 20 provides us with the greatest demonstration in the entire Bible of how elders function.

E. Sanctification (v. 32)

A common term in Paul's vocabulary, this word appears very rarely in Acts. *Sanctification* simply means being set apart by God and for God. In one sense it happens to every believer at the time of regeneration (1 Cor. 1:30; 6:11). It also describes a continuous process of spiritual formation (John 17:17; 2 Cor. 7:1) and the ultimate placement with Christ at the time of his second coming (1 Thess. 3:12–13). Lightner writes:

> Justification and sanctification are closely related, though not identical. They are, in fact, inseparable. To be justified is to be declared righteous before God, and to be sanctified is to be set apart; the one presupposes the other. Justification has to do with the believer's righteous standing before God. Sanctification has to do primarily with the believer's holiness in life, his walk before men (Lightner, 205).

F. Quotation from Jesus (v. 35)

What passage did Paul have in mind when he ended this moving address with a quote from the Lord Jesus? No verse in the Gospels exactly matches Paul's words, but the spirit of giving is well captured in Luke 6:38: "Give, and it will be given to you. A good measure, pressed down, shaken together and running over, will be poured into your lap. For with the measure you use, it will be measured to you." Yet those words seem to emphasize giving and getting, rather than the blessing and joy which giving affords. Longenecker suggests, "While some believe the words to be a post-ascension revelatory oracle by a Christian prophet that was attributed to Jesus, it is probably truer to ascribe them to the original Jesus tradition that circulated among the churches in a collection of Jesus' 'sayings' . . . whether written or oral" (Longenecker, 514).

VII. TEACHING OUTLINE

A. INTRODUCTION
1. Lead Story: Wanted: Followers
2. Context: Acts 20 represents Luke's conclusion of the three journeys, a report he began in chapter 13. From now on the focus will be aimed at Rome, even though the road must go through Jerusalem.
3. Transition: Let's not forget our key word—encouragement. Throughout the chapter, wherever Paul went, he focused on this crucial ministry desperately needed in so many churches. In both monetary support and caring, let's indeed remember the words of the Lord Jesus: "It is more blessed to give than to receive."

B. COMMENTARY
1. Personal Encouragement (vv. 1–6)
   a. Geography of ministry (vv. 1–3)
   b. Companions in ministry (vv. 4–6)
2. Personal Ministry (vv. 7–12)
   a. Disaster at midnight (vv. 7–9)
   b. Rejoicing till morning (vv. 10–12)
3. Personal Testimony (vv. 13–24)
   a. I have lived (vv. 17–18)
   b. I have served (v. 19)
   c. I have preached (v. 20)
   d. I have declared (v. 21)
   e. I am going to finish (vv. 22–24)
4. Personal Responsibility (vv. 25–31)
   a. Guard the flock (vv. 25–28a)
   b. Shepherd the flock (vv. 28b–30)
   c. Warn the flock (v. 31))
5. Personal Example (vv. 32–38)
   a. I have taught you to feed on the Word (v. 32)
   b. I have taught you not to covet (vv. 33–35)
   c. I have taught you to love each other (vv. 36–38)

C. CONCLUSION: AUGUSTINE'S DREAM

VIII. ISSUES FOR DISCUSSION

1. How have leaders of your church been an encouragement to you in your Christian growth? How have you encouraged them?

2. What kinds of sermons does your church encourage your pastor to preach? Are there sermons that your preacher knows better than to preach? Why?

3. What is your personal testimony about God working in and through your life? When have you hesitated to speak or to do the whole will of God? Why?

Acts 21

Back to the Big Apple

I. Introduction
Leonides the Spartan

II. Commentary
A verse-by-verse explanation of the chapter.

III. Conclusion
The Values of Life
An overview of the principles and applications from the chapter.

IV. Life Application
Hitler Returns
Melding the chapter to life.

V. Prayer
Tying the chapter to life with God.

VI. Deeper Discoveries
Historical, geographical, and grammatical enrichment of the commentary.

VII. Teaching Outline
Suggested step-by-step group study of the chapter.

VIII. Issues for Discussion
Zeroing the chapter in on daily life.

_____ Q u o t e _____

"*C*ourage is a special kind of knowledge: the knowledge of how to fear what ought to be feared and how
not to fear what ought not to be feared."

B e n   G u r i o n

GEOGRAPHICAL PROFILE: RHODES

- Large island off the mainland of Caria
- Capital city also called Rhodes
- Beautiful port with a glorious history
- Contained the great Colossus, one of the seven wonders of the ancient world

CITY PROFILE: PTOLEMAIS

- Also called Acco and today, Acre
- Located on the north cove of Haifa Bay
- Ancient Phoenician seaport twenty-five miles south of Tyre
- Name derived from the Ptolemy dynasty of Egypt

I N   A   N U T S H E L L

*L*uke offers us a travelogue, quite likely a first-hand view of Paul's return to Jerusalem and events there. Luke makes this trip sound very much like Jesus' last visit to Jerusalem, going up to die because of a plot by Jews and a sentence carried out by Gentiles. At the time of writing, Luke knew Paul did not die at Jerusalem, but he reflects Paul's mindset as he describes this trip.

Back to the Big Apple

Leonides the Spartan

$\mathcal{I}$n 480 B.C., Leonides the First, king of ancient Sparta, met his death at Thermopylae only eight years after he became king. When Xerxes' Persian armies invaded Greece, Leonides met them with an army of only six thousand at a narrow pass between the mountains and the sea. They held their ground for two days before the Persians found another route over the mountains and attacked the Greeks from the rear. At that point Leonides sent most of his men to safety in southern Greece and fought at Thermopylae with 300 Spartans and 1,100 other Greeks. Most of them died in that battle.

The Council of Amphityony offered this epitaph to Leonides for the Battle of Thermopylae: "Stranger, report thy word we pray to the Spartan, that lying here on this spot we remain, faithfully keeping their laws."

Following hard on the heels of Paul's poignant farewell to the Ephesian elders, Luke will now show us several portraits of a faithful Christian leader keeping God's laws and God's Word to the end. Like Leonides, Paul fought his battles with just a few companions and could very well be described as living a Spartan lifestyle. In the final chapters of Acts, we will see him at that narrow pass, before kings and governors, not only battling for his life, but also continuing to testify to the gospel of God's grace.

Such courage and resolve seem difficult to find in our day. Too often "churchianity" replaces Christianity. The Lord's people seem more interested in saving their lives than laying them down for his sake.

At the National Religious Broadcasters' Convention in Washington, D.C. in 1985, someone asked Billy Graham what he wanted as his epitaph. Graham responded, "He never lost his integrity." That could very well be said of Paul, as Luke takes us with him back to Jerusalem, where the rabbi from Tarsus never quite felt comfortable, but where he must now defend himself against the charges of his enemies.

II. COMMENTARY

Back to the Big Apple

MAIN IDEA: *Courage is always important in the Christian life, but never more important than when one thinks loyalty to the faith might lead to death.*

Across the Mediterranean (vv. 1–9)

SUPPORTING IDEA: *A disciple of Jesus has to go and do what God commands, no matter the danger involved.*

21:1–3. Luke emphasizes how difficult it was to leave the Ephesian elders at Miletus and then describes in some detail the journey back to the Phoenician coast. The first stop was Cos, about forty miles south of Miletus and home of the famous Hippocrates. Then on to Rhodes, site of the famous Colossus, and then Patara, capital of Lycia. Here Paul exchanged the smaller coastal vessel for a larger ship to make the journey across the Mediterranean, four hundred miles in approximately five days—if the weather was favorable.

One can picture Luke on the port side of the vessel taking slides of Cyprus as they passed and then photographing their docking at Tyre, the main port for sea traffic between Asia and Phoenicia. Doubtless, the ship also had significant cargo to unload in that Syrian port.

21:4–6. We know about the church at Tyre, planted through the travels of the Christian Hellenists (11:19), so we are not surprised that Paul found disciples there. We certainly do not expect him to stay seven days in view of his rush to Jerusalem. Presumably, he found himself captive to maritime schedules, especially if the ship arrived earlier than expected and, therefore, would spend more time tied up at Tyre before heading on to Caesarea.

The believers' appeal to Paul both touches and confuses us. If the Spirit was leading Paul back to Jerusalem as he had previously asserted, why would the same Spirit lead these people to try to stop him? We will encounter that problem again in verse 14 (and treat it at length in "Deeper Discoveries"). The best understanding reflects their awareness of the suffering which lay ahead. They apparently decided this was sufficient reason for Paul not to carry out his plan. Luke gives so little attention to it here, we should not make any rash judgments, such as disobedience on the part of Paul or theological confusion among the disciples.

Christianity is always a family faith, so the scene on the beach at Tyre reflects the close relationship between brothers and sisters. Notice, Luke carefully says that the entire missionary team participated in this farewell, not just the apostle. Verse 5 offers one of the few references to children in Acts.

21:7–9. Luke's words **we continued our voyage** suggest they stayed on the same ship which probably had unloaded and reloaded at Tyre. Ptolemais was only twenty-five miles south. There they found another church started by those Hellenistic refugees (11:19). Either the ship made a one-day stop, and they continued on to Caesarea with it, or perhaps the missionary team walked the thirty-two miles from Ptolemais to Caesarea. In any case, they ended up at the house of Philip who had dropped from the pages of the New Testament for twenty years (Acts 8). Luke's reference to **one of the Seven** obviously takes us back to chapter 6, so Philip's reputation as a significant leader in the early church at Jerusalem had not abated during his years in Caesarea.

Here we find not only Philip, but his **four unmarried daughters who prophesied**. Eusebius claims these ladies provided Luke with information about the early days of the Jerusalem church. Luke tells us nothing about their use of this significant gift, but we should not overlook the fact that women in the early church had the gift of prophecy which, at this point in the transition, could have been the foretelling of future events or the explanation of written Scripture. This is not the first female prophetess Luke has mentioned to Theophilus. In his Gospel he described Anna (Luke 2:36–38), and already in Acts has recorded Peter's words about prophesying daughters (Acts 2:17).

B Agabus from Judea (vv. 10–16)

SUPPORTING IDEA: *Sometimes even our friends don't understand God's will for our lives; but when that will is clear to us, we must press forward despite their good intentions to stop us.*

21:10–11. Luke chooses this chapter to introduce characters he has dealt with earlier. Agabus, you recall, appeared at Antioch (11:27–30) to prophesy the coming famine in Judea and, thereby, unleash the generosity of the Antiochan church. The words **came down** indicate he lived somewhere in the area of Jerusalem. On this occasion he behaved much like Ezekiel as he took Paul's belt which held his outer cloak, tied his own hands and feet, and offered a much more specific prophecy of what lay ahead than we have seen heretofore. Again, the Holy Spirit is said to be the origin of the prophecy. Death is not mentioned, but the obvious demonstration indicates imprisonment of some kind. As we indicated earlier, Luke seems to be drawing a close parallel with Jesus' return to Jerusalem (Matt. 20:18,19; Luke 18:32).

21:12–13. The response of the Caesarean believers was like that of the Tyrians, but this time Luke emphasizes that the missionary team joined in and **pleaded with Paul not to go up to Jerusalem**. In the agony of the moment Paul finally brought up the fear in the back of their minds but not yet verbalized—he was willing to die if God wanted him to. His words to the Ephesian elders in 20:24 came close to intimating a readiness for death, but here he actually voices the dreaded word. Marshall captures the emotion of the scene.

It is hard for a man to make a sacrifice which is going to be unpleasant for himself; it is even harder when the people whom he loves are going to be hurt by his action and plead with him to act differently. The grief displayed by Paul's friends had the effect of pounding at his *heart* as they attempted to dissuade him. But for himself Paul was quite prepared not merely for what was prophesied but also for possible death at Jerusalem. It was not that there was any virtue in such sufferings for their own sake, but only if they were accomplished on behalf of the name of Jesus, i.e., as a necessary part of Christian service (Marshall, 341).

21:14. The believers' words echo the sincere prayer of Jesus in the garden (Luke 22:42), as they commit it to the Lord. But what did they mean by **The Lord's will be done**? How could they say that in view of their earlier statement and the words of the Tyrians which members of the missionary team traveling with Paul had also heard? This is no small problem for some commentators, and we shall deal with it in "Deeper Discoveries." Suffice it here to say that the group came to unity by acquiescing to Paul's firm determination.

21:15–16. The journey to Jerusalem was about sixty-four miles. **We got ready** could mean the preparation of horses and provisions for the trip. Remember, too, they were heading for the Feast of Pentecost, so we are not surprised to see disciples from Caesarea going along with the members of the team. They deposit the missionaries at the home of the Cypriat Mnason, who appears only here in the New Testament. Some suggest that he was a Hellenist since Paul would have been less than welcome in the homes of Palestinian Jewish Christians. The phrase **one of the early disciples** may indicate that his relationship with the Christians went all the way back to Pentecost. Luke's fascinating interest in hosts and hospitality (9:11,43; 16:15; 17:5; 18:3,7; 21:8) explains why Mnason's name has been preserved for two-thousand years.

The third journey ends right here; the missionaries never made it back to Antioch. The ministry in Greece has finished. Back in chapter 19, Luke reported Paul's words **I must visit Rome also** (v. 21). Now Luke will detail for us how that takes place.

Arrival at Jerusalem (vv. 17–26)

SUPPORTING IDEA: *If you have decided to be "all things to all men," that commitment may lead you into unusual behavior, surely to be criticized by some and heralded by others.*

21:17–19. Paul and the missionary team received a warm welcome at Jerusalem and followed appropriate protocol in visiting chairman James and **all the elders**. As he had previously done at Antioch, Paul reported the results of this third journey among the Gentiles. We know nothing about the number of these elders, though some have surmised there may have been seventy in a group patterned after the Sanhedrin. The missionaries must have handed over the offerings from the Gentile churches. Luke mentions it only in passing (24:17) even though this appears to have been Paul's main reason for coming to Jerusalem at this time (1 Cor. 16:1–4; Rom. 15:25–27).

Quite possibly Paul's fears at the receipt of the offering from Gentiles were at least partially realized. Luke, not wanting to explain this matter to Theophilus, stayed with his main theme, Paul's definitive movement toward Rome. The "we" section ends at verse 18, only to reappear again in 27:1. Scholars think it unlikely that Luke left Jerusalem in the intervening time. He merely pushed himself into the background to focus on Paul's trials and speeches.

21:20–22. In six Greek words Luke describes the reaction of the church to the Gentile mission and then raises another issue of Jerusalem politics. While Paul was off evangelizing Gentiles, **many thousands of Jews** had come to faith in Christ. Various experts place the number of Jewish Christians in Judea between 25,000 and 50,000. The year was probably A.D. 56 or 57, a time of great Jewish nationalism and anti-Gentile attitudes. Many of the new converts were **zealous for the law** having been influenced by the remaining Judaizers, the same group that challenged Peter upon his return from Caesarea (Acts 11).

Word went out all over the city that Paul had been turning Gentiles away from Moses, circumcision, and other Jewish customs. His return, even with the offerings he had so carefully gathered and guarded over hundreds of miles, presented a public relations embarrassment for the elders. Paul's position had argued for tolerance and the right of each group to its own views. He had Timothy circumcised (16:3) and argued for the veiling of women at worship (1 Cor. 11:2–16), but the distortion of his teaching, especially at Jerusalem, had become standard operating procedure.

The question **What shall we do?** seems quite rhetorical. They had the situation all set up in anticipation of Paul's return. Perhaps the criticism is unjust since they faced a real problem, but one must feel Paul's exasperation that leaders of the church in Jerusalem seemed so deeply concerned with public relations while he had risked his life all over the Mediterranean world for the cause of evangelism.

21:23–24. We are already familiar with this Nazirite vow which required letting the hair grow and then cutting it and offering it at the temple (18:18). The leaders asked Paul to join these four men, not in the vow itself (there was no time for that), but in the purification ceremony and in the payment of their expenses. According to Polhill:

> Paul thus underwent ritual purification to qualify for participation in the completion ceremony of the four Nazirites which took place within the sacred precincts of the temple. This would be a thorough demonstration of his full loyalty to the Torah, not only in his bearing the heavy expenses of the vow but also in his undergoing the necessary purification himself (Polhill, 449).

As we know from 1 Corinthians 9:20–21, such behavior would not have violated Paul's principles of grace-living.

21:25. The church leaders hastened to add that this unusual request of Paul in no way changed the validity of the Jerusalem Council decision. In other words, what they asked Paul to do now in Jerusalem, had no bearing whatsoever on Gentiles in Asia Minor and Greece where he had ministered.

21:26. Apparently without protest, Paul went along with the plan, symbolically identifying with the Jews in carrying out this act of piety. The plan didn't work of course, leaving us to decide whether the vow was a good idea or not. We'll discuss it further in "Deeper Discoveries."

Ⓓ Anarchy in the City (vv. 27–32)

SUPPORTING IDEA: *Scripture hardly applauds totalitarianism, but the Bible reserves its most severe criticism for anarchy, the lawless rebellion of people who refuse to abide by rules and authority.*

21:27–29. The public relations strategy backfired. Asian Jews (most likely from Ephesus) saw another chance to get at Paul in an environment more conducive to their criticism than was their home city. They recognized Trophimus, a hometown Gentile, and claimed Paul had taken him beyond the barriers separating the court of the Gentiles from the temple court. No Gentile was permitted to enter that holy place upon penalty of death, a conclusion ratified by Roman authorities. Since Trophimus was seen in the city as Paul's companion and since Paul entered the temple in connection with this vow, they assumed this wild-eyed liberal had taken Trophimus with him and thereby **defiled this holy place**.

Bruce answers the charge in one sentence: "It is absurd to think that Paul, who on this very occasion was going out of his way to appease Jewish susceptibilities, should have thus wantonly flaunted Jewish law and run his own head into danger" (Bruce, 434). Some conclude that Paul deserved this accusation because of his behavior in verse 26, but Luke gives not the slightest hint that was the case. He clearly tells us Paul had not taken Gentiles into the restricted area of the temple.

Perhaps the events that followed were bound to occur whether or not Paul took the vow. Perhaps the accusation of the Asians or some other issue would have stirred up thousands of zealous pilgrims milling around the city for the Feast of Pentecost.

21:30–32. Here again we have Lucan hyperbole, though one can imagine that the majority of Jews in the city wanted some of this action. What follows is the sixth riot incited by Paul's behavior and preaching (Lystra, 14:19; Philippi, 16:22; Thessalonica, 17:5; Berea, 17:13; Ephesus, 19:29). The mob physically dragged Paul from the temple and closed the gates to prevent any other violence or desecration of the temple grounds. Interestingly, Luke's record of the gates being shut affords the last mention of the temple in Acts.

Roman troops were stationed at the Tower of Antonia on the northwest corner of the wall. Quite possibly a sentry saw the developing riot and sent word to his commander. Before the officer arrived, Luke tells us **they were trying to kill him.** How long would it take for scores of adversaries to kill one unarmed man? Perhaps we should remember that this occurred in the temple area, and the perpetrators, also unarmed, beat Paul mercilessly but not fatally. Furthermore, let's not underestimate the swift retaliation of a Roman commander who understood his duties to protect the *Pax Romana.*

He was a Chiliarch (leader of a thousand men) whom Luke names in 23:26 as Claudius Lysias. He had been told that the whole city of Jerusalem **was in an uproar** so he headed down himself, taking both soldiers and centurions. This show of Roman force stopped the violence immediately.

We dare not miss the hatred and ugliness in the second part of our chapter. Luke uses words like **stirred up** (v. 27); **aroused** (v. 30); **dragged** (v. 30); **kill** (v. 31); **beating** (v. 32); **uproar** (v. 34); and **mob** (v. 35). The Romans knew full well that any disturbance among the Jews would likely be religious and therefore probably take place at the temple; the urban SWAT team was always at the ready.

Arrest by the Troops (vv. 33–40)

SUPPORTING IDEA: *Government is God-ordained; and although its excesses and evils frustrate us, Scripture clearly states that it exists for protection and peace.*

21:33–36. Let's remember that Claudius Lysias was a law enforcement officer, not a judge. His duty was to stop the riot—immediately—and he chose to do that by arresting the obvious cause without concern for his guilt or innocence. Only after Paul was chained (as Agabus had predicted, 21:11) did the tribune ask the crowd for an explanation. Of course, in a mob of anarchists, one cannot hope to get any kind of rational response, so the tribune chose to take Paul back to the barracks.

The rioters had no intention of giving up their quarry so easily. They pressed the soldiers so closely that Paul **had to be carried**. Quite an amazing record! If we surmise that the presence of more than one centurion assumed the involvement of at least two hundred Roman troops, this mob tackled quite a contingent of trained and armed Romans.

As they carried Paul up the steps (perhaps the same place Christ had stood twenty-seven years earlier), the crowd screamed **Away with him!** which in Luke's writing certainly means **kill him** (Luke 23:18; Acts 22:22). Angry mobs at Jerusalem treated Paul exactly the way they had treated his Lord.

21:37–38. What follows next surprises Claudius and us. In polished and polite Greek, Paul asked permission to speak to the commander, a startling sound from the mouth of this bruised and battered prisoner. Our surprise comes in Claudius' conclusion that Paul was the Egyptian terrorist who had led thousands up the Mount of Olives just three years earlier. Insurrections happened all the time during the watch of Felix; why the commander should pick out this particular character to associate with Paul seems startling.

Josephus tells the story of the Egyptian false prophet (though he talks about thirty thousand followers, quite possibly an inflated figure) who claimed if his "army" gathered on the Mount of Olives the walls of Jerusalem would fall down at his command. Instead, Felix sent his troops up the hill to kill several hundred, capture two hundred more, and chase the rest out of the area. The leader, however, escaped. Perhaps Commander Lysias thought that charlatan had returned, this time attacked by the thousands he had swindled.

21:39–40. Like Luke, Paul was proud of his city and identified himself quite precisely for the commander in requesting permissions to speak to the people. Here we read the first of Paul's five defenses in the latter chapters of Acts. It will encompass the major portion of chapter 22.

Paul has not yet mentioned his Roman citizenship—that will come later. Though he was under false arrest, all these happenings fell into God's plan. The crowd, so out of control just minutes earlier, became silent as Paul addressed them in their vernacular Aramaic. Remember, this was a mob. The initial instigators knew well who Paul was, but the people who came rushing from every corner of the city might not have heard or seen anything. They seem as surprised to hear their victim speak fluent Aramaic as the commander was to hear him speak Greek. We need not see a miracle in the silence of the crowd, just the overall hand of God controlling events in Paul's life and ministry as he has from that day on the Damascus Road.

MAIN IDEA REVIEW: *Courage is always important in the Christian life, but never more so than when one thinks loyalty to the faith might lead to death.*

III. CONCLUSION
The Values of Life

Throughout this chapter we have seen what Paul valued and what he did not. He obviously did not value his own life, a fact he made clear to the Ephesian elders in 20:24. He also did not value his freedom, at least not to the extent of avoiding Jerusalem and the captivity he knew full well would wait for him there. He did value any opening to proclaim the gospel. At a time when he was physically damaged and certainly emotionally upset, he grasped an opportunity to speak truth to his tormentors.

Sometimes people consider strange things important. I heard about a child who visited his grandparents in Africa. While there, they took him on a safari. He saw lions, giraffes, elephants, monkeys, and all sorts of exotic animals roaming in the wild. He ate African food and visited places other children his age could only read about in *National Geographic*. When he returned home, his parents asked him what he remembered. What stuck out in his mind as the most unusual thing he had seen in Africa? To their amused surprise he responded, "Granddad can take his teeth out." Children are like that: impressed by the most unusual things and not the least bit ashamed of saying so. Mobs are like that, too, because mobs resemble children, swayed by others and capable of the most irrational behavior.

Values govern human behavior. Christians who value prayer go to prayer meeting or meet with other groups of Christians for informal prayer times. Christians who value the Scripture spend time reading their Bibles. Like Paul, Christians who value opportunities for witness go out of their way and even endure inconvenience and perhaps sacrifice to share the gospel with other people. Throughout this chapter Paul has moved through Jerusalem as a shining example of that courage.

Along the way let's not forget two negative forces introduced by Luke: compromise and anarchy. He depicts the latter as by far the worst, but we are surely not to misunderstand the importance of standing firm for the gospel of grace. In that kind of lifestyle, we demonstrate solid citizenship with obedience to the law—whether we like it or not.

PRINCIPLES

- Christian faith brings families together.
- Women have a significant role in church ministry.
- Whenever there is a questionable decision, it is best to say—and mean—"the Lord's will be done."
- Sometimes compromise is positive; sometimes it is not.

Anarchy is never God's way of doing things.

If you want to be like Jesus, plan for some suffering.

APPLICATIONS

- Obey God's will, even if it leads to prison and death.
- Listen to other Christians, but not when their opinions contradict what you believe God really wants you to do.
- Recognize that the rebellion which marks our time represents serious sin.
- Always speak politely to public officials, especially those in law enforcement.

IV. LIFE APPLICATION

Hitler Returns

As this chapter clearly indicates, religion is not Christianity. The legalistic traditions of the Jews drove them to rebellious anarchy more than once. On this occasion it occurred because people believed the worst and allowed themselves to be incited to riot by things they didn't know anything about. In our own day, people elect known drug dealers and felons to public office and consistently turn the other way when politicians live immoral and even illegal lives. We learn from all this that *people generally get the leaders they deserve.*

While in the German city of Munich to shoot the film *Appointment with Destiny,* Lee Frick thought it would be an amusing idea to walk through town dressed and made up as the character he played, Adolph Hitler. The public relations people of the movie picked up on the idea and announced that Hitler would be coming. In an amazing, indeed almost unbelievable demonstration of emotion, old men showed their medals and women wept. At the end of the evening Frick reportedly remarked, "The Germans still have Hitler in their hearts."

Today people follow the most bizarre religious cults led by the most immoral and antibiblical "prophets." We shouldn't be surprised that after working in Jerusalem for several years, Claudius Lysias had no esteem for the Jews: riot after riot, terrorist after terrorist, people willing to form a mob at the first shout of agitation.

Christians are ambassadors of peace and protectors of law and order. Cruel Roman justice formed a better vehicle for Paul's communication of the gospel than the riotous religious mobs he faced in city after city. If civility has become a lost art as some suggest, Christians ought to be among those most interested in returning it to the public arena. If our churches have pastors and officers who shout and call attention to themselves unduly, we ought to move to red alert as a congregation and immediately recognize that change may be necessary.

V. PRAYER

God, give us the courage to face whatever you have in store for our lives, knowing that the hand of God controls all human events, even the behavior of people who do not recognize you. Amen.

VI. DEEPER DISCOVERIES

A. Who Is Right? (vv. 4,14)

Commentators disagree on the attempts of two different groups of Christians to thwart Paul's return to Jerusalem. Did they think Paul understood God correctly or not? Focusing on verse 14, we could ask the question, "What do the people mean by **The Lord's will be done**? Marshall, Bruce, and Longenecker are among those who believe God really wanted Paul in Jerusalem. They conclude that these believers grieved at the potential suffering but did not intend to relay to Paul a variation of God's will. In that scenario, **The Lord's will be done** would essentially mean, "We understand he is in God's will." Marshall argues, "Faced by Paul's determination, his friends could only give up their persuasion and acquiesce in the *will* of God for him" (Marshall, 341).

Other Bible students believe Paul misunderstood God's command. They consider his desire to go to Jerusalem more of a selfish act, in which case **The Lord's will be done** would basically mean "Let the suffering come." Some who take that position claim that Luke shows us what can happen to a man of God misled by an urgent hunger to accomplish a goal God has not given him. Barnhouse gets downright critical: "By this time Paul was an opinionated, stubborn man and was determined to have his own way. It's a great, yet sad, picture of what happens in the lives of far too many Christians" (Barnhouse, 190).

This is one of those occasions in Scripture where Bible students need to be convinced in their own minds (Rom. 14:5). I have indicated that I side with Marshall, Bruce, and Longenecker on this issue. Luke never hints that Paul was wrong, and the Bible usually points out error in the lives of God's people when it occurs.

B. Philip's Daughters (v. 9)

In this most interesting passage the text tells us so little that we must avoid conjecture. When Luke describes the daughters as **unmarried**, he essentially tells us they are virgins. Unmarried or widowed women sometimes held special status in the early church (1 Tim. 5:3–16), but we would be stretching the text to make a connection between virginity and prophetic powers. Interestingly, the daughters said nothing about Paul's future problems though Luke introduces Agabus in the very next verse with his dramatic visual demonstration of imprisonment. Longenecker sees this as an interesting commentary on Luke's careful historical style.

> Had he been in the habit of making up speeches for the characters in Acts, this would have been a prime opportunity for doing so. Perhaps these prophesying maidens and their father gave Luke source material for his two volumes, possibly on women for his Gospel or on the mission in Samaria and the Ethiopian Eunuch for Acts. He could have received this matter from them during this visit and during the two-year period of Paul's imprisonment in the city. . . . Eusebius tells us that Philip and his daughters eventually moved to Hierapolis in the province of Asia (probably fleeing the Roman antagonism toward the Jews in Palestine from the mid-sixties on), and that his daughters provided information on the early days of the Jerusalem church for Papias, the author of five books (not extant) on "Our Lord's Sayings" (cf. *Ecclesiastical History* 3.39) (Longenecker, 517).

C. Another Vow? (v. 26)

Criticism mentioned above with respect to Paul's decision to continue on to Jerusalem seems nothing compared with the attacks leveled at his acceptance of James' proposal in Jerusalem. Three sample reactions indicate the problem:

1. Paul's action would make it clear that he lived in observance of the law, but many scholars have doubted whether the historical Paul would have agreed to this proposal. A. Hausrath put the objection most vividly by saying that it would be more credible that the dying Calvin would have bequeathed a golden dress to the mother of God than that Paul should have entered upon this action. Luke, it is claimed, has invented the incident to show that Paul was a law-abiding Jew (stated in Marshall, 346, though Marshall does not agree with Hausrath's view).

2. [Paul] seems to have lost his spiritual discernment, for, not only does he not castigate James and these law-keeping Christians, he joins them in their heresy. This is one of the saddest sections in the Bible.

The great apostle of freedom was returning to bondage willingly. James and his coworkers in the Jerusalem church were thus talking to Paul and were asking him to deny everything he had written in the Epistle to the Galatians and the Epistle to the Romans. They were about to ask him to deny the heart of Christianity (Barnhouse, 193).

3.   Directly we turn from the advice of these men which was that of policy and of dishonesty withal, to the consent of Paul, and begin to look at the purpose of his consent, we have moved on to an entirely differently level. I put that emphatically, because I hold that Paul made the greatest mistake of his ministry on this occasion. Yet we have to recognize the fact that the reason of his consent was not that of expediency merely, not that of policy, but that of devotion. The reason of his consent was his desire to win his brethren (Morgan, 485).

There you have it: 1) The incident is so preposterous that Luke could not have written it; 2) Paul was already out of the will of God being in Jerusalem so we should expect him to take another step downward with this vow; and 3) Paul was wrong but his motives were right.

My position sounds exactly like my comments on verses 4 and 14. God could have told us about Paul's "error" just as he identified David's sin in numbering the people or Jonah's disobedience in running the other way. He does not do that. It appears that Paul has once again become "all things to all men" in order that some advance of the gospel might come out of his act.

D. "No Ordinary City" (v. 39)

Local civic pride apart, Paul was probably right. Tarsus, the ancient seat of a Persian provincial governor, became a lumbering and linen industrial center under the Greeks. A university town with a philosophical school, its whole intellectual atmosphere reflected Greek thought. Furthermore, it stood at the confluence of East and West where Roman government met Greek culture. Jews had been in Tarsus since 171 B.C., and Paul's family could have held Roman citizenship for over a hundred years, probably since the time of Pompeii. An educated rabbi from Tarsus would stand a considerably better chance with a Roman tribune than would an Egyptian anarchist.

VII. TEACHING OUTLINE

A. INTRODUCTION

1.   Lead Story: Leonides the Spartan
2.   Context: Like his Lord before him, Paul has set his face to Jerusalem. More than once he has been warned about the dangers facing him there, and before the chapter ends, the words of Agabus have been fulfilled. Luke wants us to see that Paul willingly placed his life on the

line, quite ready to face whatever Jerusalem would offer, if he can only have the opportunity to proclaim the gospel there—and in Rome.

3. Transition: This chapter talks a great deal about the will of God and we might well ask, "How can we know God's will for our lives?" Three answers surface, quite easy to remember, but much more difficult to implement. We know God's will *by his Word* which sometimes tells us precisely what to do or not to do. We also learn God's will *through the wisdom of others.* That does not focus much in this chapter, but in the Old Testament, people regularly understood God's plan for their lives by listening to prophets or judges. Primarily though, we know God's will *through inner witness,* and that is exactly what Paul demonstrated in Acts 21. The Holy Spirit had convinced Paul's heart and mind that he should move undeterred to Jerusalem, and that is precisely what he did—regardless of the consequences.

B. COMMENTARY
1. Across the Mediterranean (vv. 1–9)
   a. Decisions in Asia (vv. 1–4)
   b. Farewells at Tyre (vv. 5–6)
   c. Visit to Philip (vv. 7–9)
2. Agabus from Judea (vv. 10–16)
   a. Prophecy of imprisonment (vv. 10–11)
   b. Pleading of the believers (vv. 12–14)
   c. Progress to Jerusalem (vv. 15–16)
3. Arrival in Jerusalem (vv. 17–26)
   a. Greetings and reports (vv. 17–19)
   b. Law and grace (vv. 20–25)
   c. Purification and piety (v. 26)
4. Anarchy in the City (vv. 27–32)
   a. Anarchy can originate in religious fervor (vv. 27–29)
   b. Anarchy appeals to mobs in the streets (vv. 30–32)
5. Arrest by the Troops (vv. 33–40)
   a. Deliverance by the commander (vv. 33–36)
   b. Identification of the prisoner (vv. 37–40)

C. CONCLUSION: HITLER RETURNS

VIII. ISSUES FOR DISCUSSION

1. What is the most difficult thing you have ever done for God? How did you get the courage and strength to do it? What resulted from your doing it?
2. Can you imagine a situation where you might have to die to serve Jesus? Are you willing to die for Jesus?
3. What does it mean to be all things to all people in order to win some? Have you ever had to make a compromise in order to lead some people to God? Where would you draw the line and refuse to compromise?

Acts 22

❦

Testimony
of a Roman Citizen

I. Introduction
Martin Luther Comes to Faith

II. Commentary
A verse-by-verse explanation of the chapter.

III. Conclusion
Religion to Regeneration
An overview of the principles and applications from the chapter.

IV. Life Application
Duty to Others
Melding the chapter to life.

V. Prayer
Tying the chapter to life with God.

VI. Deeper Discoveries
Historical, geographical, and grammatical enrichment of the commentary.

VII. Teaching Outline
Suggested step-by-step group study of the chapter.

VIII. Issues for Discussion
Zeroing the chapter in on daily life.

❦

Quote

"*No* man can give at one and the same time the impression that he himself is clever and that Jesus Christ is mighty to save."

James Denney

BIOGRAPHICAL PROFILE: GAMALIEL

- Grandson of Hillel and first rabbi to be given the title "Rabban"
- Pharisee and eminent doctor of the law
- A voice of reason in the Sanhedrin
- After his death the Talmud wrote of him, "Since Rabban Gamaliel died, the glory of the Law has ceased"

I N   A   N U T S H E L L

On the steps of the temple in Jerusalem Paul gave his own first-hand account of his conversion. The speech reinforced his total commitment to Judaism, yet strongly emphasized his personal contact with Jesus.

Testimony of a Roman Citizen

I. INTRODUCTION

Martin Luther Comes to Faith

*B*orn in 1483, Luther enrolled at the University of Leipzig in 1501, receiving his B.A. in 1502 and M.A. in 1505. That July he joined the Hermits of St. Augustine because of a vow he had made to God when thrown to the ground by lightning during a thunderstorm. Ordained a priest in 1507, the next year his order transferred Luther to the University of Wittenberg, where he lectured on moral theology until he earned a doctorate in 1512.

Throughout his education, Martin Luther wrestled with the problem of his own salvation. He dutifully studied theology, went to confession, and performed penance and all the other requirements of the church.

Some time between 1514 and 1518, through the careful reading of Romans and Galatians, Luther saw that all his efforts availed nothing; he was still a sinner who could not save himself. He had no Damascus Road experience, and apparently no other individual or group assisted in his conversion. In the quiet of his own study he trusted Jesus Christ and, though a respected churchman and theologian for years, finally became a Christian.

On October 31, 1517, Luther nailed his famous Ninety-Five Theses to the door of the Castle Church at Wittenberg, and the Protestant Reformation quietly began. Thesis #62 stated, "The true treasure of the church is the most holy gospel of the glory and grace of God." Luther found righteousness in God's grace. "The righteousness of another, instilled from without, the righteousness of Christ by which he justifies through faith."

When we think of what the church today owes to Martin Luther and the other Reformers, we recognize that their single most important contribution was to lift up the holy Scriptures and restore again the biblical doctrine of justification by faith alone. Yet, everything Luther did depended upon his understanding of God's truth from the pen of the rabbi from Tarsus whose conversion to Christianity was considerably more dramatic.

Sometimes we think that unless conversion looks like events on the Damascus Road, it isn't real. Luther's turning to Christ demonstrates that God has set no specific format, no pattern to which coming to faith must conform. Some accept Jesus in church; others, at home while talking with parents. Some understand the gospel during a city-wide evangelistic crusade; others hear a radio program while driving alone in a car. Though the format differs widely, the message does not: recognition of need, awareness that human righteousness cannot commend us to God, and dependent faith on the finished work of Christ through God's grace—these alone produce eternal life.

II. COMMENTARY

Testimony of a Roman Citizen

MAIN IDEA: *God not only saves people through Christ, he also gives them a mission for life and provides Holy Spirit power to accomplish that mission.*

Ⓐ Paul the Pharisee (vv. 1–5)

SUPPORTING IDEA: *The worst enemy of the church may use his experiences for God's kingdom after God has brought him to salvation.*

22:1–2. Remember the charge: "You are a Jewish apostate." In the formal pattern of apologetics (see "Deeper Discoveries"), Paul answered that charge by casting his life in a completely Jewish context with a special emphasis on God's direct revelation. This formal introduction **brothers and fathers** appeared in Stephen's sermon (ch. 7). His words and even his choice of language emphasized Jewishness and quieted the crowd.

Paul was a witness on trial for the gospel, and Luke devotes the remainder of his book to this image. The conversion narrative first appeared in chapter 9, now occupies this entire chapter, and will appear again in chapter 26, demonstrating how important Luke considered it in his overall portrait of Paul. Luke spends more time in Acts on defense speeches than he does on missionary messages. Bock has calculated the difference:

> There are 97 verses of defense speech, which represents 39 percent of the prison-defense section. This compares to 47 verses of Pauline missionary speech, which is 21 percent of the missionary section. There are 239 prison verses and 226 missionary verses. This shows that Paul as defender of the faith is as important, if not more important, than Paul as preacher of the faith. This fits with the goal of Luke. Part of the reassurance that Theophilus needs is seen in the reassurance Paul gives about the roots of the faith. The Way is rooted in God's promise and is moved by God's direction. Paul's defense speeches are not only his defense, but that of the Way, since he represents the natural extension of what the promise calls for, taking the message to all men (Luke 24:47) (Bock, 151).

22:3. Paul plunged into his resumé, using a familiar ancient triad of birth, rearing, and formal training. Some think his words indicate that he spent his early childhood in Jerusalem, but certainly the verse can be understood to place him in Jerusalem only during his formal rabbinical training under Gamaliel. Only here does the New Testament refer to Paul's education under Gamaliel, but it is the credential which would have certified his legitimacy in Jewish scholarship.

Having been born in Tarsus, Paul was a Jew without Palestinian roots, a maverick from the Hellenistic world. In this context, he had to overcome the false image of a confused Hellenist with Jewish theology tainted by the outside world. As today, one's credentials do not constitute the message, but they may secure a hearing.

22:4–5. Paul told the crowd what we already know from chapters 8 and 9, but what many of them would not have known because of the intervening years. Yet some there would have remembered the notorious young rabbi so zealous to persecute Christians. We find it strange that Paul refers to "the Way" instead of the gospel or Jesus. Polhill helps us understand why:

> A key concept that runs throughout this section is that of "the Way" (cf. 22:4; 24:14,22; 25:3). It is a sectarian type of term that describes Christianity not as a separate entity but as a group, a "way," in fact, Paul would say, the only *true* way within Judaism. In their own manner the Roman officials attested to this concept, maintaining that the whole dispute between Paul and the Jews was a theological difference within their own religion (25:19; 23:29) (Polhill, 442–43).

Heritage, education and religious zeal—all equal to any in the crowd and certainly, in his vigorous persecution of The Way, surpassing almost any in that wild mob at the temple. Every time Paul gave his testimony he reminds again that religion does not bring salvation. Only faith in Jesus Christ can produce new life.

B Paul the Believer (vv. 6–13)

SUPPORTING IDEA: *People may doubt your theology, but your own story of personal conversion is the heart of convincing testimony—especially when you back it up by godly living.*

22:6–9. As Paul retold the conversion experience, we learn that the light appeared at noon, something Luke did not tell us in chapter 9. A light strong enough to outshine the midday sun is considerably different than light seen in the darkness of night. He also adds the geographical reference in connection with **Jesus of Nazareth**, perhaps fixing clearly in the minds of these Jews the one of whom Paul spoke.

In verse 9 we find another difference between this account and the narrative of chapter 9. Here Paul told his audience that his companions saw the light but did not understand the voice. In chapter 9 Luke indicated the others heard the sound but didn't see anyone. These minor variations pose no textual problem at all; each account aims at a different audience and, therefore, picks up slightly different emphases, much in the way we would do with speeches today.

22:10–11. This second question **What shall I do, Lord?** also did not appear in chapter 9. Paul's explanation of Jesus' answer indicates his acceptance of Jesus as Lord, something the audience that day would certainly not have acknowledged. We have regularly talked about "messianic Christology"; here we see it in embryonic form. The term simply means acknowledging that Jesus fulfilled all Old Testament prophecies of the coming Messiah, equating him with Yahweh of the Old Testament, the LORD (*Adonai*) of the Hebrews.

Paul's emphasis on the brilliance of the light also differs from Acts 9 and reminds us of 2 Corinthians 4:6 (cf. John 1:4–9; 1 John 1:5–7).

22:12–13. The mention of Ananias is crucial here since Paul did not repeat this portion of his story in chapter 26. There he had a Gentile audience, and the fact that his first contact after a heavenly revelation was a devout Jew would have no meaning to the crowd. Here it offers yet another mark of Paul's confirmed Judaism. Of course, he does not mention that Ananias was already a Christian disciple when Paul first met him.

Paul the Witness (vv. 14–21)

SUPPORTING IDEA: *When God brings a person to faith, he already knows how he will use that one in his service, though sometimes we are slow to understand that plan and perhaps may even resist it.*

22:14–16. Paul continued his Jewish explanation of Christian conversion by using phrases like **the God of our fathers** and **the Righteous One**. His witness for Jesus these many years directly resulted from God's message given him through a devout Jewish brother. Paul accurately related Ananias' word from God **to all men**, but apparently this Jewish crowd could only see this in the context of their own nation and did not react in any way to the idea that **all men** might include Gentiles as well.

From what Luke has told us in Acts, we know that baptism is an illustration, not an agent of salvation. If this were the only verse the New Testament provided on the subject, we might wonder about a greater role for baptism. In Christian faith, as in Jewish religion, the use of water symbolized the forgiveness of sins.

As noted in the commentary on chapter 9, Paul came to faith in Christ sometime during the discussion with Ananias, and baptism followed that change of heart. Barnhouse however, always dependable for some unusual slant on a passage, suggests that Paul's salvation did not occur in conjunction with the Damascus Road experience at all.

> I refuse to believe that Paul was saved on the road to Damascus. He had been saved years before as he tells Timothy and the Galatians. He said, "I was set apart before I was born" (Gal. 1:15). In other words, he had been circumcised as a child and he had been a member of the tribe of Benjamin as he tells the Philippians, and he says, "As to righteousness under the law, I was blameless" (Phil. 3:5, 6). He had offered the blood sacrifices and day by day he had followed

as God had ordained in the Book of Leviticus. So Paul had been saved just as John the Baptist had been saved and the time came when Paul had to be transferred out of Israel and into the church; that's what took place on the road to Damascus. He stopped being "a saved Jew" and became "a saved Christian." He wasn't a Philistine becoming a Christian. He was under the Old Testament covenant of God entering the New Covenant (Barnhouse, 200).

Interesting idea, but certainly out of sync with the way Paul continually targeted the Damascus Road experience. In fact, Paul was not in the era of John the Baptist who died before the crucifixion. He came to faith some years after the crucifixion and the resurrection, well into the era of the new covenant. One could just as well argue that all the Jews and proselytes Paul found around Asia Minor and Greece did not accept Christ but just stopped being "saved Jews" and became "saved Christians." The text of the New Testament will simply not tolerate the extension of Old Testament conditions this far into the Acts.

22:17–18. Hold everything. Here is information we have not seen before. We know Paul returned to Jerusalem after his conversion, but here he tells us he went into the temple and into a trance! This occurred some three years after his conversion (9:26–29; Gal. 1:18–19), and the danger, as we have already seen in chapter 9, came from Hellenists. Again Paul depicts himself as a loyal and pious Jew who prayed in the temple and received visions from God. How could such a person be a Hellenistic apostate? Furthermore, far from being a blasphemer of the temple, he obviously held it in the highest regard.

Notice the continued use of the name LORD throughout this speech. It appears in verses 8, 10, 18, 19 and 21 and solidly links Jesus of the Christian faith with Yahweh of the Jewish religion.

22:19–20. Obviously, this vision was not a one-way revelation but a conversation with Deity. The crowd by the temple steps would have understood such protestations in light of the Old Testament. Moses argued with God that he should not go back to Egypt. Isaiah argued with God about his unworthiness. Since Paul had been commissioned as a witness for the Lord, why wouldn't Jerusalem be the perfect place to do that? Here people knew his reputation as a rabbi and his role in the martyrdom of Stephen. Here they would remember his persecution of Christians and, having seen his complete about-face, would surely pay attention to his description of an encounter with Jesus Christ.

22:21. Fasten your seat belt! Here it comes, the hated word which will again unleash the frenzy of this crowd—**Gentiles**. They seem to listen respectfully throughout the whole conversion narrative, not blinking an eye at two personal conversations with Deity. When Paul claimed that God sent him out of Jerusalem to proclaim a divine message to Gentiles, he stepped beyond the boundaries of their tolerance. So the departure from Jerusalem did not just save Paul's life, nor did he leave only because people rejected his testimony there. God had a greater duty—**far away**. The word for "send far away" is *exapostelo*. One could say Paul became the "out apostle" in contrast to the "in apostles" who stayed at Jerusalem.

This had been Paul's procedure for years—first to the Jews, then upon their rejection, to the Gentiles. Now he made it clear that God established this pattern long before Paul ever embarked on that first missionary journey from Antioch. The racism of first-century Jews was so rigidly established they could not imagine God's concern for any other people; therefore, in their view, this former rabbi now spoke blasphemy. Their first impressions must have been right—kill.

𝔻 Paul the Prisoner (vv. 22–30)

SUPPORTING IDEA: When everything turns against you and there seems to be no hope of escape, God has not abandoned you and will work out his plan for your life.

22:22. With the word **Gentiles** the speech ended. The thought that Jews and Gentiles could stand on equal footing before God was completely intolerable. The audience became a mob again as anarchy and prejudice filled the air. Earlier they had screamed **away with him** (21:36). Now the same cry with slightly more detail: **Rid the earth of him! He's not fit to live!**

22:23–24. No one knows exactly what the crowd had in mind by **throwing off their cloaks and flinging dust into the air**. Polhill ponders that, "They either tore them as a gesture of horror at blasphemy (14:14), or they threw them off their bodies as if ready to stone Paul (cf. 7:58), or they shook them out as if trying to rid themselves of the contamination of his blasphemy, or they waved them wildly in the air to express their collective outrage" (Polhill, 464). To which one is tempted to add, "all of the above or none of the above."

This was no orderly group following some predetermined pattern of symbolic gestures. Totally out of control, they acted like animals whose various behavior patterns do not always need explanation. Did they throw the dust at Paul or on themselves? Luke does not bother to explain their behavior, for it lay beyond the boundaries of explanation. The mob was so threatening, the commander ordered Paul to be taken into the barracks and then decided to flog the victim to determine why he had been victimized!

When it came to interrogation, the Romans never bothered with "good cop—bad cop" techniques. They discovered scourging as an effective means to get any prisoner to talk—and we should not confuse Roman scourging with Jewish. The Jews used rods; the Romans, leather thongs in which they had imbedded pieces of metal or bone. Many had been crippled and killed during such a beating. Paul had been beaten five times with thirty-nine lashes by Jewish authorities and three times with rods by Roman magistrates, but the *flagellum* was far more brutal, precisely the kind of beating given to Jesus in Pilate's hall (John 18:38–19:1). Paul describes his beatings in 2 Corinthians 11:24–25.

22:25. As common soldiers stretched him out for the beating, Paul addressed the centurion presiding over the event. The question is completely rhetorical; it was indeed legal. Roman laws (*Lex Baleria* and *Lex Porcia*) prohibited this beating as well as the chaining Paul had previously received. Furthermore, no one would challenge a person claiming Roman citizenship. Such a claim was accepted at face value. Those who claimed Roman citizenship and had their claims later disproved faced considerably worse punishment.

22:26–29. The centurion had no option but to report immediately to his commander, who also wasted no time getting to the scene of what could have been a miscarriage of justice. He himself had purchased citizenship for **a big price**, but Paul **was born a citizen**. The commander had already committed a crime by placing a Roman citizen in chains. To have scourged him with the *flagellum* would have been unthinkable, especially since he still had no idea who he was or of what crime he might have been guilty.

Since one generally took the name of the patron responsible for obtaining one's citizenship, Claudius Lysias may well have purchased his Roman citizenship under the reign of Claudius. Perhaps when he raised the issue of price, he expected Paul to say something like, "I know what you mean; buying citizenship nearly bankrupted my family." Learning he was a free-born Roman citizen must have stunned the tribune.

How Paul's family obtained this citizenship we do not know, though there are numerous speculations. Longenecker conjectures, "Most likely one of Paul's ancestors received Roman citizenship for valuable services rendered to a Roman administrator or general (perhaps Pompei) in either the Gischala region of northern Palestine or at Tarsus" (Longenecker, 528).

22:30. Lysias found himself in a bind. He had avoided the crime of scourging, but he still held a Roman citizen in custody. Of course, he could always argue it was protective custody since he had literally saved Paul from the Jewish mob. But who was he? Why were hundreds of people incensed that he was allowed to live? Doubtless he pondered the dilemma overnight. The next morning he ordered a meeting of the Sanhedrin. If this fellow were such a devout Jew, surely this group of scholars could get the truth out of him.

Some argue that a Roman tribune could not have called the Sanhedrin into session, but Luke does not imply that this was an official meeting, only an information-gathering time. Lysias just needed some advice. He went to the people he thought could best provide it. Like Gallio, he obviously considered this a Jewish matter. Since he had officially taken Paul into custody, the burden of seeing the case through rested upon him.

By now Luke's readers have become accustomed to the Sanhedrin. They heard witness from the apostles (4:15; 5:21), from Stephen (6:12,15), and now Paul. What is about to unfold covers six chapters in Acts and four years of Paul's life. Through it all he stands firm and bold, arguing consistently that he is a good Jew and the logical outcome of that is to accept the Messiahship of Jesus.

MAIN IDEA REVIEW: *God not only saves people through Christ, he also gives them a mission for life and provides Holy Spirit power to accomplish that mission.*

III. CONCLUSION

Religion to Regeneration

I shall never forget Fritz Frickinger. During the summer after my sophomore year in college, I spent nearly three months in southern Germany as part of an evangelistic team conducting tent campaigns in smaller towns throughout Bavaria. One of those towns was Hassloch, where I was a guest of a farmer in his small house right in the village. The animals were kept scarcely six feet away from the open doorway to the kitchen, and the fragrance of the stable filled the house.

We conducted two weeks of meetings in Hassloch, with three sessions a day—a children's meeting, a youth meeting, and an evening evangelistic rally. Dozens of people came to Christ. The last Sunday, we invited anyone who wished to come to the platform during an afternoon meeting and briefly tell the audience what Christ had done in their lives. Our limited faith was dramatically pumped up as scores of people formed a line around the side of the tent, waiting to come to the microphone and witness for the Lord.

One of those who came was my host. Though my German was not flawless, I had no difficulty understanding him as he explained his new-found faith in the gospel. A brief paraphrase in English would look something like this:

> You all know me. I have lived in this town all my life and have been a faithful member of the local church. I have always believed that religion was not only a preparation for heaven, but a part of my

civic duty. This week I have realized that Jesus Christ died to save me and that church membership or involvement with any organized religion would never take me to heaven. Now I am no longer just a church member or a "Christian" in name only. I have trusted Jesus Christ as my Savior and belong to Him.

I can't remember hearing before or since any more precise explanation of how one moves from religion to regeneration. It was precisely the journey of Paul, described so poignantly in this chapter. The message remains exactly the same today. Affiliation with a church may indeed fulfill some sense of civic duty, but it can never change hearts. Heart change comes through faith and the power of the Holy Spirit who plants the new birth within us.

PRINCIPLES

- Christians should always be ready to answer for their faith (1 Pet. 3:15).
- Baptism is still an obedient witness to that faith.
- Religious zeal may often be misguided and sometimes even fatal.
- Salvation by grace is not always a dramatic experience.
- When faced with persecution for the name of Christ, Christians should use all legal means at their disposal to avoid punishment.

APPLICATIONS

- Be ready for the Lord to break into your life at any time.
- Be obedient to whatever he tells you to do.
- Be baptized as a symbol of your faith in the Savior.
- Be calm even in the face of danger and violence.
- Be faithful to your commitments, and leave the problems to God.

IV. LIFE APPLICATION
Duty to Others

Increase Mather, pastor of the Second Church of Boston during the 17th century, wrote a Puritan tract entitled "The Duty of Parents to Pray for Their Children." His eldest son, Cotton Mather, served as his father's assistant and then became senior pastor of the same church. During the second half of his life he wrote over four hundred publications and exerted influence not only among the Puritan constituency but among Protestant churches at large, and even in politics. Interestingly, he also wrote a tract paralleling his father's title, "The Duty of Children to Their Parents Who Have Prayed for Them."

Our chapter raises the question, "For whom do you live?" Paul lived to proclaim the gospel to the Gentiles. Some people live for themselves. Greed has become a popular motivator in our day. Others live for family. Some live and even die for the church. Like Paul, some modern Christians live for Christ. Someone has written a prayer based on Psalm 119.

Oh God, I want so very much to please you.
To walk in your ways,
And carry out your purposes.
There is nothing as important to me
As being in the center of your will
And living within your design for my life.
Not only have you fashioned me with your hands, Oh Lord,
And created me for your purposes,
But you have stamped your image upon my heart.
Therefore my deepest longings are met only in you
And in the dedication of my life
To the accomplishment of your objectives.
(Source unknown)

I am not able to identify the author of those gracious words, but they certainly reflect the life force of the apostle Paul as we shall continue to see right up to the end of this wonderful history book about the early church.

V. PRAYER

God, please give us grace and peace under pressure and the ability to articulate our Christian faith to others whenever you open opportunities for us to do so. May our lives be completely dedicated to the Savior so that people can see how much we love him and how much we love you. Amen.

VI. DEEPER DISCOVERIES

A. Apologetics (vv. 3–21)

According to Ronald S. Wallace, apologetics can be formally defined as "the use of theology in order to justify Christianity before men, in the claims it makes to be ultimate truth, in the demands it makes on its followers, and in its universal mission." Though "apologists" for the Christian faith did not arise until the second century (Justin, Tatian, Athenagoras, Tertullian, and others), the presentation of an *apologia* takes place right here in our chapter by Paul's own choice of words.

In Greco-Roman culture the kind of defense speech called an apologia took on specific structure: *Exordium* (also called the *Proemium*), self-commendation to the audience; *Narratio*, recounting events; *Probatio*, proof by eyewitnesses, signs, or omens; and the *Refutatio*, direct personal answer to charges (Bock, 150).

Christian thinkers have debated the role of apologetics in contemporary theology, particularly as to its function in leading people to faith in Christ. Some have concluded (and I agree) that the primary purpose of apologetics is not evangelism but rather a strengthening of believers. We achieve this through demonstrating that Christianity can be substantiated by documentable evidence such as archaeological discoveries, historicity, etc. If apologetics plays too large a role in evangelism, we stand in danger of convincing people's minds but not their hearts.

B. Comparative Conversion Accounts (vv. 3–16)

Though source critics attribute the repetitions of this account to a plurality of sources, it is not unlike Luke or any other Bible writer to emphasize and reemphasize important portions of his work. Throughout his entire ministry Paul repeatedly had to defend his decision to take the gospel to the Gentiles, and his defense centered in God's call for him to do precisely that. In each of the three records of his conversion (chaps. 9, 22 and 26), that feature surfaces as the major point. As Longenecker puts it:

> It was not a strategy Paul thought up or a program given to him by another; it was a compelling call that came directly from Christ himself. Nor can it be explained psychologically or as an evolution of ideas whose time was ripe. Instead, it came to him by revelation, and he had no choice but to obey (Longenecker, 367).

One can pick at minor details, but, as we have already noted in the commentary section, the differences in the accounts occur because of two basic reasons: one is told by Luke and two by Paul; and each takes place in a different setting with a different purpose.

C. Brought Up in Jerusalem (v. 3)

Obviously at some point in his young life, Paul moved from Tarsus to Jerusalem. Some take his word here to mean that he was born in Tarsus but spent all his childhood and youth in Jerusalem, presumably right up to the time we find him in Acts 8. But *anatrepho* need not be understood in the narrow modern definition. It appears only three times in the New Testament, all of them in Acts. We find the other two in Stephen's speech: for three months Moses was **cared for in his father's house** and then **brought . . . up** by Pharaoh's daughter (Acts 7:20–21). In *The Ministry and Message of Paul*, Longenecker explains it like this:

At thirteen a Jewish boy became a *bar mitzvah* (son of a commandment), at which time he took upon himself the full obligation of the Law and the more promising lads were directed into rabbinic schools under abler teachers. It was probably at this age, or shortly thereafter, that Paul came to Jerusalem to further his training, perhaps living with the married sister spoken of in Acts 23:16. . . . It is some indication of Paul's youthful ability, and perhaps also of his parents' importance, that not only was he selected for further rabbinic study, but that he came to Jerusalem to study under one of the greatest Rabbis of the first century—Gamaliel I (Acts 22:3) (Longenecker, 22).

D. Rights of a Roman (vv. 25–29)

Paul's status as a Roman citizen surfaces right here, but comes to a head in 25:11 with his words, **I appeal to Caesar!** According to first-century Mediterranean law, Paul's Roman citizenship was more important than any other aspect of his nationality, however he might stress his Jewishness. It would have placed him among the aristocracy in Tarsus and probably indicated that his family was one of distinction and perhaps some wealth. Ramsay observes,

It also implies that there was in the surroundings amid which he grew up, a certain attitude of friendliness to the imperial government (for the new citizens in general, and the Jewish citizens in particular, were warm partisans of their protector, the new imperial regime), and also of pride in a possession that ensured distinction and rank and general respect in Tarsus. (Ramsay, 31).

Ramsay also thinks that Paul's family did not simply reside in Tarsus but were Tarsians, citizens with full colonial rights. Furthermore, the family might have lived in that city for almost two centuries before Paul's time, possibly settled along with other Jews by the Seleucid emperor Antiochus IV.

VII. TEACHING OUTLINE

A. INTRODUCTION
1. Lead Story: Martin Luther Comes to Faith
2. Context: In chapter 21 Luke began the final lap of his record in which he will take Paul from the Asian coast to Rome via Jerusalem and Caesarea. The trials have begun, and Paul will be a prisoner, or at least under guard, for the rest of this book. We will find no lack of excitement for the rest of Acts, but we will hear no more missionary

journeys, no more prayer meetings with brothers and sisters in Christ, and no more evangelistic sermons appealing to Gentiles. The events of the last six chapters consumed four years of Paul's life and probably taught him a great deal of patience and dependence upon the Lord, lessons we would do well to learn from reading about his experiences.

3. Transition: As we open Acts 22, we see a courageous man able to clearly articulate how Christ drew him to salvation. He can also explain how he attempted all his life to follow God's will and do God's work. In the face of murderous mobs and the cruel interrogation of Rome, he remains calm and clear, expecting that God's will, which he has already ascertained, will be carried out. In these thirty verses we learn courage, clarity of witness, and commitment to God's call in our lives.

B. COMMENTARY

1. Paul the Pharisee (vv. 1–5)
   a. His heritage (vv. 1–3a)
   b. His education (v. 3b)
   c. His religious zeal (vv. 4–5)
2. Paul the Believer (vv. 6–13)
   a. The light on the road (vv. 6–9)
   b. The visit to Ananias (vv. 10–13)
3. Paul the Witness (vv. 14–21)
   a. Selected by God (vv. 14–16)
   b. Warned through prayer (vv. 17–18)
   c. Sent to the Gentiles (vv. 19–21)
4. Paul the Prisoner (vv. 22–30)
   a. Anger of the crowd (vv. 22–23)
   b. Action of the commander (vv. 24–25)
   c. Appeal to citizenship (vv. 26–29)
   d. Appearance before the Sanhedrin (v. 30)

C. CONCLUSION: DUTY TO OTHERS

VIII. ISSUES FOR DISCUSSION

1. What happened in your life before you became a Christian to prepare you for more effective Christian ministry?
2. What is the difference between loyal church membership and being a Christian?
3. Describe your conversion experience to another person. What mission did God choose you for as he saved you?

Acts 23

Cavalry Escort

I. Introduction
Rethinking the Resurrection

II. Commentary
A verse-by-verse explanation of the chapter.

III. Conclusion
Romeward Bound
An overview of the principles and applications from the chapter.

IV. Life Application
Miracle at Cape Finisterre
Melding the chapter to life.

V. Prayer
Tying the chapter to life with God.

VI. Deeper Discoveries
Historical, geographical, and grammatical enrichment of the commentary.

VII. Teaching Outline
Suggested step-by-step group study of the chapter.

VIII. Issues for Discussion
Zeroing the chapter in on daily life.

Q u o t e

"*We* should give God the same place
in our hearts that He holds in the universe."

a n o n y m o u s

GEOGRAPHICAL PROFILE: CAESAREA

- Built between 25 and 13 B.C. by Herod the Great
- Named in honor of Augustus Caesar
- Splendid harbor on the Mediterranean about twenty-five miles northwest of the city of Samaria
- Headquarters for Roman military forces

BIOGRAPHICAL PROFILE: FELIX

- A Greek subject freed by Claudius sometime after A.D. 41
- Married a Jewish woman, Drusilla, who was actually the wife of the King of Emesa
- As a "procurator," he held the duty of gathering funds for Rome

I N   A   N U T S H E L L

In Acts 23 Paul stirs a riot by claiming the Sanhedrin has *him on trial because of his hope in the resurrection, leading the Roman commander to send him to Felix, the governor, in Caesarea. We will learn again that God controls all circumstances, keeping watch over the affairs of his people. These thirty-five verses expose us to humanity, humility, and hope; the key is verse 11.*

Cavalry Escort

I. INTRODUCTION

Rethinking the Resurrection

During Easter Week 1996, an amazing thing happened in the secular press. All three major news magazines—*Time, Newsweek* and *US News and World Report*—depicted Jesus on the front cover. The occasion was not just a Christian holiday that comes around every year. In 1996, the Christian celebration of resurrection followed hard on the heels of a new wave of criticism leveled against the historicity of that central biblical event. Kenneth Woodward's article in *Newsweek* (Apr. 8, 1996) entitled "Rethinking the Resurrection" detailed the problem along with quotes from modern critics: "In their relentless search for 'the historical Jesus,' various Biblical scholars argue that the Gospel stories of the empty tomb and Jesus' post-resurrection appearances are fictions devised long after his death to justify claims of his divinity. To hear them tell it, the Resurrection is an embarrassment to the modern mind and a disservice to the itinerant Jewish preacher from rural Galilee."

These so-called "biblical scholars," using text-bashing, speculation, and the presuppositions of their own vacuous theology, try to reconstruct the life of Jesus as social reformer; the resurrection just gets in their way. To Gerd Ludemann at the University of Göttingen, for example, no one holding a scientific world view could continue to believe in the resurrection. In *What Really Happened To Jesus: A Historical Approach to the Resurrection* (Louisville: Westminster/John Knox, 1995), Ludemann tells his readers that Jesus' body "rotted away" in the tomb. The risen Christ was a "vision" produced by the grief and guilt of the apostles, and the appearance to more than 500 was "mass ecstasy" (Ludemann, 62).

Australian author Barbara Thiering in *Jesus and the Riddle of the Dead Sea Scrolls* equates Jesus with "the wicked priest" of the Essene sect and claims he was actually crucified at Qumran, but not actually killed. Later, Simon Magus (see Acts 8:9) revived Jesus, who went on to marry Mary Magdalene, father three children, divorce her, and marry Lydia! (see Acts 16:14; Thiering, 65). You thought blasphemy was old-fashioned!

We could multiply these illustrations ten times and always come up with the same nonsense. *When people have chosen not to believe the Bible, the danger is not that they will believe nothing, but that they will believe anything.* Obviously, education and religious position mean nothing. The speculations above represent no more than the diatribe of highly skilled pagans.

After examining the evidence, Woodward's conclusion is fascinating: "After 150 years of scholarly research, there are signs that the quest for the 'historical' Jesus has reached a dead end. There have been no new data on the person of Jesus since the Gospels were written. And though scholars continue to piece together information from archaeology and other disciplines, these are valuable chiefly for fashioning a better understanding of Christian origins and how the Gospels, in particular, were composed." Woodward goes on to cite an author who establishes again the importance of the resurrection and ascension and concludes, "Not everyone can or will accept that belief. But without it there is no Easter."

In Acts 23, verse 11 with its word from the Lord is pivotal because the chapter basically talks about God's control of issues in Paul's life. The centerpiece of Paul's brief remarks to the Sanhedrin appears in verse 6: **I stand on trial because of my hope in the resurrection of the dead**. Today, Christian faith in the resurrection is not on trial. Scornful writings of modern scholars who deny the Bible wither in the face of evidence that Jesus of Nazareth was crucified, rose again, and sits at the Father's right hand today. When secular news magazines doubt the doubters, our faith rises stronger. Like Paul, we grasp hold of the central feature in the preaching of Acts—*God raised Jesus from the dead, and we are witnesses of these things.*

II. COMMENTARY

Cavalry Escort

MAIN IDEA: *God is in control of our lives even when those lives take us through difficult and dangerous circumstances.*

A Defense Before the Sanhedrin (vv. 1–11)

SUPPORTING IDEA: *God is present when we have to testify before him in front of unfriendly and unbelieving audiences.*

23:1. Often Bible chapter breaks seem intrusive. Luke did not write in chapters, of course. Those who eventually inserted chapter and verse numbers chose to include the beginning of this event as the last verse of chapter 22. We already know Paul has been brought to the Sanhedrin by Claudius Lysias. We are as surprised as they when, rather than waiting for some invitation, Paul immediately begins speaking.

He used the common formal address for assembled Jews and affirmed his commitment to godly duty as a Jew (Rom. 15:19b; Phil. 3:6b; 2 Tim. 1:4–7). As innocent as this line may seem, we must understand it in light of what the Sanhedrin knew full well about this man from Tarsus: an outspoken Christian, totally convinced of the messiahship of Jesus. Since they believed none of his Christian faith and had attempted to suppress it ever since they murdered Stephen, their only conclusion could be that he intended to condemn their consciences. The reaction of the high priest in verse 2 obviously indicates anger at what Paul had just said.

23:2. Ananias, son of Nedebaeus, was appointed priest in A.D. 48 and held that office for approximately ten years. Famous for bribery and plunder of temple offerings, he was assassinated by Jewish guerrillas in A.D. 66. His order to strike Paul on the mouth was illegal since, before the Sanhedrin as before our own western courts of law, the prisoner was innocent until proven guilty. Luke assumes Theophilus will know about Ananias, so he lets the incident stand.

23:3. Paul's response astonishes us as much as Ananias' order. We look for Paul to act like Jesus: "When they hurled their insults at him, he did not retaliate; when he suffered, he made no threats" (1 Pet. 2:23). Instead, Paul spoke the truth prophetically (though probably not consciously on this occasion), for God did smite Ananias. The phrase **whitewashed wall** accused Ananias of hypocrisy (Matt. 23:27). The reason for this charge? One appointed to uphold the law had just ordered it broken. How could a trained rabbi publicly condemn a high priest in this fashion? We have several interpretation options:

1. Paul was justified in his remark because of Ananias' character and behavior.
2. Paul was justified in expressing righteous anger.
3. Paul spoke calmly and delivered a prophecy of God's judgment on Ananias.
4. Paul lost his cool. Stretched beyond the breaking point by the previous day's events, he said something he should not have said.

Any of the above seem possible, but I opt for number 4 in view of Paul's apology in verse 5. Remember, we have been defending Paul against commentators who claimed him wrong on various other occasions in Acts. The argument has been that the text does not indicate a wrong. Here Paul seems to acknowledge his own mistake and admit wrongdoing by quoting Exodus 22:28.

23:4–5. It would seem we could infer from Luke's remark about **those who were standing near Paul** that the high priest sat some distance away. Seventy-one people in addition to Paul would have occupied the room if all the Council showed up for this hastily-called meeting. Upon being challenged regarding his angry words, Paul retreats to his opening line and calls the Council, **Brothers**, once again. He explains his behavior by saying, **I did not realize that he was the high priest**. The question of why Paul did not know Ananias was high priest is much debated (see "Deeper Discoveries").

23:6–8. Time to change tactics. Exchanging ill behavior with the high priest would achieve nothing in the Sanhedrin. Paul knew the group's make-up, since he had once been part of it. The controlling Sadducees (including Ananias) were constantly besieged by the Pharisees, particularly on the issue of the resurrection. If Paul could create a doctrinal civil war, he might divert attention away from himself to an ongoing internal debate.

For the third time Paul addresses the group as **brothers**. This time he states his sterling religious credentials: **I am a Pharisee, the son of a Pharisee**. Then he cuts to the bottom line—the resurrection. Some argue that Paul could no longer have called himself a Pharisee because he spent his life spreading the gospel to Gentiles. This man baptized Timothy, cut off his hair on a vow, paid for the purification of four Jewish brothers, and had just rushed back to Jerusalem in time for the Feast of Pentecost. He still considered himself very much a Pharisee, and obviously the Pharisees present that day considered the issue of resurrection of greater importance than the prisoner brought in by Lysias. Some Pharisees had become Christians (15:5), but the New Testament contains no record of a Sadducee ever trusting Christ.

Luke's explanation in verse 8 is interesting. No other source informs us that Sadducees did not believe in angels or spirits. They did affirm inspiration of the Pentateuch, and the Pentateuch repeatedly refers to angels. What could Luke possibly mean here? Polhill suggests:

> He may have meant that the Sadducees rejected the eschatology of the Pharisees, which involved an elaborate hierarchy of good and evil angels. Or perhaps it was the idea that an angel or a spirit can speak through a human being as an agent of revelation that Luke depicted the Sadducees as rejecting (cf. v. 9). A final possibility is that the reference was a further elaboration of their rejection of the resurrection—they rejected an after life in an angelic or spiritual state (Polhill, 470).

Whatever the correct interpretation of Luke's remark, two things rise to grab our attention. First, this remark would only have been made to a Gentile (Theophilus), since any Jew would know what the Sadducees and Pharisees believed and how their beliefs differed from one another. Second, this passage is not about Sadducee/Pharisee theology, but about a divided house which has forgotten its duty assigned by a Roman officer to investigate whether the prisoner has broken any Jewish laws.

23:9–10. A minority group of the Sanhedrin **argued vigorously** for Paul's release. Let us not stretch the line. **We find nothing wrong with this man** cannot mean they accepted his ministry among the Gentiles and his defense of the resurrection of Jesus. None of that has entered the argument at this particular meeting. They merely defended a brother Pharisee who affirmed a cardinal principle of their doctrinal system.

In the latter part of verse 9 we find out why Luke raised the point of angels and spirits in verse 8. Either he has not given us a full account of the discussion up to this point, or these Pharisees have already heard the story of Paul's Damascus Road experience. In the spirit of Gamaliel (Acts 5:39), they warn of the possibility that **a spirit or an angel has spoken to him**. Obviously, that enraged the Sadducees even more, and the meeting became complete bedlam. In the typical pattern of the Sanhedrin, they could not contain their arguments in words alone and apparently pulled at Paul from two sides until Lysias intervened and had him taken back to the barracks.

23:11. Not that night, but the night following the next day Paul experienced the fourth of five visions he received in Acts (16:9; 18:9–10; 22:17–21; 27:23–24). This message emphasized God's control over all these events and offered courage. Mainly, Jesus informed Paul that these trial appearances have not been defenses for his life, but rather witness of the truth. Furthermore, this witness would continue all the way to Rome. Finally, the missionary rabbi received confirmation from heaven regarding plans he had already expressed (19:21). The eloquence of Morgan captures the moment:

> What a night it was. How full of light, how full of glory. His Master's word of cheer to chase away the dejection of his spirit; his Master's word of commendation astonishing him, and yet comforting him in view of his failure; his Master's word of appointment, filling him with certainty that in spite of all the difficulties in front of him, he should preach in Rome (Morgan, 497).

As an aside, let's not forget Lysias. Though probably not in the council chamber during the debate, when the riot began, he immediately sent his troops **down** (likely from the Fortress of Antonia) to rescue his prisoner. We know the Romans detested the Jews, and this commander had good reason. Yesterday, he had to break up a riot in the temple grounds, and today the highest court of the land squabbled like children fighting over toys in a sandbox.

Many people outside the faith know Christians best for their ability to fight. I shall never forget an interview I had many years ago with the dean of education at a major state university. I was considering doctoral study there. We got into a discussion about my position at a Christian college. Lifting his head and staring at a blank spot on the wall in front of his desk, the dean mused, "I used to go to church." I inquired further about his previous experience with religion, and he volunteered, "I remember one thing about church people—they fight." Without further word on the subject, he looked back down at his papers and continued the discussion of my application.

I have thought scores of times over the years of the many things he could have remembered—beautiful buildings, the organ music, some good deed a church member had done for him—but apparently none of these stuck in his mind. Even allowing for whatever effect he may have wanted his words to have on me, the condemnation still hurt. We should make every effort to ensure that such words never correctly describe the congregations in which we serve.

𝔅 Plot in Jerusalem (vv. 12–22)

SUPPORTING IDEA: *God does not always accomplish his purposes through visible miracles. Sometimes the most casual and normal happenings really reflect divine interference in our lives.*

23:12–15. The radical Jews, perhaps still the Asian conspirators who started the riot at the temple, took an oath **not to eat or drink** until Paul was dead. This kind of oath in Jewish custom carried wording such as: "May God do to us the same and more" or perhaps: "May we be cursed if . . ." Paul was no stranger to such plots (9:24; 20:19).

The wording of verse 14 is important: **They went to the chief priests and elders.** Avoiding the minority Pharisees who had spoken in Paul's behalf, they approached Ananias and his cohorts to involve them in this "pretext." Though Luke does not specifically say so, the passage intimates strongly that the Sanhedrin hierarchy agreed and, thereby, entered into a murder conspiracy with anarchists.

So much for law and justice in the Sanhedrin. We should see here how hatred confuses people's minds. They based efforts to do away with Paul on religion, on their great love for the law and their desire to protect its purity. They were quite prepared to break one of the Ten Commandments to achieve that "religious" goal.

The day before I wrote these words, national news telecast live pictures of Hezbollah volunteers, "hundreds of them," lined up in battle gear with explosives strapped to their bodies. These human bombs represented the Arab response to continuous Israeli bombing of terrorist positions in southern Lebanon. I mention it to demonstrate that fanaticism has been a way of life in the Middle East for hundreds of years. Apparently, it doesn't make any difference whether terrorist acts are carried out by Arabs or Israelis, as long as one's own goals are advanced.

In our passage, these men seem quite prepared to face the wrath of Rome. If caught murdering a Roman prisoner, they would surely have been executed to a man; so great was their hatred of Paul and so enflamed their religious emotions that they worried not at all about themselves.

23:16–22. Any plot so well known in the city had little chance of success. We get the impression from Paul's letters that family ties had been broken (Phil. 3:8), but such connections do not die easily. Furthermore (the forty henchmen notwithstanding), preservation of life was the greatest value in Judaism. So God used a hitherto unknown nephew as an agent of deliverance. The mention of this nephew is all we know of Paul's family.

Some have argued that Romans would not have allowed the nephew such access to the prisoner. Such Bible students forget what Luke has already told us. At first the Romans arrested Paul as a troublemaker, but by this time Lysias had become his guardian, holding the apostle "in protective custody." We know of no restrictions the Romans placed against family and friends visiting prisoners. The latter chapters of Acts will show us they could be quite lenient when they had a mind to do so.

This whole narrative reads like a suspense story. If the life of Paul constituted an ongoing weekly television serial, producers could draw out this simple narrative for long minutes as viewers wonder what would happen next. Why would a Roman commander take the word of a young man, possibly a teenager? Because this particular commander was a seasoned veteran of Jerusalem duty! After what he had seen, even just in the past few days, he could believe the Jews capable of anything. Remember the Roman law about losing a prisoner. Lysias could not afford to ignore this piece of espionage and had every intent of acting upon it immediately.

Transfer to Caesarea (vv. 23–35)

SUPPORTING IDEA: *Sometimes God delivers his children by the simple word of a young relative. Sometimes he has to call in the cavalry. At all times, he is ultimately in charge.*

23:23–24. Can't you see the opening scene? Two minutes earlier we saw the thoughtful commander staring into space after the nephew left the room. Now after a few hard-sell commercials, the black screen breaks open the scene outside the Roman barracks. At 9:00 P.M. under cover of darkness, 470 Roman soldiers escort Paul to the provincial capital at Caesarea, headquarters of Governor Felix. The Romans were nothing if not efficient. Lysias called up two centurions with their two hundred infantry, seventy cavalry troops and two hundred *dexiolaboi*, a fascinating word which appears only here in the New Testament. Obviously it means "spearman," but it comes from a root meaning "right-handed" because in the Roman army spears were commonly thrown with the right hand.

Some scholars scoff at this account because of the overkill escort, but Lysias would take no more chances with these Jewish anarchists. Though only forty may have been involved in the plot, he could well remember the hundreds or even thousands in the temple area. This would have been nearly half the Jerusalem force, but the foot soldiers went only thirty-five miles and then returned to their barracks. In any case, Paul starts for Rome in style. The narrative reminds us of Elisha's words to his servant Gehazi when pursued by Benhadad: "Don't be afraid . . . those who are with us are more than those who are with them . . . Oh Lord, open his eyes so he may see" (2 Kgs. 6:16).

23:25–30. How could Luke possibly have known the content of private and official correspondence between a Roman commander and the procurator of Judea? Of course, he could not; that is why verse 25 says, **He wrote a letter as follows.** Luke's summary obviously came from Paul who also only learned it from whatever Felix revealed in the questioning of chapter 24.

We have been using the name Claudius Lysias throughout the narrative of these events, but this is the first time it appears in the text. Following standard letter format of the day, the commander addressed the letter **To His Excellency, Governor Felix.** Many in the first century would have doubted the excellency of this man. A freed slave, his rule of violence alienated nearly everyone, and his rise to power as a procurator surprised nearly everyone. Tacitus, the Roman historian, said of Felix, "He is a master of cruelty and lust who exercised the power of a king with the spirit of a slave."

Here we have the only secular letter in the New Testament. Generally, its text summarizes events of the last several days. Actually, the first time Lysias saw Paul he didn't rescue him but arrested him. In light of subsequent events, that fine point seems unimportant, so Luke does not split hairs on the matter. What we do learn new is that Lysias had also **ordered his accusers to present . . . their case against him.**

Lysias would not send every questionable case of Jewish agitation off to Caesarea for Felix to deal with. This special situation arose because of Paul's Roman citizenship, a problem Lysias rarely saw in Jerusalem.

Of significance again in this letter is the Roman attitude toward Christianity. Nothing about Paul's life or message challenged anything in Roman law. Lysias had no reason to imprison him, much less to execute him. This was a matter of Jewish theology—**the accusation had to do with questions about their law.** The finding of Lysias confirmed the conclusion of Gallio years before: Christianity was no threat or offense to Rome. Remember they spirited Paul out of town under cover of darkness so when Lysias wrote **I also ordered his accusers,** he described something that would occur before Felix read the letter but certainly not before Lysias wrote it. That notification would have been delivered sometime the next day with Paul well on his way to Caesarea.

23:31–33. This is the third time Paul sneaked out of a city at night. The foot soldiers stopped at Antipatris, doubtless resting there for awhile before returning to the barracks. On his horse, Paul accompanied the cavalry all the way to Caesarea, about sixty miles from Jerusalem and thirty miles northwest of Antipatris.

23:34–35. As we read these verses, we find ourselves wondering what difference Paul's place of origin had in this case? When Felix learned Paul came from Tarsus and Seleucia, he delayed the case for the arrival of accusers. Perhaps we should assume that if Paul had been from Judea, Syria, or even Asia Minor, Felix might have consulted local authorities to "check his record." Essentially, Felix attempted to determine his jurisdiction. Since both Judea and Seleucia fell under his rule, he had no problem hearing the case himself. We should not make too much of Paul's "palace" residence in Caesarea. Originally it was a royal palace, but now in A.D. 56–57 it had become a civic building containing the governor's headquarters and cells for prisoners.

MAIN IDEA REVIEW: *God is in control of our lives even when those lives take us through difficult and dangerous circumstances.*

III. CONCLUSION

Romeward Bound

Paul began the chapter waking up in a Roman barracks; then taken to the Sanhedrin, he ends the chapter bedding down in a cell at Felix's *praetorium*. It has been an exciting few days for him and for us, Luke's readers. The central theme of the chapter quickly unfolds—God's control over human events and God's protection of his people. From the moment Jesus appeared to the apostle in a vision (v. 11), Paul knew he would not die in Jerusalem nor in Caesarea. He is Romeward bound, a goal he has treasured in his heart for some time.

We already know that Paul liked to sing in adversity (chap. 16), so we can picture him both in the barracks at Jerusalem and the prison cell at Caesarea. Doubtless many of the psalms came to his lips during these years of adversity. Had he known of it, he could well have mouthed the words of Charles A. Tindley's gospel song:

> When the storms of life are raging,
> Stand by me.
> When the storms of life are raging,
> Stand by me.
> When the world is tossing me
>   like a ship upon a sea,
> Thou who rulest wind and water,
> Stand by me.
> In the mist of faults and failures,
> Stand by me.
> In the midst of faults and failures,
> Stand by me.
> When I do the best I can,
> And my friends misunderstand,
> Thou who knowest all about me—
> Stand by me.

PRINCIPLES

- God controls all circumstances of our lives.
- Even great Christian leaders like Paul can make mistakes on occasion.

- The resurrection was the crucial issue in first-century Christian proclamation.
- God can turn the wrath of our enemies into a safe trip to where he wants us to go.

APPLICATIONS

- Trust God in struggles, and expect his deliverance.
- Know that Jesus stands by you in trouble even if you don't see visions or hear voices.
- Understand again that God has raised up secular government to protect the peace and save lives from anarchy.
- Be grateful that God knows all about you, even your failures and your fears.

IV. LIFE APPLICATION

Miracle at Cape Finisterre

This chapter describes intervening providence, the way God can use a Roman commander and an unknown relative to protect a life. In *The Bible in Spain*, George Barrow tells of the miraculous deliverance he experienced aboard a ship fast driven toward the dangerous coast of Cape Finisterre:

> We were now close to the rocks when a horrid convulsion of the elements took place. The lightning enveloped us as with a mantle; thunders were louder than the roar of a million cannons; the dregs of the ocean seemed to be cast up, and in the midst of all this turmoil, the wind, without the slightest intimation, veered right about and pushed us from the horrible coast faster than it had previously driven us to it. The oldest sailors on board acknowledged that they had never witnessed so providential an escape. I said from the bottom of my heart, "Our Father, Hallowed be Thy name" (Robertson, 441).

At the risk of overemphasis, let's notice one more time the two very different types of "miracles" God used to deliver Paul. Claudius Lysias represents a visible and obvious intervention. God works through civil government which he has ordained not only to save Paul's life, but to send him on his way to Rome. Paul's nephew seems a less obvious touch of God's hand, but surely Luke intends us to see it that way nonetheless.

In a world under the control of a sovereign God, things do not "just happen." At least not things which represent life and death deliverance. Let's not push the point too far. If we go to the grocery store and select 1 percent milk instead of 2 percent, we should hardly attribute that decision to a revelation from God or his power guiding the hand that picked up the carton. Events of this chapter hardly deal with such minimal consequence. Paul's life was constantly at stake during the latter chapters of Acts, and surely the Holy Spirit intends us to see the prevailing winds of verse 11 blowing over the entire chapter: **Take courage! As you have testified about me in Jerusalem, so you must also testify in Rome.**

V. PRAYER

God, please give us the confidence of Paul to believe that you will control and direct the events of our lives.

VI. DEEPER DISCOVERIES

A. Paul's Astonishing Response (v. 5)

We join other Bible scholars for a moment to ponder what Paul could possibly have meant when he said, **Brothers, I did not realize that he was the high priest.** Let's list the options and briefly discuss each one.

1. Ananias was not dressed in his priestly robes. Remember, a quickly called meeting of the Sanhedrin was not official. All the council members may have attended dressed in "street clothes" so they all looked somewhat alike, especially since Paul started speaking before any presiding officer took charge of the meeting.

2. Paul meant, "He doesn't behave like a high priest so I won't treat him as such." Marshall takes this view when he says, "Paul was speaking in bitter irony: 'I did not think that a man who could give such an order could be the high priest.' This is the most probable solution, even though the ironic tone might have been conveyed more clearly" (Marshall, 364).

3. Because of poor eyesight, Paul could not see far enough down the room to recognize Ananias. Teachers and preachers have made much of Paul's eyes, much more than the Scripture tells us. Paul talks about some kind of illness in Galatians 4:13–14, and in verse 15 says, **You would have torn out your eyes and given them to me,** which has led many to believe he suffered from some form of eye disease. Certainly possible, but hardly enough of a case to support this view of our problem in Acts 23. Furthermore, Luke's pen was quite ready to excuse his hero whenever possible, and it's unlikely he would not have mentioned the eyesight problem here had that been the deciding issue.

4. Paul spoke to Ananias as a person ignoring his office. This is possible, but certainly seems a bit stretched in the text. The Greek of verse 5 contains no tricky words, except that the definite article (*the*) does not appear. In reality, this view sounds like number 2, depicting Paul as saying something other than what he really meant.

5. Paul really did not recognize Ananias. At first glance it's difficult for us to imagine a rabbi who did not keep up with changing events in the Sanhedrin, but this was no ordinary rabbi. He had maintained a rigorous travel schedule for twenty years, visiting Jerusalem only occasionally. During that time the high priestly office had passed not only from one person to another, but to different families. Even if Paul would have known the name of Ananias, he would have no occasion to recognize him by sight.

In a media age we find this conclusion difficult, but imagine yourself for a moment without television, newspapers, or news magazines. You know from letters or word of mouth who is majority leader in the House of Representatives, but you have never seen this person on television; you have never seen a picture in a newspaper or magazine; you only know the name. Now we gather seventy-one people in a room, and somebody tells a person near you to hit you in the face. Would you immediately conclude the order came from the Majority Leader?

We should know by now from C-Span that our Senate and House of Representatives, like the British Parliament, are scarcely more orderly than the Sanhedrin. People can shout anything at any time—and usually do. I take Paul at his word; I believe he did not recognize or realize that the first person who spoke in that meeting was the high priest. As soon as he did, he apologized and quoted Scripture to acknowledge his wrongdoing.

B. Types of Vows (v. 12)

From the information Luke gives us we could picture these forty plotters dying of dehydration, starvation, or both. In fact they had taken a vow which need not be fulfilled. Longenecker explains:

> The rabbis allowed four types of vows to be broken: "Vows of incitement, vows of exaggeration, vows made in error, and vows that cannot be fulfilled by reason of constraint" exclusions allowing for almost any contingency. The conspirators' plan, though violating both the letter and the spirit of Jewish law pertaining to the Sanhedrin . . . was in keeping with the character of the high priest Ananias (Longenecker, 533–534).

VII. TEACHING OUTLINE

A. INTRODUCTION
1. Lead Story: Rethinking the Resurrection

2. Context: As we approach Acts 23, look for evidence that God's hand protects his people at all times. Study the chapter in light of its key verse (11), and see how God uses people to take care of other people.

3. Transition: In this chapter we find evidence of fallen humanity—in the Sanhedrin, in Paul, in the Jewish conspirators, even in the letter of Claudius Lysias. That ought to give us humility about our own lives and shortcomings, coupled with hope that God can use us despite those failures. As we find Paul dependent totally upon God, we may want to review the hymn by Charles Tindley,

> Nothing between my soul and the Savior,
> So that his blessed face may be seen;
> Nothing preventing the least of his favor,
> Keep the way clear! Let nothing between.

B.   COMMENTARY
1. Defense Before the Sanhedrin (vv. 1–11)
   a. Clash with the High Priest (vv. 1–5)
   b. Conflict between the Pharisees and Sadducees (vv. 6–10)
   c. Courage from the Lord (v. 11)
2. Plot in Jerusalem (vv. 12–22)
   a. The plot built (vv. 12–15)
   b. The plot blown (vv. 16–22)
3. Transfer to Caesarea (vv. 23–35)
   a. Military escort (vv. 23–25)
   b. Official letter (vv. 26–30)
   c. Safe arrival (vv. 31–35)

C.   CONCLUSION: MIRACLE AT CAPE FINISTERRE

VIII. ISSUES FOR DISCUSION

1. What testimony can you give to a nonbeliever that God is in control of your life?
2. What have you done for God that would cause anyone else to oppose you? How do you respond when people oppose you because you are a Christian?
3. Do you know people so dedicated to false beliefs or wrong religion that they are willing to kill people who oppose them? What causes people to be so fiercely loyal to falsehood? What would make you so fiercely loyal to the truth of Christ?

Acts 24

༺ঌৡঌ৶ঌ৽

Politician on the Take

I. Introduction
Hugh Latimer before Henry VIII

II. Commentary
A verse-by-verse explanation of the chapter.

III. Conclusion
Furious in Religion
An overview of the principles and applications from the chapter.

IV. Life Application
Procrastination Is a Loser
Melding the chapter to life.

V. Prayer
Tying the chapter to life with God.

VI. Deeper Discoveries
Historical, geographical, and grammatical enrichment of the commentary.

VII. Teaching Outline
Suggested step-by-step group study of the chapter.

VIII. Issues for Discussion
Zeroing the chapter in on daily life.

"*O*ften the test of courage
is not to die but to live."

A l f i e r i

BIOGRAPHICAL PROFILE: DRUSILLA

- The youngest of the three daughters of Herod Agrippa I
- At fourteen she married Azizus, king of Emesa, then left her husband to marry Felix
- Their son, Agrippa, died in the eruption of Mount Vesuvius

BIOGRAPHICAL PROFILE: ANANIAS

- Son of Nedebaeus and high priest from A.D. 38 to about 58
- Known for violence and greed
- Hated by Jewish nationalists for his pro-Roman stance

BIOGRAPHICAL PROFILE: PORCIUS FESTUS

- Governor of Judea from about A.D. 60 to 62
- Died in office at the age of sixty-two
- Nothing is known of him prior to his assuming this post

IN A NUTSHELL

*I*n Acts 24, Luke gives almost equal space to charges against Paul, Paul's defense against those charges, and the response of Governor Felix. He seems to want to demonstrate again that Christianity has done nothing to break the laws of Rome nor the religious code of Israel.

Politician on the Take

I. INTRODUCTION

Hugh Latimer Before Henry VIII

In Oxford, England, which I visited recently, stands a striking statue of three men burned at the stake there in October of 1555: Thomas Cramner, Thomas Ridley, and Hugh Latimer, three of the most visible victims of Queen Mary's persecution. Latimer had been twice imprisoned for the faith in the latter years of Henry's reign, but he had remained a staunch defender of the Reformed doctrine of justification. He once wrote, "If I see the blood of Christ with the eye of my soul, that is true faith that his blood was shed for me."

Most famous for his preaching at St. Paul's Cross, Latimer was called before the king one day and demanded to offer public apology for what Henry found offensive in Latimer's message. As the story goes, he read the same text he had used the previous Sunday and then said aloud,

> Hugh Latimer, dost thou know before whom thou art this day to speak? To the high and mighty monarch, the king's most excellent majesty, who can take away thy life if thou offendest: therefore, take heed that thou speakest not a word that may displease. But then consider well, Hugh, dost thou not know from whence thou comest—upon whose message thou art sent? Even by the great and mighty God, who is all-present and who beholdeth all thy ways, and who is able to cast thy soul into hell! Therefore, take care that thou deliverest thy message faithfully.

With that, Latimer began the same sermon he had preached to his congregation.

In a very significant sense all the Reformers were much like the apostle Paul both in doctrine and behavior. In this chapter we find Paul before a formal court of law presided over by the officially appointed Roman governor. Yet his message hasn't changed. With deep conviction and holy energy he proclaimed his faith that day.

II. COMMENTARY

Politician on the Take

MAIN IDEA: *Through the power of God, Christians can deliver calm witness even in the most stressful of situations.*

◬ Tertullus for the Prosecution (vv. 1-9)

SUPPORTING IDEA: *Enemies of the gospel will use all skill and process possible to oppose Christian believers.*

24:1. As chapter 24 opens Paul had been a prisoner in Caesarea for five days. During that time Felix awaited the arrival of the prosecution team from Jerusalem which, as we should have known, was headed by Ananias along with **some of the elders** and a rhetorician (lawyer) by the name of Tertullus. All we know about the latter comes from this passage. He could have been a Roman, a Hellenistic Jew, or a Greek. Whatever his ethnic or religious persuasion, no one doubted his competence.

24:2-4. In the custom of the day, attorneys would praise the presiding judge and also promise to be brief, both guidelines followed with precision by Tertullus. Customary to be sure, but not true. During Felix's rule insurrections and anarchy had increased throughout Palestine. His brutal attempts to put down popular uprisings had only further inflamed the people. Most Jews living at that time would have been horrified to hear what the high priest's mouthpiece had to say to Governor Felix though it certainly was politically expedient. The land hardly knew peace; Felix demonstrated no foresight; no significant reforms took place during his jurisdiction; he did not deserve the title **most excellent**; and most Jews had no intention of expressing gratitude. Other than that, Tertullus spoke the truth.

Most experts believe that we have only a summary of the total address. That accounts for why these opening words of flattery occupy such a large portion of the overall case. This would be typical not only of Luke's handling of speeches in Acts, but throughout the New Testament by other Bible writers as well. Since Felix had a record of crucifying reactionaries, Ananias may have felt that he and his flashy lawyer had every chance to get rid of Paul once and for all.

24:5-9. Here it comes—this troublemaker has stirred up riots thereby threatening the *Pax Romana*. Like Jesus, Paul was accused of political sedition (Luke 23:2,5). We may assume that Ananias wanted Felix to treat this latest rebel as he had many before him. Not only did Paul stir up riots, but apparently he was a worldwide terrorist, for in the language of Tertullus, he had done this **among the Jews all over the world**.

The second charge looks most interesting, **He is a ringleader of the Nazarene sect**. Only here in the New Testament do we find the word **Nazarene** describing Christians, though it was applied to Jesus himself (Acts 2:22). We have no idea why Tertullus used this phrase instead of "the Way" or "the Christians"; perhaps he wanted to evoke the old line that nothing good could come out of Nazareth (John 1:46).

In verse 6, Tertullus gets to the real issue, taking us all the way back to the trumped-up charges by the Asian Jews in 21:29. Interesting, however, that the earlier charge claimed Paul actually *did* defile the temple by taking Trophimus beyond the wall. Tertullus only claimed that he *tried* to do so but was seized by the Jews to protect their holy property. Since the Romans had given the Jews authority over temple matters, perhaps Tertullus, Ananias and company wanted to emphasize again how much they were within their rights to bring these charges against this pestilent fellow.

Notice verse 7 does not appear in the NIV text (see "Deeper Discoveries").

Bringing his case to a close, Tertullus invited Felix to examine Paul personally, thereby affirming that all the charges brought by the Jews were true. We have no idea how many people Ananias brought with him from Jerusalem, but they now joined in one voice to affirm the charges identified by Tertullus.

B Paul for the Defense (vv. 10–21)

SUPPORTING IDEA: *Whenever you are brought up on charges in any kind of court of law, stay calm, and simply tell the truth.*

24:10. Paul also began with a brief complimentary remark, although this time it was true—he merely acknowledged Felix's ten-year connection with Israel and familiarity with religious events in and around Jerusalem. Felix had only been in Caesarea for two or three years, but he had previously been stationed in Samaria; therefore, he brought nearly a decade of awareness about "the Jewish problem" to this trial.

24:11. Whereas Tertullus spoke in general condemnatory statements, Paul invited Felix to check out the facts. Only twelve days earlier he had gone to Jerusalem to worship at the feast, and virtually all of those days had been spent in Roman custody. When would he have had time to foment a rebellion? Where were the others who would have assisted in this worldwide terrorism? What kind of evidence did his accusers bring to this trial to substantiate their charges?

24:12–13. Yes, his accusers seized him at the temple, but not because he was arguing with anyone, or stirring up a crowd, or doing any of the other things they claimed. We must recognize here that *Paul did not go to Jerusalem to evangelize.* We lose sight of that fact because that was his central purpose almost everywhere else in the world. According to Galatians 2:7–9, he would have only engaged in evangelism at Jerusalem if invited to do so by the Jerusalem church which, as we know from Acts 22, did happen.

24:14–16. Having denied the charges brought against him, Paul established that this whole squabble was a religious, not a political issue. He admitted to several things quite precisely:

1. He worshiped the God of the Hebrews.
2. He was a follower of **the Way**.
3. He believed everything in the Law and the Prophets.
4. He had hope in God.
5. He believed in the resurrection.
6. He worked hard to keep his conscience clear before God and   man.

All of that squares with what we know about Paul throughout Acts—except the phrase **as these men**. Should we not assume that Ananias brought only Sadducees with him, and, therefore, the accusers would not have hope in the resurrection? Not necessarily. Remember, the Pharisees who supported Paul in Jerusalem were only a minority, and Ananias could surely have found some loyal Pharisees to make this trip, perhaps even some who owed him political favors.

Perhaps Paul ignored the views of the Sadducees and spoke rather of the widely-held views of Jews in general though it is difficult to get by the words **these men** to support that view. Longenecker suggests that "though Sadducees did not share with Pharisees the hope of a resurrection, Paul as a Pharisee was probably sufficiently self-confident to believe that it was the Pharisaic hope that characterized—or, at least, should characterize—all true representations of the Jewish faith" (Longenecker, 540).

Let's not miss Paul's switch from defense to witness in this trial. In three short verses (11–13) he dealt with the charges. In the next three longer verses he witnessed of his Christian faith. Jesus had told him about giving testimony in Jerusalem and Rome. Caesarea, after all, was only a stopping place between the two.

24:17. Now for the first time Luke introduces the issue of the offering as a second reason for Paul's appearance in Jerusalem (Rom. 15:25–27,31; 1 Cor. 16:1–4). Probably we should understand the word **gifts** in this verse as a reference to the Gentile collections for Judea and the word **offerings** as the payment Paul made on behalf of the four men (21:23–26).

24:18–20. Paul's actual visit to the temple was not accompanied by any trouble at all. Some Asian Jews, conspicuous by their absence from this present trial, later accused him of something that cannot be proved because it did not happen. Furthermore, if Paul had committed some sacrilege during his time with the Sanhedrin, then let Tertullus raise that point and provide the evidence. Throughout this point of the discussion Paul stood on solid ground, for plaintiffs failing to show up in a Roman court placed themselves in danger of heavy penalties. In actuality, the Sanhedrin had broken off its examination of Paul when a theological argument broke out between the Pharisees and Sadducees. At that particular meeting no accusations were brought against him, so Tertullus had nothing to say.

24:21. Here it is again. Somehow preachers in the Acts get to the resurrection before they finish. Paul claimed to be a good Jew, practicing Jewish customs, and expecting the Jewish hope of resurrection. What possible crime could Rome find in that? Here we have the key verse of our chapter and the unifying message of Acts.

Felix with the Verdict (vv. 22–27)

SUPPORTING IDEA: *Whatever the situation, however alien the surroundings, when God gives you the opportunity, don't hesitate to speak about faith in Christ Jesus.*

24:22–23. I have entitled this section "Verdict," but in reality Felix postponed the verdict in Paul's case. He needed a much more detailed report from Lysias. Paul was right. Felix was **well acquainted with the Way.** We can criticize Felix for not releasing Paul, but the anticipation of further word from Lysias certainly seemed legitimate. On the other hand, we learn before the chapter ends that Governor Felix was just another hack politician on the take, waiting for a bribe and trying to curry favor with those he ruled. So Paul stayed under house arrest, but his Christian friends were permitted to visit him and **take care of his needs.**

Some argue that Felix was concerned for Paul and provided protective custody here as did Lysias earlier. That does not fit the information at the end of the chapter and may portray Felix in too positive a light. As for Lysias' report, we find no indication in the text that Lysias ever came. Since Felix already had a letter in his hands which fully explained Lysias' point of view on the matter, that whole line may have been a smoke screen.

24:24–26. In a surprising turn of events, Felix showed up at the Praetorium with his young wife, the Jewish Drusilla. For reasons Luke does not tell us, Felix wanted to hear Paul again but likely was not prepared for a direct sermon on **righteousness, self-control and the judgment to come.** Apparently, the Holy Spirit drove home the point to people in whose lives this particular message had unique relevance. Luke tells us **Felix was afraid** and decided to get rid of this preacher so he didn't have to listen to anymore convicting talk.

Whatever conviction Felix may have felt at Paul's preaching, it did not make a dent in his greed; he called for Paul repeatedly **and talked with him** hoping for a bribe. Bribes, of course, were against Roman law, but they occurred quite commonly throughout the empire. Some have speculated that Paul's discussions of the offerings in verse 17 provoked Felix's persistence on this matter, but that is speculative at best. Perhaps Felix just acted like Felix, carrying out his office with usual disregard for ethics, morality, and righteousness.

24:27. Acquittal was the only action available to Felix, but that would have upset the Jews, something he had done all too frequently during his time in the province. From Luke's account, it would appear that Rome merely transferred Felix to another command, but Josephus tells us otherwise. Longenecker summarizes Josephus:

> Felix's downfall came through an outbreak of hostilities between Jews and Greeks at Caesarea, with both claiming dominant civil rights in the city—the Jews because of their greater numbers and wealth and because Herod the Great, a Jew, had rebuilt the city; the Greeks because they had the support of the military and because they claimed the city was always meant to be a Gentile city. . . . Using the Syrian troops under his command, Felix's intervention took the form of military retaliation upon the Jews. Many were killed, taken prisoner, or plundered of their wealth; and a delegation of Jews went to Rome to complain. Felix was recalled to Rome and would have suffered severe punishment had not his brother Pallas interceded for him before Nero (cf. Jos. Antiq. XX, 182 [viii.9]). Felix was replaced by Festus in A.D. 60 (Longenecker, 542).

Paul spent another two years in prison because of the whim and political agenda of a Roman governor. Many scholars believe Luke was with Paul all this time and took opportunity to gather information for his writings, perhaps both Luke and Acts.

MAIN IDEA REVIEW: *Through the power of God, Christians can deliver calm witness even in the most stressful of situations.*

III. CONCLUSION

Furious in Religion

William Penn, that much persecuted Quaker, once wrote, "A devout man is one thing, a stickler is another. To be furious in religion is to be irreligiously religious. It were better to be of no church, than to be bitter for any . . . nor can spirits ever be divided that love and live in the same divine principle."

With the exception of the verbal blast at Ananias in chapter 23, Paul stayed completely calm under stress throughout all these trial narratives. The Sanhedrin became "furious in religion" and, therefore, "irreligiously religious." Paul accepted his circumstances as part of God's control on his life and found no reason to shout or whine at his trials.

His behavior still stands as a model for us. No matter how much people taunt Christians, retaliation is not an option. No matter how many antigovernment militants hide out in cabins and spout the name of God while shooting automatic weapons at police, thinking Christians know such irresponsible and violent behavior does not follow the pattern of the Bible. We see a clear articulation of Christian principles and message with, as we have said so many times throughout this study, a particular emphasis on the resurrection.

PRINCIPLES

- Christians should never be truthfully charged with disturbing the peace.
- Through God's Spirit, Christians can stay calm even under stress.
- Christian witnesses focus on the resurrection whenever possible.
- Courageous Christians do not fear to tell the truth, even to political authorities.

APPLICATIONS

- Stick to the basic message when witnessing for Christ.
- Avoid greed, especially if you are in a position to command the benevolence of others.
- Be patient—even in prison—God has not forgotten you.

IV. LIFE APPLICATION

Procrastination Is a Loser

On March 1, 1985, the International News Network released the results of a survey taken the previous year in the United States workplace. The central conclusion focused on the finding that the average American worker wastes nine weeks a year procrastinating. Nine weeks! Just by failing to do what needs to be done at the time it should be done. Nine weeks putting off decisions or delaying actions.

Those of us who have studied leadership process know that procrastination is also one of the major time-wasters among individuals. We might call it the "Felix Syndrome," the unwillingness to make a decision even though it seems clearly obvious what that decision should be. Had the INN survey reflected a nine-week loss through illness, tardiness, or laziness, we would not have been surprised. But procrastination, though an unlikely candidate, is the real loser in both individual and corporate time.

In the latter chapters of Acts we normally associate indecision with King Agrippa, and we'll certainly see that in chapter 26. Luke paints Felix with the same brush; like Pilate, a man unwilling to decide for right, he, thereby, decides not to decide.

An old piece of verse for which I have no known source, pinpoints this acute problem of procrastination.

> He was going to be all a mortal should be—tomorrow.
> No one would ever be better than he—tomorrow.
> Each morning he stacked up the letters he'd write—tomorrow.
> Who can say what a credit he might have been—tomorrow.
> The world would have known him if only he'd seen—
>   tomorrow.
> But the fact is he died and faded from view,
> And all that was left when his living was through,
> Was a mountain of things he intended to do—tomorrow.

V. PRAYER

God, please help us to be like Paul and not like Felix. Give us the calm courage to speak the truth and to make decisions which represent righteous and godly choices.

VI. DEEPER DISCOVERIES

A. The Nazarene Sect (v. 5)

We should not be thrown off by the word *sect*; in the first century it did not contain the negative connotations we attach to it today. Remember Luke has already used the same Greek word of the Sadducees (5:17) and the Pharisees (15:5). Likely the term *Nazarene* did connect derisively to Jesus' hometown, and, therefore, it stuck to the Christians throughout the first century. The Talmud often refers to Christians in this way, and later Jewish Christian sects actually adopted the name themselves.

Bock sees it as:

> a charge of sedition. There are no witnesses brought forward. But by being called a sect, the "Nazarenes" are still seen as Jewish in origin . . . The rising foment among politically oriented Jews, who eventually produced the troublesome 'Zealot' movement, may serve as background to the charge. Christians were being compared to others who would cause Rome headaches, though it should be noted that the temple charge does not fit the picture of political zealots for Israel (Bock, 164).

B. The Missing Verse (v. 7)

In the NIV margin we read these words: "Some MSS add *and wanted to judge him according to our law.* [v. 7] *But the commander, Lysias, came and with the use of much force snatched him from our hands* [v. 8] *and ordered his accusers to come before you.*" Many commentators believe that this addition clarifies the position of Tertullus and should appear in the text. If it did, of course, the word *him* in verse 8 would then refer to Lysias, not to Paul.

Most evangelical scholars prefer the shorter text supporting the argument that manuscript evidence seems insufficient to include the additional verbiage.

C. Twelve Days (v. 11)

Luke's time references are often very helpful in the flow of the text, but at other times we're not exactly sure what he means. Polhill summarizes the quandary nicely.

> The reference to twelve days has caused interpreters no end of problems. It would seem to cover the period from his arrival in Jerusalem up to the moment he was making his defense. One can arrive at the figure simply by adding the seven days of Paul's purification (21:27) to the five days of 24:1, but other days are involved. The purification did not begin until at least the third day after his arrival in Jerusalem (cf. 21:18,26). The most likely solution is to construe the rather awkward Greek expression in v. 11 as meaning that not more than twelve days were involved in his worship in Jerusalem, thus referring to the time between his arrival in Jerusalem to his arrest. This best fits Paul's response to the charge of sedition; obviously he could not stir up many crowds after his arrest—that period was hardly germane (Polhill, 482).

D. The Way (vv. 14,22)

We keep encountering this term in Acts. Luke likes to use it in reference to the early Christians. It is very tempting to link this name with Jesus' words in John 14:6, so tempting that I am reluctant to surrender some connection with that popular self-designation by the Lord and how people described his followers in later years. Marshall, however, sees the term as designating

> the true way of worshiping and serving God, for the Christians believed that the God of their Jewish ancestors was being rightly worshiped by them. Their understanding of true religion was based on the Old Testament, which they regarded as laying down the essentials of Christian faith and practice. The church was claiming in fact that the Old Testament was a Christian book (Marshall, 377–378).

True enough, but that in itself does not seem to explain why they chose this particular name. Surely Christians did emphasize that there was only one way to the Father, one way to heaven, but it is not likely they would seize upon that specific designation just to emphasize their adherence to Old Testament Scripture.

The very common word is *hodos*. It appears 102 times in the New Testament. John used it to warn people that they should prepare for the way of the Lord (Matt. 3:3); Pharisees told Jesus that he taught the way of God in accordance with the truth (Matt. 22:16); Hebrews talks about coming to God by a new and living way (10:20); and Peter writes about the way of truth (2 Pet. 2:2). None of these passages carry the drama of this word that appears in the opening lines of Jesus' "Father message" in John 14.

> "Do not let your hearts be troubled. Trust in God; trust also in me. In my Father's house are many rooms; if it were not so, I would have told you. I am going there to prepare a place for you. And if I go and prepare a place for you, I will come back and take you to be with me that you also may be where I am. You know the way to the place where I am going." Thomas said to him, "Lord, we don't know where you are going, so how can we know the way?" Jesus answered, "I am the way and the truth and the life. No one comes to the Father except through me" (vv. 1–6).

E. The Twofold Resurrection (v. 15)

The idea of a twofold resurrection appears as early as Daniel 12:2. In the New Testament, we find it in John 5:28–29 and Revelation 20:12–15. Luke himself has already talked of it in Luke 14:13–14. The first category of resurrection refers to those who are Christ's at his coming and seems to include dead saints of the church age (1 Thess. 4:16); dead saints of Old Testament times (Dan. 12:2); and tribulation martyrs (Rev. 20:4). These different segments all constitute the first resurrection which we might call the resurrection of the righteous.

The resurrection of unsaved dead will occur before the Great White Throne judgment and results only in a sentence of death with consignment to the lake of fire (Rev. 20:11–14).

VII. TEACHING OUTLINE

A. INTRODUCTION

1. Lead Story: Hugh Latimore Before Henry III
2. Context: As we approach Acts 24, we find three types of political authority: religious (exemplified in Ananias); legal (represented by

Tertullus); and civil (Felix the governor). In that context, so obviously alien to the gospel, we also observe Paul's calm witness under stress, and the key line of the chapter, **It is concerning the resurrection of the dead that I am on trial before you today** (v. 21).

3. Transition: We can hardly imagine ourselves on trial before a civil authority, but it still happens to many Third World Christians. In this chapter Paul tells us not so much what to say, but how to say it. With dignity and clarity, we speak **about faith in Christ Jesus**.

B. COMMENTARY

1. Tertullus for the Prosecution (vv. 1–9)
   a. We Jews really appreciate Roman law (vv. 1–4)
   b. But this Christian causes riots (v. 5)
   c. And he violates the Jewish religion (vv. 6–9)
2. Paul for the Defense (vv. 10–21)
   a. My religious record is clear—no lawbreaking (vv. 10–16)
   b. My civil behavior is blameless—no riots (vv. 17–20)
   c. My personal message is the issue—Jesus is alive (v. 21)
3. Felix with the Verdict (vv. 22–27)
   a. Rest without freedom (vv. 22–23)
   b. Review of the faith (vv. 24–25a)
   c. Reaction of the judge (v. 25b)
   d. Reason for the injustice (v. 26)
   e. Refusal of a pardon (v. 27)

C. CONCLUSION: PROCRASTINATION IS A LOSER

VIII. ISSUES FOR DISCUSSION

1. What charges could opponents to God bring against you? How would you respond if you had to testify in court as to your activities for God?
2. Can you honestly say you believe and try to follow everything written in Scripture? How often do you read and study Scripture?
3. If important government officials asked you to tell them the basic truths of your faith in Christ, what kind of report would you give to them?

Acts 25

❧❧

Festus—
Foot Soldier for Rome

I. Introduction
A Freedom from Fear

II. Commentary
A verse-by-verse explanation of the chapter.

III. Conclusion
A Dead Funeral
An overview of the principles and applications from the chapter.

IV. Life Application
Worldly Values

Melding the chapter to life.

V. Prayer
Tying the chapter to life with God.

VI. Deeper Discoveries
Historical, geographical, and grammatical enrichment of the commentary.

VII. Teaching Outline
Suggested step-by-step group study of the chapter.

VIII. Issues for Discussion
Zeroing the chapter in on daily life.

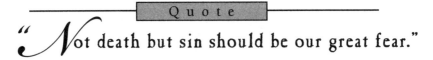

Q u o t e

"*Not* death but sin should be our great fear."

A . W . T o z e r

BIOGRAPHICAL PROFILE: PORCIUS FESTUS

- Served a two-year term as procurator of Judea
- Died from illness in A.D. 62
- Suppressed the terrorists who were active during the Felix administration
- Generally fair and totally loyal to Rome

BIOGRAPHICAL PROFILE: NERO

- Roman emperor born in A.D. 37
- First ten years of his reign were quite placid and reasonable
- Faced the apostle Paul in approximately A.D. 63
- Became a murderer of Christians as well as family members and Roman officials
- Died by suicide in the summer of A.D. 68

I N   A   N U T S H E L L

As we watch Paul slowly but intentionally make his way to Rome for the various trial experiences, we learn that to live, we need to be free of the fear of dying. The chapter opens in approximately the year A.D. 60.

Festus—Foot Soldier
for Rome

I. INTRODUCTION

A Freedom from Fear

$\mathcal{L}$es Flynn tells the story of a little girl at Camp Hope, New York, a facility which serves mentally and physically handicapped children.

> She rebelled against going to bed each night. The counselors had to struggle with her, for she would fuss and fight. When finally they asked her why she struggled so against going to bed, she explained, "I have a disease that could take my life at any moment. When I go to bed at night, I could go to sleep and never wake up. This is why I am afraid." The counselors knew she was right.
>
> A few days later she accepted Christ as her Savior. She maneuvered her wheel chair down to the front of the tabernacle to make this decision. That night, and every night thereafter, there was no struggle when she went to bed. She said to her counselor, "If I die tonight, I'll go right to be with the Lord" (Flynn, 141–42).

Throughout most of Paul's ministry, particularly during the third journey and the trial narratives, we have repeatedly observed his courage and his total absence of fear at the prospect of death. Now, with the Jews threatening death and certainly capable of making that happen back in Jerusalem, Paul continued to press without hesitation to the supreme court of Rome. In verse 11 we find him saying, **If, however, I am guilty of doing anything deserving death, I do not refuse to die.** . . . Paul, having been exonerated before Roman judges before, may well have believed that life rather than death awaited him in Rome. He may have thought that the farther away from Jerusalem he managed to get, the more secure his life would be.

Whatever his intentions, we cannot miss the basic principle here: *Paul was able to minister effectively because he had no fear of death.* Many modern Christians are paralyzed by fear of dying and, therefore, never quite experience the freedom of living. Think of the release of life it must take, the total dependence upon God, to enter a known danger area as a missionary, perhaps invade a witch doctor's tribal enclave. Hundreds of God's servants have done just that in this century—and scores of them have died in the process.

They put their total trust in God, whatever the outcome. If God chose death, they were quite prepared, like Paul, to move earlier to a heavenly home.

Let's not confuse this with some morbid striving for martyrdom. Paul showed precisely the reverse of that when he repeatedly appealed to his Roman citizenship to save himself from punishment, imprisonment, and death. The Father never asks us to stand in traffic on an interstate highway to prove that we trust him. He expects us to use God-given common sense, but at the same time acknowledge that our lives and our times rest in his hands.

God has great plans for each of his people, plans which include lives of godliness and service. To live out those plans, we must be free of the fear of dying.

II. COMMENTARY

Festus—Foot Soldier for Rome

MAIN IDEA: *When God has set his seal upon a plan for our lives, we should move single-mindedly toward that goal. For Paul, that meant testifying to the gospel in Rome.*

A Trial before Festus (vv. 1–12)

SUPPORTING IDEA: *Nothing should deter a believer from following the path of obedience which God has revealed to him.*

25:1–2. Porcius Festus wasted no time in attempting to cement relationships with the Jews. Roman procurators always had to establish a working relationship with the high priest in the Sanhedrin, or governing Judea would be a nightmare. Festus faced an even greater burden—succeeding the very unpopular Felix whose behavior toward the Jews had antagonized the local countryside for years.

Virtually unknown before his time in Judea, Festus' tenure was so short that Luke's account in Acts represents the most we know of this "foot soldier for Rome." He seems the perfect politician, quite willing to consult local authorities while trying not to offend anyone, an appropriate posture since his predecessor had just been summarily fired by Nero.

Why does Luke use "chief priests" in the plural? It may reflect the ongoing influence of Ananias, even though Ishmael, the son of Phabi, now sat in the head chair. Imagine all the local and regional matters the Sanhedrin would have had on its hands during the transition of a Roman procurator. High on that list loomed their constant nemesis—Paul—who, for two years, had languished in the prison of Herod's palace at Caesarea.

25:3–5. Will the Jews never tire of these execution plots? Whether they hoped to use Festus' inexperience against him (and against Paul), we cannot know. They were not the least bit bashful in asking for a favor from a Roman official whom they had just met; a favor linked to a murder conspiracy with which they had now become quite comfortable. In chapter 23 they had merely agreed to a murder plot presented by the Asian zealots; here they themselves apparently designed the strategy.

Festus apparently had no desire to rescue Paul; he just wanted things done decently and in order. The prisoner was already in Caesarea; he had barely had time to acquaint himself with the two major cities of his jurisdiction; he was hardly in a position to make promises to a group of religious authorities—but a man's life could be at stake.

Pure conjecture of course, but it would seem that Festus did not yet know of Paul's Roman citizenship, nor had he discussed anything with Claudius Lysias who could have told him an earful about dealing with these Jerusalem types.

25:6–9. Paul had no reason to be on trial here at all. Felix's incompetence in failing to declare an acquittal when he had no evidence to retain the prisoner now caused another trial for the apostle. Luke paints an angry picture of Jewish officials circling Paul and hurling charges, yet none of the charges could be sustained by either proof or witnesses. We assume the charges have not changed: offending the law (21:28); defiling the temple (21:28; 24:6); and planning treason against Rome (24:5). Paul denied them all (v. 8) and for the first time argued that he had not offended Caesar in any way.

Still Festus wanted to get this thing out of his hair. Doing the Jews a favor would be a good way to start his stint in Caesarea. The key words in verse 9 are **before me** which clearly suggest political compromise. If the Sanhedrin had its choice, it would have tried Paul and brought a charge of capital punishment for his desecration of law and temple. Nevertheless, getting him out of Caesarea gave them an opportunity to carry out the conspiracy mentioned earlier in the chapter. Festus thought he could mediate the situation by choosing Jerusalem as venue but presiding over the trial himself. He obviously never considered the Jews capable of a murderous ambush.

25:10–11. Things were getting shaky. One could not trust a politician in the first century, especially when the issue of favoritism kept surfacing during his early days in office. Paul had finally come to the bottom line and wanted to silence this talk about going back to Jerusalem once and for all. Let's not miss the contrast here with Jesus' trial at which he stood silent in the face of all charges. Paul was not only verbal, he became downright defiant in telling Festus that he knew **very well** that these trumped-up charges were nonsense.

Was Paul wrong because he didn't behave like Jesus? Jesus was headed for the cross, and he knew it; any discussions with Pilate or anyone else would have been futile in the Father's plan. Paul, though not afraid of dying, certainly did not have that in his plans at this point. If he would have to face a death sentence, it would have to come from a Roman court, not a frenzied Sanhedrin in their holy city. Apparently in Paul's view all other appeals had been exhausted, so he declared the Roman fifth amendment (see "Deeper Discoveries") and appealed to the emperor, an appeal reflected several more times before Acts ends (25:11–12,21,25–26; 26:32; 28:19).

25:12. All indications at this point suggested that Nero could have been a model emperor. Besides, Paul wasn't going to Nero as much as he was going to Caesar—the law, not the emperor, was the major focus here. Let's not credit Festus with any great wisdom. Once Paul had delivered his *caesaren appello* (appeal to Caesar), a provincial governor had no choice. Paul had effectively designed an end-run around Festus' authority, whether in Jerusalem or Caesarea, and whatever further delays might come in his path, he was underway for Rome.

Ⓑ Appeal to Caesar (vv. 13–22)

SUPPORTING IDEA: *The purpose of government, like the purpose of the police, is to protect and serve. As we have said so frequently, in the Roman Empire officials and their offices existed to impose the Pax Romana. Using Roman laws, Romans roads, and Roman shipping, the gospel of Jesus Christ would now make its way to the heart of the empire.*

25:13–15. Herod Agrippa II (A.D. 27–100) was still a young man the day he visited Festus. Approximately thirty-three years of age, he had become king of Chalcis in A.D. 48 and had advanced to control over Abilene, Trachonitis, Acra, Tarichea, and Tiberias. His sister Bernice was one year younger and had come to live with her brother after the death of her husband, who was also her uncle. Throughout the Roman Empire people assumed an incestuous relationship, probably an accurate analysis of the strange situation.

Herod did not rule over Judea but had been appointed by Claudius as "Curator of the Temple." He could insert or depose a high priest and also held responsibility for the temple's treasure and priestly vestments. Longenecker tells us, "Agrippa II, in fact, was looked upon by Rome as an authority on the Jewish religion. And it was for this reason that Festus broached the subject of Paul's case when Agrippa visited him" (Longenecker, 548).

25:16–22. Beginning with the first visit to Jerusalem, Festus explained to Agrippa what reads like a Roman version of the case against Paul. Luke's record was based on whatever word-of-mouth report he might have received as well as on the outcome of events. Obviously, he was not an eyewitness to this political conversation.

We find precisely what we expected because we have seen it before from the lips of Gallio and Felix. The key comes in verse 18: **When his accusers got up to speak, they did not charge him with any of the crimes I had expected**. The Jews' dispute with Paul had always been over theology, particularly interpretation of the Old Testament. At the center of it stood this **dead man named Jesus who Paul claimed was alive**. Some have accused Festus of lacking the courage to free Paul, but that would really confuse him with Felix.

The former procurator had every opportunity to acquit the prisoner in the absence of valid charges but chose not to do so. Festus had barely begun to look into the case when Paul cut him off with his appeal to Caesar. From that point on Festus had no chance to consider what he would or would not do with Paul; the matter was out of his hands.

In this casual conversation with Agrippa which existed only for informational purposes, Jesus became the center of the dispute, something lacking in earlier trial summaries. Marshall correctly observes,

> It is interesting that by this stage the question of Paul's alleged desecration of the temple has quite disappeared from sight, and the topic of the resurrection (23:6; 24:21) has replaced it. Festus talks about it as something that he fails to comprehend, and indeed it is difficult to see how it could have become a point on which to hang a criminal charge. But this is precisely the point. The real ground of dispute is that Paul preaches the resurrection of Jesus, something which the Sadducees refused to believe on principle and which the Pharisees likewise refused to believe although they admitted the fact of a final resurrection of all men. Such an opinion might be unacceptable to the Jewish leaders, but ultimately it was a matter of "questions about words and names and your own law" (18:15), and as such it could scarcely come within Roman cognizance as a ground for a criminal charge. The Jews had managed to convert their religious charge against Jesus into a political charge when they brought him before Pilate. They had not succeeded in proving it (Luke 23:4, 14, 22), but they were even less successful in the case of Paul (Marshall, 388–89).

Like the word *Christian,* we would expect the word *emperor* to appear frequently in the pages of the New Testament. After all, the entire account took place against the backdrop of Roman authority and Rome appears from the soldiers of the gospel to references to the city itself in the Book of Revelation. But the word *emperor* (*sebastos*) appears twice in this chapter, its only use in the entire New Testament. At this time Romans did not yet equate the emperor with Deity, but certainly acknowledged a high level of majesty.

Festus, in his ignorance, had stumbled over the philosophy of the resurrection which argues, "There is more to life than life." Perhaps this message never affected him, but it was precisely the testimony Paul would take to Caesar's court.

Presentation to Agrippa (vv. 23–27)

SUPPORTING IDEA: *We have repeatedly seen Paul's innocence affirmed among Roman authorities, but now that same position would be taken by a Jewish king.*

25:23. We can hardly miss the parallel between Paul standing before Herod Agrippa II and Jesus before Herod Antipas, a scene which Luke alone records (Luke 23:6–12). In each case the prisoner was first arraigned before a Roman governor and then brought before the Jewish king.

This is the longest of five defenses Luke records in Acts. Luke may have been a firsthand observer. A bona fide historian, he had already chronicled the life of Christ and may have used a first-century equivalent of a "press pass" to attend public festivities. The Romans knew all about pomp, and Agrippa had picked up a thing or two himself; so we see this high drama building though there is nothing legal at stake. These two could decide absolutely nothing about the fate of the prisoner; the whole council convened just for show and the convenience of Agrippa to hear Paul's side of the story. An interesting word for "pomp" is *fantasia*. Luke attempts here to paint a picture displaying the mood of the event. Finally, when all the robes were unfurled and the trumpets had sounded their last note, Paul was brought in.

25:24–25. In a fine piece of rhetorical exaggeration which could have been appreciated by both Romans and Greeks, Festus announced **the whole Jewish community** in Jerusalem and Caesarea wanted Paul dead. He had hardly been in office long enough to get many variant opinions on this subject, but as a Roman, he assumed that the leaders of any people (in this case the Sanhedrin) spoke for that people. Here Festus set himself up as Paul's deliverer, even though it had been necessary to stand against all the Jews in Judea. Politicians must always make an impression, always give the message that they have achieved something, preferably defending the constitution and national legal system. Again Festus declared Paul's innocence but didn't quite tell the truth in saying, **I decided to send him to Rome**; that decision did not belong to him.

The honorific term "emperor" was first conveyed on Octavian, adopted heir of Julius Caesar in 27 B.C. Nero (A.D. 54–68) added *kyrios* (lord or majesty), and the imperial court grew until the end of the Roman Empire.

25:26–27. Since Paul had broken no Roman law, what could this governor write when he sent the prisoner to Rome? We find no hint early in the chapter that he has looked to Agrippa for help on this matter, but here it comes in verse 26. To be sure, it would be unreasonable to send a prisoner to the emperor without specifying charges. It would also be dereliction of duty, incompetence, and probably cause for removal from office. Festus' conundrum had lessened, since he no longer had to deal with the Jews; but he still had to figure out what papers Roman soldiers would take to the imperial city along with this nuisance of a prisoner.

This whole ostentatious hearing reminds me of the visual hypocrisy I once saw while watching the Rose Parade on television. Usually timed to the minute, on this particular occasion America's longest and most expensive parade stopped dead. Band instruments pressed against tired lips as the players halted with a jolt. Horses were barely restrained from running into the float in front of them. The cause? Just one float in that entire parade had run out of gas and, therefore, brought the entire proceedings to a standstill. That float had been designed by the Standard Oil Company!

Up to this point Festus had been somewhat low key and reasonable, if not aggressively just, in this case. This whole charade, calculated to bring prestige to his new regime as well as impress a neighboring king, paints him as the hack politician he probably was. As Polhill puts it, "He had no charges against Paul because there were none to be found. Paul's need to make the appeal, his continued confinement, the entire situation was 'unreasonable'; and it was very much the procurator's own doing" (Polhill, 496–97).

MAIN IDEA REVIEW: *When God has set his seal upon a plan for our lives, we should move single-mindedly toward that goal. For Paul, that meant testifying to the gospel in Rome.*

III. CONCLUSION

A Dead Funeral

Burne Jones attended the funeral for Robert Browning, famous British poet. Though I have no current documentation for the quote, I have read of Jones' discomfort with the proceedings because of his familiarity with Browning's attitude toward life, an attitude reflected in so many poems. Browning as you recall once wrote,

Grow old along with me!
The best is yet to be,
The last of life, for which the first was made:
Our times are in His hand,
Who saith, "A whole I planned,
Youth shows but half; trust God: see all, nor be afraid!"
(Browning, 400)

Apparently the funeral service reflected none of that joy nor hope, and the coldness of the event disturbed Jones so deeply that he wrote,

As I sat there and listened to that dead funeral service, I thought of the intensive life of Robert Browning, who, all of his days down to his old age, was alive and young in his heart and spirit. I just wished someone would come out of the triforium with a trumpet and blast the sound, raise the dead, wake the people, and speak of victory and resurrection.

PRINCIPLES

- To live, we need to be free of the fear of dying.
- There is more to life than life.
- Christians should look to God for deliverance and support, never to the secular state, and certainly not to religious authorities.
- Politicians too often place personal power above justice and right.

APPLICATIONS

- Be careful of worldly security; for Christians it may very well be a trap.
- Expect the worst in politicians, and hold them accountable for the law you know protects you.
- Disregard worldly ostentation, and focus on Jesus whenever you have opportunity to speak in a public setting.

IV. LIFE APPLICATION

Worldly Values

Religion is not the only field which rejects brilliant representatives of its own group. In our chapter, the Jews continued to press for the execution of one of the greatest rabbis who ever taught. They had exiled him from their holy city and their religion, but that was not enough. They wanted him dead, so they would hear no more about this Messiah who died and rose again and whose death had been caused by the emotional and volatile temperaments of his own people.

In 1968, a young man earned a degree in zoology from Syracuse University. He applied to medical schools all across America and was rejected by every one. He chose to attend the University of Bologna but spent only two years on that campus before dropping out. Finally, some years after graduating from Syracuse, he earned a medical degree from the University of Utah. His name was Robert Jarvik. He used his medical brilliance to create the first permanent artificial heart and, thereby, revolutionized the way the medical community handled heart disease.

Perhaps it is not an exaggeration to think of thousands upon thousands of Christians in churches around the world who have "dropped out" of serving the Lord because they have been disappointed or perhaps even mistreated by other Christians. Often that abuse comes from superiors, even from pastors who have been commissioned by God to care for the flock.

Or perhaps we could look at the shattered lives of hundreds of pastors who, disheartened and depressed because of their abuse by church members and defenders of denominational policy, were driven out of the ministry and with crushed spirits now sell real estate or used cars.

We can deplore such a situation, and we can ask God never to allow us to be part of discouraging the life and ministry of another; but we must also watch our own lives and service. Somehow, we need to learn that Philippian joy of Paul who, as we shall see in the next chapter, took delight in his chains for they gave him such a magnificent opportunity to proclaim the message of Jesus Christ in places he could have never gone while a free man. Can the Holy Spirit give us that kind of positive outlook today? Of course; but we will have to be just as committed to Jesus and just as dependent upon God's grace as was Festus' prisoner in A.D. 60.

V. PRAYER

God, please give us greater joy in our service for you and help us thwart discouragement by casting all our problems and all the criticism of others upon you as we keep focused on our mission and ministry in the world.

VI. DEEPER DISCOVERIES

A. Rome's Fifth Amendment (v. 11)

The *Ad Caesarem Provoco* (appeal to Caesar) protected Roman citizens from mistreatment and legal hanky-panky in all parts of the empire.

Sometime after the New Testament era, Roman citizens were automatically sent to that city from all the provinces for trial. In the third century the *Ad Caesarem Provoco* was commonly allowed to everyone but slaves. Here, however, it became necessary to appeal officially for trial at the imperial court in Rome. Such an appeal was usually required only for cases that transcended normal provincial jurisdiction. The right itself dated back to almost 500 B.C. Verdicts could be appealed out of a formal court to a jury of fellow-citizens, a very Greek process. Polhill describes the transition:

> Under the empire the emperor himself became the court of appeal, replacing the former jury of peers. Although governors seem to have had the right to pass capital sentences and even to deny appeal in instances involving established laws, in cases not involving well-established precedent (*extra ordinem*) such as Paul's, the right of appeal seems to have been absolute; a procurator such as Festus would not have been in the position to deny it. Though appeal was generally made only after a verdict had been reached, Paul's appeal *before* condemnation seems to have been in order (Polhill, 491).

Conybeare and Howson suggest that Festus was probably surprised by this move and emphasize again the significance of what Paul said: "By the mere pronunciation of these potent words, 'I appeal unto Caesar,' he instantly removed his cause from the jurisdiction of the magistrate before whom he stood, and transferred it to the supreme tribunal of the Emperor at Rome" (Conybeare, 669).

The appeal to Caesar, unlike the Fifth Amendment in process, still intended the same protection for citizens against lawyers and judges who might entrap them with their own words or by means of some local interpretation of law. Certainly Paul's experience demonstrates the usefulness of understanding basic laws that apply to Christians (including such matters as taxes and donations) as well as more crucial matters of imprisonment and punishment.

B. The Herodian Clan (v. 13)

It all began with Antipiter in 47 B.C. who was somehow linked to services rendered to Julius Caesar by Hyrcanus, a high priestly ruler of Galilee, Samaria, Judea, and Perea. The connection between the two gave Antipiter the procuratorship of Judea. Before the aged Hyrcanus passed off the scene, Antipiter arranged the appointment of Herod, his second son, to the governorship of Galilee.

Antipiter was murdered in 43 B.C., the year after Caesar's assassination, and the Parthians marched west against the vulnerable eastern front of the Roman Empire. Somehow in all of this, Herod made his way via Egypt to

Rome and gained the support of both Octavian and Antony. During the thirteen years between the assassination of Caesar and the emergence of Octavian, Herod solidified his reign in Palestine and governed for thirty-four years.

Herod the Great left four sons who appear in the Gospels: Archelaus, Antipas, Philip the Tetrarch (Luke 3:1) and Herod, son of Mariamne (Matt. 14:3). The latter is of no consequence, and the royal line beginning with the original Antipiter passed from Herod the Great to Herod Antipas I (who killed John the Baptist) to Herod Agrippa I (eaten by worms in Acts 12); and now to Herod Agrippa II who conversed with Paul in Acts 26.

We should not confuse this long line of kings with the Herodian party. Andrews explains this latter group:

> The Herodians were those among the people who, though hating the Roman rule, favored the pretensions of Herod's family to kingly power . . . . In case of national independence, this family should reign rather than the House of the Maccabees, or any other claimant. They were never numerous, for the great body of the nation looked upon that family as foreigners and usurpers (Andrews, 261).

C. Did Paul Fail to Trust God?

Some have criticized Paul for constantly claiming his Roman citizenship and, on this occasion, appealing to Caesar. Why not the humble silence of Jesus? Where was the apostle who was unafraid to die, the testifier of such wonderful words in Acts 20:24? Some scholars find fault with Paul's attitude as well as his words since he defiantly refused any involvement by Festus and says, **No one has the right to hand me over to them [the Jews]. I appeal to Caesar** (v. 11).

Although the situation was considerably different, a passage in Nehemiah sheds light on the dilemma of Acts 25.

> But when Sanballat, Tobiah, the Arabs, the Ammonites and the men of Ashdod heard that the repairs to Jerusalem's walls had gone ahead and that the gaps were being closed, they were very angry. They all plotted together to come and fight against Jerusalem and stir up trouble against it. But we prayed to our God and posted a guard day and night to meet this threat (Neh. 4:7–9).

Notice the "double coverage" used by Nehemiah—we prayed to God, and we posted a guard. There was not the slightest evidence that Paul had transferred his dependence from God to Nero—that would have been a foolishness far beyond his capability. Without ceasing to pray, and still totally resting on God's grace for deliverance, Paul added to that prayer a modern "posting of the guard" by appealing to the highest Roman court.

VII. TEACHING OUTLINE

A. INTRODUCTION
1. Lead Story: A Freedom from Fear
2. Context: As we approach Acts 25, we find Paul two years older than he was at the end of chapter 24, and he has spent that two years in prison. The behavior of Felix had taken the empire closer to the Jewish wars which would explode in just eight more years and result in the destruction of Jerusalem in A.D. 70. Now a new politician has taken the governorship of Judea. Standing before Festus, Paul will finally issue his appeal to Caesar, thereby assuring a continuation of this irreversible movement to Rome.
3. Transition: As we struggle with Paul through beatings and trials, we want to see his unfailing and unflagging loyalty to the Savior. We also want to see his total dependence upon God to carry him through any difficulty along the way and ultimately produce divine results and fulfill divine promises in his life.

B. COMMENTARY
1. Trail Before Festus (vv. 1–12)
   a. Plot for murder (vv. 1–5)
   b. Politics and courts (vv. 6–9)
   c. Plea to Caesar (vv. 10–12)
2. Appeal to Caesar (vv. 13–22)
   a. Politician's dilemma (vv. 13–15)
   b. Politician's decision (vv. 16–22)
3. Presentation to Agrippa (vv. 23–27)
   a. The festive setting (v. 23)
   b. The flowery speech (vv. 24–27)

C. CONCLUSION: WORLDLY VALUES

VIII. ISSUES FOR DISCUSSION
1. If placed on trial for Christian beliefs, what kind of verdict would you face? What kind of testimony could you give for yourself?
2. If friends involved you in a dispute about a dead man named Jesus, what would you say to them?
3. What letter of recommendation could your church write for you? What specific evidence would they have to cite in the letter?

Acts 26

Apostle before a King

I. **Introduction**
Mummies or Miracles?

II. **Commentary**
A verse-by-verse explanation of the chapter.

III. **Conclusion**
Closing Rome's Arenas
An overview of the principles and applications from the chapter.

IV. **Life Application**
John R. Mott—Ambassador
Melding the chapter to life.

V. **Prayer**
Tying the chapter to life with God.

VI. **Deeper Discoveries**
Historical, geographical, and grammatical enrichment of the commentary.

VII. **Teaching Outline**
Suggested step-by-step group study of the chapter.

VIII. **Issues for Discussion**
Zeroing the chapter in on daily life.

"He is no fool who gives up what he cannot keep to gain what he cannot lose."

Jim Elliott

BIOGRAPHICAL PROFILE: HEROD AGRIPPA II

- Great-grandson of Herod the Great and son of Herod Agrippa I
- Raised in Rome at the court of Claudius
- Sided with Rome during the Jewish wars of A.D. 66–70

BIOGRAPHICAL PROFILE: BERNICE

- Younger sister of Herod Agrippa II
- Later the wife of King Polemo of Cilicia for three years
- Mistress to the Roman general Titus during the Roman war in Palestine

IN A NUTSHELL

Acts 26 contains the last and the longest of Paul's five testimony speeches. It offers the fullest exposition of the resurrection and again ends in an affirmation of Paul's innocence. This time Paul actually ends his address and gives a clear presentation of the gospel and its application.

I. INTRODUCTION

Mummies or Miracles?

The pseudoscience of cryogenics reaches new popularity each year in North America. One retired psychologist, dying of cancer, wanted his body preserved by freezing for later revival. His will included $4,200 for a steel capsule and liquid nitrogen to keep the body frozen at 200 degrees below zero centigrade. The capsule containing the frozen body remains in Phoenix in storage until cures for cancer are discovered.

Yet we have no solid evidence that higher life forms can survive freezing and thawing. This process is not even used for the preservation of individual human organs. If it were, the medical process of heart and liver transplants could be drastically revised.

Preservation of bodies, of course, is nothing new. The Egyptians mummified pharaohs and priests thousands of years ago expecting that their dead would reincarnate. At least one modern scholar, Dr. Elof Carlson, a zoologist at the University of California, believes that Egyptian hopes will find some fulfillment in another century or two. He argues, however, that the process will be *reconstitution* instead of *reincarnation*.

If future generations of geneticists can copy the genetic codes or gene patterns in the dried tissue of mummified bodies and place it in fertilized egg cells, those cells could grow into physical copies of the mummies except, of course, for memories and emotions. Carlson argues, however, that this could only be done with mummies, since the bodies of persons buried or cremated could not be reconstituted because their cells have been destroyed (Paul Lee Tan, *Encyclopedia of 7700 Illustrations,* [Rockville, Md.: Assurance Publications], 1146).

All of that would have been so much mumbo jumbo to Paul who understood quite clearly that whether a dead body is frozen, mummified, cremated, or buried and turned to dust, resurrection will restore it into a glorified body which will live forever. He argued for over twenty years that Christ was the original demonstration. This basic doctrine, the resurrection of Jesus of Nazareth, largely accounted for Paul's imprisonment and the speech to Agrippa we find in this chapter. Of course, nothing in Acts compares with 1 Corinthians 15 in detailing Paul's view of the resurrection, but his words to Agrippa represent the most thorough description of this crucial doctrine we find in Acts.

We should never forget that this book opened with the ascension of the resurrected Christ. Luke set a tone at the beginning of the first chapter which he has maintained throughout the book. When most modern preachers deal with the gospel, they talk about the cross. No believer doubts the importance of atonement and Christ's substitutionary death for all humankind. The resurrection assumes the cross. Paul had already written to the Romans, "He was delivered over to death for our sins and was raised to life for our justification" (Rom. 4:25). This heart of the gospel was the heart of Paul's testimony before Agrippa. The better we understand resurrection, particularly the resurrection of Christ, the more we understand Christ's work on earth in our behalf.

Mummies? Cryogenics? People will try to beat death as long as they have life, but only God can destroy this terrible enemy. He has already told us death will be the last enemy to go. Meanwhile, rather than devise clever human means to sustain our own lives beyond the grave, we trust in the miracle of resurrection to give us bodies infinitely superior to the ones we now possess. In them we will live with the Lord for eternity.

II. COMMENTARY

Apostle before a King

MAIN IDEA: *Paul's dedication to the message of Christ, based upon Old Testament Scripture, had caused all his troubles with the Jews. Yet Old Testament Scripture had foretold Christ's suffering and resurrection, the heart of Paul's gospel.*

A Testimony of Accusation (vv. 1–8)

SUPPORTING IDEA: *Dedication to the faith of the fathers can bring a believer into trouble with government and religious authorities.*

26:1–3. The spotlight shifted from the speech of Festus to the prisoner. Paul would soon experience the fulfillment of Jesus' promise that he would witness before kings (Acts 9:15). We have every reason to believe that Agrippa paid careful attention to what he heard. For one thing, the Romans considered him an authority on Jewish religion, and he had that reputation to maintain. Second, he had specifically asked for the privilege of hearing the prisoner (25:22). Most important, Festus had already suggested that the king had a responsibility to provide some information for the official papers to be sent to Rome along with the prisoner.

Luke tells us that Paul **began his defense**; in reality there was no ongoing trial. All official procedures in Caesarea ended with Paul's appeal to Caesar, so despite the pomp and grandeur, this hearing was quite informal. Nevertheless, Paul gained another opportunity for an *apologia*. As we learned earlier, *apologia* ("defense") stands today for a very important branch of theology called "apologetics." Its purpose is to explain and, yes, defend the foundations of the Christian faith. For Paul that foundation stood in the resurrection of Jesus.

We have understood throughout Acts that we probably do not have the entirety of any sermon Luke recorded. He has provided summaries in every case, but perhaps the length of the summary suggests the length of the original address. In this case, with an assembly gathered primarily for this purpose and no murderous Jews ready to stone him at the first opportunity, Paul would have had the leisure to develop his gospel without interruption and without time restraints. Since Luke was likely present, he could describe such minute details as Paul's hand motion, probably the outstretched arm of a Greek orator ready to deliver his address.

In formal politeness, Paul directed his remarks to the king and considered himself **fortunate** to have this opportunity. That interesting word (*makarios*) is associated with the Beatitudes of Jesus ("blessed"). Paul also suggested that he defended himself **against all the accusations of the Jews**. In fact, accusations of sedition and rioting had been dismissed (25:18), and the accusation of defiling the temple never brought forward any competent witnesses (24:18–19). That really left Paul free to deal with one central issue—that he taught against Jewish law and perverted the doctrines of the Old Testament. Few officials in the Mediterranean world would have been more competent to hear an explanation of that charge than Marcus Julius Agrippa II.

26:4–6. Reputation has always been a crucial aspect of Christian behavior. Paul went well beyond his conversion to remind Agrippa that he (Paul) was not an unknown quantity in Jewish circles. Indeed, he began his career as a high-profile Pharisee serving the Sanhedrin by persecuting and imprisoning Christians, a segment of his life which he would shortly develop in greater detail. At this point he simply wanted Agrippa to remember that he was "a Pharisee of the Pharisees." As a Pharisee, he believed in resurrection which, as Paul has stoutly maintained throughout all the trials, held center stage in this entire debate.

The point, of course, emphasized that everyone should expect a Pharisee to believe in resurrection. It should startle Agrippa and any knowledgeable Jew to find a Pharisee who did *not* believe in resurrection, so why was everybody upset because Paul treasured that doctrine so highly?

Some have argued that **my own country** and **Jerusalem** were one and the same, but this raises again the question of how early in his life Paul went to Palestine's religious center. It seems much more likely he referred first to his years in Cilicia and then Jerusalem.

26:7–8. The key word throughout these early verses is **hope**. It appears here in verses 6 and 7, but also surfaces in other trial defenses (23:6; 24:15; 28:20). In the words of Marshall, "It refers to the believing expectation that God will fulfill the promises and prophecies made in the Old Testament, and for Paul it refers specifically to the belief that these promises have been and will be fulfilled in Jesus. The question at issue is thus whether the Jews believe in the fulfillment of God's promises" (Marshall, 392–393).

Not only is resurrection a hope, it is also a promise. Some will be startled to find Paul's reference to **twelve tribes**. Some have argued only remnants from Judah and Benjamin made up the New Testament Jewish nation, but minimal evidence supports that view. Though tribal distinctions were not nearly as important as they had been in the Old Testament, the concept of twelve tribes composing the entire nation still held strong influence among the Jews in Paul's day.

So far so good. No one could quarrel with Paul's rabbinic connections, and no one could dispute that the Jewish nation as a whole prayed consistently for resurrection and redemption. Now all of a sudden Paul seemed to address the wider assembly (the word *you* is plural) and asked what looks like a rhetorical question. In light of the gathered assembly, the apostle surely intended a challenge to what they did *not* believe.

> Was he putting this question to Jews or to the mainly Gentile gathering in the chamber or to all? Perhaps it was to all. Gentiles like Festus could not comprehend the idea of resurrection at all. Except for the Sadducees, the Jews believed in resurrection, fervently hoped in it, but rejected Paul's conviction that it had begun in Christ. Ultimately, it was Christ's resurrection that Paul had in mind, and all of them—Jew and Gentile alike—found it incredible (Polhill, 500).

🅑 Testimony of Persecution (vv. 9–11)

SUPPORTING IDEA: *Sometimes it helps people understand the gospel when we explain some types of sin from which we ourselves have been delivered.*

26:9. Paul made a quick shift to proceed from general resurrection to the resurrection of Jesus. In short, he admitted that he, too, once thought the resurrection of Jesus incredible. Here again we find the name of Jesus representing his presence and power (2:38; 3:6,16; 4:10,12; 5:41).

26:10. Paul's authority as a Sanhedrin hitman came directly from religious officials appointed by Agrippa's father, Herod Agrippa I. We have clear record in Acts regarding Paul's imprisoning many, but more than one Christian put to death because of his efforts is new at this point. Surely Stephen must be included, but who were the others? Since Luke gave such press to Stephen's death, how could he have failed to mention other Christians killed during the early persecution?

Certainly it is possible Paul spoke rhetorically and metaphorically here and that words like **I cast my vote** could mean "I gave my approval." Scholars cannot agree on the meaning of this important verse, but they do acknowledge the terminology Paul uses here could indicate that he had been a member of the Supreme Sanhedrin in Jerusalem at the time of Stephen's death.

26:11. Forcing people to recant through cruelty is an established practice of brutal religion whatever its name. Authorities always do it in the name of God, but it always reflects the character of sinful fallen humanity. It hardly matters whether we find Jews beating Christians, Christians beating pagans,

Catholics beating Protestants, or Protestants beating Catholics. Cruelty has always been contrary to the spirit of Jesus! Certainly such cruelty represents one of the major failings of faith which has turned thousands away from the Scriptures in disgust. Any attempt to bring people to "truth" by torturing them clearly indicates that the persecutors themselves have long since abandoned truth.

Interestingly, Paul tells us he **tried** to force Christians to abandon the faith, indicating that he was not commonly successful. Whether his reference to **foreign cities** includes anything other than Damascus we do not know, for there his persecuting activities came to an abrupt halt.

⟨C⟩ Testimony of Confrontation (vv. 12–18)

SUPPORTING IDEA: *When God has met you in some personal way, don't be afraid to talk about it again, again, and again.*

26:12–14. Luke's threefold record of the Damascus Road experience shows its importance in his thinking as well as the verbal testimony of Paul. In this particular telling, Paul omitted details which would confuse a largely pagan audience such as the blindness and the encounter with Ananias. Today we call this *contextualization of the gospel*, but Paul was doing it two thousand years ago. It simply refers to proclaiming the message of Christ in a way that would be most understandable to any given audience. Missionaries must do this, and wise pastors practice it on a regular basis.

Here Paul emphasized the light **brighter than the sun, blazing around me and my companions**. Here we find the first textually valid mention of the **goads**. A goad is a pointed stick used to prod cattle. The reference seems to imply early convictions from Stephen's speech and quite likely, from the way he died. Others argue, however, that the goads represented the new breakthrough in his life—the light, the voice, the interruption Jesus created that day on the road to Damascus. Still others see in the goads Paul's destiny and his inability to stop the divine sovereignty pressing him toward becoming the apostle to the Gentiles. Perhaps all these can be found in the metaphor, though Greek literature of the time best supports the latter.

A look at the NIV text tells us Jesus spoke in Aramaic, but the marginal note gives the option of Hebrew. In actuality, the text says the words were heard in the Hebrew dialect. Since this was conversation and not the reading of Old Testament Scripture, this most likely suggests Aramaic.

26:15–18. Paul moved directly to the commissioning words of Jesus the Lord. What the gathered audience at Caesarea heard that day sounded very much like Old Testament prophetic calls (Ezek. 2:1,3; Jer. 1:7,8; Isa. 42:6b,7). Grammatically, this presents a most interesting paragraph. It includes a stack of infinitives: to open eyes, to turn from darkness to light, to turn from the authority of Satan to God, to receive forgiveness of sins, to receive an inheritance among those who believe in Jesus.

Furthermore, it offers an interesting array of dualities, some of them standing in stark contrast.

Get up	Stand on your feet
Appeared to you	To appoint you
As a servant	As a witness
What you have seen	What I will show you
Rescue from Jews	Rescue from Gentiles
To open their eyes	To turn them
From darkness to light	From the power of Satan to God
Receive forgiveness of sins	Receive a place among those who are sanctified

As we say on a seminary campus, "That will preach!" It may just seem like something that happened one day, but in these words of Jesus to Paul, we have the essence of a clear-cut call to proclaim the gospel. As Longenecker says, "Paul's mission was a prophetic one that perpetuated the commission originally given to God's Righteous Servant, Jesus Christ. And Christians today, as God's servants and prophets, are called to the same kind of ministry" (Longenecker, 553).

Let's not forget Luke's purpose in both his New Testament books—to proclaim the gospel of Jesus Christ. With its emphasis on conversion, forgiveness, and sanctification, this paragraph has clearly established not only Paul's call, but the message he had faithfully presented all across Asia Minor and Greece for over two decades.

Testimony of Resurrection (vv. 19–23)

SUPPORTING IDEA: *If you ever have any doubt what to say when called to defend your faith and witness the gospel, you can't go wrong by heading right for repentance and resurrection.*

26:19–21. Paul's geographical lineup sounds a bit like Acts 1:8 with the substitution of Damascus for Samaria. This basically describes the pattern of Paul's ministry—to Jews first and also to Gentiles (Rom. 1:16). His message of repentance reminds us of John the Baptist who called upon people to **prove their repentance by their deeds** (Luke 3:8). We know that Paul began in Damascus (9:19–22, 27) and went to Jerusalem (9:28, 29), but the reference to Judea needs further treatment (see "Deeper Discoveries").

Though Paul certainly held a positive view of Christian behavior as the result and demonstration of faith (Eph. 2:10; Titus 2:14; 3:8), we should not take too strongly the NIV rendition **prove their repentance**, which more literally reads "doing works worthy of repentance." Both versions have problems if they stand alone since they imply that repentance might come through works or that one is obligated to prove salvation before it is of any significant value. The whole New Testament provides a backdrop for this verse, clearly teaching that salvation comes by faith alone. Salvation founded on faith produces life change which demonstrates its fruits in daily conduct that brings glory to God.

26:22–23. Paul had been delivered more than once by Roman intervention, but he understood clearly that all help ultimately came from God. God's deliverance in the past enabled Paul to be present at Caesarea that day and proclaim the gospel to such an assembly of dignitaries. Who were the **small and great** in that audience? Perhaps rather than taking that as a reference to the greater significance of the governor and king and perhaps the five tribunes, contrasted with lesser members of the audience, we should focus on the word **alike**.

Paul's ministry knew no geographical or ethnic boundaries; he proclaimed the same gospel to all regardless of social or cultural standing. Perhaps, surrounded as he was by the royal robes of the king and the ostentatious splendor of Rome, Paul allowed himself just a moment to remember the wild peasants at Lystra who tried to make him a god.

Verse 23 leaves Jewish tradition behind and focuses specifically on the Christian gospel. The first part of the verse, though spoken in just a few words, emphasized that Christians believe that the suffering and reigning messianic passages of Old Testament prophecy refer to one and the same Christ and that Jesus himself is that Christ (Luke 24:44–49; Acts 3:18,24; 10:43; 13:15,27; 15:15; 24:14). No evidence suggests that first-century Judaism expected Messiah to suffer. The Jews of Jesus' day had no inclination to recognize Jesus of Nazareth in any messianic role.

The second part of the verse emphasizes the resurrection as the firstfruits of those who believe (1 Cor. 15:20). This resurrected Messiah would light his people and all people (Isa. 42:6; 49:6; 60:3). On this theme of the suffering servant, you may want to study further comparisons between Luke 24:44–49 and Acts 26:19–23.

E Testimony of Application (vv. 24–32)

SUPPORTING IDEA: *Never forget that when you teach, preach, or witness the gospel, specific application to your hearers forms an important part of the process.*

26:24. Festus could contain himself no longer and interrupted Paul with a shout. He had already complained earlier to Agrippa that he had no intellectual grasp of this business **about a dead man named Jesus who Paul claimed was alive** (25:19). Now to have this whole story surface again in such theological terms was too much for a thinking Roman. He didn't doubt Paul's intellectual capacity; in fact, that might have been his problem. Too much study had made him something of a religious maniac. Any sensible person in the Greco-Roman world understood that people did not rise from the dead so all this nonsense merely showed what can happen to a person who spends too much time reading the Old Testament scrolls.

26:25–27. Far from being maniacal, Paul's testimony was **true and reasonable**. He could find no value in arguing this with a Roman governor, so Paul turned immediately to the Jewish king. Paul assumed Agrippa's familiarity with the Jesus message **because it was not done in a corner**. This is one of my favorite expressions in Acts and a common Greek idiom of the day.

How often we hear people talk about the Christian faith as some kind of secret cult whose people meet in special places at special times to share their esoteric knowledge and experiences. To be sure, that kind of behavior occurs among people who call themselves Christians, but that was hardly the pattern of churches in the New Testament. In Florida they call it "government in the sunshine"—no secrets, nothing to hide, everything out in the open.

Paul didn't wait for Agrippa to respond, since he assumed his knowledge of the Christian message. So he switched the topic ever so slightly with a rhetorical question: **King Agrippa, do you believe the prophets? I know you do**. He assumes that belief in the prophets should logically bring one to Christ. Surely Paul did not suggest that Agrippa was a Christian believer. Rather Paul indicated that Agrippa honored the message of the prophets. In the words of Marshall, "At most he must be suggesting that Agrippa believed that the prophets foretold the coming of the Messiah. But the way in which Christians saw the fulfillment of the prophecies was not necessarily the way in which Jews viewed them" (Marshall, 399).

26:28–32. The Jewish king, a most astute politician, was never "almost persuaded." His response represented the only diplomatic way in which he could have addressed Paul's question, namely, with another question. He certainly couldn't have said he did not believe the prophets; that would have been an affront to the people he had been appointed to rule. To admit that he did believe the prophets in this volatile theological atmosphere would surely have led Paul to another dimension of application, an embarrassment Agrippa certainly wanted to avoid. This king had been in politics for over ten years. He wasn't about to change his religious viewpoints on the basis of one sermon in a Roman hall.

Paul's quick mind had no trouble picking up on Agrippa's response. His last word sent a direct evangelistic appeal. Agrippa's belief in a few minutes, an hour, weeks, or months was of no concern to him—the ultimate issue was that he and everyone else listening that day would eventually believe. We can see Paul holding up his chains as an object lesson, perhaps making eye contact with most of the people in the room. They had heard the message; the choice now belonged to them.

I want to weep when I picture this scene in my mind. Beaten and persecuted by Jews, ridiculed by Greeks and Romans, Paul still wanted them to accept his Savior. He certainly did not wish for them, representatives of his tormentors, to be prisoners in chains. Even at this high point of rhetorical fervor, Paul's caring heart breaks through into words. Paul probably would have proclaimed more words, but the king had heard enough and terminated the event by rising to leave. He neither considered Paul guilty of crime nor intended to become a Christian, so why listen further?

Polhill sees in Agrippa "the tragedy of the Jews in Acts." He notes, "They were God's people; the prophets were their prophets; Christ was their Messiah; his resurrection fulfilled their hopes. Still, in large part, they were not persuaded. This tragic story continued to the last chapter of Acts" (Polhill, 509). In this informal hearing—not a trial—no one could render an official verdict, nor was anyone expected to. Bernice and Agrippa agreed with what Festus had already decided—Paul had broken no Roman laws, nor any Jewish laws worthy of death or even imprisonment. Had he not appealed to Caesar, he could have been set free.

Agrippa enjoyed an interesting time; Festus prepared his report for Caesar's court; and Paul had opportunity to proclaim the gospel at greater length and with more freedom than any other formal setting in Acts. All in all, it was a good day—with one exception—Paul was still a prisoner headed for Rome.

MAIN IDEA REVIEW: *Paul's dedication to the message of Christ, based upon Old Testament Scripture, had caused all his troubles with the Jews. Yet Old Testament Scripture had foretold Christ's suffering and resurrection, the heart of Paul's gospel.*

III. CONCLUSION

Closing Rome's Arenas

The Rugby School in England was founded in 1567 through a bequest of Laurence Sheriffe. His playground gave the world the founding of rugby football in 1823, and for that the school gained fame. Five years later (1828) Rugby became one of England's leading public schools (the equivalent of an American private academy) under its headmaster Thomas Arnold, whose real-life experiences formed the basis for the character in *Tom Brown's School Days* by Thomas Hughes.

Dr. Arnold was more interested in truth than rugby. A historian by academic discipline, he once said of Christ's resurrection, "No fact of ancient history is so well attested—if it were not a miracle, no one would think of doubting it."

The basic idea of Acts 26 is Paul's gospel, and the basic idea of Paul's gospel centers in the resurrected Lord. Once again we have learned that deep involvement in religion is not enough and can even be destructive. We have also learned that God can reach into the hearts of official fanatics to bring them to faith. Through Luke's pen, Paul has told us all about repentance, atonement, and resurrection. He has set the gospel against the backdrop of one of the cruelest empires of ancient times.

We should not let the reasonably mild-mannered Festus distort the historical fact that Rome gave the world neither hospitals nor orphanages but rather crosses and arenas of death. In those arenas thousands of Christians went to be with the Lord in the years beyond this chapter. Eventually, the gospel closed the arenas and opened those missions and hospitals because ultimately truth triumphs over terror.

PRINCIPLES

- Biblical testimony centers on Scripture.
- Biblical testimony focuses on Christ.
- Biblical testimony results from God's work in your life.
- Biblical testimony always requires response.

APPLICATIONS

- Know what you will say when people call on you for reasons supporting your faith.
- Articulate your personal testimony even though it is hardly as dramatic as Paul's Damascus Road experience.
- Understand and explain repentance and resurrection often to your family, Sunday school classes, Bible study groups, and anyone who will listen.
- Let your Christian faith be known to all; don't keep your personal witness "in a corner."

IV. LIFE APPLICATION

John R. Mott, Ambassador

Born in 1865, John Raleigh Mott became general secretary of the Student YMCA in 1888 and later chairman of the Student Volunteer Movement for Foreign Missions. A world-renowned missionary statesman, he chaired the International Missionary Council in 1921 and focused his life on promoting the unity of believers and church groups.

While serving in Japan, Mott was chosen by President Calvin Coolidge to be U.S. Ambassador to that country. He responded to the president, "God has called me to be an ambassador from the courts of heaven; since that call I have been deaf to all other invitations."

Can we demonstrate that kind of allegiance to God's call on our lives? Paul certainly could. This chapter reiterates his complete allegiance to the claims of Jesus on his life and the unique ministry those claims had given him. Christians don't talk much about a "call" anymore, but passages like Acts 26 still dominate the Bible.

In the materialistic, increasingly secularistic culture of our postmodern society, the emphasis, even among Christians, seems to be on financial security and comfortable lifestyle. Forty, thirty, perhaps even twenty years ago, students would enter a Christian college eager to learn the Scriptures and quite ready to give their lives for missionary service or some other type of Christian vocation. That rarely happens today because many parents discourage it.

Talented and dedicated high school graduates head for state universities to major in business, law, pre-medicine, or some other "hot" field in which experts project a good number of high-paying jobs for years, if not decades, to come. To disturb such people with the call of Christ to live as Paul lived, and perhaps to die as Paul died, seems out of character with our *modern* world.

I remain convinced that if genuine revival is ever to embrace America, two things will have to change. First, Christians will have to pay much more attention to their Bibles, studying and reading them with a fervor virtually unknown in today's selfish times. Second, sensitized by feeding upon God's Word, Christians of all ages must offer themselves to do whatever God has called and gifted them to do, whether a lifetime of service in some remote foreign field or the use of one's business as a marketplace ministry, a public pulpit for the proclamation of the gospel.

V. PRAYER

God, revive us again; break through our stubborn selfishness; disturb our lifeless lethargy; and give us the conviction and fervor of Paul—with or without his chains. Amen.

VI. DEEPER DISCOVERIES

A. Resurrection in the Old Testament (vv. 7–8)

Repeatedly in Acts the apostles and others equate their understanding of Jesus' resurrection with the prophets' promise of resurrection. Rarely do they expound upon that. It may be worth our while to take a look at some of those texts. In the Old Testament David elaborated resurrection hope (Ps. 16:9–11;

cf. 49:15; 73:24). Some of the most poignant resurrection passages appear in Job.

"I know that my Redeemer lives, and that in the end he will stand upon the earth. And after my skin has been destroyed, yet in my flesh I will see God; I myself will see him with my own eyes—I, and not another. How my heart yearns within me!" (Job 19:25–27).

The prophets, particularly after 750 B.C., emphasized resurrection. One of the clearest passages occurs in Isaiah 26:19: "But your dead will live; their bodies will rise. You who dwell in the dust, wake up and shout for joy. Your dew is like the dew of the morning; the earth will give birth to her dead." In 536 B.C. Daniel wrote, "Multitudes who sleep in the dust of the earth will awake: some to everlasting life, others to shame and everlasting contempt" (Dan. 12:2). In the words of J. Barton Payne, "God's . . . grace will thus not rest until His testamental promise of reconciliation has become effective in the restoration of all His saints, made glorious both in soul and in body" (Payne, 462).

B. "In all Judea" (v. 20)

Bible scholars find this phrase out of sync with the rest of verse 20 and an unusual description that seems to conflict with evidence in Acts 9:20–30 and Galatians 1:18–24. Even a conservative scholar like Longenecker suggests, "'and in all Judea' was an early gloss that entered the text through a false reading of Romans 15:19" (Longenecker, 553). Marshall complains, "It does not fit grammatically into the sentence (the other phrases are in the dative case, while this one is in the accusative), nor does its content correspond with the earlier description of Paul's activity in Acts . . . .. It seems probable that the text is corrupt" (Marshall, 397). Polhill adds, "There is no mention of a larger witness of Paul 'in all Judea.' There are grammatical and textual problems with this reading, and it may well be that the text originally referred to Paul's preaching 'in every region among both Jews and Gentiles'" (Polhill, 504).

It would seem we have only two options here—either accept the conclusions of the scholars that the text represents some later additions or subtractions, or decide that Paul here describes a time of ministry in Judea not mentioned anywhere else in Scripture.

C. "Almost Persuaded"?

Older Christians have been singing it for years. The words and music by Philip P. Bliss (1838–1876) are based on the King James Version text of Acts 26:28: "Almost thou persuadest me to be a Christian." The translation gives the impression of an eager Agrippa, on the verge of trusting Christ but held back by the trappings of royalty or perhaps the alien surroundings of a Roman hall. From those words Bliss created a song that has surely been sung tens of thousands of times as an invitation hymn at the end of an evangelistic service.

"Almost persuaded" now to believe;
"Almost persuaded" Christ to receive:
Seems now some soul to say,
"Go, Spirit, go Thy way,
Some more convenient day
On Thee I'll call."

Poignant words and quite possibly used by God many times to bring people to faith or at least to promote that last step of action based on the proper presentation of the gospel from Scripture. Neither the song nor the familiar rendering of the verse fit the text itself. The Greek spoils many good sermons on Acts 26:28 and throws cold water on Bliss's persistent song. To be sure, many people do come to the point which the song describes—but Agrippa was not one of them.

E. Could Paul Have Withdrawn His Appeal?

This is what we wonder as we close Acts 26. Since Paul had done nothing to deserve death or imprisonment, since both a Roman governor and a Jewish king agreed he was not guilty, why not let that verdict set aside Paul's appeal to Caesar? Marshall suggests, "In strict law, according to Sherwin-White (p. 65), acquittal at this stage would have been possible, but 'to have acquitted him despite the appeal would have been to offend both the emperor and the province'" (Marshall, 401).

From everything we know about Roman law at that time, provincial governors had the authority to set a prisoner free even after that prisoner had appealed to Caesar. If Paul's case had dealt with robbery or sedition and he had been proved not guilty, that conclusion would have been more likely. However, the cloud hanging over this former rabbi had strong political implications, at least the way the Jews told the story. The safest thing for a fledgling procurator would be to "send it downtown."

All this may very well be moot. Luke does not tell us whether Paul would have wanted his appeal revoked or whether, by this time, he had so set his face toward Rome that he intended to ride that appeal right into Caesar's court. Perhaps a bit of both played a role in the outcome of this situation.

VII. TEACHING OUTLINE

A. INTRODUCTION
1. Lead Story: Mummies or Miracles?
2. Context: In Acts 26 the Christian message is set before high-powered authorities of both Romans and Jews. However, it is very unlike Paul's speech on the Areopagus before Greek intellectuals and centers precisely on the Christian gospel. Paul argues that a message of repentance and resurrection got him into trouble in the first place

and explains, from the beginning, how God called him to be a Christian and what God told him to say.

3. Transition: As we look into this chapter, we see Paul's testimony one more time. We feel the beat of his heart as he talks again about the Damascus Road and explains the Christian message of repentance and forgiveness because of the resurrection. As the chapter ends, we notice how difficult it is to convince high-powered people, dependent upon their authority and wealth in life, to accept the humble claims of a suffering Messiah.

B.   COMMENTARY
1. Testimony of Accusation (vv. 1–8)
   a. Formal introduction (vv. 1–3)
   b. Personal history (vv. 4–6)
   c. Central issue (vv. 7–8)
2. Testimony of Persecution (vv. 9–11)
3. Testimony of Confrontation (vv. 12–18)
   a. The light from heaven (v. 12–13)
   b. The voice from heaven (vv. 14–18)
4. Testimony of Resurrection (vv. 19–23)
   a. Preaching repentance caused my problems (vv. 19–21)
   b. Trusting in God brought about my deliverance (vv. 22–23)
5. Testimony of Application (vv. 24–32)
   a. Pagan rejection (vv. 24–27)
   b. Religious rejection (vv. 28–32)

C.   CONCLUSION: JOHN R. MOTT—AMBASSADOR

VIII. ISSUES FOR DISCUSSION

1. Recall the religious experiences you had as a child. Who are the people responsible for leading you to know Christ? Have you been faithful to the heritage they gave you? Why? Why not?
2. How would you answer Paul's question, "Why should any of you consider it incredible that God raises the dead?"
3. What experience with God has had the most influence on your life? How has that experience affected your life? How would your life be different if you had not had that experience?

Acts 27

❦

Mediterranean Cruise

I. **Introduction**
Sailboat Disaster

II. **Commentary**
A verse-by-verse explanation of the chapter.

III. **Conclusion**
The Oxygen of the Spirit
An overview of the principles and applications from the chapter.

IV. **Life Application**
"Thy Sea Is Great; Our Boats Are Small."
Melding the chapter to life.

V. **Prayer**
Tying the chapter to life with God.

VI. **Deeper Discoveries**
Historical, geographical, and grammatical enrichment of the commentary.

VII. **Teaching Outline**
Suggested step-by-step group study of the chapter.

VIII. **Issues for Discussion**
Zeroing the chapter in on daily life.

❦

Q u o t e

*E*ternal Father, strong to save,
whose arm has bound the restless wave,
who bid'st the mighty ocean deep,
its own appointed limits keep;
Oh hear us when we cry to Thee
for those in peril on the sea."

W i l l i a m   W h i t i n g

GEOGRAPHICAL PROFILE: CRETE

- A Mediterranean island located just southwest of Rhodes
  Approximately 156 miles long and from 7 to 30 miles wide
- A large Jewish colony was established here around 140 B.C.

BIOGRAPHICAL PROFILE: ARISTARCHUS

- His name means "the best ruler"
- A Macedonian from Thessalonica
- One of Paul's traveling companions
- Paul's fellow-prisoner for the sake of the gospel

I N   A   N U T S H E L L

*A*cts 27 describes Paul's sea voyage to Rome, especially the storm-caused shipwreck that God predicted and in which God prevented the loss of human life. The chapter centers on the sovereignty of God in the life of Paul. We probably find the key in verse 24 where an angel spoke to Paul and said, **Do not be afraid, Paul. You must stand trial before Caesar; and God has graciously given you the lives of all who sail with you.**

Mediterranean Cruise

I. INTRODUCTION

Sailboat Disaster

We laugh about it now, but it wasn't funny at the time. Shortly after our daughter married, our son-in-law gave me his old Sunfish sailboat. We never quite figured out whether he didn't have any place to keep it or he considered it something of a reverse dowry. We live near a large lake, and he took me out one day for a training session, showing me all the various parts of the fourteen-foot craft, including how to "right it" in the water should it overturn.

Sometime after that I took my very hesitant wife on the boat which I, amateur that I was, had loaded with our sandals, a half-gallon jug of iced tea, suntan lotion, and assorted other picnic-type items. That warm summer day, a prevailing south wind kept driving us toward the northern part of the lake. Despite all my best efforts to tack against the wind and reposition the boat, I could make no headway whatsoever. In the process, however, I managed to flip the boat five times, losing everything we had on board. Four of those times I actually pulled it back up, but the last time, thoroughly exhausted, I was unable to right the boat.

After much thrashing about, we managed to pull it with us into a cluster of trees still growing up through the water in the man-made reservoir. From that humble perch, I flagged down a passing motorboat who towed us both, one embarrassed, one angry, back to land. As you can imagine, it was weeks before my wife set foot on that sailboat again.

The point of this miniature "shipwreck" story is that we found ourselves totally helpless, stranded about a half mile from shore at a point in the lake where we could see neither houses nor people. We were totally dependent upon someone else to rescue us from the water.

That's the basic spiritual lesson in Acts 27. Humanity flounders helplessly; and without God, hopelessly. Jesus had already told Paul he would witness in Rome (23:11). Here the apostle received a reaffirmation of that promise in a frightening, life-threatening situation. That's the way we live our lives, though not always in physical danger. So many struggles, so many decisions leave us both helpless and hopeless. In those lonely hours we throw ourselves upon God's sovereignty and trust his providence to provide whatever rescue we need.

II. COMMENTARY

Mediterranean Cruise

MAIN IDEA: *Cruising on ancient ships was rather like human life—sometimes slow, sometimes calm, sometimes dangerous, and even disastrous—but always full of surprises.*

A The Ship (vv. 1–12)

SUPPORTING IDEA: *The believer may have a word from God but still not be able to determine the course of action that affects his life.*

27:1–2. Here the fourth "we" section of Acts appears, indicating Luke accompanied Paul across the Mediterranean and could, therefore, give us an eyewitness report. The expedition was under the command of Centurion Julius of the Imperial Regiment, a group particularly useful to Caesar in times of military intrigue.

Their ship sailed from Adramyttium, a harbor on the west coast of Asia Minor, just southeast of Troas. Obviously, Paul's party boarded the ship at Caesarea. Aristarchus, **a Macedonian from Thessalonica**, was part of the party. Paul mentions him in Colossians 4:10 and Philemon 24. We should probably think of him as a member of the missionary team, though surely he appeared to Julius and his troops as Paul's servant. It would not be unusual for a well-educated Roman citizen, even one being sent to Rome as a prisoner, to travel with his friends, perhaps even a personal physician.

27:3. Their first stop lay seventy nautical miles north of Caesarea, the old Phoenician port of Sidon. While the crew took care of the cargo, Paul visited Christians in that town. Perhaps the Sidonian church was founded by the scattered Hellenists (11:19).

Julius behaved much like Lysias in Jerusalem, a thoroughly professional officer with a tendency toward kindness when it seemed warranted. The word **needs** surely refers to food and other items Paul's party may have required on board. I use the word *cruise* jokingly in the title; on these Spartan ships it was every passenger for himself.

We find **friends** interesting, since Paul had never been to Sidon. Some suggest Christians commonly used this term of themselves (3 John 14), based on the disciples' experience with Jesus (Luke 12:4; John 11:11; 15:13–15).

27:4–5. Luke had been on enough voyages with Paul to pick up some sailor talk, so he tells us that they **passed to the lee of Cyprus** which means they stayed close to the long east coast of the island because of westerly winds. Two-and-a-half years earlier, Paul's ship had sailed with that prevailing west wind to Tyre, passing Cyprus on the south. This time tacking would have been important (directing a ship first starboard and then port so that one does not try to sail directly into the wind); protecting the vessel by using Cyprus as a shield made a lot of sense. Most experts agree that the voyage from Cyprus to Myra could well have taken about fifteen days and covered over four hundred nautical miles.

In the first century, Myra had become an increasingly popular port (particularly for grain ships sailing from Alexandria to Rome). It would have been impossible to set a direct northwesterly course for that important commercial journey, so a 90-degree angle at Myra had become a popular pattern. Longenecker tells us that Myra "was the most illustrious city in Lycia, with distinguished public buildings, a very large theater, and many evidences of wealth" (Longenecker, 558).

27:6–8. Apparently an Alexandrian grain ship was available, so Julius transferred his party on board. Polhill describes the type of vessel.

> Such ships seemed to have been privately owned and leased by the Roman government. Adequate supply of grain was absolutely essential to the stability of the empire and seems to have been closely regulated by the state. Grain ships were usually quite large, sometimes in excess of a thousand tons and over a hundred feet in length (Polhill, 517).

Regardless of its size, the ship was no match for Mediterranean weather. With difficulty, it reached the Asiatic coastal city of Cnidus, another 130 miles from Myra. There the west winds would not allow the pilot to make port, so they headed south for the safety of Crete and hugged its southern coast until they reached Fair Havens, just about the center of the 160-mile long island. The normal route for an Alexandrian grain ship would have taken them across the northern coast of Crete, but this ship was apparently fighting for its life already and probably thrilled to make port at Fair Havens, the modern-day town of Limeonas Kalous. Twice Luke has used the word **lee** which does not mean left or right, north or south, but a position which offers shelter from a prevailing wind.

27:9–10. Up to now Luke has given us meticulous geographical detail so that we can reconstruct the journey on an ancient map. Now he drops in a time reference to tell us winter was rapidly approaching. By **Fast** Luke refers to the Day of Atonement (*Yom Kippur*) sometime toward the end of September or the beginning of October of either A.D. 59 or 60. The ship had lost precious time struggling from Myra to Fair Havens, so it seemed impossible to cross the open sea for Italy and arrive there before winter. Longenecker is quite precise in describing the problem: "Navigation in this part of the Mediterranean was always dangerous after 14 September and was considered impossible after 11 November" (Longenecker, 559).

Paul was a seasoned traveler in these waters, though he had not yet seen anything like the late fall Mediterranean between Crete and Italy. Nevertheless, he felt compelled to give the others his viewpoint and predicted disaster if they sailed any farther. We should understand that Paul did not pretend to be a nautical genius; he merely based his viewpoint on what all knowledgeable people in the Mediterranean world understood as the shipping patterns and dangers of that threatening body of water.

We wonder, to whom might Paul have addressed this remark? Since verse 10 begins with a plural, we assume it was not just the centurion alone. Perhaps by this time Paul's wisdom had become obvious, so that both officers and sailors listened to him.

27:11–12. If this council, either formal or informal, was intended to convince the centurion of the best decision, we can hardly fault him for following **the advice of the pilot** instead of the opinions of a prisoner. In 1 Corinthians 12:28 Paul used **pilot** (*kubernete*) to describe the gift of administration. The pilot (or captain) would have been in charge of all navigational decisions, though in this particular case the **owner of the ship** happened to be on board. We can certainly see why he would press for a tighter schedule for reasons of commercial profit. Even he did not favor going on to Rome, but **the majority decided** to head for Phoenix, a larger and safer port about forty miles west.

Scholars have mused over Luke's description of the harbor at Phoenix, **facing both southwest and northwest**. Most agree he describes modern Phineka Bay on the west side of Cape Mouros. We can picture it as a half-moon harbor with entrance from the west and, therefore, shelter from strong northeast winds. Up to this point the ship's problem had come from westerly winds, but that was about to change very quickly.

🅱 The Storm (vv. 13–26)

SUPPORTING IDEA: *In the face of disaster, when all hope is gone, trust in the promises of God.*

27:13–15. At first the plan seemed solid. With a gentle south wind the ship edged along the coast making its way west to Phoenix. **Before very long** a "**northeaster**" hit them from over the top of the island and simply took over the ship. Different places call such storm winds different things. In Texas we keep an eye on the northwest sky for a "blue norther" during which the skies turn a frightening dark purple and the temperature can plummet fifty degrees in an hour or two. In the Pacific it's a typhoon; in the Atlantic or Gulf of Mexico, a hurricane. Here it was *Euroquilo*, derived from the Greek word for "east wind" and the Latin word for "north wind." They intended to head ever so carefully northwest, but with *Euroquilo* behind them they could only let the ship drift southwest toward the African coastal city of Cyrene. Though we cannot be sure, by his words **we gave way to it**, Luke may mean they trimmed all sails but the foresail which would have been essential to steer the boat away from the coast of Africa.

27:16–17. Having survived this storm, Luke would enjoy every minute telling about it. The small island of Cauda lay about twenty-three miles from Crete. The ship passed **to the lee**, meaning the sheltered east and south side of the island. The large commercial vessel would have towed a small boat which apparently interfered with its progress and had to be taken on board. Not only that, but the sailors actually tied up the ship with ropes to keep it from being shattered to pieces by the storm.

The next step was to lower **the sea anchor**, though the Greek word *skeuos* could be translated "equipment," a possible reference to any kind of rigging. Nevertheless, they did this because they feared the sand bars of Syrtis, still hundreds of miles away but clearly in the path they believed the wind was pushing them. Syrtis represents a long stretch of desolate banks along the northern Africa coast near Tunis and Tripoli. By lowering the anchor, they would have slowed their progress lest this violent wind blow them all the way to those dreaded shoals.

27:18–20. The next two weeks (v. 27) must have been hell on water. They saw no light by day or night. Despite every effort to save the ship, **we finally gave up all hope of being saved**. In good nautical tradition they jettisoned their cargo, or at least part of it (v. 38). The third day out, **they threw the ship's tackle overboard with their own hands**. We can debate what **tackle** means; but since it translates precisely the same Greek word as **anchor**, we are back to the broad English term *equipment* and have to assume they threw over whatever they could spare to lighten the load.

With their own hands fascinates us since, presumably, in the first century they would have had no other way to do it. Ramsay takes a slightly different manuscript reading and substitutes "we" where the NIV offers "they." Nevertheless, his description is worth reading.

> The sailors threw overboard part of the cargo; and the passengers and supernumeraries, in eager anxiety to do something, threw overboard whatever moveables they found, which was of little or no practical use, but they were eager to do something. This makes a striking picture of growing panic; but the third person, which appears in the great MSS., is ineffective, and makes no climax (Ramsay, 332).

27:21–22. Doubtless they retained food on board, but in such a storm, who could eat? Furthermore, they had rushed from one end of the ship to the other with ropes, hooks, and boxes—sleeping and eating were the least of their worries during those awful two weeks. Let no one claim the Bible paints its characters with too holy a brush. All of a sudden a very human prisoner shows up on deck to tell the crew, "I told you so." Probably the last thing they needed at that point was a missionary rabbi nagging, "If you had only listened to me." He had earlier warned them that there would be loss **to our own lives also**; now he changed that threat in view of the heavenly message he had received the night before. For this reason we are perhaps best advised not to take Paul's words in verse 10 as a prophecy but merely his usual habit of giving advice whenever and wherever he thought people could use it.

27:23–26. Here's the heart of the chapter. We will discuss Luke's extensive nautical narrative in "Deeper Discoveries," but here we need to see the light of heaven shining on a dark and driven ship and on its lost and lonely passengers. Paul already knew he would make it through (23:11). Like Abraham interceding for Sodom, Paul likely pleaded with God to save the lives of his traveling companions. Now, presumably in response to his prayers for his traveling companions, he reports the angel's message: **God has graciously given you the lives of all who sail with you.**

Doubtless many gods had received repeated appeals during that two weeks; in a situation like this, the most calloused pagan can all of a sudden find words addressed to some kind of deity who might intervene in a time of obvious disaster. Only one God answered! The angelic messenger was quite precise—they would not only be saved, but the ship would **run aground on some island.**

How poignant Paul's words as he referred to **the God whose I am and whom I serve.** What a strong and solid witness at a frightening moment in a terrifying place. Disaster will turn to deliverance, and hopelessness to hope, because of God. I cannot resist the comparison with the Jonah narrative of the Old Testament—God's servant in a small minority on a pagan ship facing the fury of a storm. In Jonah's case the storm's cause was the prophet; in this story the missionary brought salvation.

Luke records no response to Paul's promise. Had the men cheered or fallen on their knees on the deck to worship Paul's God, we can be sure Luke would have told us. Instead, they would wait to see whether this promise of hope had any substance.

C The Shipwreck (vv. 27–44)

SUPPORTING IDEA: *The true anchors in any storm—physical, emotional, or spiritual—can only be found in faith, hope, prayer, and the sovereignty of God.*

27:27–29. Luke confuses us just a bit by referring to **the Adriatic Sea** when undoubtedly Paul's ship moved across the Mediterranean. They sailed on the Sea of Adria, a first-century reference to the north central Mediterranean between Crete and Malta. Today we use the term "Adriatic Sea" to describe water between the eastern coast of Italy and what has become Bosnia Herzegovina.

At midnight on the fourteenth day seasoned sailors sensed land, perhaps from the sound of the surf, a change in the winds, or some other such indication. Checking the water's depth, they found Paul's words about running aground could very well come to pass so **they dropped four anchors from the stern and prayed for daylight**. The anchors would likely have been stones or perhaps lead weights; ancient vessels carried multiple anchors, and this ship surely had more than four.

> Anchoring by the stern was unusual; but in their situation it had great advantages. Had they anchored by the bow, the ship would have swung around from the wind; and, when afterwards they wished to run her ashore, it would have been far harder to manage her when lying with her prow pointing to the wind and away from the shore. But, as they were, they had merely to cut the cables, unlash the rudders, and put up a little foresail (v. 40); and they had the ship at once under command to beach her at any spot they might select (Ramsay, 335).

27:30–32. Obviously, the sailors' faith in their gods was insufficient. Contrary to the law of the sea, they tried to escape, leaving all their passengers to face the storm's fury. If Ramsay is right when he suggests that anchoring the stern was the only move that made any sense in this situation, even a nautical layman like Paul could figure out they were up to no good when they pretended to drop anchors from the bow. Had they succeeded, all experienced hands who could beach the ship (the storm had not abated) would be gone, leaving only soldiers and passengers—and without a dinghy.

Why did Paul say it was necessary for them to stay on board? If God had promised to deliver all lives, what did it matter who took the dinghy and who stayed on board the main ship? Perhaps we best conclude that God had included this word in the angel's message, or perhaps Paul simply applied common sense to the situation he saw developing.

It would appear that the soldiers acted a bit impetuously in cutting away the lifeboat which could have been used to ferry passengers ashore in the morning. Certainly posting a guard for the remaining hours of the night would have accomplished the intended purpose more effectively. We can hardly be critical and picky about the behavior of men who had been battered for two weeks by such a storm. Quite possibly, the angry centurion shouted at the nearest soldier to pull his sword and cut the ropes. In any case, they were now all "in the same boat."

27:33–38. Twice Paul had been right and had emerged as the leader of the group. Hard work awaited daylight's appearing for these men who had been starving themselves for days. Marshall indicates they may have been fasting, but there is no such suggestion in the text. Seasickness along with frenetic busyness seem to provide better reasons for their failure to eat.

Paul had already told them about his God. Now he offered a visible demonstration, doubtless an audible prayer to the sovereign Lord of Creation, surely including thanks for deliverance as well as for the food. We are reminded of Luke 9:10–17 and 22:19 as we watch the serenity of the moment, a stark contrast to the confusion and hyperactivity of the past two weeks. Polhill describes it well:

> The breaking of bread and giving of thanks was the customary Jewish form of blessing a meal, and Jesus was observing that custom in the Lord's Supper. Paul also was observing that custom and in the presence of a predominantly pagan group. It was scarcely a eucharistic celebration. . . . In short, the eucharistic language of the meal on the ship may not be so much an indication that they celebrated the Lord's Supper there as that Paul and the other Christians were reminded of how Jesus broke bread with his disciples and continues to do so, continues to be present in the lives of his people. The meal thus had a meaning for them it could not have had for the pagans— their lord continued to be present with them. He was present in that time of particular need. For them the meal was more than needed sustenance—it reassured them of their Lord's presence to deliver them (Polhill, 527).

Do you feel embarrassed bowing your head to thank God for food in a public restaurant? Don't. Just think about Paul off the coast of Malta.

All of a sudden Luke counted heads; perhaps he was involved in the food distribution, and the number of passengers only became important at this point. At any rate, we discover 276 witnesses to the veracity of Paul's prophecies. Everyone took care of his hunger; everyone seemed content that deliverance lay ahead. They took the final step to make land, increasing the draft by throwing the rest of the grain into the sea.

27:39–41. We have no question what happened in this paragraph, for Luke tells it in amazing detail. They didn't know where they were, but they saw a place to run the ship onto the beach. Picture them cutting loose the anchors, lifting the rudders, and heading straight in. Remember, the storm was still blowing, so the bow of the ship aimed southwest when it hit an unseen sandbar and wedged fast. Now, rather than being blown ahead across water, the ship absorbed the winds from behind and the pounding of the surf around. Slowly it fell apart. While the ship was drifting, the rudders had been tied up. Now the sailors needed to steer for the sandy beach they had chosen, so they untied those ropes. Tourists today can visit St. Paul's Bay on the northeast coast of Malta, though not everyone agrees it is the designated spot where Paul's ship actually ran aground.

27:42–44. We should have no trouble at all picturing frantic men rushing to the bow, scrambling down rope ladders, or perhaps even diving into the surf. Remember the Philippian jailer (Acts 16)? With prisoners besides Paul on board, Roman soldiers knew their duty. Julius protected him, however—yet another intervention by a Roman centurion in Paul's life. Some swam to shore, some floated on pieces of wood, and **in this way everyone reached land in safety**.

Surely Luke intends us to see throughout this chapter that God's sovereign providence governed every specific detail of this voyage. The safe deliverance of all lives came only through obeying him and listening to the words of his servant. That servant, like all true servants of the Lord to the present hour, knew how to practice the presence of Christ, especially under the pressure of crisis. I like the way Morgan puts it: "Here is the secret. Here was a man on two ships, one after the other, in storms, in stress and danger, with howling winds and creaking timbers and rending ropes and buffeting waves. Why was he quiet? Because the Lord was with him, and he knew it" (Morgan, 534).

MAIN IDEA REVIEW: *Cruising on ancient ships was rather like human life—sometimes slow, sometimes calm, sometimes dangerous, and even disastrous—but always full of surprises.*

III. CONCLUSION

The Oxygen of the Spirit

Though I have been down in several abandoned mines, I have never visited a working mine and, thank God, certainly never been trapped in one. I understand, however, that trapped miners need just two things to survive: hope and oxygen. Without oxygen they will be physically dead in minutes; without hope, they may last longer, but their spirits will eventually give up, perhaps before struggling rescuers can get to them. To put it another way, *hope is the oxygen of the spirit.*

This chapter is about hope. We have seen Paul preaching, but this is not a passage about sermons. We have seen Paul defending the faith, but Paul had no time for eloquent apologetics on board this ship. We have seen Paul before the Sanhedrin, but pagans surrounded him here. We have seen Paul in prison, but here he faced the potential of almost instant death.

Luke has given us this wonderful chapter to show a sovereign God still in control of the wind and the waves he had created millennia before. His divine sovereignty, his total providence engineered the deliverance not only of Paul and his party, but more than 270 others. We cannot leave Acts 27 without visiting again those wonderful verses tucked right into the middle of the chapter.

> But now I urge you to keep up your courage, because not one of you will be lost; only the ship will be destroyed. Last night an angel of the God whose I am and whom I serve stood beside me and said, "Do not be afraid, Paul. You must stand trial before Caesar; and God has graciously given you the lives of all who sail with you." So keep up your courage, men, for I have faith in God that it will happen just as he told me (vv. 22–25).

PRINCIPLES

- Christians know disaster is coming in this world.
- There may be hope for individuals along the way, but for society only at the second coming of Jesus Christ.
- Your safety depends on the strength of your anchor.
- Christians are a universal family of friends.

APPLICATIONS

- Don't make rash decisions and then expect God to bail you out.
- Never give up hope.
- Remember God's personal concern for his children.

IV. LIFE APPLICATION

"Thy Sea Is Great; Our Boats Are Small"

Certainly we must see in this chapter God's capacity to deliver his children from danger and death. In a broader sense, can we not see our lives as the swirling Mediterranean—sometimes calm, often stormy; sometimes directed, often confused? Three things surface beyond question in this shipwreck narrative:

1. God's personal concern for his children.

2. God's powerful capacity to deliver his children.
3. God's purposeful claim upon his children.

We see physical living out of magnificent spiritual truth recorded by Paul in his letter to the church at Rome: "And we know that in all things God works for the good of those who love him, who have been called according to his purpose" (Rom. 8:28).

Henry Van Dyke (1852–1933) was an American Presbyterian clergyman, educator, and poet. His book of collected poems released in 1911 included the following reflection so appropriate to Paul's voyage and to our lives.

> Oh Maker of the mighty deep
> Whereon our vessels fare,
> Above our life's adventure keep
> Thy faithful watch and care.
> In Thee we trust, whate'er befall;
> Thy sea is great; our boats are small.
> We know not where the secret tides
> Will help us or delay
> Nor where the lurking tempest tides,
> Nor where the fogs are gray.
> We trust in Thee, whate'er befall,
> Thy sea is great; our boats are small.
> Beyond the circle of the sea,
> When voyaging is past,
> We seek our final part in Thee;
> Oh bring us home at last.
> In Thee we trust, whate'er befall;
> Thy sea is great; our boats are small.

V. PRAYER

God, thank you for delivering Paul, Luke, Aristarchus, and the others on that fateful journey across the Mediterranean. Please deliver us from the storms of our lives, and help us always to place our hope in you. Amen.

VI. DEEPER DISCOVERIES

A. Day of Atonement (v. 9)

Described in detail in Leviticus 23:26–32, the Day of Atonement (*Yom Kippur*) signifies the reconciliation between God and humanity after sin had separated (Isa. 59:2) and alienated them (Col. 1:21). The sacrifices of Leviticus 1–7 offered opportunity for fellowship but also for forgiveness.

Sinners pled the mercy of God (Ex. 34:6–9) and anticipated forgiveness based on a specified "substitute." In the Old Testament Day of Atonement they meant the sending away of the second goat (Lev. 16:20–22); in the New Covenant, we find forgiveness in the finished work of Christ. Kaiser writes,

> Therefore, the principle of Leviticus 17:11 meant that God provided this substitutionary way of dealing with sin to show humanity that they owed their lives as a forfeit for their sins against God. Hence the animal substitutes. Ultimately, animals would never effect a permanent reconciliation, so the need still remained for the perfect God-man to sacrifice his life. In the meantime, subjectively real efficacy was authoritatively provided, based on God's plan to eventually provide objective efficacy in the death of his Son (Kaiser, 296).

B. Narrative Theology

In approaching a chapter like this, we may wonder why Luke would spend so many words and describe so many details when no gospel was preached and no one came to Christ. Only when we understand the significance of narrative theology can we grasp not only this chapter, but large sections of Acts. Repeatedly we have noticed how Luke emphasizes the sovereignty of God and his providential deliverance throughout the story.

Such detail would not have concerned Jews; but Luke was writing to a Greek, and the Greeks loved the Mediterranean. Sea voyage stories abound in ancient Hellenistic literature. Greeks reading Luke's book, or even Hellenistic Jews like the author himself, would have reveled with delight in the way Luke tells the story of these last two chapters. Luke captures his intended readers and at the same time shows them God working through the life of one of his children to bring deliverance not only to that individual, but to an entire ship's roster.

Some challenge the authenticity of the story, arguing that Luke took a popular shipwreck story of his day and just added Paul's name. We have many chapters from Luke's hand to show us his concern for literary detail and geographical references. This is precisely the way he would write an eye-witness account which this claims to be. Paul is Luke's hero and is treated that way even in contrast to Paul's demeaning words about himself in some of his letters (e.g. 2 Cor. 1:9–10).

In Acts 27, Paul's confidence came not from within himself but from his trust in God who can allow his children to descend into danger or depression or both before offering them deliverance. Polhill extols the chapter:

> Luke was at his literary best in this account, building up suspense in his dramatic portrayal of the violence of the storm, the desperation of the sailors, the abandonment of all hope. But at each

point when the situation seemed most desperate, there came a word of encouragement from Paul—his God would not abandon them, take heart, eat, be of good cheer. Then final deliverance came. All were saved. Paul's God had indeed not abandoned them to the anger of the seas. One cannot miss the emphasis on the divine providence, and it is precisely through the detailed telling of the story that the lesson has its greatest impact (Polhill, 514).

VII. TEACHING OUTLINE

A. INTRODUCTION
1. Lead Story: Sailboat Disaster
2. Context: As we enter Acts 27, we encounter one of the great stories of the Bible, an account not unlike the Old Testament record of the prophet Jonah. Sea stories have always made good reading from the ancient world to our own postmodern one, and Luke gives us one of the best. We should remember two things as we study: God sent Paul to Rome under orders; and God would make sure that he arrived safely.
3. Transition: In the Mediterranean storm we see our own lives, the frustrations and fears we so often encounter in trying to make progress toward a goal. Above all we see God's personal, powerful, and purposeful sovereign control of events in our lives.

B. COMMENTARY
1. The Ship (vv. 1–12)
   a. Departure from Caesarea (vv. 1–2)
   b. Delay in Fair Havens (vv. 3–8)
   c. Decision to enter the open sea (vv. 9–12)
2. The Storm (vv. 13–26)
   a. Helpless in the hands of men (vv. 13–20)
   b. Hopeful in the hand of God (vv. 21–26)
3. The Shipwreck (vv. 27–44)
   a. Final despair (v. 27–38)
   b. First signs of delivery (vv. 39–44)

C. CONCLUSION: "THY SEA IS GREAT; OUR BOATS ARE SMALL"

VIII. ISSUES FOR DISCUSSION

1. How do you react when you find yourself a minority opinion and cannot do what you know is the right course of action?

2. In what situations have you depended on God for protection? In what ways has he provided protection for you?

3. Recall the scariest, most dangerous situation you have ever faced. What emotions did you feel? Where did you find God in the situation?

Acts 28

God's Man in Rome

I. Introduction
Island of the Barbarians

II. Commentary
A verse-by-verse explanation of the chapter.

III. Conclusion
An Unfinished Story
An overview of the principles and applications from the chapter.

IV. Life Application
When I Consider How My Light is Spent
Melding the chapter to life.

V. Prayer
Tying the chapter to life with God.

VI. Deeper Discoveries
Historical, geographical, and grammatical enrichment of the commentary.

VII. Teaching Outline
Suggested step-by-step group study of the chapter.

VIII. Issues for Discussion
Zeroing the chapter in on daily life.

CITY PROFILE: SYRACUSE

- Located on the east coast of Sicily, the most important and prosperous Greek city on the island
- Founded in 734 B.C.
- Contained two large harbors which made it an important commercial port

CITY PROFILE: RHEGIUM

- A Greek colony on the toe of Italy, founded in 712 B.C.
- Only six miles across the strait from Sicily's Massana
- A difficult harbor which required a south wind for ships to enter

CITY PROFILE: PUTEOLI

- An Italian seaport located on the Bay of Naples
- Closest harbor to the city of Rome
- Modern name is Pozzuoli

I N   A   N U T S H E L L

*A*cts 28 centers on bold proclamation as Paul finally reaches Rome after escaping a snake attack on Malta. In Rome he defends and proclaims his gospel even as a prisoner. We find the key verse at the very end of the chapter (and the book) and might literally translate it in this manner: "Preaching the kingdom of God and teaching concerning the Lord Jesus Christ with all boldness, unhindered."

I. INTRODUCTION

Island of the Barbarians

$\mathcal{E}$ighteen miles long and eight miles wide, Malta lies 58 miles south of Sicily and 180 miles northeast of the African coast. The Phoenicians had colonized it a thousand years earlier, so the language we find there in the first century was a Carthaginian dialect.

Assuming control in 218 B.C., the Romans placed a governor on the island to protect the empire's interest and supervise the population. The name Malta (Melita) meant "a place of refuge" in the Phoenician language, and it certainly became that for Paul and his traveling companions.

The NIV kindly translates **islanders**, but Luke's Greek word is *barbaroi* from which we get our English word *barbarian*. Perhaps only a Greek like Luke would have chosen that word, quite possibly because of the unfamiliar language spoken there. Ramsay says, "It does not indicate rudeness or uncivilised habits, but merely non-Greek birth; and it is difficult to imagine that a Syrian or a Jew or anyone but a Greek would have applied the name to the people of Malta, who had been in contact with Phoenicians and Romans for many centuries" (Ramsay, 343). The word itself is interesting; literary experts would call it *onomatopoetic*, a word which creates the sound it attempts to convey. To educated Greeks and Romans all strange languages sounded like bar-bar-bar, so they commonly referred to the people who spoke them as barbarians.

Many would agree that the North American continent contains many cities which serve as "islands of barbarians," not because of ethnicity or language, but because of behavior. We need not pick on the cities. A few years ago a small compound outside Waco, Texas, became an island of barbarians, and more recently Montana has captured the spotlight for the same reasons.

Police officers and psychologists alike warn us of the barbarous nature of our civilization as we change centuries. Sin runs rampant, and life holds little value to some who will kill for the slightest motive (a set of hubcaps or a pair of basketball shoes), or perhaps for no reason at all.

Less than twenty-four hours before I sat down to prepare this chapter, a four-month-old infant in Richmond, California, was dragged from a bassinet and brutally beaten by robbers who had broken into his home to steal a tricycle. The police captured three "criminals," taking into custody two eight-year-olds and a six-year-old. They charged the six-year-old with attempted murder.

We so often use the words *barbarian* and *civilization* as opposites, but some warn that we may well be a barbarian civilization. As violence escalates and safety wanes, Christians have an ever-growing responsibility to point to the only one who can bring peace to the islands of barbarism all across our continent. That's what happens in our study of Acts 28. A veteran missionary, dumped out on shore by a violent storm, brings the message of truth and hope to the island of the barbarians.

What about Malta today? It contains a population of about 335,000 and is listed in the *World Christian Encyclopedia* as 100 percent "Christian," of which 97 percent are Roman Catholic and less than 1/10th of 1 percent evangelical (pp. 479–480). Every year on February 10, the island celebrates the shipwreck of the apostle Paul.

II. COMMENTARY

God's Man in Rome

> **MAIN IDEA:** *Along with Paul, Christians have victory over sin and the world both in life and in death.*

Ⓐ Miracles on Malta (vv. 1–10)

> **SUPPORTING IDEA:** *Christ's resurrection removes our fears and gives hope for living and for dying.*

28:1–4. By now Luke has convinced us that Paul sailed under God's protection every nautical mile of this journey, and the viper incident confirms that. In fact, despite two weeks of battering and darkness, the ship was scarcely 60 or 70 miles off course, and we can imagine 276 happy people warming themselves around what must have been a very large fire.

In picking up some sticks to assist in keeping the warm blaze roaring, Paul was bitten by a snake, likely revived from its cold weather stiffness just as Paul approached the fire with his hands full of fuel. (See "Deeper Discoveries.") The local natives put immediate spiritual meaning to the event and argued that this man (Paul) had obviously only escaped the terror of the sea in order to meet death on land since **Justice has not allowed him to live**.

The capital letter at the beginning of **Justice** suggests that the natives were not talking about Paul getting his due, but referring rather to a god or goddess whom they revered. Luke uses the word *Dike*, referring to the Greek goddess of justice. Likely the Maltese had their own equivalent which, even if Luke would have inquired about it, would have been strange to the ears of Theophilus.

28:5–6. Why doesn't Paul rebuke these people as he did those at Lystra (14:15–18)? Perhaps because though they **said he was a god**, they made no attempt to worship him, so Paul shook off the incident much in the manner he had the snake. Luke's obvious point is the acquiescence of the islanders who, in reality, observed God's protection. Yes, God rescued Paul from the sea, and he had no intention of killing him on land.

28:7–10. In our day everybody wants to be number one. Here we meet a man who was. Publius served as **the chief official of the island**, literally, "the first man of the island." Presumably because of the viper incident, this Roman invited Paul's team to his home. I cannot say definitively that Luke's use of the word **us** (v. 7) referred only to Paul's immediate party, but we have some difficulty imagining 276 guests on Publius' estate even for the short span of three days.

Living with Publius was his father who suffered **from fever and dysentery**. Paul's response to the situation presents the only occasion in Acts when both prayer and laying on of hands accompanied a healing. Longenecker ponders the nature of the illness:

> The malady the father of Publius was suffering from may have been Malta Fever, which was long common in Malta, Gibraltar, and other Mediterranean locales. In 1887, its cause, the micro-organism *Micrococcus Melitensis*, was discovered and traced to the milk of Maltese goats. A vaccine for its treatment has been developed. Cases of Malta Fever are long-lasting—an average of four months, but in some cases lasting two or three years. Luke uses the plural *pyretois* ("fevers") in his description, probably with reference to the way it affects its victims with intermittent attacks (Longenecker, 565).

In verse 9, Luke recaptures his flare for hyperbole and portrays everyone on the island sick with any disease coming to be cured. Luke painted this beautiful picture, rather reminiscent of the Gospels (Luke 4:38–41), to describe general healing rather than ridding the island of all sickness and disease. Two different words for "heal" appear in verses 8 and 9, *iasato* and *therapeuo*. Whether the use of the latter term means that Luke was able to assist as a physician in some cases while Paul as an apostle healed others, we cannot be certain.

The missionaries spent three months on Malta and obviously were involved in a number of healing miracles. What of the gospel? Why no reference here to Paul's witnessing the gospel or to anyone putting faith in Christ? The only possible conclusion is that for reasons we do not know Paul did not preach and no one trusted Christ on Malta. We need to jot this down as a reminder of one of the many things we want to ask Luke when we get to heaven.

All in all, the three months at Malta seemed to be a highlight of the trip despite the way they got there. These courteous barbarians not only took care of their "guests" but furnished them with supplies for the next and final leg of their journey. Toussaint suggests that "these supplies were no doubt given in gratitude for Paul's services" (Toussaint, 429). Since that is likely the case, we see again how much Paul blessed everyone who traveled with him from Caesarea to Rome.

B Welcomes Along the Way (vv. 11–16)

SUPPORTING IDEA: *God has people everywhere, and Christians are never strangers to one another.*

28:11. The time was probably nearing February of 61 A.D. The storm had driven their ship six hundred miles west from Crete to Malta. They spent the winter months (November through January) on that island. Also on the island for those non-navigable months **was an Alexandrian ship with the figurehead of the twin gods Castor and Pollux.** Castor and Pollux were the patron saints of sailors, the Gemini, twin sons of Zeus. Ancient mariners considered seeing the Gemini constellation during a storm a good omen for the journey. Perhaps Luke used a bit of wry humor here as we picture the three Christians joking about the name as they board "the good luck ship" after the adventures described so fully in chapter 27.

28:12–13. Back in the early chapters Paul would frequently go "on the road again." Here at the end of Acts he goes "on the sea again," island-hopping on his way to Rome. The first stop after only ninety miles is Syracuse on Sicily, once called by Cicero, "the loveliest city in the empire." The home of Archimedes about 200 B.C., its strategic location and strong fortifications defied Roman onslaught for three years before they conquered it.

Finally a trip of about seventy miles landed them on Italy itself, at Rheggium on the very toe of the boot. Then they sailed on up the west coast of Italy to Puteoli, yet another 210 miles. Still 130 miles from Rome, Paul had reached the resort city on the Bay of Naples. From the sulfur springs at Puteoli, one can see Vesuvius, the mountain which erupted just seventeen years after Paul's visit.

28:14. No longer dependent on ships' schedules, Paul could spend a week with **brothers** at Puteoli before walking northwest on the *Via Domitiana* toward Rome. This seems unusual liberty for a prisoner, and perhaps we should assume a soldier was with him at all times. An ancient Jewish community existed in Puteoli, and Paul found a Christian group there as well. We should remember that Paul did not take the gospel to Rome; he found believers in Italy when he arrived.

So important was Rome in the thinking of both Paul and Luke that Luke felt it necessary to emphasize this final leg of the trip by saying essentially the same thing at the end of verse 14 and again at the beginning of verse 16. In actuality, the Greek text of verse 14 reads: "And so we came to Rome," perhaps indicating that in Luke's view, arrival at Puteoli was almost consonant with arrival at Rome itself.

28:15. Watch the text carefully here. Paul had visited for a week with **brothers** at Puteoli, but the reference to **brothers** in verse 15 describes Christians from Rome. They had walked down the famous Appian Way to meet the apostle at Three Taverns, thirty-three miles south of the imperial city. Doubtless, the believers at Puteoli had sent word ahead which prompted this welcome-wagon approach. Apparently two groups of Roman believers reached Paul. One came to **the Forum of Appius**, a rest stop along Italy's "Pennsylvania Turnpike," and another, to Three Taverns. The former group would have traveled forty-three miles to meet Paul, and the latter, thirty-three.

Only here does Luke mention Christians in Rome. They do not appear in the narrative of the rest of the chapter as Paul debates with the Jews. However, the last part of verse 15 certainly indicates that they provided prayer, encouragement, and support for Paul during his entire stay in Rome. Longenecker includes a colorful note on this stage of the journey. While walking the *Via Domitiana* between Puteoli and Neapolis, "Paul would have passed the tomb of the poet Virgil (Publius Vergilius Maro, 70–19 B.C.). The Mass of St. Paul celebrated at Mantua, Virgil's birthplace, until the fifteenth century, included this Latin poem about Paul at Virgil's tomb:

> Virgil's tomb the saint stood viewing,
> And his aged cheek bedewing,
> Fell the sympathetic tear;
> "Ah, had I but found thee living,
> What new music wert thou giving,
> Best of poets and most dear" (p. 567).

What an interesting thought. To review Virgil's human longings and suggest that Paul's gospel could provide the only final answer strikes a responsive chord in our hearts. On the one hand, we can imagine Paul rushing to Rome (though his speed would have been ultimately governed by Julius). On the other, however, we can easily picture the philosophical apostle accompanied by the inquisitive physician stopping at every monument and historic site along the way.

28:16. Acts 28:16 represents the last of the "we" sections in the book. By this time, Paul's credibility and integrity were so well established with Julius that he likely convinced Roman officials to keep him out of prison, allowing him to live privately with a good bit of freedom. Far from being a flight risk, Paul had pushed to come to Rome. Though he had something of an earlier reputation of escaping from cities at night, that would not likely be a problem at Rome.

Acts 23:11 had been fulfilled. Paul was at Rome and, for the moment, at liberty to do and say what he wished. Though the text does not tell us so, perhaps we can assume that Luke and Aristarchus stayed with Paul in Rome with Epaphras, John Mark, Demas, Timothy, and others coming and going over the next two years.

Ⓒ Jesus and the Jews (vv. 17–24)

SUPPORTING IDEA: *When God has identified a plan for ministry, we stay with it despite chains, guards, or shipwreck.*

28:17–20. Right up to the last, Paul never surrendered the pattern—first the synagogue, then the streets. Now he had considerably more "clout" and, rather than slipping into a synagogue as a guest, called the Jewish leaders of Rome together. He presented his case with special focus on the reason for his imprisonment found at the end of verse 20: **It is because of the hope of Israel that I am bound with this chain** (23:6; 24:21; 26:6–8). Note, too, that Paul was under house arrest and, therefore, unable to meet with the Jews in some place of their choosing.

The central theme of this first encounter with the Jews focused on Paul's innocence. Luke summarizes the trial narratives in just a few words, though Paul may have carried out this lengthy explanation far beyond the boundaries of what we find in the text. We learn something new in verse 19. Not only were the charges against Paul groundless, but Paul had no counter charges to bring against the Jews. In this "clean slate" atmosphere he wanted to discuss with the Roman Jewish leaders his status as a prisoner and the hope of the resurrection.

Paul had no martyr complex; he had not come to Rome to die. From everything we read in these last chapters of Acts, he expected release and perhaps a long ministry in Rome and even points west. Everything continued to center on **the hope of Israel** which, as Toussaint says, "was more than a resurrection; it meant fulfillment of the Old Testament promises to Israel (cf. 26:6–7). Paul firmly believed Jesus is the Messiah of Israel who will return some day and establish Himself as the King of Israel and Lord of the Nations (cf. 1:6)" (Toussaint, 430).

28:21–22. We need to remember that the Jews had been expelled from Rome approximately ten years earlier (A.D. 50) and only began returning about A.D. 54. Their lack of communication with the mother country and general fuzziness regarding Christianity can be accounted for, to some extent, by their own insecurity in the city of Rome. Nevertheless, it is somewhat surprising that they didn't show greater awareness of events and issues surrounding Paul's appearance in Rome. Perhaps they knew more than they felt comfortable saying in light of their shaky status in the city.

To Romans, as we know by now, Christianity was just another Jewish sect, so they used that term in responding to Paul. The word **sect** is *hairesis* from which our word *heresy* derives.

Keep in mind, too, that Paul's ship was among the first to arrive after winter, so Jews in Jerusalem and Caesarea had had little chance to communicate with their counterparts in Rome since this whole trial sequence began during the riot at the temple in chapter 21.

28:23–24. A large group came to visit Paul and stayed all day. He **declared to them the kingdom of God and tried to convince them about Jesus from the Law of Moses and from the Prophets.** Perhaps we could find a model for these remarks in Paul's address at the synagogue in Pisidia in Antioch (13:17–41), to say nothing of the epistle to the Romans itself. Paul preached Jesus from the Old Testament. His view of the kingdom dealt with the origin, death, resurrection, and coming reign of the Lord.

The result? We've seen it before, and so had he. **Some were convinced by what he said, but others would not believe.** Perhaps the former group was only convinced of Paul's innocence, but more likely they actually accepted the gospel and became Christians though Luke does not precisely tell us that. In either case, a divided synagogue following proclamation of the gospel has become a staple in Acts.

Ⅾ The Gospel to the Gentiles (vv. 25–31)

SUPPORTING IDEA: *When God has called us to a distinctive role, such as Paul's mission to the Gentiles, we should waste no time getting right to the task wherever he sends us.*

28:25. The wording of the verse is important. Luke seems to want us to understand that though this argument continued, no one actually got up to leave until Paul began to quote Isaiah 6:9–10. In doing so Paul affirmed again the inspiration of the Old Testament text by the Holy Spirit (1:16; 4:25). His reference to **my own people** in verse 19 now changed to **your forefathers** as he began to distance himself from these unbelieving Jews. This quotation from Isaiah 6 had been used by Jesus (Luke 8:10; Matt. 13:13–15; Mark 4:12) and Paul had written it in Romans 11:8.

28:26–27. Jesus had employed this text to explain to the disciples why he spoke in parables. Here Paul used it to demonstrate Israel's stubbornness and their unwillingness to understand how God's providence brought redemption. This warning not only applies to Israel as a nation but to individuals then and now. As Marshall puts it:

> God's Word brings the diagnosis of sin, which is painful to hear and accept, but at the same time it wounds in order to heal. Once a

person deliberately refuses the Word, there comes a point when he is deprived of the capacity to receive it. It is a stern warning to those who trifle with the gospel (Marshall, 425).

28:28. Here again we see the overarching plan—the gospel to the Gentiles. Remember, each time we have seen this, it has not been a permanent turning away from the nation of Israel, but a movement from Jews in a given city to Gentiles in that same place (13:46; 18:6). It seems clear that no national return to Christ occurred. Though Paul prayed and hoped for that, he would not see it in his day nor in any day until the second coming of the Messiah. Some versions include a verse 29, but the NIV correctly omits it in view of insufficient manuscript evidence.

28:30. Obviously Rome was in no hurry to deal with this trial, so Paul, using his own resources, ministered to **all who came to see him.** During this time Paul wrote four epistles, Ephesians, Philippians, Colossians, and Philemon. Among those who visited him were Tychicus, Onesimus, and Ephaphroditus in addition to those we mentioned earlier. From the Prison Epistles we learn that Paul expected to stand trial (27:24) and expected to be released. In Longenecker's chronology he dates a release about A.D. 63 and says,

> Accepting the Pastoral Epistles as genuine, we may believe that after Paul's release from this Roman imprisonment he continued his evangelistic work in the eastern portion of the empire (at least in lands surrounding the Aegean Sea)—perhaps even fulfilling his long cherished desire to visit Spain (Rom. 15:23-24; cf. 1 Clement 5). And since 2 Timothy 4:16-18 speaks of an approaching second trial and a tone of resignation, we may conclude that Paul was rearrested about 67 and, according to tradition, beheaded at Rome by order of the Emperor Nero (Longenecker, 572).

Luke did not write Paul's biography. He wrote a record of the early church's expansion. Luke obviously finished his book before Paul's release, or he would have described the release and the continued expansion of the church; so we date the writing of Acts somewhere around 63, probably just prior to Paul's release. The Roman statute of limitations on accusations would have run out in eighteen months, and Luke might very well have expected Theophilus to pick up on that implication.

Not everyone accepts this early dating of the Book of Acts. Some suggest Luke assumed the knowledge in the Christian community of what happened to Paul and therefore didn't include it in his book. Some even argue that Luke wrote a third volume to complement and conclude Luke and Acts.

28:31. Luke ends the book on a ringing note of victory. During these two years Paul boldly **preached the kingdom of God and taught about the Lord Jesus Christ** and he did so *akolutos*, **without hindrance.**

Whatever the conclusion about dating Luke's writing, he surely wants us to grasp the reality that God's message, the gospel of Jesus Christ, will proceed unhindered throughout the world regardless of what happens to courageous messengers.

MAIN IDEA REVIEW: *Along with Paul, Christians have victory over sin and the world both in life and in death.*

III. CONCLUSION

An Unfinished Story

Music lovers the world over are familiar with the famous "Unfinished Symphony" (Symphony No. 8 in B Minor) composed by Franz Schubert. The abrupt ending of this piece of music has made it world famous. Luke has also given us an unfinished story, but from all evidence, that is precisely what he intended. We can only speculate about a third volume, but he clearly wrote at a time when further information about Paul was unavailable or, if for some reason he did know more, he chose not to include it.

In his typical style, much in the way he ended his Gospel, Luke emphasizes the positive and healthy forward movement of the gospel and the message of the kingdom of God. Rome may bind the preacher, but the message goes on. That is the precise message of Acts. We may only have twenty-eight chapters here, but one could argue that each year in the life of the church another chapter is added. If Luke were still writing, he might describe your church or mine, or he might write about present missionary activity in Africa or Latin America. No, Acts is not an unfinished story. It finishes precisely where the author intended to end and trumpets the victory of Christ and his message right at the close of the book. In the final analysis, Christ, not Paul, is the hero of Acts.

PRINCIPLES

- Christians have victory over sin and the world in life and in death.
- Kingdom citizens owe allegiance to the King—only then to this world.
- The message of the gospel is not bound by the fate of the messengers.
- The true Christian servant is never off duty.

APPLICATIONS

- Expect to find Christians wherever you go; followers of "The Way" form a global community.
- Encourage and support other Christians, especially those who find themselves in some kind of difficulty.
- Be bold and stand firm despite the opposition.
- Practice faithfulness in God's service no matter how difficult that may be at times.

IV. LIFE APPLICATION

When I Consider How My Light Is Spent

John Milton (1674) was an English poet and the composer of the great epic *Paradise Lost*. His sequel, *Paradise Regained*, written four years later, depicts Christ overcoming Satan's temptations. Milton was a Puritan who studied the Bible faithfully and based much of his writing on its very words. From 1640 to 1660, Milton supported the Puritan movement in England, believing the Church of England corrupt and arguing that bishops should be deprived of power. In 1652 John Milton lost his sight and three years later wrote "On His Blindness." Here is the entirety of that poetic work:

> When I consider how my light is spent
> Ere half my days in this dark world and wide,
> And that one talent which is death to hide
> Lodged with me useless, though my soul more bent
> To serve therewith my Maker, and present
> My true account, lest He returning chide,
> "Doth God exact day-labour, light denied?"
> I fondly ask. But Patience, to prevent
> That murmur, soon replies, God doth not need
> Either man's work or his own gifts. Who best
> Bear his mild yoke, they serve him best. His state
> Is kingly: thousands at his bidding speed,
> And post o'er land and ocean without rest;
> They also serve who only stand and wait.
> (Williams, 106–107)

Yes, they also serve who only stand and wait, but that is not the central message of this sonnet. It focuses clearly on faithfulness despite one's surroundings and circumstances, and that is precisely what we see from Paul.

Certainly, it's difficult for us to identify with beatings and imprison-ments, though Christians in every age have endured these. In more modern settings however, we might struggle with raising godly children in a single-parent household, pastoring a church which seems to rest lazily in a no-growth mode, or struggling with the frailties and disabling diseases of age. All these and more fit well into the pattern, if not the experience, of Paul's life and ministry. Perhaps his magnificent testimony from Miletus can serve as our ringing connection with this book: **However, I consider my life worth nothing to me, if only I may finish the race and complete the task the Lord Jesus has given me—the task of testifying to the gospel of God's grace** (Acts 20:24).

V. PRAYER

God, please allow us to finish our lives on earth with a solid allegiance to your Word and a willingness to serve you despite the difficulties and struggles all around us.

VI. DEEPER DISCOVERIES

A. Snake Miracle (v. 5)

Many have argued that Luke invented this story to provide a little color to the narrative and a little more heroism for Paul. Some of those arguments seem based on the absence of poisonous snakes on the Island of Malta today. Ramsay attacked this view long ago: "The objections which have been advanced, that there are now no vipers in the island, and only one place where any wood grows, are too trivial to deserve notice. Such changes are natural and probable on a small island, populous and long civilised" (Ramsay, 343).

Others have suggested that the snake was probably a constrictor (still found in Malta today) and have pictured it clinging to Paul's hand rather than actually biting him. However, one does not **swell up or suddenly fall over dead** from a constrictor so small it only surrounds one's arm.

Truly the natural reading of the text is best. Luke lets us see this event through the eyes of the islanders who certainly knew their snakes better than their 276 surprise visitors and considerably better than modern commenta-tors. The islanders expected Paul to have serious reaction to his encounter with this snake, but there was none. Rather than argue his immunity or some other explanation, can we not just accept a miracle which God performed, opening the door to wide social ministry on the island?

B. Castor and Pollux (v. 11)

Paul left Malta on another Alexandrian ship, quite possibly headed to Rome like the first one. Ships, like inns, were named for their figureheads, and this one carried on its prow a painted carving of Castor and Pollux, sons of Leda, queen of Sparta. In Greek mythology, these two had been transformed by Zeus into twin gods represented to this day by the constellation Gemini. Longenecker tells us, "The cult of the Dioscuroi (lit., "sons of Zeus") was especially widespread in Egypt and the Gemini were considered by sailors a sign of good fortune in a storm. For an Alexandrian ship, the figurehead was an appropriate one" (Longenecker, 566).

C. Rome (v. 14)

Along the Appian Way, just north of Aricia, Paul would have caught his first glimpse of Rome. As Coneybeare and Howson describe it,

> St. Paul would see a vast city, covering the Campagna, and almost continuously connected by its suburbs with the villas on the hill where he stood, and with the bright towns which clustered on the sides of the mountains opposite. Over all the intermediate space were the houses and gardens, through which aqueducts and roads might be traced in converging lines towards the confused mass of edifices which formed the city of Rome. Here no conspicuous building, elevated above the rest, attracted the eye or the imagination. Ancient Rome had neither cupola nor campanile. . . . It was a widespread aggregate of buildings, which, though separated by narrow streets and open squares, appeared, when seen from near Aricia, blended into one indiscriminate mass: for distance concealed the contrasts which divided the crowded habitations of the poor, and the dark haunts of filth and misery, from the theaters and colonnades, the baths, the temples and palaces with gilded roofs, flashing back the sun (Coneybeare, 732).

We are told "Rome was not built in a day," a vast understatement. Settlements began to form the original town shortly after 600 B.C., but Rome did not become a large, heavily populated city until some 200 years later. Within a hundred years after that, the squalor of which Conneybeare and Howson wrote became a characteristic feature. Experts believe that in time one-fifth of the population of Rome became Christian; but after ten generations of persecution, the city killed and buried well over a million followers of "The Way." In A.D. 64, the year after Paul was freed, parts of Rome were destroyed by fire for which history has made Nero responsible. In any case, the Scripture ends with numerous proclamations against the vile behavior of Rome and symbolic condemnations of its punishment.

D. How Many Imprisonments?

Perhaps it began with Eusebius, but tradition claims that Paul was released after his first defense and enjoyed another two or three years of ministry, quite possibly roaming again over Asia Minor, and this time heading west to Spain. This viewpoint rests largely on material in the Pastoral Epistles (1 and 2 Tim.; Titus) which cannot be fitted into the information we have in Acts. Polhill says:

> It is thus highly likely that the personal events related in the Pastorals date from a period after Paul's first Roman confinement and are thus themselves testimony to Paul's release and subsequent ministry. In this view Paul would have arrived in Rome sometime in 59 or 60 and been released in 61 or 62. His return to Rome, second imprisonment, and martyrdom would have taken place under the Neronic persecution of the Roman Christians in A.D. 64 or 65. According to early tradition, Paul was martyred under Nero, being taken about a mile outside the city walls along the Ostian Way and beheaded (Polhill, 548).

Marshall is not so sure, but Polhill's explanation is accepted by many evangelical scholars and Bible students. Indeed, Ramsay says essentially the same thing, adding:

> At his second trial the veil that hides his fate is raised for the moment. On that occasion the circumstances were very different from his first trial. His confinement was more rigorous, for Onesiphorus had to take much trouble before obtaining an interview with the prisoner (2 Tim. 1:17): "He fared ill as far as bonds, like a criminal" (2:19). He had no hope of acquittal: he recognized that he was "already being poured forth as an offering, and the time of his departure was come." The gloom and hopelessness of the situation damped and dismayed all his friends: at his first hearing "all forsook" him; yet for the time he "was delivered out of the mouth of the lion." In every respect the situation thus indicated is the opposite of the circumstances described on the first trial (Ramsay, 360).

Assuming that pattern is correct, Paul could well have written 1 Timothy and Titus during his period of release (approximately from A.D. 63–66, and 2 Timothy from the Mamertine prison just prior to his death in A.D. 67.

VII. TEACHING OUTLINE

A. INTRODUCTION

1. Lead Story: Island of the Barbarians
2. Context: We have come to the end. Everything Luke has written up to this point has prepared us for Paul's arrival at Rome. Yes, we are

surprised by the ending of the book, and the commentary speaks briefly to that; but Paul's witness in Rome was clearly established, and Luke ends the book on a note of victory.

3. Transition: In Acts 28 we'll find people encouraging one another again, highlighted in the steadfast and resolute determination of Paul to boldly proclaim the name of Jesus in Rome.

B. COMMENTARY
1. Miracles on Malta (vv. 1–10)
   a. Paul and the snake (vv. 1–6)
   b. People and their sickness (vv. 7–10)
2. Welcomes Along the Way (vv. 11–16)
   a. Brothers at Puteoli (vv. 11–14a)
   b. Brothers at Rome (vv. 14b–16)
3. Jesus and the Jews (vv. 17–24)
   a. Introduction to the Jewish community (vv. 17–20)
   b. Ignorance in the Jewish community (vv. 21–22)
   c. Instruction of the Jewish community (vv. 23–24)
4. Gospel to the Gentiles (vv. 25–31)
   a. Prophecy of Gentile salvation (vv. 25–27)
   b. Proclamation of Gentile salvation (v. 28)
   c. Preaching of Gentile salvation (vv. 30–31)

C. CONCLUSION: WHEN I CONSIDER HOW MY LIGHT IS SPENT

VIII. ISSUES FOR DISCUSSION

1. Have you ever found yourself in a situation where strangers offered you unexpected kindness? How did you respond? Did you use the opportunity to witness for Christ?
2. When have other Christians welcomed you in a way that brought encouragement and hope to your life? How did you respond? Did you give God thanks for bringing these people into your life?
3. When people ask you about Jesus, how do you convince them to turn to him for salvation? How do you respond if the people do not believe your witness?

Glossary

1. **Agrippa, Marcus Julius II** (A.D. 41–44)—Last member of dynasty of Herod, ruling Judah; son of Herod Agrippa I and grandson of Herod the Great; heard Paul's defense (Acts 25:13–27; 26:32).

2. **Anarchy**—State of lawlessness caused by absence of government; total disorder.

3. **Angels**—Heavenly messengers who either deliver God's message to humans, carry out God's will, praise God, or guard God's throne.

4. **Antinomianism**—False teaching that claims that since faith alone is necessary for salvation, a person is free from the moral obligations of the law; accusation leveled against Paul (Rom. 3:8; 6:1,15).

5. **Antioch**—Third largest city in Roman Empire after Rome and Alexandria; on Orontes River in Syria; home of Christian church that sent out and supported first missionaries (Acts 11:19,26; 13:1–3).

6. **Antonia, Fortress of**—See Fortress of Antonia.

7. **Apocalyptic**—Writings from God that employ symbolic language to tell of a divine intervention soon to take place to bring an end to world history; the doctrinal system explicit in these writings; and the movement(s) that produced the writings and doctrine.

8. **Apology/apologetics**—Formal presentation defending a set of beliefs or course of action against a competing belief system or an attack on one's own system.

9. **Apostasy**—Act of rebelling against, forsaking, abandoning, or falling away from what one has believed.

10. **Aramaic**—North Semitic language originating in Syria among the Arameans; became international language of Persian Empire; was spoken language of most Jews in Palestine at time of Jesus.

11. **Ascension Commission** (Acts 1:7)—Christ's missionary command to his followers immediately before he ascended to heaven.

12. **Atonement**—Reconciliation between God and humans effected by the death, burial, and resurrection of Jesus Christ; associated in Old Testament with sacrificial offerings and, especially the Day of Atonement ritual.

13. **Bernice** (b. about A.D. 28)—Daughter of Herod Agrippa I; married to Marcus—the Jewish magistrate in Alexandria, then to her uncle Herod of Chalcis; then allied in questionable relationship with her brother Herod Agrippa II, then married to Polemo of Cilicia briefly before returning to Agrippa; financed Vespacian's bid for power in A.D. 68; linked romantically with Titus.

14. **Bishop**—Overseer; officer in early church usually seen as identical with elders and pastors; after A.D. 100 came to be leader of a major church and then over central church and outlying rural churches.

15. **Blasphemy**—Attitude of disrespect that finds expression in an act directed toward the character of God; person who denied the messianic claims of Jesus and rejected his unity with the Father (Mark 15:29; Luke 22:65; 23:39).

16. **Break Bread**—To begin a meal; used in connection with love feast early church celebrated along with the Lord's Supper as well as to the Lord's Supper itself.

17. **Call**—God's act of summoning people to salvation (1 John 3:1; cf. 2 Thess. 2:13–15), to the Christian life (Eph. 1:18; 4:1; 2 Tim. 1:9; Heb. 3:1; 2 Pet. 1:10), and to special vocational ministries (Mark 1:20; Acts 13:2).

18. **Christ**—*see* Messiah.

19. **Church**—Group of persons professing trust in Jesus Christ; meeting together of persons to worship Christ and seeking to enlist others to become his followers; normally refers to local group of believers (1 Cor. 1:2); can refer to all believers (Eph. 1:22–23).

20. **Circumcision**—Ritual act of removing foreskin of male genital performed on eighth day after birth (Lev. 12:3); center of controversy in early church concerning its relationship to a person becoming a disciple of Jesus; Council of Jerusalem said it was not required for Gentiles (Acts 15).

21. **Clement**—1. Elder in church at Rome who wrote 1 Clement in Apostolic Fathers about A.D. 95; 2. Theologian in church at Alexandria about A.D. 200.

22. **Collection for the poor**—Offering Paul took up among Gentile churches in Philippi, Thessalonica, Corinth, and Galatia to help impoverished church at Jerusalem; delivered to Jerusalem after third missionary journey.

23. **Common grace**—God's bounty poured out on all people regardless of their faith or righteousness.

24. **Congregation**—Assembled people of God, the church.

25. **Contextualization**—Missionary strategy by which gospel message is presented in terms that can be readily understood by the people to whom it is addressed.

26. **Conversion**—The experience of an individual in which a person turns from sin and trusts in Jesus Christ for salvation, resulting in an outward change in daily life.

27. **Council**—*see* Sanhedrin.

28. **Council of Jerusalem**—See Jerusalem Council.

29. **Deacons**—Church officers who serve the church; by A.D. 100 they had become assistants to pastors/elders; apparently served the poor, assisted in baptism and Lord's Supper, and performed practical ministerial tasks.

30. **Diana (Artemis)**—Roman (Greek) goddess of the moon; daughter of Zeus; cared for nature; mother goddess; fertility goddess; identified with Ephesus (see Acts 19:28).

31. **Disciples**—Persons who follow and learn from Jesus Christ; sometimes used more specifically as alternate designation for twelve apostles.

32. **Dispensation**—In some theological systems a period of time during which people are tested according to a specific revelation of God's will; popularized in system of J. N. Darby featuring seven dispensations related to Gen. 1:28; 3:23; 8:20; 12:1; Exod. 19:8; John 1:17; Eph. 1:10.

33. **Dispersion/Diaspora**—Jews scattered in lands outside Palestine as a result of fall of Samaria in 722 B.C. and of Jerusalem in 586 B.C.; gave rise to Jewish communities and Jewish synagogues in which Paul began his ministry in cities he visited.

34. **Drusilla**—Jewish wife of Felix, the Roman governor of Judea; youngest daughter of Herod Agrippa I; originally married to King Azia of Emesa (see Acts 24:24).

35. **Ecclesiastical**—Pertaining to the church and its organization and processes.

36. **Elders**—In the church, spiritual leaders and ministers, usually equated with bishops and pastors; became a decision-making council.

37. **Eschatology**—Teaching concerning the last things in world history and inauguration of eternal kingdom.

38. **Eusebius**—Bishop of Caesarea (313–339); wrote early church history and so known as Father of Church History; studied early chronology; compared Gospel parallels.

39. **Exclusivity of the gospel**—Christian belief that the gospel provides the only way to salvation, thus that belief in Jesus is necessary for any person to be saved.

40. **Exorcism**—Practice of expelling demons by means of some ritual act.

41. **Fasting**—Refraining from eating food to devote time to religious devotion and/or mourning.

42. **Felix**—Roman procurator of Judea (A.D. 52–60) at time Paul visited Jerusalem for last time; presided over one of Paul's trials (Acts 23:24; 24:26–27).

43. *Flagalantes*—Persons who in the name of religious devotion and penitence beat themselves, scourge themselves, or otherwise torture themselves to win God's favor and forgiveness; Catholic church first approved and then later under Clement VI disapproved of the practice.

44. **Fortress of Antonia**—Defense tower Herod the Great built near the northwest corner of the temple about A.D. 6 as his palace residence and as barracks for up to six hundred Roman troops; also used to store high priest's robe and to provide arena for public speaking.

45. **Gamaliel**—Leading Pharisee in Sanhedrin; counseled Sanhedrin not to kill the apostles so they would be sure they did not oppose God (Acts 5:34); Paul's teacher (Acts 22:3); died about A.D. 52.

46. **God-fearers**—Gentiles who worshiped Israel's God without undergoing circumcision and becoming Jewish proselytes; observed Sabbath and food laws.

47. **Governor**—Chief administrative official over a province with tax and military authority, representing and responsible to Roman emperor.

48. **Grace**—Undeserved acceptance and love received from another, especially the characteristic attitude of God in providing salvation for sinners who do and can do nothing to earn it.

49. **Grace-living**—Early Christian lifestyle of depending on God's grace rather than on strict obedience to law to maintain relationship with God after the salvation experience.

50. **Greek**—Language introduced to Near East by Alexander the Great; became international language of commerce, government, and literature; used even during Roman Empire.

51. **Hebraic Christians**—Believers in early church who came from Palestine with a Hebrew culture; most worshiped in Hebrew, lived in Aramaic, and probably knew Greek.

52. **Hebrew**—Language of ancient Israel in which Old Testament is written; by time of Jesus it had become language of worship and Scripture, replaced in daily life by Aramaic.

53. **Hellenistic**—Pertaining to the culture of Greece spread into Near East by Alexander the Great; Jews outside Palestine were raised in Greek/Hellenistic culture rather than Hebrew culture.

54. **Heresy/Heretical**—Opinion or doctrine not in line with the accepted teaching of a church; opposite of orthodoxy.

55. **Hermeneutics/Hermeneutical**—Science of interpreting literature, especially sacred literature like the Bible.

56. **Hermes**—Greek god (Latin, Mercury); messenger of gods, associated with eloquence in speech (see Acts 14:12).

57. **Herodian**—Member of aristocratic Jewish group who favored the policies of Herod Antipas and thus supported Roman government rather than seeking Jewish independence.

58. **Homiletics/Homiletical**—Study of creation and delivery of sermons explaining and applying Scripture.

59. **Hyperbole**—A literary style using a deliberate exaggeration to make a point.

60. **Incarnation**—God becoming human; the union of divinity and humanity in Jesus of Nazareth, qualifying him to be agent of God's saving plan for humanity.

61. **Inheritance**—Humanly, a legal transmission of property after death; theologically, the rewards God gives his children who are saved through Jesus Christ.

62. **Jerusalem Council**—Meeting in Jerusalem at which the apostles and elders of Jerusalem church agreed to claims and teachings of Paul and Barnabas that Gentiles could receive the gospel and be saved without being circumcised as Jewish proselytes first (Acts 15).

63. **Josephus**—Jewish military commander in Galilee who moved to Rome and became historian of Jewish life and our most important source for the history of the Jews in the Roman period; died about A.D. 100.

64. **Judaizers**—Jewish church members who opposed Paul, demanding that Gentiles be circumcised and be full Jewish proselytes before they were accepted as believers in the church; lost the argument at the Jerusalem Council.

65. **Justification**—The act/event by which God credits a sinner who has faith as being right with him through the blood of Jesus (Rom. 3:21–26; 4:18–25; 5:10–21; 1 Pet. 3:18).

66. **Latin**—Language of ancient Italy and the Roman Empire; used on cross of Jesus (John 19:20); language of early Bible translation called the Vulgate; never replaced Greek as language of culture and commerce.

67. **Legalists**—*see* Judaizers.

68. **Levite**—Order of Jewish priests descended from priestly tribe of Levi.

69. **Lysias, Claudius**—Roman tribune or army captain who helped Paul escape Jews and appear before Felix (Acts 23:26).

70. **Martyr**—Person who witnesses for Christ by dying rather than deny Christ.

71. **Messiah**—Transliteration for Hebrew, "anointed One," translated into Greek as Christ; king God promised to send from line of David to save his people Israel and through them the nations; role taken by Jesus with emphasis upon suffering and self-sacrifice rather than on ruling and kingship.

72. **Ministry**—Self-giving service intended to honor Jesus and meet the needs of people.

73. **Monotheism**—Belief and practice that only one God exists and is alone to be the object of worship and praise.

74. **Natural revelation**—God's communication through nature of things about himself that we would not otherwise know (Rom. 1:21–23); gives people responsibility before God for their actions, but content insufficient for salvation.

75. **Nazirite**—Member of class of individuals especially devoted to God; based on vow made either for specific period or by parents at birth for lifetime (Num. 6:1–21; Acts 18:18; 21:22–26).

76. **Omnipotent**—Being all-powerful and thus able to accomplish anything desired; attribute of God and of no one else.

77. **Oral tradition**—Materials preserved from past generations by repeated telling rather than by writing; source of much of Jewish law taught by Pharisees but rejected by Sadducees.

78. **Origen**—Leading theologian from Alexandria (about 185–254); Greek church father; text critic; biblical commentator; author of early statement of faith; published *Hexapla*, version of Old Testament in Hebrew and several Greek translations.

79. **Palestinian Christians**—*See* Hebraic Christians; distinguished from believers whose original home was not Palestine.

80. **Passover**—Most important Hebrew festival, celebrating the delivery from Egypt.

81. **Pastor**—Shepherding office of the church closely associated with teaching; usually seen as identical in early church with bishops and elders.

82. **Patriarchs**—Israel's founding fathers—Abraham, Isaac, and Jacob with whom God established his original promises for Israel.

83. *Pax Romana*—Roman government's establishment and maintenance of international peace that allowed empire to prosper without widespread rebellion; threat to such peace constituted major crime against the government.

84. **Pentateuch**—First five books of Hebrew Bible: Genesis, Exodus, Leviticus, Numbers, Deuteronomy; only Scriptures recognized by Samaritans and by Sadducees.

85. **Pentecost**—Israel's feast of weeks at time of wheat harvest; celebrated fifty days after Passover; time of year when Holy Spirit came in power for first time on Christ's disciples (Acts 2).

86. **Pesher**—Jewish commentary on biblical book or biblical theme, as seen in commentaries among Dead Sea Scrolls; identifies biblical subject with modern figure or situation; often points to end time.

87. **Pharisees**—Jewish party or sect that used oral law and tradition to help Jews obey God in new situations not explicitly covered by the law; major opponents of Jesus.

88. **Polytheism**—Belief in existence of and practice of worshiping more than one god.

89. **Praetorium**—Barracks in Jerusalem where Jesus was taken and mocked (Mark 15:16); apparently the official residence of the Roman governor in any city (for example Caesarea (Acts 23:35; Phil 1:13).

90. **Pre-evangelism**—Teaching and witnessing done to prepare people to be able to understand meaning and message of the gospel of Christ.

91. **Priesthood of believers**—Belief that every person has direct access to God without any mediator other than Christ so that each person can respond directly to God and can minister to other people in the name of Christ.

92. **Principle of proportion**—Assumption in studying Scripture that God invests longer portions of Scripture in happenings or teachings he considers highly important.

93. **Proconsul**—Office in Roman government that oversaw administration of a province; responsible to the senate in Rome (Acts 13:7; 18:12; 19:38); comparable to a governor.

94. **Progressive revelation**—God's act of revealing himself in a developing disclosure of himself, his will, and his truth with new revelation always being complementary and supplementary to what has come before and being suited to the needs and capabilities of the persons to whom it is revealed.

95. **Proselyte**—Convert to a religion; non-Jew who accepted the Jewish faith, completed Jewish rituals including circumcision, and adhered to Jewish law.

96. **Providence**—God's faithful and effective care and guidance of everything which he has made toward the end which he has chosen.

97. **Puritan**—Member of movement within English Church under Queen Elizabeth I seeking to implement a full Calvinistic reformation in England; then a way of life emphasizing personal regeneration, sanctification, household prayers, and strict morality.

98. **Regeneration**—Radical spiritual change in which God brings an individual from a condition of spiritual death to a condition of faith and responsiveness to God.

99. *Religio Licita*—A religion sanctioned by the Roman Empire as legitimate.

100. **Remnant theology**—Biblical teaching that God disciplined his disobedient people and reduced the chosen ones from the nation of Israel to an obedient minority remaining after judgment to the Obedient One, Jesus of Nazareth.

101. **Repentance**—A feeling of regret, a changing of the mind, and a turning from sin to God.

102. **Revelation**—The content and process of God making himself known to people, God bridging the gap between himself and his people, disclosing himself and his will to them.

103. **Righteousness**—The actions and positive results of a sound relationship within a local community; the right relationship created by God between himself and a person of faith.

104. **Sabbath**—Day of rest God ordered from his people at creation; day people set aside to worship God; for Jews, the seventh day of the week for which the Pharisees strictly regulated acceptable conduct.

105. **Sadducees**—Jewish priestly party that controlled the Sanhedrin and accepted only the Pentateuch as Scripture.

106. **Saints**—Holy people; all God's people of faith.

107. **Salvation**—God's acutely dynamic act of snatching sinners from death and providing them eternal life through Jesus Christ.

108. **Samaritan**—Originally inhabitants of Samaria; then of northern kingdom; in Jesus' day, inhabitants of Samaria who worshiped there instead of in Jerusalem and main-

tained their own religious tradition built around their version of the Pentateuch (Luke 9:52–54; 10:25–37; 17:11–19; John 8:48; Acts 1:8; 8:5).

109. **Sanctification**—Process of God making the believer holy resulting in a changed lifestyle.

110. **Sanhedrin**—Highest Jewish council in time of Jesus composed of seventy-one members including Sadducees and Pharisees (Acts 5:34; 6:12–15; 7:54–60; 22:30; 23:1–28).

111. **Scribes**—Persons trained in writing skills and in interpretation of the Mosaic law and its oral tradition; usually Pharisees; led in plans to kill Jesus (see Acts 4:5; 6:12; 23:9).

112. **Sedition**—Rebellion against lawful authority; accusation against Paul (Acts 24:5).

113. **Septuagint**—Oldest translation of Hebrew Old Testament into Greek; often quoted in the New Testament.

114. *Shema*—Transliteration of Hebrew imperative meaning, "Hear" (Deut. 6:4); applied to Deut. 6:4–9 as basic statement of Jewish law and basic Jewish confession of faith; gradually supplemented to include Deut. 11:13–21; Num. 15:37–41.

115. **Sign**—An object, occurrence, or person that points to something else and through which one recognizes, remembers, or validates something. Signs may impart knowledge, identify, signify protection, motivate faith, recall God's saving acts in the past, witness to God's covenant, and confirm or authenticate prophecy.

116. **Soteriology**—Statement of biblical teaching or doctrine of salvation.

117. **Sovereignty of God**—Biblical teaching that God is source of all creation and thus that all things come from and depend upon God.

118. **Substitutionary atonement**—Biblical teaching that Jesus Christ is God's substitute sin offering through his death on the cross making it possible for believers to be at one with God and experience his forgiveness and salvation.

119. **Suetonius**—Gaius Suetonius Tranquillus (born about A.D. 70)—Government officer under the Roman emperors Hadrian and Trajan; wrote *Lives of the Caesars.*

120. **Synagogue**—Meeting place and prayer hall of Jewish people since Babylonian exile; place where Paul normally began his ministry in a new city.

121. **Synagogue of the Freedmen**—Greek-speaking synagogue in Jerusalem involved in instituting the dispute with Stephen (Acts 6:9); members apparently from North Africa; may have been descendants of former prisoners of war freed by Pompey in 63 B.C.

122. **Tabernacle**—Sacred tent built by Moses as portable and provisional sanctuary where God met his people (Exod. 33:7–10).

123. **Tacitus** (about A.D. 50–117)—Roman orator, lawyer, and government official; most significant Roman historian on Roman and Jewish history for period between A.D. 14 and 68.

124. **Talmud**—Jewish commentaries written between A.D. 200 and 500 on the Mishnah, the oral interpretations of the law of Moses; different editions collected and published in Babylon and Palestine; central document for Judaism.

125. **Tetrarch**—Political position in the early Roman Empire with administrative control over one fourth of a province; title given Herod Antipas and Herod Philip.

126. **Theophilus**—Gentile to whom Luke addressed his Gospel and Acts (Luke 1:3; Acts 1:1).

127. **Torah**—Teaching or instruction; Jewish name for five books of Moses: Genesis, Exodus, Leviticus, Numbers, and Deuteronomy.

128. **Totalitarianism**—Centralized control by absolute state authority with citizens totally subordinate.

129. **Transfiguration**—Transformation of the outward appearance of Jesus in company of Moses and Elijah; witnessed by Peter, James, and John (Matt. 17:1–13; Mark 9:1–13; Luke 9:28–36; compare 2 Pet. 1:16–18).

130. **Tribune**—Roman official charged with protecting citizens and their rights from arbitrary actions of the judges or magistrates.

131. **Type/typology**—Method of interpreting some parts of Scripture by seeing a pattern which an earlier statement sets up by which a later statement is explained; seeing a correspondence in one particular matter between a person, event, or thing in the Old Testament with a person, event, or thing in the New Testament.

132. **Tyrians**—Inhabitants of or citizens of Tyre.

133. **Unleavened bread**—Agricultural festival Israel celebrated in connection with Passover (Exod. 12:8,15,20; 13:3, 6–7).

134. *Via Ignatia*—Roman road that eventually ran from Byzantiun on the Bospour in the east to Dyrrhacium on the Adriatic. It provided easy communication between Rome and Macedonia.

135. **Western Text**—A Greek form of the New Testament represented by a variety of manuscripts generally originating in North Africa, Italy, and France and characterized by paraphrase; earliest witnesses to this form of the Greek text come from about A.D. 150.

136. **Zealots**—Jewish superpatriots in time of Jesus; extreme wing of Pharisees, believing only God had right to rule over the Jews and so opposing all foreign governments; arose about A.D. 6. (see Luke 6:15; John 18:40).

137. **Zeus**—Chief god of Greek pantheon; god of the sky; controlled weather (see Acts 14:8–12).

Bibliography

Andrews, Samuel J. *The Life of Our Lord Upon the Earth*. Grand Rapids: Zondervan, 1954.

Arrington, French L. *The Acts of the Apostles*. Peabody, Mass.: Hendrickson Publishers, 1988.

Barnhouse, Donald Grey. *Acts: An Expositional Commentary*. Grand Rapids: Zondervan, 1979.

Barrett, David B. "Malta." *World Christian Encyclopedia*. Oxford: Oxford University Press, 1982.

Bock, Darrell L. *The Acts of the Apostles* (An Independent Study Course). Grand Rapids: Institute of Theological Studies, 1994.

Browning, Robert. "Rabbi Ben Ezra." In *Immortal Poems of the English Language*, edited by Oscar Williams. New York: Washington Square Press, 1952,

Bruce, F. F. *The Book of Acts*. New International Commentary on the New Testament. Grand Rapids: Eerdmans, 1988.

————.*The Epistle to the Galatians*. Grand Rapids: Eerdmans, 1982.

Constable, Thomas L. "Notes on Acts." Dallas, Tex.: Dallas Theological Seminary, 1991.

Conybeare, W. J., and J. S. Howson. *The Life and Epistles of Saint Paul*. Hartford, Conn.: S.S. Scranton and Company, 1895.

Criswell, W. A. *Acts: An Exposition*. Grand Rapids: Zondervan, 1978.

Davies, W. D. *Paul and Rabbinic Judaism*. London: SPCK, 1962.

Douglas, J. D. *The New International Dictionary of the Christian Church*. Rev. ed. Grand Rapids: Zondervan, 1978.

Eims, Leroy. *Disciples in Action*. Wheaton: Victor Books, 1981.

Ellis Smith, Marsha A., general ed. *Holman Book of Biblical Charts, Maps, and Reconstructions*. Nashville, Tenn.: Broadman & Holman Publishers, 1993.

Flynn, Leslie B. *The Other Twelve*. Wheaton: Victor Books, 1988.

Gaebelein, Frank E., editor. *The Expositor's Bible Commentary*. Grand Rapids: Zondervan, 1979.

Gangel, Kenneth O. *Unwrap Your Spiritual Gifts*. Wheaton: Victor Books, 1983.

Haenchen, E. *The Acts of the Apostles*. Translated by B. Noble and G. Shinn. Oxford: Basel Blackwell, 1971.

Kaiser, Walter C., Jr. "The Theology of the Old Testament." In *The Expositor's Bible Commentary*. Vol. 1. Grand Rapids: Zondervan, 1979.

Kelso, James L. *An Archaeologist Follows the Apostle Paul*. Waco, Tex.: Word Books, 1970.

Lightner, Robert P. *Evangelical Theology—A Survey and Review*. Grand Rapids: Baker Book House, 1986.

Longenecker, Richard N. "The Acts of the Apostles" in *The Expositor's Bible Commentary*. Vol. 9. Grand Rapids: Zondervan, 1981.

————.*The Ministry and Message of Paul*. Grand Rapids: Zondervan, 1971.

Machen, J. Gresham. *The Origin of Paul's Religion*. Grand Rapids: Eerdmans, 1925.

Marshall, I. Howard. *The Acts of the Apostles*. Tyndale New Testament Commentary. Leicester, England: Inter-Varsity Press, 1980.

Morgan, G. Campbell. *The Acts of the Apostles*. New York: Fleming H. Revell, 1924.

Nock, Arthur Darby. *St. Paul*. New York: Harper & Row, 1938.

Ogilvie, Lloyd J. *Acts: The Communicator's Commentary*. Edited by Lloyd J. Ogilvie. Vol. 5. Waco, Tex.: Word Books, 1983.

Payne, J. Barton. *The Theology of the Older Testament*. Grand Rapids: Zondervan, 1962.

Polhill, John B. *Acts*. Vol. 26 of The New American Commentary. David S. Dockery, editor. Nashville: Broadman Press, 1992.

Pollock, John. *The Man Who Shook the World*. Wheaton: Victor Books, 1972.

Ramsay, W. M. *St. Paul the Traveler and the Roman Citizen*. London: Hodder and Stoughton, 1895.

Robertson, James D., ed. *Handbook of Preaching Resources from English Literature*. New York: The MacMillan Company, 1962.

Ryrie, Charles C. *Basic Theology*. Wheaton: Victor Books, 1986.

Schaeffer, Francis A. *The Church at the End of the 20th Century*. Downers Grove, Ill.: InterVarsity Press, 1970.

Schaller, B. "Passover." In *The New International Dictionary of New Testament Theology*. Collin Brown, ed. Vol. 1 (pp. 632-634). Grand Rapids: Zondervan, 1979.

Sweeting, George. *The City: A Matter of Conscience*. Chicago: Moody Press, 1972.

Toussaint, Stanley D. "Acts." In *The Bible Knowledge Commentary—New Testament*, edited by John F. Walvoord and Roy B. Zuck. Wheaton: Victor Books, 1983.

Unger, Merrill. *Demons in the World Today*. Wheaton: Tyndale House, 1971.

van Baalen, J. K. *The Chaos of Cults*. Rev. ed. Grand Rapids: Eerdmans, 1956.

Williams, Oscar, ed. *Immortal Poems of the English Language*. New York: Washington Square Press, 1952.